THE REICHSTAG FIRE

FRITZ TOBIAS

THE
REICHSTAG FIRE

With an Introduction by A. J. P. TAYLOR

G. P. Putnam's Sons

NEW YORK

Translated from the German
by Arnold J. Pomerans

FIRST AMERICAN EDITION 1964

English translation © 1963
by Martin Secker & Warburg Limited

First published in Germany under the title *Der Reichstagsbrand*,
© 1962 by G. Grote'sche Verlagsbuchhandlung

*Library of Congress Catalog
Card Number: 64-10428*

PRINTED IN THE UNITED STATES OF AMERICA

Contents

Illustrations

The author gratefully acknowledges the help of:

the Wiener Library, London;

the International Institute for Social History, Amsterdam;

the Federal Archives, Koblenz;

the Federal Information Office, Bonn;

the State Office for Political Education, Hannover;

Chief Police Inspector J. C. Hofstede, Leyden;

Herr Ernst Torgler, Hannover;

Herr Gustav Schmidt-Kuester, Hannover;

Herr Karl-Heinz Dobbert, Berlin;

and many others.

The extracts quoted from *The Invisible Writing* are reprinted by kind permission of Mr. Arthur Koestler and The Macmillan Co.

The extracts quoted from *The God That Failed* (edited by Richard Crossman) are reprinted by kind permission of Mr. Arthur Koestler and Harper & Row, Publishers, Inc.

Introduction by A. J. P. Taylor

THE fire in the Debating Chamber of the Reichstag on 27 February 1933 has a place in all the history books. Historians, who find so much to disagree about, are for once in agreement, or were until the present book was published. National Socialists – Nazis for short – started the fire, we believed, in order to cause an anti-Communist panic in Germany and so to influence the general election, due on 5 March. The trick succeeded. The German electors took alarm. The Nazis got their majority, and Hitler was able to establish his dictatorship. The Reichstag fire not only explained the initial Nazi success. It also set the pattern for explanations of all Hitler's later acts. We saw at every stage – over rearmament, over Austria, over Czechoslovakia, over Poland – the same deliberate and conspiratorial cunning which had been first shown on 27 February 1933. Historians, writing about Nazi Germany, did not look closely at the events of that night. They took the central fact for granted: Nazis set fire to the Reichstag, and there was an end of it. Most historians were less sure how the Nazis did it. They used some equivocal phrase: 'we do not know exactly what happened'; 'the details are still to be revealed' – something of that sort. Much evidence was in fact available: police reports, fire inspectors' reports, large excerpts from the proceedings of the High Court at Leipzig, kept by Dr Sack, Torgler's counsel. Herr Tobias was the first to look at this evidence with an impartial eye. He took nothing for granted. He was not concerned to indict the Nazis, or for that matter to acquit them. He was that rare thing, a researcher for truth, out to find what happened.

His book sticks closely to the events of 27 February and to the legal or sham-legal proceedings which followed. Some knowledge of the political background may be useful. The republican constitution, created at Weimar in 1919, gave Germany an electoral system of proportional representation. No single party ever obtained an absolute majority in the Reichstag. A series of coalitions governed Germany between 1919 and 1930. Coalition broke down under the impact of the world depression. The Social

9

Democrats refused to carry through deflation; their former associates insisted on it. Brüning, a member of the Centre (Roman
Catholic) Party, became Chancellor and imposed deflation by
emergency decrees, without possessing a majority in the Reichstag. Discontent mounted. Nazis and Communists fought in the
streets. In May 1932 Brüning proposed to dissolve the private
armies of these two parties by emergency decree. The elderly Field-
Marshal Hindenburg, President since 1925, refused. He feared that
conflict with the private armies would bring the real army into
politics; and this he was determined to avoid. Brüning was dismissed. Papen, another member of the Centre, became Chancellor.
He, too, relied on emergency decrees. He dissolved the Reichstag
in the hope of winning wider support. His hope was not fulfilled.
The Nazis won 37.3 per cent of the votes cast on 31 July – their
highest vote in a free election – and 230 seats in the Reichstag.
Papen tried to tempt Hitler with an offer of subordinate office.
Hitler refused. Papen dissolved the Reichstag again. This time the
Nazis did not do so well. On 6 November they received only 33
per cent of the vote and 196 seats. Once more Hitler was offered
office. Once more he refused. Papen now proposed to prorogue
the Reichstag and to govern solely by Presidential decree. The
army leaders declared that they would be unable to maintain order.
Papen resigned. Schleicher, Hindenburg's military adviser, took
his place.

Schleicher tried to strengthen his government by negotiating
with trade union officials and with a few Nazis who had lost faith in
Hitler. The negotiations came to nothing. On 28 January 1933 he
confessed to Hindenburg that he, too, would have to rule by
emergency decree. Meanwhile Papen, still intimate with Hindenburg though out of office, had been negotiating more successfully
with Hitler. Hitler agreed to join a coalition government of
National Socialists and Nationalists. On 30 January he became
Chancellor. This was not a seizure of power. Hitler was intrigued
into power by respectable politicians of the old order – principally
by Papen and also by more obscure advisers round Hindenburg.
Papen had, he thought, taken Hitler prisoner. There were only
three Nazis in a cabinet of eleven; the key posts of foreign minister
and minister of defence were in the hands of non-political experts,
loyal to Hindenburg; and Hitler was not to visit Hindenburg
except in the company of Papen, the Vice-Chancellor. Nazis and

Nationalists together did not have a majority. Hitler urged that yet another general election would give them a majority, and thus relieve Hindenburg from the embarrassment of issuing emergency decrees any longer. The constitutional system would be restored. This, after all, had been the object of making Hitler Chancellor.

Once more the Reichstag was dissolved. The Nazis now reaped the advantage of being in the government. Göring, Hitler's chief assistant, became head of the Prussian police; and the police naturally hesitated to act firmly against the Nazi ruffians in their brown shirts. Violence became one-sided. Communist and Social Democrat meetings were broken up. The Nazis made much of the Communist danger as an election cry. They alleged that the Communists were planning an armed rising. On 23 February the police, on Göring's orders, raided Communist headquarters in order to discover evidence of this plan. They found none. On 27 February the Reichstag went up in flames. Here, it seemed, was the decisive evidence against the Communists, provided perhaps by Heaven. Hitler announced the existence of a revolutionary conspiracy. Emergency decrees were passed, authorizing the arrest of dangerous politicians. Communists and others were sent to labour camps. As a matter of fact, the fire had singularly little effect on the general election of 5 March. The Social Democrats and Centre held their previous vote practically intact. The Communists had 70 deputies instead of 100. The National Socialist vote increased to 43.9 per cent. Even with the Nationalists, who also increased their vote a little, Hitler had only a bare majority in the Reichstag.

This was not enough for him. Hitler wished to carry an Enabling Law which would empower him to govern by decrees and thus make him a dictator by constitutional process. This Law needed a two-thirds majority in the Reichstag. The Communists were prevented from attending. The Social Democrats attended, and were solid against the Enabling Law. Decision rested with the 102 deputies of the Centre. They were lured by promises of security for Roman Catholic schools, and voted for the Law. Hitler obtained his two-thirds majority. He soon pushed aside the restrictions which Papen had tried to place upon him. He dislodged, or discredited, the Nationalist ministers; banned all parties in Germany except the National Socialist; and gradually engrossed all power in his own hands. The consequences for Germany and the world are known to us all.

On a cool retrospect, the burning of the Reichstag occupies a comparatively small place in the story of Hitler's rise to absolute power. He was Chancellor before the fire occurred; it did not much affect the electors; and they did not give him the crushing majority which he needed. The passing of the Enabling Law, not the general election, was the moment of decision. But these were not cool days. A democratic system was being destroyed in the full glare of publicity. Berlin was thronged with newspaper correspondents from foreign countries, eager for stories. With nerves on edge, everyone expected conspiracies by everyone else. The fire at the Reichstag supplied the most dramatic story of a dramatic time. It was naturally built up beyond its merits. For instance, we talk to this day as though the entire Reichstag, a great complex of rooms and building, was destroyed. In fact, only the Debating Chamber was burnt out; and the burning of a Chamber, with wooden panels, curtains dry with age, and a glass dome to provide a natural draught, was not surprising. Many other similar halls have burnt in an equally short space of time, from the old House of Commons in 1834 to the Vienna Stock Exchange a few years ago. A prosaic explanation of this kind did not suit the spirit of the time. People wanted drama; and there had to be drama.

There was, on the surface, no great mystery about the burning of the Reichstag. An incendiary was discovered: van der Lubbe, a young Dutchman. He gave a coherent account of his activities. This account made sense both to the police officers who examined him and to the fire chiefs who handled the fire. It did not suit either the Nazis or their opponents that van der Lubbe should have started the fire alone. Hitler declared, from the first moment, that the Communists had set fire to the Reichstag. They, knowing that they had not, returned the compliment and condemned the fire as a Nazi trick. Thus both sides, far from wanting to find the truth about the fire, set out on a search for van der Lubbe's accomplices. The German authorities arrested Torgler, leader of the Communists in the Reichstag, and three Bulgarian Communists. One of them, Dimitrov, was chief European representative of the Communist International, though the Germans did not know this. The four men were accused, along with van der Lubbe, before the High Court at Leipzig. The prosecution was not interested in establishing the guilt of van der Lubbe. This was both self-evident and unimportant. The prosecution was after the four Communists. It was essential to demonstrate that van der Lubbe could not have acted alone. Most of the evidence was directed to this point. It convinced the Court, and has continued to convince most of those who examined the case later. Van der Lubbe, everyone decided, had accomplices. The prosecution, however, failed to establish that the accomplices were the four men in the dock. All four were acquitted. Van der Lubbe was convicted, and executed by virtue of a special law, made retrospective for his case. His capital crime was not to have set fire to the Reichstag, but to have had accomplices in doing so.

The opponents of the Nazis outside Germany were quick to point the moral. Everyone now agreed that van der Lubbe had accomplices. The accomplices had not been found, despite all the labours of the German criminal police and the German High Court. From this it clearly seemed to follow that the accomplices were not being sought in the right place. They were, in fact, the Nazis themselves. Here was a splendid opportunity for anti-Nazi propaganda. Communist exiles used it to the full. They organized a counter-trial in London, and provided evidence for it as lavishly as Stalin did for the great 'purge' trials in Russia later. Many of those who manufactured the evidence did so in good faith. They argued that the Nazis were immeasurably wicked (which they were) and that they had set fire to the Reichstag. They must have done it in a certain way; and the evidence before the counter-trial, though actually conjecture not fact, merely showed what this way was. In those days many of us were passionately anti-Nazi, and were ready to believe any evil of them. We had, as yet, little experience of how the Communists manufactured evidence when it suited their purpose. Men of good will accepted the verdict of the counter-trial; and though they were later disillusioned by the 'purges', by the post-war trials in eastern Europe, or by the Hungarian rising in 1956, some are reluctant to admit that they were taken for a ride by the Communists as early as 1933. Much of the evidence accepted by the counter-trial has now been discredited. Everyone, for instance, now recognizes the Oberfohren Memorandum and the confession of Karl Ernst, both discussed in detail by Herr Tobias, as Communist forgeries. The central argument remains unassailed: van der Lubbe could not have set fire to the Reichstag alone. Yet the proof of this rests mainly on the evidence placed before the Leipzig High Court. The Nazis unwittingly convicted themselves; and anyone who believes in their guilt is relying on evidence which the Nazis provided – or manufactured.

Such is the background for this book. Herr Tobias has not produced new evidence. He has merely looked again at the evidence which always existed. His examination involves much detail. This is essential if we are to judge what the evidence is worth. He has had to follow many false trails, and it is exasperating when these lead to a dead end. In the original German edition, he ran after still more false trails. Some of these have been left out, in order to spare the English reader. They do not, in my judgement, affect the general picture. I do not know Herr Tobias. He was never a Nazi; nor was his book written to please the present authorities in Germany – very much the contrary. It was written in an endeavour, whether mistaken or not, to discover the truth. In my opinion, he has succeeded, so far as anyone can succeed with the evidence we have at present. The reader will, I hope, believe me when I say that I have no desire to 'acquit' the Nazis. I welcome the investigations by Herr Tobias, solely because their conclusions seem to me right.

The case against the Nazis rested on two arguments or rather assumptions: the first that van der Lubbe was a physical degenerate who was incapable of starting the fires alone; the second that it was impossible, in any case, for the fires to have been started by a single man. Herr Tobias has shaken both these assumptions. He shows that van der Lubbe was quick-witted, ingenious, and physically active. His defective eyesight was balanced, as often happens, by sensitivity in other ways. He described precisely how he had set fire to the Reichstag; and his description tallied with the evidence. The police took him through the Reichstag with a stop-watch. He covered the ground at exactly the right times. Herr Tobias also provides a convincing explanation of van der Lubbe's motives and of his later behaviour. Van der Lubbe despaired at the lack of fight shown by the Communists and other opponents of Hitler. He wished to give a signal of revolt. When his gesture failed, when indeed it helped to consolidate Hitler's dictatorship, he fell into despair. There is a cry of human tragedy in his repeated declaration to the High Court: 'I did it alone. I was there. I know.' No one believed him.

Herr Tobias shows too that the fires were not beyond the capacity of a single man. The opinion of the 'experts' against this rested on conjecture, not evidence. Thus, there is good ground for believing that van der Lubbe did it all alone, exactly as he claimed. We can go further. There is some evidence, though naturally more conjectural, that the Nazis did not do it. If they in fact started the fire, why did they so strikingly fail to provide any evidence against the Communists or even that van der Lubbe had accomplices? The Nazi leaders certainly behaved as though they were surprised when they arrived at the scene of the fire. Indeed everyone acknowledges that Hitler had no previous knowledge of the fire, and was genuinely surprised. Yet it was his spontaneous reaction in accusing the Communists which gave the Reichstag fire political significance so far as it had any. Hence even the believers in Nazi guilt must admit that Hitler's method was to grab at opportunities as they occurred, not to manufacture them beforehand. Again, there has been total failure to show how the Nazis were associated with the fire. The strongest point in Herr Tobias's book is perhaps the firm and final demonstration that neither the Nazis nor anyone else could have come through the famous 'tunnel' from Göring's house. Use of this tunnel by the Nazis was an ingenious Communist speculation, plausible only to those who knew nothing of the physical obstacles which the tunnel and its many locked doors provided. We are thus left with two conclusions. There is no firm evidence that the Nazis had anything to do with the fire. There is much evidence that van der Lubbe did it alone, as he claimed. Of course new evidence may turn up, though this is unlikely after thirty years. The full records of the proceedings before the High Court are locked away at Potsdam under Communist control. They would surely have been released before now if they had helped to convict the Nazis. I have an uneasy feeling that van der Lubbe talked about his intentions beforehand and that he may have been egged on by Nazi companions. This does not imply that the Nazi leaders knew anything of it, and it makes no difference to the story.

Should this book have been written and published at all? Many people have been indignant at any so-called attempt to 'acquit' the Nazis of any charge, true or false. It is easy to understand why people have been indignant in Germany. Nazi guilt means innocence for everyone else. In particular, present German Ministers, who, as members of the Centre, voted for the Enabling Law in 1933, can plead that they were cheated by Hitler into believing in a Communist danger. But why should people mind in England? They are reluctant, I suppose, to confess that they were taken in the other way round – by the Communists, not by Hitler. Writers and lecturers on German history are annoyed at having to change their texts or their lecture-notes. I do not sympathize with them. As a scholar, I am just as pleased at being proved wrong as at being proved right. The essential thing is to acknowledge one's mistakes. On the Reichstag fire I was as wrong as everyone else; and I am grateful to Herr Tobias for putting me right. The Nazi (and Communist) method is to stick to every charge against one's opponents, whether it be true or false. We sink to their level if we copy their methods. Every act of fair judgement against the Nazis – every 'acquittal' of them if you like – is a triumph for the free spirit. Herr Tobias has performed a great service for all those who believe in truly free inquiry.

An essay by Sir Lewis Namier on Open Diplomacy opens with the words: 'There would be little to say on this subject, were it not for the nonsense which has been talked about it.' This is true of many topics besides Open Diplomacy. It is true of the fire at the Reichstag. Taken by itself, merely as a fire, there is little to say about it. An unbalanced Dutch boy started the fire all alone, much as Martin set fire to York Minster in 1829. Martin wanted to stop the organ buzzing. Van der Lubbe wanted to give the signal for a rising against the Nazis. Both were disappointed. The organ of York Minster still plays. Not a single German responded to van der Lubbe's call. But then everyone talked nonsense. The Nazis accused the Communists of starting the fire. Communists and others accused the Nazis. The nonsense talked about the fire illuminates, perhaps better than anything else, the political climate of the nineteen-thirties. It illuminates Nazi methods and Nazi incompetence. It illuminates Communist methods and, by comparison at any rate, their competence – particularly their competence in manufacturing legends which deceived high-minded people all over the world. It was their best stroke since the affair of Sacco and Vanzetti, where, it now appears, Sacco, though probably not Vanzetti, was guilty after all. The legends about the Reichstag fire became a cardinal part of recent history. Like all legends, they should be demolished; and Herr Tobias has gone a long way towards demolishing them.

MAGDALEN COLLEGE
OXFORD

Author's Preface

LIKE so many evils, this book had its root in 1933, when, as a direct result of the Reichstag fire, I lost my job and my home. Born in 1912, the son of a ceramic artist who later became a Trade Union official, I was working as a bookseller in a shop in the Trade Union buildings in Hamburg by 1933. On the morning of 1 April 1933, Nazi thugs battered their way in, and when all the shooting and shouting was over, my father and I were jobless and homeless.

The fire trial, which I followed from a distance while struggling to find a new job, ended with a large question-mark. Everything seemed to show that Germany's new rulers had perpetrated a gigantic swindle. A government, I argued, that had promised to base its policies on honesty, decency and truth, and yet began with what appeared so transparent a deception, deserved neither credence nor respect.

When the end of the war found me in an Italian hospital, where skilful American surgeons patched me up and pumped me full of fresh blood, I learned from American papers of many other Nazi scandals and hoped that the real truth of the Reichstag fire would soon come to light.

For years I waited in vain, and when Rudolf Diels, the first chief of the all-knowing Gestapo, had to confess in his book *Lucifer ante portas* that he too considered the fire as mysterious as before, and when even the Nuremberg Trials produced no fresh evidence (only legends obviously designed to curry favour with the Occupation Authorities) I rashly resolved to try to find out for myself.

In 1946 I was made an honorary member of the Hanover Denazification Court, and soon afterwards I was asked to join the State Denazification Commission. Then, in 1953, I became a permanent member of the State Civil Service and began to have enough leisure to carry out my resolution and began the studies of which this book is the result.

As I pursued what at first were completely unsystematic attempts to get at the facts, a new picture began to emerge, first in

17

outline and then in ever-greater detail. It differed radically from any that had been drawn before.

In the summer of 1956 I was approached by a member of the Federal Information Office who had heard by chance that I had been steadily amassing fresh evidence on the Reichstag fire, and who implored me not to keep my findings to myself. At first I refused to publish anything, partly because of laziness and partly because I knew what I should be letting myself in for. But in the end his persistence prevailed and I agreed to the publication of some extracts from this book in *Der Spiegel*.

I was not surprised when they were greeted with howls of rage, for in the course of my researches I had learned how tenaciously most people guard their familiar opinions. Many of those who attacked me in the correspondence columns of *Der Spiegel* and *Die Zeit* revealed that they are not nearly as interested in the truth as in preventing the acceptance of any facts that could possibly be interpreted as whitewashing the Nazis. In what follows I shall try to show that their fears are unjustified and that, as Kurt Stechert has put it, 'a democratic politician must declare war on all lies, for the humanitarian cause can only be advanced by the truth.'

Naturally, after all these years, including a total war and its aftermath, the picture I have been able to draw is somewhat blurred in places. On the other hand, I have managed to amass so large a volume of material that I have had to omit a great deal from a book addressed not only to the professional historian but also to the general reader. I must ask both to forgive me, and also to overlook my occasional inability to discuss sheer stupidity with the requisite scientific detachment.

F. T.

I

THE CRIMINAL CASE

1. A Case of Arson

SHORTLY before 10 p.m. on 27 February 1933, the telephone rang in Division IA, Police Headquarters, Berlin. When Detective-Inspector Heisig answered it, he was greeted by the voice of an extremely agitated Dr Schneider:

'Is that you, Heisig? Listen carefully, the Reichstag is on fire. The whole thing is a Communist job, because we've caught a Dutch Communist in the act. Göring has put the entire Prussian police on the alert, and I have just broadcast his orders over the Karlshorst police transmitter. Will you tell everyone in IA to get down to Headquarters as quickly as they can? The chief [Rudolf Diels] is bringing the criminal, and I want you to take a statement as soon as he arrives.'

Inspector Helmut Heisig had just turned thirty-one. Five years earlier, he had abandoned his theological studies to become a detective, first in Breslau, and later in Berlin. In the beginning, he had been assigned to criminal cases, but as the political tension mounted, he was increasingly drawn into the fight against Communist and National Socialist extremists. So impressed was Police President Albert Grzesinski with the work of his new inspector that he entrusted him with a number of extremely delicate and difficult political missions.

Heisig continued to do his duty by the Weimar Republic long after he realized that German democracy was doomed, that all the careerists in the force had long ago joined Nazi cells, and that they were now preparing black lists of 'unreliable elements'.

In fact, Heisig figured prominently on one such list, for in 1932 he had closed an election meeting of Captain Hermann Göring, the very man who, as Prussian Minister of the Interior, had meanwhile become his chief, and who was to complain to the Supreme Court on 4 November 1933: 'I was handed the Prussian Ministry of the Interior as a political instrument. . . . But the instrument turned out to be completely useless. What good were policemen who lived in the past, who had but yesterday beaten up our men . . .?'[1]

A typical opportunist, on the other hand, was the police officer who, on the historic 27 February 1933, attended a crowded Social Democratic election meeting in the Sportpalast. When the chief speaker, the editor of the *Vorwärts*, Friedrich Stampfer, explained the main difference between a Marxist and an anti-Marxist – 'While the former has to have a vast store of knowledge, the latter needs no knowledge at all' – the police officer leapt on to the platform and declared the meeting closed. The crowd was so incensed at this arbitrary intervention that the ushers had great difficulty in protecting the officer. There were shouts of: 'Down with Hitler', and: 'String him up'.[2]

The police had significantly counted on the sudden interruption of the meeting, and had accordingly placed the 32nd Precinct (Brandenburg Gate) on the alert. But when the door of the police station finally flew open, in came not the expected constable with an urgent request for reinforcement against the outraged demonstrators in the Sportpalast, but a panting young man in a brown raincoat.

'Come at once, the Reichstag is on fire!' he shouted.

And the duty officer, Lieutenant Emil Lateit, lost no time; together with Constables Graening and Losigkeit and the breathless young man, he jumped into the squad car whose engine had been kept running for quite a different purpose. The time was 9.15 p.m precisely.

Everything had happened so quickly that no one had found time to ask the young man for his name, let alone a signed statement. Back at the Reichstag, he kept standing about the street for a while and was then pushed back with the rest of the huge crowd which had meanwhile assembled. He went home, presumably satisfied that he had done his duty.

The squad car took no more than two minutes to reach the Reichstag building. When Lateit, whom the young man directed to the West Wing, observed a glow to the right of the main staircase, he hastily scribbled a note: '9.17 p.m. Reichstag blazing. Reinforcements needed', and sent Constable Graening back to the station. Graening returned a few minutes later with a large contingent of policemen who immediately cordoned off the area.

The Reichstag itself was quite deserted on this dull and wintry day – the temperature was 22 degrees F. and there was a sharp easterly wind. The last deputy to leave the building had been the chairman of the Communist parliamentary group, Ernst Torgler, who had passed through Portal Five (Northern Entrance) accompanied by the Communist deputy, Koenen, and the group secretary, Anna Rehme. Their late departure was not in the least unusual, for not only was Torgler a member of many Reichstag Committees, but his Reichstag rooms had become the Berlin Communist headquarters ever since the closure of the Karl Liebknecht House. The Reichstag was, in fact, the Communists' last legal refuge, for here alone did their leaders enjoy any kind of immunity. As Torgler passed through Portal Five he handed his keys to the night watchman, Rudolf Scholz. Scholz, who had known the affable and popular Torgler for many years, exchanged a few pleasantries with him before Torgler and his companions left the House.

Just under half an hour earlier, at 8.10 p.m. to be precise, Scholz had started on his customary round of inspection. It was his job to turn off any lights that had been left on and to close any open doors and windows. At about 8.30 p.m. he had passed the Session Chamber, and a quick look had showed him that everything was in order. Then he had heard footsteps in the dark, had switched on a light, but had continued on his round when he found that it was only Fräulein Anna Rehme on her way to the Communist Party rooms, where – as she explained – she wanted to pick up election material for Koenen. Scholz finished his rounds at about 8.38 p.m., just in time to take possession of Torgler's keys.

A few minutes later – at 8.45 p.m. – the Reichstag postman, Willi Otto, passed night porter Albert Wendt at Portal Five. Wendt told him that all the deputies had left. As was his custom, Otto lit his lantern and went up the main staircase leading to Portal Two (south), and to the Reichstag Post Office, where he emptied the post-boxes. Otto, too, neither heard nor noticed anything suspicious in the deserted building. Ten minutes later, at about 8.55 p.m., he left the Reichstag again through Portal Five, the only entrance still open.

At about 9.03 p.m., Hans Flöter, a young theology student, was making his way home from the State Library. As he turned the south-western corner of the dark and deserted Reichstag and headed across the square in front of the main entrance, he heard the sound of breaking glass. When he spun round to look in the

23

direction of the noise, he saw a man with a burning object in his hand on the first-floor balcony outside a window to the right of the Main Portal. Flöter wasted no time but sprinted off to the north-western corner of the building where he knew he would find a police officer. The officer (Sergeant Karl Buwert) seemed unable to take in what Flöter was trying to tell him, so that Flöter, in his excitement, felt impelled to give him a thump in the back to emphasize his words. Then the policeman trotted off in the correct direction and Flöter – who was no friend of the new government – continued on his way home. As he later put it, he had pressed the button and had started the machine but was not at all concerned to watch it run its course. However, before he walked off, he looked at his watch. It was 9.05 p.m.

When Police-Sergeant Buwert reached the front of the building, he at once noticed a broken window and a red glow behind it. He thought that Flöter was still with him, when in fact he had been joined by someone else. The two men gaped speechlessly at the weird spectacle behind the Reichstag windows.

Then a third passer-by appeared on the scene. He was twenty-one-year-old Werner Thaler, a typesetter, who had rounded the south-western corner of the Reichstag on his way to the Lehrter Bahnhof. He had previously heard the noise of breaking glass, had jumped up on the balustrade in the centre of the carriageway, and had gained the impression that two persons, and not one, were trying to break in. (It appeared later that this might have been an optical illusion, caused by reflection.) Remembering that he had passed a policeman a short way back, he raced off in the direction of Portal Two (Southern Entrance) and shouted into the night: 'Quick. Someone's trying to break into the Reichstag.' Then he ran back to the carriageway where he found Buwert and his unknown companion. Thaler's wrist-watch, which was usually fast, read 9.10 p.m.

For a moment all three of them looked on in paralysed astonishment. Then, as the man inside could be seen rushing from window to window waving a flaming torch, the three men started after him. Buwert had meanwhile drawn his pistol, and as the flickering light appeared in the last window but one, Thaler shouted: 'For goodness' sake, man, why don't you fire?' Buwert aimed his gun, pulled the trigger, and ran towards the window. Seeing that the mysterious intruder had disappeared, he now turned to the (unidentified) second young man, and asked him to alert the Brandenburg Gate police guardroom:

'Tell them the Reichstag is on fire and to call the fire brigade.'[3]

The young man did as he was told, while Buwert himself ran off towards the Simsonstrasse. On the way he met a Reichswehr soldier and, having a rather poor opinion of civilians, he asked him, too, to report the fire to the Brandenburg Police Station. The soldier, who had no intention of doing anything of the kind, agreed, and – continued on his way. Later, a bus conductor, Karl Seling, recalled that a Reichswehr soldier had, in fact, boarded his bus at the Bismarck Memorial stop, at about 9.15 p.m.

Meanwhile Buwert had been joined by other passers-by: Messrs Karl Kuhl and Hermann Freudenberg, and their respective spouses. They had all been out walking, had noticed a suspicious glow from far away, and had rushed to the scene with loud shouts of 'Police! Fire!', arriving just in time to see the flames lick up the curtains. Buwert, who at last grasped the fact that someone was deliberately setting fire to the Reichstag before his eyes, now ordered Kuhl and Freudenberg to make sure that the fire brigade had been called.

Together with Frau Wally Freudenberg, the two men ran off down the Simsonstrasse. When they saw a number of people coming out of the German Engineering Institute (V.D.I.), they rushed up to the caretaker, Otto Schaeske, shouting:

'The Reichstag is on fire. Call the fire brigade!'

Completely taken aback, Schaeske opened the telephone book, and started a vain and nervous search for the right number. Eventually, Emil Lück, who had been helping out in the cloakroom that night, snatched the book from him, quickly found the correct entry, and dialled.

Meanwhile Buwert's shot had brought two patrolmen to the scene. When Buwert told them briefly what had happened, one of them decided to make absolutely certain, and ran off to sound the fire alarm in the near-by Moltkestrasse.

Buwert's shouting and waving had also attracted the attention of Constable Helmut Poeschel, who was on duty at the north-eastern corner of the Reichstag. When he heard Buwert's: 'Fire! Tell the doorkeeper of Portal Five,' Poeschel set off at a gallop. Gasping for breath, he ordered the completely stupefied Albert Wendt to pull the fire alarm which, as Poeschel knew, was kept in the doorkeeper's lodge. But Wendt refused to believe the constable without

25

seeing for himself. He rushed outside, carefully locking the door behind him. When he saw the blaze, he exclaimed: 'It's the restaurant!' and when Lieutenant Lateit, who had meanwhile arrived on the scene, told him that the fire brigade had already been called, he ran back to his lodge and tried to ring up Chief Engineer Eugen Mutzka and House-Inspector Alexander Scranowitz. In his excitement he must have misdialled, for he failed to get hold of either of them, though he did manage to contact the Chief Reichstag Messenger, Eduard Prodöhl, and Paul Adermann, the night porter at the Speaker's Residence. While he was still talking to Prodöhl, Wendt could hear the jangle of an approaching fire engine.

Adermann, for his part, immediately notified the Director of the Reichstag, Geheimrat Galle. Then he rang up the Prussian Ministry of the Interior to report the fire to Hermann Göring, the Speaker. The call was taken by Göring's secretary, Fräulein Grundtmann.

Immediately on his arrival at the Reichstag, Lieutenant Lateit asked Buwert whether the fire brigade had been called. When Buwert told him it had, he asked further whether the full-scale alarm had been sounded. Buwert said no, and Lateit told him to see to it, but also to keep a close watch on the Reichstag windows and to fire at anything suspicious.

Lateit then tried to enter the Reichstag, first through Portal Two (south) and then through Portals Three and Four (east), but found them all locked. He ran on to Portal Five (north), where Wendt, the porter, told him that House-Inspector Scranowitz was on his way with the keys to the inner doors.

Scranowitz had been having his supper in his near-by flat, when he suddenly heard the fire engines. Fearing the worst, he rushed to the telephone and called Wendt, quite unaware of the fact that Wendt had been trying to get hold of him. When Wendt told him that the restaurant was on fire, Scranowitz yelled at him: 'And why the dickens didn't you report it to me?'

He banged the receiver down and raced across to Portal Five. Once there, he opened the inner doors and rushed up the staircase, followed by Lieutenant Lateit, and Constables Losigkeit and Graening. As they dashed into the large lobby, they noticed a red glow coming from beyond the Kaiser Wilhelm monument. When Lateit looked through an open glass door into the Session Chamber, he saw a large flame. In the doorway he spotted a blazing 'cushion', which turned out to be a folded overcoat. In addition, the thick plush curtains on either side of the glass door were burning, and so was some of the wooden panelling.

It was about 9.22 p.m. when Lateit entered the Session Chamber. The whole Chamber was softly lit up by a steady, continuous sheet of flame over the tribune. The effect was that of a brightly illuminated church organ. (Lateit was unaware that its 'pipes' consisted of three blazing curtains.) He observed no other fires in the Chamber, nor did he notice any smoke. Constable Losigkeit, on the other hand, who went farther into the Chamber, saw other flames in the stenographers' well, below.

Lateit, now fully convinced that an incendiary was at work, ordered the two policemen to draw their revolvers. Meanwhile, House-Inspector Scranowitz had switched on the light in the corridors and in the lobby. Lateit, who had been present during the Blücher Palace fire in April 1931, was still firmly convinced that the Chamber could easily be saved by the fire brigade.

On his way back to Portal Five, Lateit noticed a number of small fires: here a carpet was in flames, there a wastepaper basket. Everywhere bits of material were lying about – he counted some twenty-five of these, each roughly the size of the palm of his hand. He thought 'they might have been the charred remains of table-cloths', for all of them were giving off a lot of smoke. On the floor of the lobby, he found a cap, a tie, and a piece of soap.

Near Portal Five he encountered a number of firemen who were busy extinguishing fires in the western lobby. To other firemen standing there he cried:

'It's arson. The place is one great mass of fires.'

He ordered one of the firemen to go back to the Session Chamber with Constable Losigkeit. Then he told his own men to make a careful search of the whole building for the intruder, while he drove back to the Brandenburg Gate for reinforcements. His arrival at the guardroom was recorded as 9.25 p.m. He had been away for a total of ten minutes.

While Lateit, Losigkeit, and Graening had been looking at the fire in the Chamber, they had been joined by Constable Poeschel. Lateit ordered him to accompany House-Inspector Scranowitz, who, after he had switched on the lights in the lobby and corridors, was about to light up the Chamber as well. Behind the Kaiser Wilhelm monument, Scranowitz noticed one of the many small fires Lateit had already observed, and stamped it out. Then he ran to the restaurant, opened the door, and was met by a mass of flames. When he made his way back to the lobby, he noticed that the curtains and a wooden panel leaning against the wall had caught fire.

Scranowitz, too, now looked into the Session Chamber – shortly after Lateit had done so. A single glance showed him that the curtains behind the Speaker's Chair had caught fire, but that the panelling was still untouched. But then he observed – or claimed that he observed – a completely different picture from that described by Lateit: on the first three rows of deputies' benches Scranowitz counted some twenty to twenty-five small fires, each about eighteen inches wide, and all of roughly the same shape. In addition, the Speaker's Chair and the Orators' Table were ablaze, and so were the curtains in the stenographers' well. Here the flames, however, were flickering and 'spluttering' violently. Scranowitz shut the door to the Chamber and, with Constable Poeschel, who had been looking over his shoulder, ran across the thickly carpeted southern corridor to the Bismarck Hall. Just as they passed under the great chandelier, a man, bare to the waist, suddenly shot across their path from the left, i.e. from the back of the Session Chamber. The man stopped dead in his tracks and then started to run back, but when Poeschel raised his pistol, shouting 'Hands up!', he obediently raised his arms. He was a tall, well-built young man, completely out of breath and dishevelled. All Poeschel found on him was a pocket knife, a wallet, and a passport. While Poeschel was leafing through this document, House-Inspector Scranowitz, shaking with rage, yelled at the stranger: 'Why did you do it?'

'As a protest,' the man replied.

Scranowitz, a tall, athletic man, hit out at him in blind fury.

Meanwhile, Poeschel had gathered from the man's passport that his name was Marinus van der Lubbe, that he came from Leyden in Holland, and that he was born on 13 January 1909.

The time was 9.27 p.m.

Then Poeschel marched his prisoner to Portal Five, where someone flung a rug over his naked shoulders, before they took him away to the Brandenburg Gate Police Station.

The fire alarm from the German Engineering Institute was received at Brigade Headquarters at 9.13 p.m. At 9.14, this call

28

was duly transmitted to the Linienstrasse Fire Station, whence a section of pumps under Chief Fire Officer Emil Puhle was sent out at once. It arrived at the north-eastern corner of the Reichstag at 9.18 p.m. At 9.19 p.m. another section, led by Fire Officer Waldemar Klotz, drew up. It had been sent out from Turmstrasse Station in response to the fire call from Moltkestrasse. Each section consisted of four fire engines. At about 9.23 p.m., Puhle used ladders to climb up to, and break into, the restaurant; so great was his hurry that he failed to notice that one restaurant window was already broken. The door leading to the lobby and the entire panelling were now ablaze; the curtains had completely burnt down. There were a number of small fires – for instance, a window curtain which threatened to flare up in the draught from the broken window – and these were quickly extinguished. At 9.27 p.m., Puhle crossed to the Session Chamber where he was met by Fire Officer Waldemar Klotz. Klotz, who had seen Puhle's section parked at the western side, had not bothered to stop but had gone on to tackle the fire elsewhere. He made a brief stop at Portal Two (south) but, finding it locked, he drove right round the building to Portal Five (north), leaving Fire Officer Franz Wald and one vehicle behind.

At about 9.20 p.m., Klotz gave orders to make a hose ready, while he, with Firemen Kiessig and König carrying hand pumps, hurried into the lobby. Here they dealt with a burning carpet, the curtain of a telephone box, the telephone box itself, and the ornamental panelling of a door. At about 9.24 p.m., Klotz entered the Chamber, and noticed a tremendous draught and a tremendous wave of heat. The Chamber itself was full of thick smoke, so that all he could make out was a glow in the north-eastern corner. Since he was afraid of increasing the draught, he quickly shut the doors.

A little later, when he looked into the Chamber a second time, the whole place was a sea of flames. At 9.31 p.m., the tenth-grade alarm was given (each grade calling for one section of four pumps). A few minutes later, eight further sections started towards the Reichstag. With them came Chief Fire Director Gempp, the head of the Berlin Fire Department, accompanied by Fire Directors Lange and Tamm, and Chief Engineer Meusser. Quite separately, both Gempp and Lange gave the full-scale (15th grade or grand) alarm at 9.42 p.m. Within minutes, therefore, fifteen sections of pumps with more than sixty vehicles had been thrown into the fire-fighting. At the same time, a number of fire-boats began tackling the fire from the river Spree.

By the time the fire was finally put out at 11 p.m., the Session Chamber was completely gutted. The panelling was gone, and so were the three-tiered tribune, the glorious carvings, and the glass dome, which now offered an unimpeded view of the night sky.

It was also at about 11 p.m. that Paul Bogun, an engineer, reported to Lieutenant Lateit at the Brandenburg Gate Police Station. He told the lieutenant that, at about 9 p.m., he had come out of a lecture at the Engineering Institute, near the Reichstag, and finding that his tram had just left, he had decided to walk home. When he was some twenty yards from Portal Two, he heard a 'rattle', and then saw a man step out of the swinging doors. The man hesitated while looking across at two women, one of whom had appeared to give him a signal. The man had run off towards the Königsplatz, peering back at the Reichstag 'most suspiciously'.

Lateit told Bogun to report the matter to Police Headquarters at once. Bogun, however, preferred to wait for another three days before doing so.

Another person to come forward, Frau Kuesner, who passed the Speaker's Palace at about 8.55 p.m. on her way to the National Club, also alleged that she had seen a man running off. Later, it emerged that the man in question had, in fact, been an innocent pedestrian, who had taken shelter from the icy wind in Portal Two while waiting for a bus. When the bus came into sight he had made a dash for it.

2. The Arsonist

MARINUS VAN DER LUBBE

In September 1955 – twenty-two years after the Reichstag fire – Johan van der Lubbe of Amsterdam petitioned the Berlin County Court to repeal the sentence passed by the Supreme Court in Leipsig on his brother Marinus on 23 December 1933. Three years later, his petition was dismissed for purely formal reasons.

Thus disappeared what little chance there still was of having the mysterious events of 27 February 1933, and the enigma of Marinus van der Lubbe, examined by an independent court.

What sort of man was this young Dutchman who, on the evening of 27 February 1933, was apprehended in the flaming Reichstag? Rarely has the life of any man been studied in such great detail, and yet been so deliberately distorted and misunderstood. To this day most people believe that van der Lubbe was:

1. A congenital idiot;
2. A juvenile delinquent;
3. A pathological vagrant;
4. A pathological liar;
5. A pathological boaster;
6. A homosexual prostitute in the service of the Nazis.

All attempts to describe the real van der Lubbe come up against two books published in 1933 and 1934 by Communist propagandists in Paris, with the sole aim of proving that the Reichstag was burned by the Nazis. In order to make that story stick, van der Lubbe had to be turned into a Nazi tool at all costs.

Part I, entitled *The Brown Book of the Hitler Terror and the Burning of the Reichstag*, appeared shortly after the fire; Part II, entitled *The Reichstag Fire Trial* or the *Second Brown Book of the Hitler Terror*, appeared after the trial and had a special introductory chapter by Georgi Dimitrov. In what follows, we shall refer to the two as *Brown Books I* and *II* respectively.

Soon after Inspector Heisig had given the alarm, officers of

Division IA started to report at Police Headquarters. When Diels and Schneider eventually arrived with the prisoner, everyone kept peering in to catch a glimpse of the half-naked Dutchman.

In his evidence to the Supreme Court, Heisig later described the strange situation as follows:

> The whole room was teeming with people. First of all there were the officers from my own and from near-by offices. Then there were Police President von Levetzow, the Vice-President, Ministerialrat Diels, Ministerialdirektor Daluege, together with a number of gentlemen from all sorts of Ministries. Altogether some forty to fifty people must have crowded into the little room, for it was completely packed.

All these men had come in, not only to catch a glimpse of the arsonist, but also to learn what further outrages might be expected that night. The presence of so many of his superiors naturally perturbed young Inspector Heisig, particularly when they kept interrupting his interrogation to fire questions of their own at the prisoner.

In general, the average Dutchman understands German far more readily than the average German understands Dutch, but in van der Lubbe's case Heisig had no difficulty at all in making him out, as he spoke German fluently, though with an unmistakable Dutch accent. Van der Lubbe himself insisted that he needed no interpreter, and spoke out quite fearlessly. Heisig had to interrupt him many times because most of his statements threatened to degenerate into political harangues. To begin with, Heisig asked him to explain his motives, so as to decide whether or not the crime fell within the province of the Political Branch. Van der Lubbe replied that his motives had been political: he wanted to encourage the German workers to fight for their freedom. His deed was meant as an example.

Heisig deduced that the man was a Communist, though van der Lubbe denied having any connection with the Communist Party.

During the discussion of his finances, van der Lubbe volunteered the information that he had used part of his extremely meagre resources to buy firelighters and matches for a number of other fires as well. When pressed by the astonished Heisig, van der Lubbe confessed that he had set fire to the Welfare Office in Neukölln, a Berlin suburb, two days before.

Detective-Inspector Walter Zirpins took over from Heisig. After another few hours, van der Lubbe grew visibly tired. By 3 a.m. he was completely exhausted, and Zirpins had him put in a cell for the night.

Meanwhile Heisig rushed off a letter to the police in Leyden, van der Lubbe's home town. Van der Lubbe was known so well there that the Dutch authorities were able to send back an immediate reply. In it Detective-Inspector N. G. Weyers confirmed that Marinus van der Lubbe was a dangerous Communist.

At about 8 a.m. next morning, van der Lubbe was fetched for further interrogation. Once again, a host of curious people popped in to have a look, but this time the atmosphere had grown a great deal less informal. All van der Lubbe's statements were now taken down verbatim. Because of the special interest the case was bound to excite, Heisig asked his secretaries to make as many copies as possible; van der Lubbe signed each page of every one.

The impression van der Lubbe made on his interrogators can be gathered from the police report dated 3 March 1933 and from the evidence of Inspector Heisig and Dr Zirpins before the Supreme Court. In the police report we read:

> He is endowed with a great deal of (admittedly very one-sided) intelligence, and, appearances to the contrary, he is a very bright fellow. His grasp of the German language is so good that he can follow even finger shades of meanings, though his own speech is slurred. Thus he could not only follow the examination but remember entire sentences and repeat them word for word. [Especially during the discussion of his motives] he kept correcting those phrases which, he thought, did not fully reflect his real meaning.

And this is what Dr Zirpins stated in evidence before the Supreme Court:

> . . . he corrected the statement, going into questions of style, and rejecting certain passages out of hand. In short he had no need of an interpreter.

Dr Zirpins also mentioned another characteristic:

> He had a remarkable capacity not only for repeating dates, but for remembering numbers in general. There are some people who cannot remember numbers, but he had, as it were, a genius for numbers, could remember dates and times, etc.

33

Few believed Zirpins when he went on to say:

> I gave him a small piece of paper to sketch on. First he drew a plan of
> the Welfare Office. At the time I did not know the layout, but, in fact,
> his plan was perfectly correct. . . . I had been in the Reichstag only
> twice before, and did not know the precise set-up, but van der Lubbe
> drew everything so perfectly that afterwards, when we inspected the
> scene of the crime, everything fell into place. I myself would – quite
> frankly – have been quite unable to reconstruct the scene nearly as well
> as he did. I gave him a red and a blue pencil with which he traced his
> path in and out of the building with perfect facility.

Marinus van der Lubbe was a bricklayer by trade and had
learned drawing at night school. In addition he had an almost
phenomenal memory. In the final police report we are told: 'He
had a remarkable sense of direction, which he probably acquired in
the course of his travels. Although he has been in Berlin for only
eight days, he is able to describe long walks, street by street . . .'

During his evidence before the Supreme Court, on 27 September
1933, Heisig was asked whether he was present during the reconstruction of the crime. Heisig replied:

> Yes, and van der Lubbe led us. We neither indicated the direction nor
> influenced him in any way. He was almost delighted to show us the
> path he had taken. He said he had an excellent sense of direction
> because of his poor eyesight. Another sense had taken the place of his
> eyes.

All these statements by Heisig and Dr Zirpins were given little
credence – they simply did not fit into the general scheme of things.
For one thing, they ran counter to the public image of van der
Lubbe as an apathetic moron; for another, they bore out van der
Lubbe's claim that he was the sole culprit when all the experts said
he could not have been.

We can form a good idea of Marinus van der Lubbe's real
character from the statement he made to the police on 3 March
1933:

> At the outset, I must insist that my action was inspired by political
> motives. In Holland I read that the National Socialists had come to
> power in Germany. I have always followed German politics with
> keen interest and I read all the articles I could get hold of on Brüning,
> Papen and Schleicher. When Hitler took over the Government, I
> expected much enthusiasm for him but also much tension. I bought

all the newspapers on this subject, and found that they were of my opinion. I myself am a Leftist, and was a member of the Communist Party until 1929. What I did not like about the Party is the way they lord it over the workers, instead of letting the workers decide for themselves. I side with the proletariat in the class struggle. Its own leaders must stand at the head. The masses themselves must decide what they ought to do and what they ought not to do. [These were in fact the views of the *Rade* or International Communists, a tiny Dutch splinter group completely unknown in Germany.] In Germany a National Coalition has now been formed, and I think it holds two dangers: (1) it oppresses the workers, and (2) it refuses to submit to other countries so that it is bound to lead to war. I watched on for a few days and then I decided to go to Germany and to see for myself. I made the decision without anyone else, and I came to Germany all by myself. Once here, I intended to observe how the National Coalition affects the workers and what the workers think about the National Coalition. I started in Düsseldorf, where I spoke to workers in the street. I did the same thing in other towns. In Berlin, I also studied the pamphlets of the various parties and then went to the Welfare Offices in Lichtenberg, Wedding, and Neukölln. I also went to the Labour Exchange, but it was closed because of the elections. I found out that whereas the National Coalition has complete freedom in Germany, the workers have not.

Now, what the workers' organizations are doing is not likely to rouse the workers to the struggle for freedom. That is why I discussed better ways and means with the workers. The privileges which the National Socialists enjoy today must also be enjoyed by the workers. That is the reason why I asked the workers to demonstrate. But all I was told was to take the matter to the Party – the Communist Party. But I had heard that a Communist demonstration was disbanded by the leaders on the approach of the police, and that the people listened to these leaders instead of carrying out their own resolutions. I realized then that the workers will do nothing by themselves, that they will do nothing against a system which grants freedom to one side and metes out oppression to the other. In my opinion something absolutely had to be done in protest against this system. Since the workers would do nothing, I had to do something by myself. I considered arson a suitable method. I did not wish to harm private people but something that belonged to the system itself: official buildings, the Welfare Office for example, for that is a building in which the workers come together, or the City Hall, because it is a building belonging to the system, and further the Palace, because it lies in the centre of the city, and if it goes up, the huge flames can be seen from far away. . . . When these three

35

fires failed to come off, that is to say when my protest did not come off, I decided on the Reichstag as the centre of the whole system. . . .

And finally, van der Lubbe's answer to the crucial question:

As to the question whether I acted alone, I declare emphatically that this was the case. No one at all helped me, nor did I meet a single person in the Reichstag.[1]

Thus did the young radical explain his motives to the police, to the Examining Magistrate, the Public Prosecutor, and finally the Supreme Court Judges. Not one of them was prepared to listen to him, partly because his theories transcended their narrow political horizons, and partly because of their hatred of everything that smacked of Communism.

CHILDHOOD AND BACKGROUND

In the year 1904, Franciscus Cornelis van der Lubbe, a forty-one-year-old hawker, married Petronella van Handel-Peuthe, a divorcée, in Leyden. From her first marriage, she brought him four children – one girl and three boys – who were joined in time by three children from the new marriage: Johan, also called Jan; Cornelis and Marinus (Rinus). By the time Marinus was born on 13 January 1909, his parents had ceased to get on with each other. Soon afterwards they separated. The father took to the road and to drink, leaving his asthmatic wife to fend for her many children and herself. She opened a small shop in 's Hertogenbosch, and did all her housework, of which there was a great deal with so large a family, in the evenings. In short, her life would have been very hard for a healthy woman, let alone for a semi-invalid. As a result, the children were left to themselves most of the time and it was no wonder that Marinus, the youngest, ran wild and had to be sent to a home for neglected children – for a 'few weeks' as he himself put it. One of his teachers during that period, van der Meene, has described him as a 'talented boy of average application'. Marinus gave him little cause for complaint and at no time did he have to punish the boy severely.

Fate struck Marinus a severe blow in 1921: his mother died when he was only twelve years old and he joined the household of his stepsister, Annie Sjardijn, who lived in Oegsgeest near Leyden. She herself had three children of her own, aged two, four and six years respectively. Marinus, who, according to those who knew him at the time, was a charming, alert and respectful young lad, naturally acted the big brother to his small nephews.[1]

Marinus continued to attend the Christian School in Leyden for eighteen months after his mother's death, and then his brother-in-law apprenticed him to a builder. After work Marinus went to night school to continue his studies. At the age of sixteen Marinus was so healthy and strong that all his friends called him 'Dempsey'.

It was from his workmates that he first learned the new revolutionary gospel with which he quickly replaced all he had been taught by his Calvinist teachers, and which opened up to him an entirely new world of ideas, concepts and words.

Marinus, the boy who grew up with a minimum of parental authority and supervision, found it easy to dismiss all authority – individual or social – as completely unnecessary. He started his fight against 'bourgeois capitalism' by becoming a member of *De Zaaier* (The Sowers), a Communist Youth Organization. In it, he first proved his great ability to sway others.

Marinus worked hard at his job and earned good money. He spent much of his spare time reading and became a familiar figure in the Leyden Public Library. Among the heavy books he borrowed were *Philosophy and Labour* and *Today and Tomorrow* by Henry Ford, and Marx's *Das Kapital*. His longing to see the world was fed by Sven Hedin's books on Tibet and China, so much so that some years later he actually left for China – on foot. Needless to say, the foundation of his self-taught knowledge was rather shaky, so that his hatred of capitalism was based less on Marxist 'science' than on youthful enthusiasm and Utopian dreams of heaven and earth.

Then fate struck him yet another blow. During a lunch break he fell victim to what was meant to be a harmless joke. Two of his friends playfully pulled an empty lime sack over his head and a piece of lime got into his eye causing a painful inflammation. Since misfortunes never come singly, both eyes were damaged by more lime a short time later. He had to spend five miserable months in Professor van der Hoeve's eye-clinic. Despite three operations, his cornea turned opaque, his eyesight became weak, and his eyelids were ever afterwards subject to all sorts of infections.

This accident was a turning point in his life: he had to break off his apprenticeship and, not surprisingly, he is said to have toyed with the idea of suicide. He had no home, no parents, and now he was near-blind. The long months in the clinic in which he could do

37

little but feel sorry for himself, were bound to increase his unrest and dissatisfaction with life, and he only saved his sanity by immersing himself completely in politics. He was awarded a very small weekly disability pension – seven gulden and forty-four cents – which was not nearly enough to live on, so that he had to do casual labour from time to time. During the intervals he lived on the dole. Among his many casual jobs, he was assistant waiter in the Railway Restaurant at Leyden (winter 1927), porter in the 'Hof van Holland' hotel in Nordwijk (summer 1928), and a potato trader on his own account. He also worked on a dredger, on a ferry plying between Nordwijk and Sassenheim, as a butcher, a messenger boy, and in the Dutch bulb trade. In short, he was anything but an idler.

In the Young Communist League, for which he worked indefatigably, his physical strength, intelligence, and lack of bourgeois prejudices marked Marinus out from the start. Very quickly he fell foul not only of the local police, but also of his ever-correct brother-in-law, Sjardijn. After countless political arguments, Marinus left Oegsgeest for good, and at the age of eighteen he moved back to Leyden to share a room with the Communist student Piet van Albada. Quite naturally, Albada and his political friends exerted a great deal of influence on him, so much so that Marinus soon attracted the attention of the Leyden police as well.

Despite his youth, Marinus was allowed to take the chair at a public meeting of the Leyden Communist Youth League on 15 November 1928. In October 1929 he rented an empty store-room, proudly baptized it Lenin House, and offered it as a meeting hall to the Youth Group. He wrote leaflets and edited factory and school pamphlets, in all of which he attacked militarism and capitalism; he was present at every strike meeting and political demonstration held in Leyden, and worked tirelessly for the revolutionary cause. His activities as public speaker and heckler soon made him a well-known figure, particularly among the unemployed, whom he led during a number of processions through the town.

Once, when his political opponents, the Dutch Social Democrats, held a rally, he organized a Communist counter-demonstration. On that occasion he launched his first direct attack on an institution against which he was afterwards to wage private war: the Welfare Office. For him the Welfare Office was the epitome of the hated capitalist system, a system in which petty officials pompously throw

crumbs from the opulent tables of the rich to the poor and dis-
possessed. Marinus 'hit back' by throwing bricks through the
windows of the Welfare Office. He was arrested and sentenced to
fourteen days in prison.

Though Marinus was quick to take offence, and quick to argue,
he was no more truculent than most young radicals. Thus he
repeatedly resigned from the Young Communist League, only to
rejoin once his anger had abated. Finally, he broke completely with
the Dutch Communist Party for reasons still shrouded in mystery
but obviously related to his independent attitude and his spontaneous identification with the working class.

Through Piet van Albada, Marinus became familiar with the
ideas of such 'left deviationists' as the LAO (Left Workers'
Opposition) the AAU (General Workers' Union) and last but not
least the PIC (Party of International Communists) or *Rade* Communists, as they were also called. This 'Party', which had only a
handful of members in Holland, was opposed to the very idea of
discipline and leadership, and saw the salvation of the working
class in spontaneous, individual action alone.

THE 'PATHOLOGICAL VAGRANT'

None of the men who later cross-examined Marinus van der
Lubbe had ever felt the urge to pull up their stakes and to go out
into the world – without money or friends. No wonder therefore
that they all looked down on him as a shiftless vagrant.

Like so many unemployed workers anxious to escape the sad
monotony of their enforced indolence, Marinus van der Lubbe
decided to change one kind of misery for what turned out to be
another, and took to the roads of Europe. He was an exceptionally
undemanding person; night after night he shared his quarters with
the flotsam of human society, and he was content – because all of
them applauded his scathing attacks on the State and on capitalism.

Marinus's first journey did not take him to Sven Hedin's
mysterious East, but only to Northern France. Then, in 1928, he
hiked through Belgium and spent a few days in the German city of
Aachen. From August to November 1930 he was in Calais, where
he conceived the idea of swimming the Channel one day. He was
young and strong, used to exertions and unusually persistent once
he made up his mind to do something. He returned to Leyden from

39

his first trip, firmly resolved to see as much of the world as he possibly could.

In the spring of 1931, Marinus and his Communist friend, Hendrik Holverda, decided to raise money for another trip by what was then a favourite method with impecunious globe-trotters: they sold postcards bearing their own likenesses. On this particular photograph Holverda had raised his clenched fist in the Communist salute. The text, which was printed in French, Dutch and German, read: 'Workers' Sports and Study Tour of Marinus van der Lubbe and H. Holverda through Europe and the Soviet Union. Start of the tour from Leyden, April 14th, 1931'.

But they could not raise enough money and, on his way back to Holland, van der Lubbe was arrested by the Prussian police in Gronau (Westphalia) for selling postcards without a licence. On 13 May 1931, the court imposed a fine of fifty marks or ten days' imprisonment, and Marinus chose prison.

Naturally he was greatly disappointed, particularly since he knew that the Communists in Leyden would gloat over this set-back; yet he would not have been Marinus van der Lubbe had he given up completely. In fact, he tried time and again to reach his great goal – the Soviet Union, and it was this very persistence which enabled his detractors to say that van der Lubbe kept talking about fantastic projects which he never carried out.

On 29 September 1931, he made his first tour of the Balkans, and wrote to Koos Vink from Yugoslavia:

> If it is at all possible, I should like to fork left in Turkey, and go on to Tiflis (Russia). However, I anticipate great difficulties. . . .

And on 14 October, he added the following reflections:

> I had intended, while on my way to China, to visit Tiflis in Russia. Since, however, I have not come far enough, I shall make, not for Tiflis, but for European Russia, say for Odessa or Rijeo [?] There I shall somehow try to smuggle myself across the Red border. . . .

A week later – on 21 October – Marinus wrote to Koos Vink:

> I thought I might try to cross into Russia from Rumania but because that too is just another vast detour and because it's probably very difficult to get across the border, I have decided against it. . . .

On 12 February 1932, when he had reached Vienna in the course of his second Balkan tour, he wrote to Koos Vink:

I have just got a Hungarian visa and shall leave Vienna straight away, since otherwise the whole thing will take far too long. I shall probably go on to Russia, that is if nothing special happens. . . .

From his letter of 19 April it became clear that something 'special' had, in fact, happened:

When you receive this letter, I shall have spent a whole week in a Polish prison. I was given three weeks, for illegal entry, and when my time is up I shall return to Holland.

Marinus himself never claimed that he had been to Russia; that claim was made 'on his behalf' by his former Party comrades anxious to show him up as a liar, particularly when it came to his attitude to the Soviet Union. It was to refute these and other slanders that Marinus's real friends, and especially the *Rade* or International Communists, published the *Red Book* (*Roodboek*) which, apart from a contemptuous and brilliant refutation of every Communist slander, also contained Marinus's diary for the period 6 September – 24 October 1931, together with a large number of his letters.

This brings us to his Channel-swimming attempts which even so sympathetic a man as Dr Seuffert, his counsel, has considered a clear sign of Marinus's boastfulness. However, we know from Mr Justice de Jongh that 'Marinus was a fine sportsman, who had swum from Noordwijk to Scheveningen'.[2] Now, a glance at the map will show that this was a very respectable achievement. Why, then, should his attempts to do what so many others have done – to swim the Channel – be considered a sign of boastfulness or a proof of his pathological need to impress others?

At the time, the Dutch newspaper, *Het Leven*, had offered a considerable prize – 5,000 gulden – to the first Dutchman to swim the Channel, and Marinus was a Dutchman and a good swimmer. And who could really have blamed him if, apart from the large prize, he was also attracted by the glory of it all?

In his diary or in his letters he never mentioned the Channel crossing in other than matter-of-fact terms:

Having re-considered my plan once again this morning, I have come to the conclusion that I had best be back home at about the end of May or the beginning of June. Then I will have time to make up my mind whether I will take part in the Channel crossing or not. From now on,

I have decided not to rush about so much but – if possible at all – to go swimming every day.

How very seriously he took this business may be gathered from the fact that on 14 October, while he was still in Rumania, he sent a letter to a Dutchman he had met in Calais asking for work near the French coast, so that he could practise swimming every day. Even then he was not too optimistic about his chances, for on the same day he made the following entry in his diary: 'I have therefore decided to return so that I can be ready for the summer. But even when I return, things won't go as smoothly as all that.'

How very unboastful the whole scheme was is further borne out by the following entry, dated 21 October: 'By the way, I have tried to cross the Danube. But I failed, for the water was too cold. If I swam every day, things might be different.'

In his letter of the same day to Koos Vink, he returned to the Channel crossing once again:

As regards the crossing, I should like to ask you if *Het Leven* has said anything at all about holding the prize open until next year. Please tell me if so, and if possible send me the article regarding the Channel crossing and the swimming. Incidentally, last week I wrote to the Dutch gentleman in France, asking about work and also if he would send his reply to your address. If you should hear from him ...

The *Red Book* also published a postcard from an Austrian swimmer who had allowed Marinus to use her boat for his Channel training.

Shortly before his second journey to Hungary in January 1932, Marinus had another clash with the hated Welfare Office. Having been refused an increase in his unemployment relief, he once again smashed a few windows as a protest. Marinus was sentenced to three months' imprisonment *in absentia*.

On his return from Hungary, he was welcomed by a special reception committee: a police escort. On 15 June 1932, he sent the following cry for help to Koos Vink:

As you can see from this letterhead I have landed in prison in Utrecht, because I was sentenced to three months on account of the windows ... I can however appeal against the sentence which costs approximately 1.0 *fl*. Would you therefore be kind enough to send me a postal order for 1.50 *fl*. at once, so that I can appeal?

After hearing the appeal on 29 June 1932, the Court upheld the original three months' sentence. As a result, Marinus was in Scheveningen prison from 12 July until 2 October 1932. After his release he paid a number of brief visits: to his father in Dordrecht, to Amsterdam, and to The Hague.

Marinus's hatred of the Welfare Office also took forms other than smashing windows. When a further request for an increase was refused, he went on hunger strike and managed to last out for a full eleven days. Then he was carted off to hospital, but only when he was promised that his request would be met in full did he finally break his long fast.

Once again he had proved his remarkable strength of purpose. At the same time he had forged a new weapon which he was to use many times again: for example, during the preliminary investigation into the Reichstag fire. But there he met an equally determined opponent: the Examining Magistrate, Paul Vogt.

It has often been asked why Marinus should have gone back to Budapest so soon after his return from Hungary. Later, in the Supreme Court, he replied to the President's question: 'Why did you visit Hungary so often? Did you have special contacts there?' – by which, needless to say, the President meant political contacts – with a curt 'No', and there is, in fact, no evidence that any such contacts were made. Even so, the *Red Book* published a photograph of a Hungarian girl not, as the authors emphasized, to disprove the Communist slander that van der Lubbe was a homosexual, but '. . . in the hope that one of the readers of this book, which is printed in four languages, may recognize the woman in the photograph and may be able to provide us with her name and present address, so that we may turn to her for some explanation about her relationship with van der Lubbe.'

In an undated letter (published in the *Red Book*) which he must have posted towards the end of October 1931, van der Lubbe had written: 'Certain circumstances force me to leave Budapest tomorrow for Hódmezövásarhely. I think I shall probably be needing some money there . . .'

It must have been exceptional circumstances indeed which drove Marinus to ask for an urgent loan of 2.5 gulden, to be sent by express to that unpronounceable town, and it seems likely that the attractive original of the photograph was somehow involved in it all.

On his return to Holland, Marinus could not wait to find out whether a letter from Budapest was waiting for him. Though he knew he would be back in Leyden on Tuesday, 8 December 1931, he wrote to Koos Vink on Thursday, 3 December, from Enschede: '. . . in case a letter from Budapest should arrive before Sunday, would you please have it translated at once and send it on to me by express? If it should arrive after Sunday, please do nothing, I shall be able to deal with it myself.'

Quite obviously, Marinus treated his love affair with extreme discretion, for otherwise the editors of the *Red Book* should not have had to appeal to the world at large for the girl's name and address.

MARINUS VAN DER LUBBE'S LAST JOURNEY

On 30 January 1933, Dutch newspapers, in common with newspapers the world over, reported the Nazi victory in Germany in banner headlines. Adolf Hitler had been appointed Reich Chancellor. Subsequent issues were full of gory reports about Nazi outrages. Only the Communist papers consoled their readers with glib assurances that Hitlerism was nothing but the death rattle of expiring capitalism. Soon the victorious workers would sweep away even this excrescence and under the leadership of the 'vanguard of the proletariat' – the Communist Party of Germany – begin to build a better and more equitable society. Marinus van der Lubbe, who bought all the papers he could, had heated discussions with his friends, and particularly with Koos Vink, about the revolutionary possibilities which might, indeed which were bound to, result from the inevitable clash between the bourgeois-fascist hordes and the revolutionary proletariat. He felt that something tremendous, something unique, was happening in Germany and, after waiting for another few days, he set out on foot for Berlin, the great centre of political events. The date was 3 February 1933.

At first everything went according to plan. Passing Kleve, Düsseldorf, Essen and Dortmund, he reached Paderborn on 10 February. On the 12th, a Sunday, he was in Hameln. Then he continued via Braunschweig, Burg, and Genthin. He spent the night of 15 February in the small village of Morsleben, and the night of 17 February in the casual ward run by Frau Hedwig Wagner in Glindow near Potsdam. On the afternoon of the following day –

a Saturday – he reached Berlin, having hitched a ride in a lorry for the last stretch. He put up in the men's hostel in the Alexandrinenstrasse which he remembered from his first visit to Berlin.

Next morning (Sunday) he went to a concert arranged by the German Social Democratic Party in the Bülowplatz, and watched the police closing this innocent function without any explanation. In the afternoon he attended a demonstration of the *Reichsbanner* (Social Democratic Corps) in the Lustgarten, and in the evening he went to see *Rebellen*, a film starring Luis Trenker.

On Monday morning he cleared the snow outside the hostel, and then wrote a few letters to Holland, including one to Koos Vink, whom he asked to forward his disability pension.

It did not take Marinus long to abandon his rosy view of the situation – nowhere had he met the anticipated resolution to fight against the brown 'mercenaries of capitalism', and though he missed no opportunity of inveighing against Hitlerism, no one seemed to care. In the wintry streets of Berlin, at the Welfare Offices in Wedding and Neukölln, in the various labour exchanges he visited – everywhere he arrived at the same disappointing conclusion: there was not the slightest hope of mass revolutionary action. He suggested spontaneous protest marches, of the kind that had proved so successful in Holland, but people either took no notice of him or else treated him with suspicion. Why did this foreign busybody rant in the street, they wondered, instead of leaving things in the hands of the great German Communist Party, who, after all, knew best. No doubt the man was a Nazi spy.

Marinus spent Monday and Tuesday nights – 20 and 21 February 1933 – in the Fröbelstrasse hostel.

On Wednesday, 22 February, at about 10 a.m., he turned up outside the Welfare Office in 'red' Neukölln, where he harangued a number of unemployed who happened to be standing about. This harangue later provided the Examining Magistrate with the much-needed 'link' between van der Lubbe and his alleged Communist contacts (the indictment devoted no less than fifteen pages to what was said on that occasion). In fact, as we shall see, Marinus's remarks were no more 'significant' than any previous or subsequent comments he made on conditions in Germany. The only thing which distinguished this occasion from all the others was that it was here, in Neukölln, that van der Lubbe first suspected the truth: among the countless unemployed and Communists he had met in Berlin, not a single one was prepared to make even the slightest sacrifice for the cause. If anything at all could still be done, he would have to do it by himself.

On Thursday morning he got dressed, drank some coffee and then went to Schlaffke's Café. At about eleven o'clock he walked to the Alexanderplatz Post Office to pick up the three gulden which Koos Vink had forwarded to him. On a billboard he saw a placard announcing a Communist Party meeting in the Sportpalast, and he immediately made for it, after having asked a newspaper-seller the way. He arrived at the Sportpalast at about 2 p.m. and obtained a ticket. Then he walked back to the Alexanderplatz, and thawed out in the warm post office in the Königstrasse, while studying the pamphlets, newspapers and election manifestos he had meanwhile collected. As he intended speaking at the meeting he made a number of notes. Then he walked about the streets, and finally reappeared at the Sportpalast at about 6 p.m. The main speaker was to be the Communist deputy Wilhelm Pieck.

As it happened, Marinus van der Lubbe was not given a chance to express his views – the meeting was closed by the police as soon as it started, and with no resistance on the part of the audience. Completely disgusted, van der Lubbe returned to his hostel, seething with impotent rage and unable to fall asleep for a long time. The great Communist Party of Germany had gone into voluntary liquidation!

On Friday morning he was back in Neukölln, a district with which he had by now become quite familiar. He had given up the idea of waiting for the German revolution, and took his leave of his new acquaintances. Then he walked back towards the Alexanderplatz. Quite suddenly he had the feeling that he must make one last attempt to persuade just a few workers to stand up to the Nazis. He retraced his steps to Neukölln and, in Prinz-Handjery Strasse, he came across a number of young people with whom he began to discuss his ideas. Again he was met with polite indifference. Dismayed, he turned his back on them and returned to the hostel in the Alexandrinenstrasse.

It was that Friday night that he finally decided to take matters into his own hands, and to begin by setting a number of public buildings on fire. Perhaps once the intimidated masses saw these strongholds of capitalism going up in flames, they might shake off their lethargy even at this late hour.

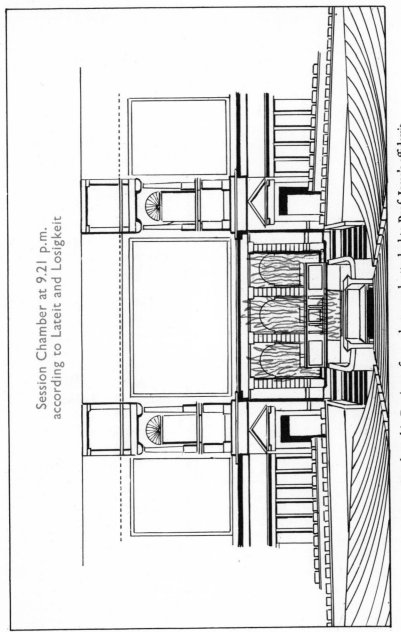

Session Chamber at 9.21 p.m.
according to Lateit and Losigkeit

FIG 1. Bundesarchiv R43/294 after a photograph attached to Prof. Josse's affidavit.

Session Chamber at 9.23 p.m.
according to Scranowitz

FIG 2. Origin as overleaf.

MAIN FLOOR

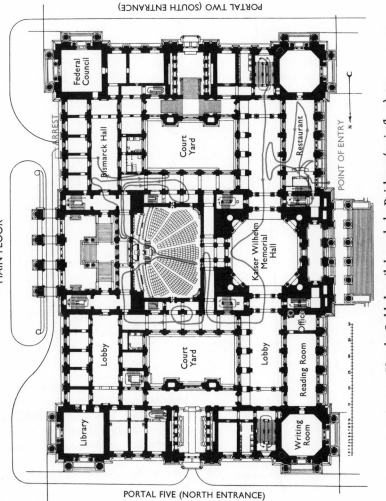

PORTAL TWO (SOUTH ENTRANCE)

ARREST

Federal Council

Bismarck Hall

Court Yard

Restaurant

POINT OF ENTRY

N

Kaiser Wilhelm Memorial Hall

Library

Lobby

Court Yard

Lobby

Office

Reading Room

Writing Room

PORTAL FIVE (NORTH ENTRANCE)

FIG 3. Van der Lubbe's trail through the Reichstag (main floor).

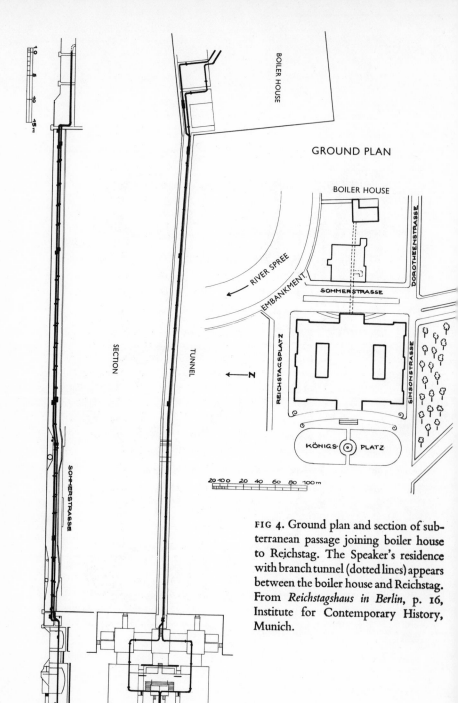

GROUND PLAN

BOILER HOUSE

BOILER HOUSE

DOROTHEENSTRASSE

RIVER SPREE

EMBANKMENT

SOMMERSTRASSE

REICHSTAGSPLATZ

SIMSONSTRASSE

N

20 10 0   20   40   60   80   100 m

KÖNIGS-   ⊙   PLATZ

SECTION

TUNNEL

SOMMERSTRASSE

10
5
10
15 m

FIG 4. Ground plan and section of subterranean passage joining boiler house to Reichstag. The Speaker's residence with branch tunnel (dotted lines) appears between the boiler house and Reichstag. From *Reichstagshaus in Berlin*, p. 16, Institute for Contemporary History, Munich.

THE FOUR FIRES

On Saturday morning at about 10 a.m., Marinus left the hostel in the direction of Neukölln, passing the Town Hall and the Palace on the way. He then bought matches at Otto Zöchert's in the Annenstrasse, and two packets of firelighters at E. Brahl's in the Neanderstrasse. He specially asked for firelighters 'with a red flame' on the wrapper, i.e. for the 'Oldin' brand.

On leaving the shop, he at once opened the packets and looked at the contents very carefully.[3]

In yet another shop, Heleski's in the Liegnitzer Strasse, he asked for two more packets of lighters. As the shopkeeper did not understand him at once, he explained: '*Dinger zum Kacheln!*' (*Kachel* = 'stove' in Dutch, but 'tile' in German). Asked whether he was a Dutchman, he quickly replied that he came from the Rhineland.

At about 4 p.m. he turned the corner to the Neukölln Welfare Office, for he had decided to make a start right there.

The wooden hut was surrounded by a five-foot fence. While examining the layout very carefully, Marinus spotted an open window and, since it was still too light, he decided to return later. He was back at 6.30 p.m., swung himself over the fence, divided one packet of firelighters in two, lit one half, and then threw it through the open window at the back, into what turned out to be the ladies' lavatory. The firelighter landed on the concrete floor and charred the lavatory door before it burnt itself out. Van der Lubbe had meanwhile climbed up on a windowsill, where he lit the remaining half of the packet and threw it on to the snow-covered roof. Then he jumped down again, threw another half packet on to the eastern side of the roof, and made his getaway.

The lighter on the roof did its job so well that a fire was noticed soon afterwards by two passers-by. They summoned Police-Sergeant Albrecht who, with another passer-by, managed to put the fire out fairly quickly. As both witnesses stated later, the roofing had caught fire despite the snow. This alone shows the effectiveness of the sawdust-and-petroleum firelighters van der Lubbe was using.

Van der Lubbe had long disappeared by the time the fire was discovered and put out: he had made for the Hermannsplatz underground station to catch a train to the Alexanderplatz. From

47

there, he walked through the Neue Königstrasse to the Town Hall which he reached at about 7.15 p.m. He had noticed an open basement window earlier during the day, and now threw a burning packet of firelighters through it – into the flat of Engineer Richard Kiekbusch.

Here, too, van der Lubbe ran away without awaiting the outcome. The fire cut a large hole into the floor, and also burned a coat-rack, the wallpaper and a large section of the skirting-board. The flames were so high that they scorched the ceiling. Kiekbusch, attracted by the smell, put out the fire just in time, for '. . . inflammable materials were stored in the adjoining rooms, and the fire might easily have eaten its way through the plasterboard walls into the other flats.'

Though he was extremely angry, Kiekbusch did not report the matter to the police. Instead he simply notified his own superiors next morning, and was told 'not to make a fuss about trifles'.[4] As Kiekbusch explained later, thoughtless or malicious passers-by had more than once thrown burning cigarette butts through the open windows, thus causing a number of minor fires.

Van der Lubbe next made for the old Imperial Palace, his third objective. As luck would have it, a scaffolding had been placed in front of the west entrance, which Marinus, the former bricklayer, had little difficulty in climbing. Once on top, he walked along the western edge of the roof, then along the southern edge until he came to a number of double windows with a common balustrade. One of the outer windows (the fourth) was slightly ajar, and he threw a burning packet of firelighters inside. It struck against the inner panes, fell down and burned the sill.

Next van der Lubbe discovered a kind of roof-arbour, belonging to a retired gentleman by the name of Schönfelder. Though he made repeated attempts to set fire to the wooden structure, the wind proved far too strong. In the end, Marinus climbed down the scaffolding and went back to sleep in the Alexandrinenstrasse hostel. At 10.10 p.m., Fireman Hermann Schulz of the Palace Fire Brigade noticed the smell of smoke during his round through the top of the Palace. He opened Room 42, and was met by thick clouds. He quickly climbed up on the roof, bent over, saw that the sill was ablaze, and immediately rang the Palace Fire Brigade, who sent up Fireman Waldemar Maass. Together they first broke a window and then put out the fire with a hose.

48

A report of this fire was published on 27 February:

> It has only now become known that a small fire broke out on Saturday
> in an office room on the fifth floor of the Berliner Schloss, which was
> quickly put out by a fireman stationed on the premises. The origin of
> the fire is not yet fully explained. But it is thought to have been an act
> of incendiarism.
> One hour before the fire started, the caretaker had made his round
> through the Schloss and had even passed through the room. At the
> time there was nothing suspicious to be seen. Soon afterwards the
> room was in flames. Investigation showed that there was a burning
> firelighter on the window-sill, and another under the window and
> also on the steam pipes.
> The police investigation has not yet been concluded.[5]

The origin of this fire might never have been discovered at all,
had the amateur incendiary, van der Lubbe, not dropped so many
spent matches on the roof, and had he not left the wrappers of his
firelighters lying about.

At the Supreme Court Trial the Assistant Public Prosecutor, Dr
Parrisius, had this to say about the first three fires:

> All the evidence suggests that he committed these crimes by himself.
> Had they produced the desired effect, the German capital would have
> been in a state of frenzied excitement as early as 25 February 1933.[6]

A comparison of the fires shows that they all had one remarkable
thing in common: all three were started successfully despite the
rather unorthodox methods used, and all three were discovered
more or less by chance.

Next day, on Sunday, 26 February, van der Lubbe walked
through Charlottenburg to Spandau. Shortly before midday, he
watched a Storm Troop demonstration, and also spoke to a
woman, who took pity on him and offered him some food. Afterwards he went on to Henningsdorf, where he reported his presence
to the police in accordance with the Aliens Law. The police then
gave him shelter for the night – a small cell in the police-station.
According to the police records, he shared this cell with another
man, to whom we shall return later.

On Monday morning, the two of them were put out very early,
and were seen to cross the street to a café, where they were given a
free cup of coffee each. It was well before eight o'clock when they
started the march back to Berlin. Marinus arrived in the centre of

the city at about 12 noon and went to Hermann Stoll's at 48a Müllerstrasse, where he bought four further packets of firelighters 'with the red flame on the wrapper'. He put one packet each into his overcoat and coat pockets, and then set off through Chaussee-strasse, Friedrichstrasse, Unter den Linden, Neue Wilhelmstrasse and Dorotheenstrasse to the Reichstag where he arrived at about 2 p.m.

Walking round the vast building a number of times, Marinus discovered that there were quite a few ways of getting in. In the end he decided on the western front, because it was the least frequented. Richard Schmal, a junior official who was just leaving the Reichs-tag, remembered noticing van der Lubbe there, dressed in shabby clothes, a peaked cap, and ridiculously short trousers.

Since it was long before nightfall, van der Lubbe walked through the Tiergarten to the Potsdamer Platz and from there through the Leipzigerstrasse and the Königstrasse to the Alexander-platz Post Office. There he stayed, in the warm, from 3.30 p.m. to 4 p.m., while reading some fresh pamphlets he had picked up in the street. Then he went to the Friedrich Gardens, and returned to the Reichstag at about 9 p.m. On the way he tore the wrappers off the firelighters, so as not to waste time later. The western front of the Reichstag was completely deserted. Marinus climbed up the balustrade to the right of the broad carriageway and expertly scaled the wall to the first floor. He landed on the balcony in front of the restaurant, i.e. in front of the window nearest the central portico on the southern side. (He left traces of his climb on the façade which were subsequently discovered and checked.) On the balcony, he took a packet of lighters out of his pocket and managed to light it, but only after he had used up half a dozen matches. As he explained later, he preferred lighting the packet outside in the strong wind to running the risk of being stopped by someone inside.

At 9.03 p.m. he kicked his foot through a pane 8 mm. thick – he had to kick more than once – and then dropped into the dark restaurant. There he flung the lighter, which had started to burn fiercely, on to a wooden table behind the bar. Then he took a second packet from his pocket, lit it from the remains of the first, snatched up the curtains over the door leading into the lobby, and set fire to them. (Both curtains were completely destroyed, and the wooden door and door-posts were badly damaged.) Then he ran back to the curtains over the second window, threw a firelighter on to a table and pulled the bottom of one curtain over it. Next he lit part of the third packet of lighters with the remains of the second, and set fire to the other curtain. Having lit the rest of the third packet from the burning curtain, he ran to the Kaiser Wilhelm monument and, finding nothing combustible there, he took off his overcoat, coat, sweater and shirt. Using the last as a firebrand, he doubled back to the restaurant, ran into the waiters' room to the left of the counter, and pulled a tablecloth out of a cabinet. He set fire to the tablecloth with his shirt, and ran down the stairs to the kitchen where he dropped the burning table-cloth. As he did so, he was startled by a shot outside (the shot fired by Buwert). Then he set fire to a number of towels in the cloak-room, and ran up the staircase back to the monument, where he picked up his coat and sweater, but left his cap, his tie and a piece of soap, all of which were later collected by Lieutenant Lateit. Near the door of the Session Chamber, he lit the sweater, and then, bare to the waist, raced through the lobby into the western corridor, saw a wooden panel leaning against a wall and tried to set fire to it. Next he set fire to a large desk standing between two doors in the northern corridor, opened the door to the Session Chamber, set fire to the curtains nearest the Speaker's Chair, tore down the curtain in the entrance of the stenographers' well, lit it from one of the other curtains, dragged it to the western corridor and dropped it. Then he went back to the Speaker's Chair for more burning material, ran out into the eastern corridor and then some yards into the southern corridor, where he set fire to a number of other curtains. At this point he suddenly heard voices, and made for the Bismarck Hall. On the way he dropped a burning brand which set fire to a door and a carpet. As he entered the Bismarck Hall, he was intercepted by Constable Poeschel and by House-Inspector Scrano-witz.

Van der Lubbe surrendered quite happily, for he knew that his fourth fire had been a great success. He had shown the German workers that even one man could strike back at the Hitler régime, and that is why his answer to Scranowitz's furious 'Why?' was: 'As a protest!'

Van der Lubbe had stampeded through a vast building with such incredible speed that most people refused to believe his story. But later, even the most sceptical had to agree that when he was asked by the Court to reconstruct the crime, while an official clicked a stopwatch, he showed that he could, in fact, have been telling the truth all along.

The fourth fire differed from the other three by only one – admittedly essential – factor: it was the only one that was not detected in time, and hence the only one that did serious damage.

THE GREAT QUESTION

All the time van der Lubbe was in the Brandenburg Gate guard-room, he was surrounded by a wall of uniformed and well-nourished policemen, who looked on him with a mixture of curiosity and revulsion. Naturally the first question everyone wanted to ask him was why he had started the fire, and why in the Reichstag of all places. Van der Lubbe told them all that he had not intended to protest against parliamentary institutions as such, that he had already set fire to a number of other buildings, and that he would have set fire to more if he had not been stopped. He mentioned the Palace, and also the Cathedral.

When the duty officer, Lieutenant Emil Lateit, returned to the station a little while later, he asked van der Lubbe whether the cap and tie that had been picked up in the Reichstag were his. Lieutenant Lateit also asked whether van der Lubbe had really set fire to the Reichstag all by himself. Van der Lubbe said yes to both questions. Had he intended to set fire to the Palace and to the Cathedral as well? Van der Lubbe said yes again. To Lateit, the correct Prussian officer, any man who rebelled against order and discipline, let alone somebody who defied authority by running about half-naked in mid-winter and setting public buildings on fire, was quite obviously a raving lunatic. That is why, like Scrano-witz before him and like everyone else after him, he kept on pressing van der Lubbe for the 'real' reasons – a question that was to break van der Lubbe's spirit in the end. As it gradually dawned on the unfortunate man that his captors, the guardians of the hated capitalist system, failed to understand him, not because they could not follow his peculiar German, but because they were quite incapable of grasping, however vaguely, what was in his mind, Marinus van der Lubbe lapsed into silence.

Unfortunately, Lateit was as incapable of understanding van der Lubbe's sudden silence as he had been incapable of understanding what preceded it. There was only one explanation: the fellow was no ordinary criminal but an obvious lunatic, one who deliberately courted notoriety and arrest, and one, what is more, who also threw his clothes away. Some kind of pyromaniac, no doubt, who liked to get his name into the papers. Shaking his head, Lateit gave up, and sent van der Lubbe to police headquarters in the Alexanderplatz.

The reader, too, may well shake his head at van der Lubbe's 'naïve' ideas, though few would care to argue that they were completely incoherent or senseless – under the prevailing conditions, they were, in fact, no more 'naïve' or 'adventurous' than those of the Nazis themselves. Ten years earlier, on the night of 8 November 1923, Hitler too had been convinced that his 'great deed' – the Munich putsch – would become a signal to all Germany and that the Weimar Republic would collapse as a result.

There are many other surprising similarities between Hitler and van der Lubbe. Each was one of seven children from different marriages. Both are said to have wanted to enter the ministry, both lost their fathers early in life – Hitler through death, van der Lubbe through desertion. Both had ailing mothers who died prematurely. Hitler was stricken with tuberculosis at sixteen, which changed the course of his life; van der Lubbe had an accident at sixteen with similar results. Both vacillated for years, unable to settle down to anything for long. Both were wild fanatics, and belonged to small political splinter groups. Both were penniless and spent much of their time drifting from one casual ward to another. Both had their heads stuffed with stupendous ideas, and both had nostrums for all mankind's major ills. Neither finished school; both had excellent memories and were excellent speakers. Both were avid readers of Sven Hedin's travel books. Both were too busy with politics and too poor to have steady girl friends, though neither was sexually abnormal. Both took political actions which, in the sober light of day, look like the actions of madmen. Finally, both Hitler and van der Lubbe died violent deaths, and saw the collapse of their most cherished political hopes.

Those who consider this comparison a little too far-fetched might do well to remember Frederick II's dictum:

> Courage and skill are shared by highwaymen and heroes alike. The difference is that the hero is a noble and famous robber while the other is an unknown rogue. One earns laurels and praise for his crimes, the other gets paid with the rope.

THE SÖRNEWITZ LEGEND

The widespread belief that van der Lubbe had close associations with National Socialists shortly before the Reichstag fire can be shown to be the result of deliberate Communist juggling with the facts. It all started with the following story, published in the *Brown Book* under the heading 'A Guest of the Nazis':

> On 1st and 2nd June (1932) he stayed the night at Sörnewitz (Saxony) where he was seen in company with the local councillor Sommer and also Schumann who owned a vegetable garden. Both are National Socialists. After the Reichstag fire, Councillor Sommer reported van der Lubbe's visit in 1932 to the Mayor of Brockwitz. This fact was recorded in a protocol, which was forwarded to the Saxon Ministry of the Interior, which notified Frick, Reich Minister of the Interior, of these facts. The facts became public as the result of an interpellation in the Saxon Diet by a Social Democratic deputy. They have not been denied by anyone. . . . Councillor Sommer disappeared a short time after he made the report.[7]

What was the basis of all this?

On 1 June 1932, on his way home from Hungary, van der Lubbe had asked the Sörnewitz parish authorities for permission to spend the night in the parish shelter. In the morning he left for Dresden, where his name was duly entered among those who spent the night of 3 June in the local poorhouse.

We shall see that, after the Reichstag fire, a reward of 20,000 marks was offered to anyone who could throw further light on van der Lubbe's 'real' motives and accomplices. Now, when this matter was discussed at a gathering of welfare officers in Meissen on 3 March 1933, the Mayor of Sörnewitz, Councillor Liebscher, told the meeting that van der Lubbe's name appeared in the register of his parish shelter. Franz Lindner, from neighbouring Brockwitz, then asked whether van der Lubbe was the crook who had also visited Brockwitz at that time, swindling the local Nazi leader Oskar Sommer. The man had given out that he was a National Socialist, and had muttered something about civil war and rebellion.

At the Supreme Court trial in Leipzig, the resulting comedy of errors took up so much time that van der Lubbe, who in any case could neither remember Sörnewitz nor fathom why they made such a fuss of his having spent the night there, had his first fit of

54

laughter. The President and the Chief Public Prosecutor, who thought that the accused was holding them in contempt, interrupted the trial, to insist on an explanation. Naturally van der Lubbe found it extremely difficult to explain what he thought of their ridiculous efforts to reconstruct conversations that he had forgotten long ago, or of the way in which the Court blew up trivialities until they assumed quite ridiculous proportions. And when all this bluster went hand-in-hand with so much pomp and solemnity, with all the trimmings of German legality, what else could he do, poor fellow, but burst out laughing in their faces? He knew that he was no Nazi, had admitted that he had no accomplices, and simply could not understand what these ridiculous bunglers in purple were trying to do to him.

Still, all the Court's lengthy and laborious investigations eventually bore fruit: it was proved beyond the shadow of a doubt that the man who had swindled the Brockwitz Nazi leader could not have been van der Lubbe. What had happened was that on 7 August 1932, i.e. six weeks after van der Lubbe himself had been in Saxony, a young man had called on the Nazi Oskar Sommer, claiming that all his money and his papers had been stolen while he had taken a swim. He was foolish enough to show Sommer an envelope with his real name: Wilhelm Barge. As Sommer later told the Court, Barge kept boasting about his achievements, and even hinted that he was a member of Hitler's inner circle. According to Barge the Nazis were planning an armed uprising for 1 October and were quite ready for civil war. Sommer took his uninvited guest to the local inn, but being slightly suspicious of him, he asked the local policeman, Max Miersch, to keep his eye on the fellow. When Miersch turned up at the inn the next morning, Barge was still asleep, but half an hour later he disappeared without a trace. Sommer then lodged an official complaint. In December 1932, Wilhelm Barge was sent to prison for nine months for fraud and forgery.

But before Lindner's vague suspicion that Barge might be identical with van der Lubbe was finally refuted, the mere suggestion of such a possibility had proved most embarrassing to the Nazis, particularly after it was seized upon by their enemies.

When the Mayor of Brockwitz, Bruno Keil, first heard about Lindner's suspicions, he immediately summoned Sommer who, astonished though he was, admitted that Lindner might possibly be right. Keil picked up the telephone and reported the whole thing to the Chief Magistrate in Meissen, who in turn notified the Reichstag deputy Dobbert. Dobbert then rang up the Saxon Minister of the Interior, and also sent a telegram to the Public Prosecutor in Leipzig. The telegram, dated 4 March 1933, read as follows:

> Reichstag Incendiary Marinus van der Lubbe stayed night of 1 June 1932 in Sörnewitz as recorded in night register. Played National Socialist to leading National Socialists in Brockwitz, viz. Councillor Sommer and nurseryman Schumann. Entertained by Councillor Sommer and disappeared. Told Sommer Germany on eve of civil war, but that National Socialist Party fully prepared.

When Dobbert's telegram was forwarded to the Examining Magistrate, Judge Vogt, in Berlin, Vogt promptly dispatched his assistant, Dr Wernecke, to Brockwitz. It did not take Wernecke long to discover that the whole story was based on an almost incredible combination of errors and confusions.

THE MOST SHAMEFUL LIE OF ALL

Far more scandalous still was the *Brown Book* lie that Marinus was a homosexual. This is what the *Red Book* had to say on that subject:

> When, in their account of Marinus's youth, they come to his twelfth year or so, these red gentry begin to hint that Marinus was a strange sort of fellow, so strange, in fact, that he was certain to turn into a homosexual. . . . The victim gets his first jab on page 46 of the *Brown Book*:
> '[His comrades] also tease him on account of his fear of girls. This characteristic was so strong and so obvious that his former classmates talk about it to this day. He simply could not be made to consort with any girls, but found his love among schoolboys and other boys of his age.'
> The second injection with homosexuality germs comes on page 47:
> 'It was all the more inexplicable to the builders' apprentices, with whom he was working, why Marinus van der Lubbe was so afraid of women.'
> It would take us too far afield to refute the *Brown Book* story of van der Lubbe's youth point by point. We shall therefore single out the

lie that he was a homosexual, a lie that becomes the more brazen, the closer the *Brown Book* comes to Marinus's so-called 'experiences' with Dr Bell.

The *Red Book* then looks at the *Brown Book* story that '. . . Izak Vink told our reporter that he often shared a bed with van der Lubbe', and points out that though Vink said just that, he also added: '. . . without my ever noticing the slightest homosexual tendencies', a phrase which the *Brown Book* conveniently forgot to repeat.

Unlike the *Brown Book*, in which the main allegations were anonymous, i.e. completely uncorroborated, the *Red Book* published signed statements by many people who had known Marinus in Leyden. All were agreed that they had never noticed the slightest homosexual tendencies in him.

The *Brown Book*'s prize exhibit was provided by a Herr 'W.S.', the 'friend of Dr Bell'. This Dr Bell, a shady international adventurer, was alleged to have kept a list of all the boys whom he procured for his friend Röhm, the notorious Storm Troop Chief of Staff. Herr 'W.S.' had this to say:

If I remember rightly, it was in May 1931 that Bell told me he met a young Dutch worker who made a very good impression on him. Bell was out in his car near Berlin or Potsdam, when he met a hiker, and offered him a lift. The hiker was a young Dutch workman, and he visited Bell later in Munich. Bell called him Renus or Rinus. He had frequent meetings with him. . . .
Dr Bell fetched a number of papers from a secret cabinet. He pointed to a sheet and said: 'This is Röhm's love-list. If I ever publish it, Röhm is a dead man.' He showed me the list, which contained some thirty names. I remember very well that one of them was Rinus followed by a Dutch name beginning with 'van der'.[8]

'Unfortunately,' the *Brown Book* continued, 'this love-list was taken away by the Storm Troopers who murdered Bell near Kufstein.'

It is typical that this 'sworn statement of Herr W.S.' published in the *Brown Book*, differs in many respects from the testimony 'Herr W.S.' gave at the London 'Counter-Trial', and which was reported in *Het Volk* on 16 September 1933. According to that testimony, Bell's list consisted exclusively of Christian names, with only one exception which, as the reader will have guessed, was

57

none other than: 'Marinus van der ... and then one or two letters which I could not quite make out: S, T, L, or H and then ... ubbe, and Holland.'

The *Red Book* rightly scoffed:

Wasn't it clever of Dr Bell, to write the name of van der Lubbe out in full, when all the other entries were Christian names or nicknames, and even to add his country of origin! Obviously, the Germans must by then have grown so super-patriotic that they insisted on distinguishing between local homosexuals and alien imports.

The *Brown Book* also had other homosexual aces up its sleeve. Thus it claimed that:

When van der Lubbe returned to Leyden in January or February 1932, he had a great deal to tell his friends about his tour. He claimed that he met a young journeyman whose sister worked in a Budapest brothel. Marinus van der Lubbe made it known that he had decided to save this girl. At her insistence he had spent one night with her but without touching her. This behaviour is so typical of homosexuals that Freud has called it the 'Parsifal-complex'.[9]

The reply of the *Red Book* was:

If it is written in the *Brown Book*, so famed for its clarity and honesty, then, of course, it simply must be true. Particularly when its authority is propped up with Professor Freud's. However, the *Brown Book* might have added that – again according to Professor Freud – this 'complex' is found among heterosexual men, as well.[10]

During his travels in Europe, Marinus van der Lubbe had many clashes with the police. All his convictions are known, and it appears that, though male homosexuality is an offence in most European countries – with the notable exception of Holland – no charge sheet contains so much as a hint that he was ever suspected of being an invert. And yet, had he been a homosexual as well as a 'penniless vagrant' he would surely have tried to solicit male customers wherever he went.

3. The Police Investigation

THE FINAL REPORT

DETECTIVE-INSPECTOR Dr Walter Zirpins submitted his final report on the Reichstag fire on 3 March 1933. In Section C, he posed and answered a crucial question, when he said:

> There is no doubt that van der Lubbe committed the crime entirely by himself. This conclusion follows from the investigations, the objective facts, and the precise answers of the suspect.

In support of this view, which refuted the Nazi story of Communist complicity and hence was bound to earn him Government hostility, Dr Zirpins adduced the following facts:

> The scene of the crime and his activities there were described by van der Lubbe right from the start [i.e. before the official reconstruction of the crime on the spot] in such detail – seats of fire, damage caused, trails left, and paths taken – as only the incendiary himself could have supplied. Had he not been there himself, he could not possibly have described, and later demonstrated on the spot, all these facts and especially the smaller fires which he had lit at random.
> The reconstruction of the crime proved that all the details he gave were absolutely correct.

So accurate were van der Lubbe's descriptions and sketches that the astonished detectives were quite unable to catch him out in a single error or omission. Had there been accomplices, some signs of their presence would most certainly have come to light.

On 27 September 1933, when Dr Zirpins gave evidence before the Supreme Court, and hence before all the world, Torgler's counsel, Dr Sack, asked him to tell the Court why, in his final report, he felt so certain that van der Lubbe must have been the sole culprit.

Dr Zirpins's reply was:

> The method used was the same with all three fires. Marinus van der Lubbe has, as I have said, given us a signed statement, explaining the

whole matter. I believe – no, I am convinced – that he did it all by himself.

Now, the very fact that all those of van der Lubbe's statements which were verifiable proved to have been absolutely correct ought to have suggested to the worthy detective that van der Lubbe might also be speaking the truth about his motives. However, Dr Zirpins's objectivity did not stretch so far. Thus, in the last section of his report, he felt impelled to leave the safe foothold of established fact for the shifting sands of speculation, that is for the allegation that van der Lubbe had acted on the instructions of the German Communist Party. He based this allegation on the following 'evidence':

> During the police investigations he kept trying to develop his Communist ideas, so that it was only with great difficulty and after hours of conversation that we managed to get down to the real business.

And this was all the 'evidence' the police could muster to prove the story that van der Lubbe was a tool of the Communists. Oddly enough therefore, this slander, which the Communists soon turned against the Nazis, was not started by the National Socialists themselves, but by Zirpins, a police officer of the old school, one who at no time belonged to the Nazi Party. It was this man who said of van der Lubbe:

> A man who is willing to carry out revolutionary intrigues on his own account is just what the Communist Party needs. In the Party's hands, van der Lubbe became a willing tool, one who, while believing he was shifting for himself, was being shifted from behind the scenes. No wonder then that the Communist Party was so delighted to use him, particularly since they knew that they would be able to wash their hands of him completely.

And Zirpins added with quite remarkable assurance:

> The strong suspicion that van der Lubbe acted on the orders of Communist leaders, is confirmed by unequivocal facts.

And what precisely were these 'unequivocal' facts? One was that van der Lubbe had made 'contact', not with the Communist Party but '... with workmen in Welfare Offices, at meetings, etc., where he started discussions with them. . . .'

Another 'unequivocal' fact was that '. . . on his arrest he was found to carry the appended Communist leaflets in his pocket.'

The third fact was even more 'unequivocal': 'When, after the interrogation on 2 March, he was taken back to the cells at 6 p.m., he promised cheerfully to deliver a stirring Communist speech to the Supreme Court.'

Then there came an 'unequivocal' incrimination of the Communist Party leadership:

> There is a great deal of circumstantial evidence to show that Communist deputies were the instigators of the crime, and especially the Deputies Torgler and Koenen, who in recent times used every conceivable occasion as an excuse for unusually frequent meetings in the Reichstag.

Quite apart from the fact that no evidence was produced to show that the two men used 'every conceivable occasion' for 'unusually frequent' meetings in the Reichstag, the fact that the President of the Communist Diet faction met the President of the Communist Reichstag faction in what, after the closure of the Karl Liebknecht House, remained their last legal refuge, was neither remarkable nor in any way suspicious, particularly at a time when a general election was being fought. No wonder that in all subsequent hearings these 'facts' were never mentioned again.

It was their Communist plot theory which encouraged the police to ignore the Criminal Procedure Code, and to allow hostile witnesses to have a good look at van der Lubbe first, and to 'describe' him afterwards. Their subsequent statements enabled Zirpins to claim:

> Three eye-witnesses saw van der Lubbe in the company of Torgler and Koenen before the fire. In view of van der Lubbe's striking appearance, it is impossible for all three to have been wrong.

Although police reports 'must restrict themselves to the established facts', Dr Zirpins's report continued:

> Witnesses who were in the vicinity of the Reichstag at the time, noticed a suspicious person fleeing the building during the fire. It seems likely that this person, whose identity remains unknown, was one of the principals keeping an eye on the progress of the crime.

Another bit of 'corroborative' evidence quoted by Zirpins was the following:

On 17 February 1933, a Russian was seen in the Potsdamer Platz in the company of two Dutchmen, to whom he handed bundles of bank-notes under suspicious circumstances.

Zirpins considered this last bit of 'evidence' so important that he quoted its sources in full:

We, the undersigned
1. Paul Merten
2. Walther Arlt
make the following statement:
A week ago we reported that on Friday, February 17th, 1933, between 11 p.m. and 11.30 p.m. we saw a Russian handing four bundles of banknotes to two Dutchmen in the Potsdamer Platz behind the news-paper kiosk (Post Office side).

We inferred the Dutch nationality of the two men from the fact that the word 'van' cropped up a number of times. The conversation was carried on softly in German, and we heard nothing of the subject matter the men were discussing. We did, however, watch the men and saw that they entered the Café Vaterland. . . . We also noticed that, as the Russian took the money from his coat pocket, he accidentally dropped a piece of paper. We picked it up later and made out a series of numbers, strokes, dots and punctuation marks. We handed this piece of paper over to the police.[1]

During the identity parade which was arranged at once, the two witnesses were unable to recognize van der Lubbe. He himself had this to say:

I am further told that on February 17th, 1933, a Russian was observed on the Potsdamer Platz handing [four bundles of banknotes] to two Dutchmen under suspicious circumstances. I myself did not arrive in Berlin until February 18th, 1933, and could obviously not have been there. I know no Dutchmen in Berlin, and have no acquaintances here.

Was Dr Zirpins dismayed? By no means! For this was his incredible conclusion:

Even though it has been established that van der Lubbe was not in Berlin on February 17th, 1933, and certainly not at the time in question – about 11 p.m., it nevertheless remains quite possible that these men were sent from Holland to pave the way for him.

The whole thing smacks of Gilbert and Sullivan, and not of a serious police investigation, particularly since the investigator-in-chief himself had only just stated that van der Lubbe had committed the crime without any assistance.

Further 'evidence' adduced by Zirpins was an unsigned newspaper article which the Police President of Essen had forwarded to him. Although even this article did nothing to prove the complicity of the other accused, Zirpins nevertheless used it against them. The article stated, *inter alia*, that:

> In the opinion of the Dutch police, the crime is undoubtedly the first of a series of individual outrages instigated by Moscow against Fascist Germany. These individual outrages are meant as substitutes for the old Communist method of starting riots, since, because of recent police measures, no great store can be set by mass actions.

Of similar validity was the next bit of 'incriminating' evidence, viz. the testimony of the ex-convict Otto Kunzack, a man whom the Supreme Court later described as an inveterate liar and informer. Yet this liar's statement was deemed worthy of being given great prominence in Zirpins's final report, where we can read:

> I knew van der Lubbe, the Reichstag incendiary, personally. He received his instructions from Cologne and Düsseldorf. Similar instructions were also received by Landtag Deputy Kerff, formerly a teacher in Cologne, and by one Josef Winterlich of Cologne.

As further evidence, Zirpins quoted a Nationalist press report alleging that the Communist Deputy Schumann had spoken of the Reichstag fire well before 8 p.m. on the eve of the fire. As it turned out, Schumann did not make the alleged remarks until after he had heard the ten o'clock news.

Yet all these bits of evidence which, taken singly or collectively, proved absolutely nothing, were deemed sufficient reason by Zirpins for '... suspecting that van der Lubbe acted on the orders of the Communist Party'.

Eighteen years later, Dr Walter Zirpins, now a senior Civil Servant, had this to say about his former theory:

> The question whether or not van der Lubbe acted under orders had to be left open by me, since my instructions were simply to examine van der Lubbe. Subsequently I have become firmly convinced that van der Lubbe had no principals.[2]

Had Dr Zirpins paused to reflect at the time, he would surely have reached the same conclusion much earlier. For when all is said and done, the very last thing German Communists wanted was to burn down their only remaining refuge in Berlin.

However, Zirpins's contentious and far-fetched conclusion, which earned him some ridicule even during the trial, was, in fact, just what Hitler needed in order to proscribe the Communist Party and to pour his brown hordes into the streets. That is, of course, the real reason why the story of van der Lubbe's untrustworthiness found its way into Zirpins's police report, whence it was handed on to the Examining Magistrate, the medical experts, the fire experts, the Public Prosecutor, and finally the Supreme Court judges.

Marinus van der Lubbe was committed for trial on the very day Inspector Zirpins published his report, and the case passed out of the hands of the police into those of Judge Vogt, the Examining Magistrate attached to the Supreme Court.

As one more astonishing example of the lengths to which the authorities were prepared to go to produce Communist 'accomplices', we need only tell the following story:

On the night of the fire, a large police force combed every conceivable nook and cranny of the Reichstag building for the alleged accomplices, and for any clues they might have left behind. All the policemen could discover, however, was the presence of some mysterious white crystals on the floor of one of Torgler's rooms. The crystals were carefully gathered up and rushed to the Prussian Institute for Food, Drugs and Forensic Chemistry. Its director, Professor Dr August Brüning (now at Münster University) carried out an analysis and reported his findings to the Police President with all the pomp and circumstance demanded by the occasion. The conspiratorial particles were – granulated sugar.

HEISIG'S INVESTIGATIONS IN HOLLAND

On 4 March 1933 Inspector Heisig was sent to Holland by his chief, Rudolf Diels, with instructions to gather what evidence he could on van der Lubbe's background.

As Heisig told the Supreme Court on 29 September 1933, the Dutch authorities proved extremely helpful. He was able to speak to many of van der Lubbe's friends and acquaintances, including Piet van Albada, Jacob (Koos) Vink, the mayor of Oegsgeest, and Marinus's former teacher, van der Meene.

64

Albada, in particular, was concerned to defend his friend against Communist slanders, though, had he known with what disastrous results, he might not have said such things as:

I have known van der Lubbe since about autumn 1929. I met him in the Dutch Communist Party. In the Party he gained his reputation by the work he did for the Young Communist League. In any case, even before he moved in with me, he was an exceptionally active member of the League. In the CPH [Communist Party of Holland] he attracted attention through discussions, lectures, and above all through his Communist work among the unemployed. The Party soon noticed his considerable influence among the unemployed, and entrusted him with ever more important tasks among them.[3]

Such explanations, far from vindicating van der Lubbe, merely confirmed Heisig's belief that Marinus was a Communist stooge and so, of course, did the following:

After I left the CPH I became convinced that van der Lubbe was just the man the Party would use for special actions. He was always willing to start an agitation, without asking whether it had any chance of success or not.

When I realized how the Party misused him, how they sent him into battle while they themselves remained safely in the background, and also that van der Lubbe was too decent to put any blame on the Party, I tried to make the whole thing clear to him and to gain him for my International Communist ideas. While he sympathized, he nevertheless refused to join us.

Once again, Albada had painted a picture of a zealot who would shield his so-called friends at any cost to himself. But Albada dealt Marinus an even worse blow when he went on to say:

I know that the Party asked van der Lubbe to resign in case they were blamed for his activities. I have heard it said that the CPH has put van der Lubbe 'on ice'. But I know that he is still doing work for the Party, although not to the same extent as before.

With that statement Albada had completely discredited van der Lubbe's own statement and that of the Dutch police, namely that van der Lubbe had resigned from the Communist Party in 1929–31.

On 10 March 1933 van der Lubbe's friend Koos Vink made a similar statement, no doubt with the same good intentions, and with the same devastating results:

I am a member of the CPH. Marinus van der Lubbe is one of my best friends. Marinus van der Lubbe was a very hard-working and keen Communist and was very much respected in the Party. He frequently organized Communist meetings, at which he was a prominent speaker. He exerted a great deal of influence on the unemployed in Leyden; whatever he said always went down well with them and was done.

At the end of September 1933, when Heisig gave evidence on his investigations in Holland to the Supreme Court, and when the world press published his statement, the Communist Party put strong pressure on Albada and Vink, no doubt by telling them that their testimony might send van der Lubbe to the scaffold. As a result, Albada and Vink immediately retracted their statements, and the Communists were able to gloat:

> No sooner was Heisig's evidence given than van Albada and Vink publicly protested. It appeared that not only had Heisig completely changed their statements but that he had included in them parts entirely of his own invention.[4]

Towards the end of his stay in Holland, the Chief of the Leyden police invited Heisig to hold a press conference which had been requested by a number of Dutch journalists. On this occasion, too, there were many questions about van der Lubbe's mysterious backers or accomplices. Now, had Heisig in fact been the Nazi hireling the Communists said he was, he could have hedged by claiming that the matter was *sub judice*, and thus have earned the gratitude of Göring and his other superiors. Instead, he gave what, in the circumstances, could only have been his honest opinion. This is how the Dutch press reported him next morning:

> By treating him [van der Lubbe] considerately and by letting him feel that he would be deemed innocent until proved otherwise, the German authorities managed to get along with him extremely well. . . . Herr Heisig had the impression that van der Lubbe was being absolutely honest. . . . Though van der Lubbe lacked intellectual training, he proved exceptionally keen and shrewd whenever the discussion turned to anything he was particularly interested in. The German police officer was struck most of all by van der Lubbe's highly developed sense of direction. He knew Berlin almost as well as the inspector himself, and described his race through the Reichstag in every last detail. . . .
> Herr Heisig was asked whether the fire might not have been started

by political opponents of the Communist Party, and whether the police had not simply let the real culprits escape. That was all a lie, was the forthright answer of the German policeman. It was absolutely impossible for any accomplices to have escaped. In Herr Heisig's opinion, van der Lubbe had started the fire entirely by himself.[5]

This surprising opinion of someone in Heisig's position caused a tremendous stir in the Dutch press, for Heisig, who had been on the case from the start, and who ought to have known the facts better than anyone else, had denied the official German view that van der Lubbe had had countless Communist accomplices. The repercussions were fast, furious, and quite predictable: the Examining Magistrate, Judge Vogt, ordered Heisig to return immediately, while he himself published the following 'correction' in the official Government newspaper:

> Various newspapers have alleged that the Communist van der Lubbe burned the Reichstag by himself. In fact, the report of the Examining Magistrate shows there is good reason to believe that van der Lubbe did not act on his own. For the time being, all details must be withheld in the public interest.[6]

The *Red Book* rightly suspected that it was

> . . . probably not too sweeping an assumption that he (Heisig) was taken severely to task by his superiors for the careless views he had expressed. For how could they continue to hold the four Communists, once the inspector in charge of the investigation had himself declared that van der Lubbe was the sole culprit?[7]

In fact, Heisig was told by Judge Vogt that his press conference had helped to discredit not only the preliminary investigation but also the policies of the Third Reich. Accordingly, Judge Vogt made it known that all future press communiqués would be issued by him alone.

As Heisig spent the rest of his life under the spell of the Reichstag fire, we shall tell his story in brief.

After the events we have described, Heisig left Berlin, shortly before Division IA changed its name to Gestapo. As a petty official, and one who was politically 'unreliable' to boot, Heisig was careful to keep his mouth shut, which he found the easier to do in that no one would have believed him in any case: the Nazis because they were absolutely convinced of the guilt of the Communists; the Communists because they were as firmly convinced of the guilt of the Nazis.

Heisig took the first chance he had of resigning from the Prussian Police, and on 1 January 1934 became head of the Criminal Police in Dessau.

But even in the provinces he quickly got into hot water because of his political reticence which, under the Nazis, was bound to attract attention. His personal file which, it must be remembered, was compiled long before anyone thought of the possibility of denazification, contains the following statement:

> On January 1st, 1934, I took charge of the Criminal Police in Dessau (Anhalt), and on September 1st, 1934, I was appointed Chief Criminal Inspector.
> At the end of March 1936, I was accused of disrespect towards the local district leader of the National Socialist Party and was suspended on half pay.
> The Special Court in Halle referred my case to the District Court in Dessau which imposed a fine of 200 marks (or forty days) with the explanation that the status of the accused called for severe punishment.

At the beginning of May 1945, Heisig, who had meanwhile been promoted to the rank of Superintendent, was taken to the Regensburg Labour Camp by the Allies. Here he shared a cell with a particularly notorious prisoner, the former Chancellor, Franz von Papen. During their conversations Heisig told von Papen that, in his opinion:

> Van der Lubbe had fired the building, not at the instigation either of the Communists or of the Nazis, but on his own initiative. He had already attempted to burn the Schöneberg Town Hall, the Neukölln Welfare Office and the Berlin Palace.[8]

After Heisig's release from the internment camp, he ran into fresh difficulties. At the time of van der Lubbe's arrest in the Reichstag, Constable Poeschel had cursorily searched van der Lubbe without spotting a Communist pamphlet which was found on the Dutchman after a more thorough search in the police station. This pamphlet – 'Towards a United Front of Action'! – was later produced as evidence that van der Lubbe was a Communist (Exhibit 54).

When Poeschel, who knew nothing about this completely unimportant pamphlet, was asked about it during the trial, he was afraid to admit that he had overlooked anything, though no one would have blamed him if he had. He insisted blandly that, if he had not found the pamphlet at the time, then no pamphlet could have been there. In the end, the Court forced him to concede that 'perhaps it might have been there all the same'.

Now, in 1936 a former National Socialist and leader of the 'National Front against Bolshevist Excesses', Walther Korodi, who had left Berlin for Switzerland in 1935, published an anonymous article in which he alleged that Heisig had planted the pamphlet on van der Lubbe in order to prove his Communist connections. Though Heisig protested his innocence, which ought to have been clear from his record anyway, Communists made this slander the excuse for a vicious campaign against him in 1948, just after he had been released from the internment camp. One pamphlet called him a perjurer, adding that 'the whole story of the pamphlet was manufactured by the political police, and above all by Inspector Heisig'.[9]

As a result, Heisig was accused of complicity in the Reichstag fire and re-arrested. And so we have come full circle: Helmut Heisig, who had steadfastly opposed the Nazi thesis of Communist complicity at no small risk to himself, was now indicted as an accomplice by the very Communists he had tried to exonerate.

When he was first interned in May 1945, Heisig was already a broken and ailing man. The camp and the odious attacks by the Communists did the rest. After his final release he found that many of his former colleagues, who had shown themselves far more receptive to Nazi demands, had been reinstated long ago. On 23 August 1954, just before he, too, was due to be 'rehabilitated' at last, Heisig was killed in an accident.

In *Brown Book II*, Heisig is described as 'one of the confidants of the National-Socialist Party in the Berlin police headquarters', whose function it was 'to furnish convincing proofs of the guilt of the Communists'. It was further alleged that Heisig's interrogation of van der Lubbe was so irregular and that the record of it proved so embarrassing that '. . . from the beginning to the end of the trial the alleged statement was neither read nor shown to any of the other accused.'

Now, the authors of the *Brown Book*, who were apparently not

familiar with the German criminal code, assumed that the statement must have disappeared simply because it was not read out
in Court. However, according to German law, the Court is not
entitled to consult police or other preliminary records, except in
very special circumstances. Only direct evidence given in Court is
considered admissible evidence.

But, in any case, the authors of the *Brown Book* knew perfectly
well that the police records had not disappeared. In particular, they
knew, or ought to have known from the Notes of Evidence, which
they analysed with so much skill, that depositions made both to
the police and to the Examining Magistrate were read out in Court,
the moment van der Lubbe decided not to answer any more
questions. Thus on 27 September 1933, the Presiding Judge, Dr
Bünger, turned to Heisig with:

> I should like to recall to you the order in which your questions were
> put. You first asked what time it was when he [van der Lubbe] arrived
> at the Welfare Office. You recorded the answer: At 6.30 p.m.

Later, Dr Bünger told Heisig's colleague, Dr Zirpins:

> Now I shall tell you which interrogation we are concerned with – the
> one that took place on February 28th – probably well after midnight,
> was it not? This interrogation is incorporated in *Prel. Exam.* Vol. I,
> page 59. Did it take place early in the morning?

Dr Zirpins replied:

> Yes, it was in the morning. Herr Heisig had interrogated him for
> two hours during the night. . . .

The depositions were further referred to on the 52nd day of the
trial, i.e. on 6 December 1933. On that day Judge Rusch dealt with
Dimitrov's request to be informed of what van der Lubbe had told
the police about his (van der Lubbe's) alleged membership of the
Dutch Communist Party. Judge Rusch said:

> As is generally known, the first interrogation was carried out by
> Inspector Heisig on the night of February 27th. The matter is
> reported in the form of questions and answers in *Prel. Exam.* Vol. V,
> page 48.

HITLER'S 'OVERSIGHT'

Hitler and his henchmen worked themselves into a lather of fury about van der Lubbe when really they ought to have been more than grateful to him. For was it not thanks to van der Lubbe's ill-considered action that they were given the chance of seizing power? Yet Göring, for instance, in his evidence to the Supreme Court on 4 November 1933 explained that the only reason he had refrained from 'making an example' of van der Lubbe was that he had hoped to catch the accomplices.

'The others are by far the worst,' he added.

Hitler himself kept harking back to this theme, particularly when world opinion laid the crime at his, or rather at Göring's, door. At a Cabinet Meeting held on 2 March 1933, Hitler explained that 'all these calumnies would have been stopped at source had the criminal been hanged on the spot'.

The subject was discussed again at the Cabinet Meeting of 7 March 1933 when Frick, the Minister of the Interior, argued that van der Lubbe should be hanged on the Königsplatz at once. Hitler concurred, and took the opportunity to deliver a harangue against those to whom nothing mattered except keeping to the letter of the law.

In his official address to the new Reichstag, on 3 March 1933, Hitler brought the matter up once again:

> The fact that a certain section of the press, particularly outside the German Reich, tries to couple the national resurrection of Germany with this evil deed, confirms my decision to wipe out the crime with the speedy public execution of the incendiary and his accomplices. (Loud applause from the National Socialist benches and the public.)[10]

Next day Hitler had an unpleasant surprise, for when Minister Frick demanded the death sentence for van der Lubbe in the Cabinet, Presidential Secretary Meissner told him: 'The Reich President [von Hindenburg] continues to have strong reservations about signing an order for the public execution of van der Lubbe.'

After this rebuff the President delivered an even more serious blow to 'that foreigner Hitler', when he said: 'The Reich President believes most strongly that public executions are not in keeping with German sentiments or with German history.'

After that, Hitler could not but proclaim that '. . . these views

of the Reich President are naturally binding on the Cabinet'.[11]
Eight years later, Hitler was still fuming about it all:

> Marinus van der Lubbe, the man who started the fire, ought to have
> been hanged within three days, if only because he was seen carrying a
> parcel from Torgler's house on the day of the fire. Had we made short
> shrift of him, we should also have been able to convict the real
> instigator, Dimitrov, who is now the head of the GPU in the Soviet
> Union.[12]

Today there seems little doubt that it was precisely by allowing
van der Lubbe to stand trial that the Nazis proved their innocence
of the Reichstag fire. For had van der Lubbe been associated with
them in any way, the Nazis would have shot him the moment he
had done their dirty work, blaming his death on an outbreak of
'understandable popular indignation'. Van der Lubbe could then
have been branded a Communist without the irritations of a public
trial, and foreign critics would not have been able to argue that,
since no Communist accomplices were discovered, the real accomplices must be sought on the Government benches.

4. Wallot's Building

THE 'SYMBOL OF THE WEIMAR REPUBLIC'

MOST post-war accounts of the Reichstag fire repeat the legend that by destroying the Reichstag the incendiary or incendiaries intended to destroy the visible 'symbol' of German democracy – not only Parliament but parliamentary government as well.

Is it true to say, then, that the Reichstag building was the 'symbol' of German democracy? Was it really the embodiment of the democratic ideal of the Weimar Republic?

It is often forgotten that the unwieldy building on the Königs-platz was completed a quarter of a century before the young Weimar Republic moved in. Its architect, Paul Wallot, had worked away at it for ten long years – from 1884 to 1894 – at a cost to his country of 87 million gold marks. When he was finished, he had created a poor imitation of the Brussels Palace of Justice.

Its bombastic Prussian pomp, the banality of its sculptures, the clash of styles, were such that, immediately after the opening, voices began to clamour for the demolition squad, and for a new building more in keeping with the spirit and the needs of a modern state. Quite apart from the aesthetic aspects, the Reichstag's impressive façade soon proved to cover up a host of annoying shortcomings. For one thing, the mammoth structure was exceedingly short of working space, most of which had been wasted on display.

In order to remedy this glaring fault, the German Government offered a prize in 1929 for the best plan of rebuilding the Reichstag. However, all the entries had to be rejected – no satisfactory solution could be found. The deputies shrugged their shoulders, and forgot the whole business, particularly since Germany had come to feel the depression and no one could be bothered with parliamentary building experiments.

But it was not only architects who detested the building. Thus the former Minister of Justice, Gustav Radbruch, has said:

I have occasionally called the Reichstag 'a house without any weather'

73

... for – no matter what the weather was outside, inside there was never anything but the insipid light of a cloudy sky.

I am convinced that the excitability of the deputies ... was based to some extent on the monstrous structure of the Reichstag.[1]

This so-called 'excitability of the deputies' was a reference to the many shameful scuffles by which German democracy was so often and so publicly degraded.

The ugliness of the Reichstag must have cushioned the blow of its destruction quite considerably. Thus when the Minister of Finance, Count Schwerin von Krosigk, was told about the fire he rejoiced at the fact that it was not a 'valuable monument'. The Nazi press officer, Dr Ernst Hanfstaengl, called the building a horror. The last Speaker of the Reichstag, Hermann Göring, said on many occasions that, though he bore no responsibility for the fire, he had no artistic objections to its results. On 13 October 1945 he astonished an American officer when, having emphatically denied his complicity in the Reichstag fire, he added that he himself would have burned the Reichstag for quite different reasons – simply '... because the large Session Chamber was so hideous, and because it had plaster walls. ...'[2]

Before the Nuremberg Tribunal Göring also insisted that:

There was no reason at all why I should have set the Reichstag on fire. True, from the artistic point of view I have no regrets that the Chamber was destroyed; I hoped to build a better one.[3]

The Reichstag building covered some two and three-quarter acres and was built of gigantic sandstone blocks. It faced true west, its road frontage was about 460 feet, and its central depth some 330 feet. Each corner had a tower, some 130 feet high. Right in the centre rose a gigantic glass cupola, which Berliners called the biggest round cheese in Europe; above it, rising almost 250 feet from the ground, shone a golden crown. From the Königsplatz which, at the time of the Weimar Republic, was turned into the Platz der Republik, a large flight of stairs led through the Main Entrance (Portal One) to the main floor. Beneath it lay the ground floor, the cellar, and two intermediate storeys, above it were two upper floors.

The main floor contained the Chamber, measuring some 95 feet by 72 feet. The three-tiered tribune (the Speaker's Chair above; the Orator's Table in the middle; and the stenographers' table below) faced the 600–700 deputies' seats, arranged in semicircles and divided into seven sectors. Successive rows were raised, in the manner of an amphitheatre. Opposite the tribune was the public gallery, with the press box, the former royal box, and the diplomatic box to the right. Daylight had to pass through the glass cupola and a glass ceiling, and was extremely faint by the time it reached the seats.

All the walls of the Chamber were richly panelled, and the panelling behind the tribune was lavishly hung with costly tapestries. In addition, there was a vast quantity of wood in the form of parapets, pillars, staircases, carvings, seats and desks. There were seven wooden doors, including a number of swinging doors. The stenographers' table stood in a well in the floor, which was reached by a small staircase, and had two doors of its own.

It was only because of the glass dome that the rest of the building was saved from destruction. For when the dome cracked, a natural chimney was formed, which sucked up all the flames and prevented the fire from spreading out.

This explains why the Session Chamber was 'cut out of the building by the fire as neatly as the stone from a peach' (Douglas Reed, *The Burning of the Reichstag*, p. 17), a fact which the former Reichstag President, Paul Löbe, was quite wrong to consider 'suspicious'.[4]

When the *Brown Book* alleged that the incendiaries – led by S.A. Colonel Heines with van der Lubbe 'fifth or sixth in line' – had entered the building through an 'underground passage', they started a rumour which grew as it fed on people's love of mystery and fable. In fact, the Reichstag tunnel was anything but mysterious: a tube six feet in diameter running some 450 feet from the Reichstag cellar to the boiler room on the Reichstag embankment. Wallot had placed the boilers at that distance from the main building 'in order that there should be no source of fire within Parliament itself', and had built the passage to carry the steam pipes across.

We know from Gustav Regler, an ex-Communist, how the *Brown Book* got hold of the plans of the Reichstag. With great (and quite unnecessary) secrecy, Regler copied the plans in the Strasbourg National Library – from Paul Wallot's *Das Reichstagsgebäude in Berlin* (Leipzig, 1899) and then offered them over the telephone to Willi Münzenberg, the leader of 'Agitprop' (Communist

75

Agitation and Propaganda Department), who had fled from Berlin to Paris.

> I explained my idea, and he grasped the importance of the documents at once. . . . A new publishing house would be founded, a *Brown Book* was to be published, and I, of course, would be expected to take part. The whole world would be aroused. 'Don't worry about money, bring all the photographs you can!' Next day I had a money order.
> Only in the train did I dare to study the photographs; I locked myself in the lavatory. They were precisely what we needed: in the cellar beneath the destroyed Parliament, a corridor ran towards Göring's residence; the incendiaries' secret entrance had been discovered.[5]

The *Brown Book* accordingly published a 'Central Section of the Reichstag Cellar' to show the 'secret' way in which the incendiaries must have entered the building.

> There is such a secret way into the Reichstag, namely the underground passage which connects the house of the President of the Reichstag (Göring) with the Reichstag building itself.[6]

The Communists themselves knew only too well that this Section Plan did not show the passage itself, but only a part of the Reichstag cellar. To my knowledge, no one has drawn attention to this deliberate deception.

The *Brown Book* also published a 'Section Plan of the German Reichstag Building' with the legend: 'The entrance to the underground passage leading to Göring's house is just above the word "Sitzungsaal".' The idea was to suggest to the reader (a) that the passage ran straight to, and only to, Göring's residence and (b) that it ended directly beneath the Session Chamber. Had they printed a genuine section of the passage, their colourful theories would quickly have been exploded, for Wallot's book, from which Regler had taken the plan, made no mention of a Speaker's residence, which was, in fact, built in 1903, nine years after the completion of the Reichstag. In order to join it to the central heating system, a special tunnel had then to be built, joining the main passage beneath the driveway of the Speaker's residence.

The passage, or tunnel, therefore, had three exits or entrances, one in the boiler house, a second in the Reichstag cellar and a third in the Speaker's residence. The Communists probably learned about this last entrance at the end of World War I when the revolutionary 'Reichstag' regiment gained a measure of notoriety:

This 'Reichstag' regiment was made up of rather suspicious characters. They kept running up and down the passage. Machine-guns had been set up in the passage, and other arms were hidden there by members of the regiment and sold in secret. Once sold, they were taken out through the boiler room or the Speaker's residence. Ever since then the passage has been extremely popular in Left circles, at least to my knowledge.[7]

On 9 May 1933 the locksmith Wingurth testified before Judge Vogt, the Examining Magistrate:

As for the rumour that the incendiaries entered and escaped through the underground passage, all I can say is that the whole thing strikes me as extremely unlikely, because too many doors would have had to be opened and shut, and I was told that all the doors were found properly locked after the fire.

The door leading to the Reichstag cellar from the drive . . . can only be opened with a spanner. The iron door behind it must be opened with an ordinary key. In the cellar itself there is another, unlocked door. A bit farther along is the door into the Reichstag (the so-called black door). At the other end of the passage there is another iron door, the so-called red door, which is kept locked. The red door leads to the passage between the Reichstag and the boiler house and thence, through two other locked doors, to the courtyard.[8]

In other words, the cellar and the passage were sealed off by a number of doors, all of which were locked every night at 7 p.m. The keys were usually handed in to the doorkeeper of the Speaker's residence, or, less frequently, to the night porter of the Reichstag.

The tunnel itself was included in the rounds of the night porter, particularly since, in 1932, the police had been warned of an intended dynamite attack on the Reichstag. They were told that the dynamite had been hidden somewhere in the cellar, and that the criminals would try to enter the Reichstag through the underground passage. At the time the whole building was immediately searched – in vain. Nevertheless it was thought necessary to take additional precautions, and it was then that the red door was first put in.

How extremely difficult it really was to find the inconspicuous door to the passage in the maze of corridors and doors of the Reichstag cellar, was demonstrated during the trial. A police officer, whom the Court had sent into the passage in order to determine whether or not he would make a great deal of noise down there, failed to return. The judges waited with increasing impatience, and finally sent a search party to look for him. They found him wandering about in the labyrinth below, hopelessly lost.[9] These facts in themselves ought to have suggested how ridiculous it was to assume that a gang of foreign incendiaries could have rushed through that maze in record time.

The main passage formed a straight T at its junction with the subsidiary passage, so that no one could have hidden himself or anything in it without being discovered. In addition, it had a peculiarity which Douglas Reed described as follows: '. . . the tunnel was floored with loose metal plates which, as I was able to satisfy myself, made a din that must have been heard by him (the porter).'[10]

Reed was able to 'satisfy himself' of this din when, during the reconstruction of the crime, the Court was led through the passage by engineer Heinrich Risse:

> The judges, the Public Prosecutor and his collaborator, counsel for the defence, all laid aside their robes and made their way to the cellars. The five accused, the relevant witnesses, and the representatives of the international press followed. . . .
> The passage was a narrow brick one, floored with loose steel plates, and there was a clatter and a jangle as some sixty newspaper representatives made their way through it.[11]

These clattering and jangling plates made nonsense of the whole passage hypothesis for, as further experiments showed, the plates resounded noisily even when people walked over them in carpet slippers. A group of seven to ten men storming through the passage would have been heard by the night porter of Göring's residence even if they had walked on tiptoe. Now when the night porter, Paul Adermann, testified on oath that he heard no suspicious noises whatsoever, the Court had to believe him – the Presiding Judge himself had participated in the demonstration witnessed by Reed. The state of the window through which van der Lubbe had entered, the marks he left on the outside wall, and the evidence of the student, Flöter, left no doubt about the real path the incendiary had taken.

II

THE POLITICAL CASE

5. Brown *versus* Red

HITLER'S FIGHT WITH WINDMILLS

WHEN Marinus van der Lubbe fired the Reichstag, he could not have chosen a more crucial moment in Germany's history. A state of civil war, that had lasted for just under fifteen years and in which thousands had fallen, had culminated in victory for the one side. Henceforth battles would no longer be waged in the street, but old scores would be settled in S.A. barracks, in quickly erected concentration camps, and in prisons. The police, recently abused as the representatives of a hated system, were turned into the new Government's trusted henchmen, almost overnight.

Even though they had climbed into the saddle, the Nazis feared that their Communist enemies had, at best, suffered a severe setback. Judging by the past, they might hit back at any moment, and the only thing to do was to expect the worst, and to pounce on them on the slightest excuse.

That is why the fire started by a young fanatic was immediately turned into a major political issue, and why he was sacrificed in the struggle between brown and red. With van der Lubbe, the German police had caught, not an incendiary, but an immense red herring. . . .

When Dr Ernst Hanfstaengl, a guest in Göring's residence, heard the jangle of fire engines outside, he rushed to the telephone and called Dr Goebbels who, as he knew, was entertaining Hitler that evening. At first, Goebbels thought the whole thing was a practical joke – Hanfstaengl's way of paying him back for a recent hoax. Goebbels therefore told him not to be so damned silly and slammed the receiver down. A little while later, Goebbels had second thoughts and decided to ring Hanfstaengl back. Hanfstaengl was furious by now, and told Goebbels to come and see for himself. In the end, Goebbels called the Brandenburg Gate police-station, where he was told that the Reichstag was ablaze.[1]

While Goebbels the diarist had this to say about the beginning of that exciting evening: 'At nine o'clock the Führer is expected to dinner. We shall listen to music or chat'[2], Goebbels the propagandist gave out a different story next morning: 'Reich Chancellor Hitler rushed to the scene [the Reichstag] straight from his arduous work. He was accompanied by Dr Goebbels and Oberführer Ernst.'[3]

Göring was waiting for them in the Reichstag. Unlike Hitler, he had, in fact, been forced to interrupt his work. At 4.15 p.m. he had attended a Cabinet meeting and had then gone on to the Prussian Ministry of the Interior, where he was just having a discussion with Ludwig Grauert, an old air-force comrade and now his Under-Secretary, when the door was pulled open and Göring's adjutant, Police Captain Jacoby, rushed in with the news of the fire. Göring was completely taken aback, and exploded: 'What the hell is going on? Get me a car at once! I'm going straight there!'[4]

After telling his private secretary, Fräulein Grundtmann, that he wanted to see Sommerfeldt, his press chief, in the Reichstag as soon as possible, Göring raced off. Near the Reichstag his car was stopped a number of times by policemen who had meanwhile cordoned off the entire area. It was from one of them that Göring first heard the word arson, and that he first realized that 'the Communist Party had set the Reichstag on fire'.[5]

Göring first tried to enter the Reichstag through Portal Three, but finding it locked he made for Portal Two which had meanwhile been opened. There he and his party – all in mufti – were quietly joined by another civilian, the Berlin correspondent of the London *Times*, Douglas Reed. Reed's joy was, however, short-lived, for he was quickly recognized as a gate-crasher and put out by the police. The same happened to two other journalists whom Göring discovered in a telephone box.

Next, Göring gave orders to notify Hitler and the Chief of Police. He also told Chief Fire Director Gempp, who had rushed up to report to the Minister, not to bother about him but to carry on with the job of putting out the fire. Then Göring went to his own Reichstag rooms where he was soon afterwards joined by Vice-Chancellor von Papen, and a little later by Hitler and Goebbels.

Meanwhile Under-Secretary Grauert, who had come along in Göring's car, was told by Albert Wendt, the night porter, that the last people to leave the House had been Deputies Torgler and Koenen – two Communists. The day porter, Wilhelm Hornemann, made things even worse for Koenen when he alleged that Koenen had tried to sneak into the Reichstag at about 7 p.m., his coat collar suspiciously turned up and his face averted. Then Robert Kohls, cloakroom attendant at Portal Two, stated that he had rung up the Communist Party rooms at about 8 p.m., but that no one had answered. He had been most surprised, therefore, when Torgler's secretary rang down only a short while later to ask for Torgler's coat. Kohls was taken to Minister Göring, who considered his story so important that he asked Kohls to come along to the Ministry of the Interior.

Vice-Chancellor von Papen had spent the early part of the evening at the Conservative Herrenklub, where he was

> ... giving a dinner in the President's honour. Suddenly we noticed a red glow through the windows.... The Field-Marshal got up, and all of us watched the dome of the Reichstag looking as though it were illuminated by searchlights.
> [Hindenburg] seemed rather unmoved and merely asked to be given further news as soon as possible ... I went straight to the burning building ... and found Göring in one of the badly damaged corridors, where as Prussian Minister of the Interior he was giving orders to the firemen. 'This is a Communist crime against the new Government,' he shouted to me.[6]

Papen, who had no reason to doubt Göring, expressed his disgust at this latest Communist outrage to the journalists waiting outside.

An official car had meanwhile brought Göring's press officer, Martin Sommerfeldt, to the Reichstag. This is how he remembered the scene:

> Göring was standing in the smoke-filled lobby, surrounded by officers of the fire brigade and the police. I reported to him, and found him quite calm. I gained the impression that, though he was worried about the fire, he did not attach too much importance to it. He told me quietly and briefly to get out full reports on the cause and the extent of the fire, and to draft an official communiqué.[7]

Sommerfeldt set to work at once.

Because of the size of the conflagration, no one present that night had the slightest doubt that a whole gang of arsonists – naturally Communists – must have been responsible for the fire. Imagine Göring's surprise, therefore, when he was told that, though the whole building had been sealed off and though every nook and cranny had been searched, not a single accomplice had been run to earth. It was then that Göring suddenly remembered the false alarm of 1932, when the political police had notified him, as the Speaker, of a threatened dynamite attack. Could not the criminals have followed the same route as the alleged dynamiters of last year? Göring immediately ordered a search of the underground passage, and his adjutant, Captain Jacoby, delegated the job to Göring's bodyguard, Walter Weber. With an escort of three policemen, chosen at random – as he testified before the Supreme Court and also told the author of this book in the spring of 1960 – Weber raced across to the Speaker's residence to fetch the keys from the housekeeper, Frau Puschke. The four of them then unlocked the door to the passage and found – absolutely nothing. Even so, Göring kept insisting that the passage must have been used by van der Lubbe's accomplices.

More fortunate by far than his colleague Douglas Reed was the Berlin correspondent of the London *Daily Express*, Sefton Delmer, who was allowed to enter the burning Reichstag with Hitler's party. Delmer heard Göring tell Hitler straightaway that the fire had obviously been started by Communists, that a number of Communist deputies had been seen leaving the Reichstag shortly before the fire was detected, that one of the Communist incendiaries had been arrested, that the entire Prussian police had been mobilized and that every public building had been specially garrisoned. 'We are ready for anything,' Göring said.

Then Hitler moved to one of the balconies to watch the raging inferno in the Chamber. Other Nazi leaders and Cabinet Ministers, including Dr Frick, Prince August Wilhelm, the Lord Mayor of Berlin, Dr Sahm, and Police President von Levetzow, had meanwhile joined their Führer, and so had the British Ambassador, Sir Horace Rumbold.

This is how Rudolf Diels described the scene:

On a balcony projecting into the Chamber stood Hitler, surrounded by a band of his faithful. Hitler was leaning over the stone parapet, gazing at the red ocean of fire. When I entered, Göring stepped towards me. His voice conveyed the full pathos of the dramatic hour: 'This is the beginning of a Communist uprising. Not a moment must be lost...'

Göring could not go on, for Hitler had swung round towards us. I saw that his face had turned quite scarlet, both with excitement and also with the heat. . . . Suddenly he started screaming at the top of his voice:

'Now we'll show them! Anyone who stands in our way will be mown down. The German people have been soft too long. Every Communist official must be shot. All Communist deputies must be hanged this very night. All friends of the Communists must be locked up. And that goes for the Social Democrats and the *Reichsbanner* as well.'[8]

This outburst was anything but a well-rehearsed act on Hitler's part. Uncertainty about Communist plans had weighed heavily upon him ever since he became Chancellor on 30 January, and had increased daily as the Communists continued to lie low. Now, the enemy had struck at last – how could it be otherwise? This fire could have only one purpose – it was the signal for a Communist uprising, first in Berlin and then in the whole of Germany. Now the Communists would make common cause with the Social Democrats and with the millions of Trade Unionists. A general strike would be proclaimed, and Hitler's dreams of empire might be shattered once again. Was the 'national rebirth' to fare no better than the nationalist Kapp putsch in 1920? Had not the German Trade Union President, T. Leipart, called Hitler's appointment as Chancellor a 'declaration of war against the workers', adding: 'Because of their determination and love of freedom the German workers will wage a life-and-death struggle, the terrible consequences of which ought to be a warning to the new rulers.'[9]

And had not *Vorwärts*, the official organ of the Social Democratic Party, told the new rulers on 30 January 1933, that they would rue the day they decided to take illegal measures? Had they not threatened a general strike, claiming that:

Striking is a legal weapon. . . . But tactical reasons tell us to be sparing with it, lest the crucial moment find us exhausted. . . . In times like these, things can change very quickly. There is only one answer to the alliance of the enemies of the working class: a United Front.

Goebbels recorded the reactions of the Nazi leaders when, on 31 January, he wrote in his diary:

During discussions with the Führer we drew up the plans of battle against the red terror. For the time being, we decided against any direct countermeasures. The Bolshevik rebellion must first of all flare up; only then shall we hit back.[10]

Göring mentioned the same plan in 1933 and again after the war. Hence it was no wonder that, when Rudolf Diels gave Hitler his own view, namely that the fire must have been started by a madman, Hitler scoffed at his artlessness and said:

'This is a cunning and well-prepared plot. The only thing is that they have reckoned without us and without the German people. In their rat-holes, from which they are now trying to crawl out again, they cannot hear the jubilation of the masses.'[11]

Diels, who was a police expert on Communist activities, took a much more realistic view of the situation. He knew better than anyone else that the Communists had no intention of staging a rebellion – that much he had learned clearly from an army of Communist turncoats and traitors. However, not only Hitler but even Göring, who as Diels's chief, ought to have known the truth, refused to listen to him, and ordered

a state of alert for the entire police, merciless use of fire-arms, and what similar emergency measures there were in his great military arsenal. I repeated that I had sent a radio message to all police authorities ordering, in his name, a general alert and the arrest of all those Communist officials who had long ago been hallmarked for arrest in case the Communist Party was proscribed.[12]

Dr Schneider confirmed his colleague Diels's description of Hitler's furious outburst in the Reichstag:

After Hitler had shaken himself out of a kind of torpor, he started what seemed an unending stream of vituperations against 'Communist monsters'. He and Göring were absolutely convinced that the Communists had intended the 'shameless burning of Germany's palladium' as a signal for their boasted mass action. Hitler quite seriously gave the police orders to hang all Communist deputies and to take other drastic steps, though only some of his instructions were practicable and hence broadcast over all police transmitters, viz:
1. All Communist members of the Reichstag, the Landtag, Municipal Councils and all Communist officials are to be arrested;
2. All Communist newspapers are to be seized.[13]

Looking back at that hectic day, Dr Schneider today believes that:

What militates most against Nazi responsibility or complicity was the extraordinary agitation which the news of the fire sparked off among members of the Government and among leading Nazis. This shows better than anything that the fire was not pre-arranged by them. I was able to watch their agitation with my own eyes.

A third eye-witness of Hitler's dismay was Sefton Delmer:

That evening, Hitler himself was not yet absolutely certain that the fire was a Communist plot. This became clear from what he said to me as we walked side by side through the burning building. 'God grant,' he said, 'that this be the work of the Communists. You are now witnessing the beginning of a great new epoch in German history.' That was the first clue. Hitler did *not* say, 'This *is* the work of the Communists', but, 'God grant this be the work of the Communists.' And a little later, when von Papen appeared, Hitler seized his hand, pumped it with much unbecoming enthusiasm, and said: 'This is a God-given signal, Herr Vice-Chancellor! If this fire, as I believe, is the work of the Communists, then we must crush out this murder pest with an iron fist.' Note the 'if'.

Like Dr Schneider, Delmer concluded:

It must be granted that what I saw of Hitler's and Goebbels's behaviour in the Reichstag does not fit in with the theory that both were party or even privy to the Reichstag fire plot.[14]

Clearly, the Reichstag fire was no brilliantly conceived plan, no ingenious stratagem by the Nazis to destroy their opponents – on the contrary it was the Nazis' fear that the fire might let loose a flood of red terror that caused them to unleash a flood of brown terror first. The world was to learn time and again with what blind fury Hitler invariably reacted to real or imaginary threats.

The fantastic spectacle of Hitler's maniacal monologue on the night of the fire may well explain the remarkable fact that Hitler himself was never incriminated by even his worst enemies. So high-pitched was Hitler's voice, in fact, and so hysterical his tirade to his henchmen that Diels turned to his colleague and said: 'This is a real madhouse, Schneider.'

Hitler's delusions, which remind one so forcefully of Don Quixote's tilting against windmills or drawing his sword at empty wineskins, also stopped the Nazi leaders from realizing that the Communist threat existed only in their own minds. Moreover, it was this very misconception which gave birth to the legend of the 'Reichstag fire mystery' – a legend which has obstinately obscured the simple truth for three decades.

That very night, Division IA became the scene of feverish activity, as warrants were issued for the arrest of all Communist Party officials. The first squads – each consisting of a detective and two uniformed constables – set out at dawn, on 28 February 1933. At 3.15 a.m., a message was sent to the airport police in Tempelhof and at 3.25 a radio message was broadcast to German border patrols, warning them to intercept all Communist officials and deputies.

Meanwhile an improvised ministerial conference was being held in the Ministry of the Interior. Among those present were Hitler, von Papen and Göring, together with the Nationalist Under-Secretary von Bismarck, Under-Secretary Grauert, Police President von Levetzow, the Head of Division IA Rudolf Diels, and other high officials. On the agenda were the measures that must be taken to prevent the expected terrorist attacks by the Communists. Grauert, who was not a Nazi, insisted on an adequate legal basis for these measures, and Dr Frick undertook to provide it.[15]

Among the many curious spectators who gaped at van der Lubbe during the police interrogation on the night of the fire were the Nazi deputies, Berthold Karwahne and Kurt Frey and the Austrian Nazi official, Stefan Kroyer. They had been out on a spree, when they heard a late-night radio message that Torgler and Koenen had fled the Reichstag at about 10 p.m., and were wanted for questioning. Despite the late hour, Karwahne and his friends decided to call on Göring at the Ministry of the Interior. They told him that they had happened to pass the Communist Party rooms in the Reichstag a number of times that afternoon, and that on every occasion Torgler had been huddled together with extremely suspicious characters. Torgler himself had looked so guilty when he felt himself observed as to leave little doubt about what he was doing: he was briefing the others for arson.

Göring thereupon sent the Nazi trio straight to police headquarters, where a thoughtless detective led them to Heisig's room. In that way they were allowed to catch a glimpse of van der Lubbe, whom, needless to say, they 'identified' as one of the men they had seen with Torgler.

In their excitement the police had committed an irreparable blunder – they had allowed witnesses to look at a police suspect, and then to describe him as someone they had seen earlier. As a result, Torgler might easily have been hanged, had he not been saved by a series of fortunate circumstances, and by the devotion of his guardian angel and defending counsel, Dr Alfons Sack.

In the blazing Reichstag, Sommerfeldt had meanwhile carried out Göring's orders to gather what information he could about the fire and its causes. What the fire officials and Diels and Schneider told him was not much, but at least it had the advantage of agreeing with the facts fairly well:

> I learned that the fire was discovered at 9 p.m. by a civilian who notified the nearest policeman. The latter alerted a police patrol, the police-station alerted the fire brigade, etc. The policeman saw a man tugging wildly at a curtain over one of the large panes in the lobby, and fired a shot at him. When the police entered the building, they found burning firelighters everywhere, which suggested arson. They managed to collect about a hundredweight of this material, and arrested a man who seemed to be running berserk in the corridors. The man was carrying firelighters on his person.[16]

Apart from the weight of the firelighters, Sommerfeldt had been told the truth, and he immediately drafted a press communiqué:

> My draft ran to some twenty lines, and contained no facts other than those mentioned.
>
> In view of the tense political situation, and the coming elections, I deliberately refrained from dramatizing what struck me as a most mysterious affair.

When Sommerfeldt submitted his draft to Göring at about 1 a.m., he found to his surprise that '... whereas Göring had been completely composed in the blazing Reichstag, he was now in a state of great excitement.'

Sommerfeldt, who had not been there to see Hitler turning scarlet in the face as he shook Göring out of his composure, Diels out of his 'artlessness', and Goebbels out of his 'wait-and-see' policy, was even more surprised when Göring glanced at the report, flung all the papers on his desk to one side, thumped the table with his fist and thundered:

'That's sheer rubbish! It may be a good police report, but it's not at all the kind of communiqué I have in mind!'

Sommerfeldt, who knew he had done his job conscientiously, was deeply hurt: 'His tone was insulting; no one had ever dared to speak to me in that way.'

Göring, for his part, could not understand how anyone could produce that kind of insipid report after Hitler's prophetic outburst in the Reichstag. Rather than convince his stubborn press attaché, he seized a blue pencil and, shouting: 'This is sheer rubbish,' again, he went on: ' "One hundredweight of incendiary material? No, ten or even a hundred." And he added two noughts to my modest one.'

Now Sommerfeldt, too, became annoyed:

'This is quite impossible, Minister! No one can possibly believe that a single man could have carried that load . . .'

Göring snapped back:

'Nothing is impossible. Why mention a single man? There were ten or even twenty men! Don't you understand what's been happening? The whole thing was a signal for a Communist uprising!'

If he thought that would floor Sommerfeldt at last, Göring was quite wrong:

'I do not think so, Minister. No one has mentioned anything of the sort, not even Diels, whom I saw in the Reichstag. He merely thought that the Communists *might* have been responsible. I must insist, Minister, that my report is based on the official findings of the fire brigade and the police.'

Göring remained speechless for a moment, and then he flung his giant blue pencil furiously on to the desk.

'I shall dictate the report myself to Fräulein Grundtmann. You can insist all you want.'

Göring started dictating to his secretary without once stopping, but glancing at a piece of paper now and then. He gave it out as an established fact that the Reichstag fire had been intended as a signal for a Communist campaign of bloodshed and arson. He ordered the police to take all Communist officials into protective custody and to confiscate all Marxist newspapers. Göring multiplied my own figures by ten, with a side-long glance in my direction.

The additional nine culprits thus introduced became an integral part of the Reichstag fire 'mystery', and even Göring forgot its real origins. His ten criminals were welcomed by the Communists, who quickly turned them into Nazis.

When Göring had finished, Sommerfeldt asked him to sign the report.

'Whatever for?' Göring asked in astonishment.

'Because this is not an official report on a fire, Minister, but a political document. The news agencies will only accept it from me if you sign it officially.'

Silently, Göring wrote his distinctive large 'G' underneath the last line.

When Sommerfeldt took the communiqué to the Government agency (Wolffs Telegrafen-Büro – WTB) he discovered that the newly-appointed commissar, Alfred Ingemar Berndt, had already released a communiqué by Goebbels. Sommerfeldt mused:

Now I realized what the piece of paper was which Göring kept looking at while he dictated his report.

At last, it dawned on him:

While I was busy questioning the experts in the Reichstag, and writing my draft report, something must have happened to turn the Reichstag fire into a political event of the first importance.

Göring's full communiqué read as follows:

Results of the official investigation
Investigations of the fire which broke out in the German Reichstag have shown that the incendiary material could not have been carried in by less than seven persons, and that the distribution and simultaneous lighting of the several fires in the gigantic building required the presence of at least ten persons.

The fact that the incendiaries were completely at home in the vast building suggests that they must have been people who have had free access to the House over a long period. Hence there are grave suspicions that the culprits were deputies of the Communist Party who have recently been assembling in the Reichstag under all sorts of pretexts.

Their familiarity with the building and with the duty rota also explains why the police caught no one except a Dutch Communist, who, being unfamiliar with the building, was unable to escape after he had committed the crime. The arrested man, whom the Dutch police describe as a dangerous radical, is known to have been present during the deliberations of the Communist Action Committee, where he insisted on playing his part during the fire.

Moreover, the arrested Dutch criminal was seen by three eye-witnesses in the company of the Communist deputies Torgler and Koenen a few hours before the fire.

Since, furthermore, the Deputies' Entrance to the Reichstag is locked at 8 p.m., and since the Communist deputies Torgler and

Koenen had asked for their coats at about 8.30 p.m., but did not leave the Reichstag, through another exit, until 10 p.m., they are suspected of complicity in the crime.

According to a false rumour, Deputy Torgler has reported to the police of his own free will. All he did do was to apply for a safe-conduct the moment he realized that he could not escape. His application was refused, and Torgler was arrested.[17]

The figures quoted, and particularly the number seven, readily suggested that the police had obtained them after a scrupulous investigation. That figure was, however, merely the result of a spontaneous – and as he himself came to recognize soon afterwards – precipitate exclamation by House-Inspector Scranowitz, who had let slip during the night of the fire that at least six to eight persons must have been responsible. Now since 'six to eight' gives an average of seven, seven was the number which was generally adopted. Göring himself reported to the Cabinet on 2 March 1933 that, according to the experts, at least six to seven persons must have started the fire.

On the other hand, it seems incredible that as late as 1 March official reports still alleged that Torgler and Koenen had left the Reichstag at about 10 p.m., when that *canard*, based on a confusion of Torgler with the National Socialist deputy, Dr Albrecht, had already been exploded on 28 February. No wonder that official German reports were henceforth treated with so much scepticism abroad.

THE ARREST OF THE 'RINGLEADERS'

On leaving the Reichstag, Torgler, Koenen, and Torgler's secretary, Anna Rehme, who suffered from phlebitis, started walking very slowly to the Friedrichstrasse station. There Fräulein Rehme took her leave of them, and the two deputies went to dinner in the Aschinger Restaurant, where Torgler had arranged to meet the Communist deputy Birkenhauer. About an hour later, they heard the news that the Reichstag was on fire. At first Torgler thought that the whole thing was a joke, but he soon changed his mind, and tried to get back to the building. But trams were no longer allowed to stop near the Reichstag, and Torgler decided to return to Aschinger's. Meanwhile Koenen had left, but Torgler met him again at Stawicki's Beer Hall, near the Alexanderplatz, where they had previously arranged to play cards. Torgler, who was convinced the fire had been started by some careless fool, was completely stunned when he heard from Walter Oehme that he, Torgler, had just been described as an incendiary over the radio, and the fire as a signal for a Communist uprising. Torgler and his friends quickly put their heads together in Stawicki's Bar, and all of them concluded that, since the Government was blaming completely innocent people, the fire could only be a deliberate Nazi plot to prevent the Communist Party from fighting the coming elections. After a number of telephone conversations, Torgler decided to call the Nazis' bluff and to report to the police. He knew that he would have no difficulty in proving his complete innocence.

Had he had the least suspicion that the whole campaign, far from being a carefully planned provocation, was simply one of Hitler's many misjudgements against which it was useless to argue, Torgler, as he admits today, would have followed the example of Pieck, Ulbricht and Koenen, to mention only a few Communist leaders, and have fled abroad instead of bearding the brown lion in his den. Had he done so, however, his disappearance would have been considered a clear admission of guilt.

When Torgler eventually rang Division IA to announce his visit, he caused a tremendous stir, the ripples of which quickly reached Göring and Hitler. For meanwhile Detective Karl Spietz had reported that Torgler was away from home, that his wife claimed she knew nothing of his whereabouts, and that there was good reason to assume that he had made a quick getaway. And now the alleged fugitive had decided to turn up at police headquarters with two lawyers: Dr Kurt Rosenfeld and Rosenfeld's daughter, Frau Dr Kirchheimer. No wonder Goebbels felt impelled to dispel this 'rumour' in his press communiqué.

After he had been kept waiting for hours at the police-station, Torgler was told by Superintendent Reinhold Heller that he would have to stay there. And stay there he did.

While the Reichstag was still ablaze, the Munich-Berlin night express carried a passenger whose passport showed him to be a Dr Rudolf Hediger from Reinach. In fact, that passport was a forgery, one of many such churned out in a special Communist workshop in 48a Kaiserallee, Berlin-Wilmersdorf. Frau Rössler, from Berlin, would most certainly not have looked twice at the impressive middle-aged gentleman who was paying her compliments with so

93

much southern dash, had she had the least suspicion that he was none other than Georgi Dimitrov, head of the West European Section of the Comintern. As it was, Frau Rössler declared her readiness to continue the acquaintance and agreed to a rendezvous in West Berlin.

Dimitrov's comrades and later co-accused, the Bulgarians Blagoi Simon Popov, and Vassili Tanev, spent the afternoon of 27 February 1933 in various Berlin cafés and finished the evening in an UFA cinema in the Nollenbergplatz, where they saw *Demon Islands*.

By the beginning of March, van der Lubbe's picture was plastered all over public hoardings and published in newspapers with the promise of a reward of 20,000 marks to anyone who could provide information leading to the capture of his accomplices.

On 3 March, Johannes Helmer showed the evening paper (*Nachtausgabe*) to his fellow-waiters in the Bayernhof Restaurant in the Potsdamerstrasse, and asked them whether they did not recognize van der Lubbe's picture. He reminded them about those 'Russians' who had repeatedly entered the restaurant – which was a Nazi haunt – by mistake. The other eight waiters shook their heads – not one of them could remember the face. Still, Helmer wanted the 20,000 marks badly, and he decided to go to the police. This is what he told them:

> In my opinion this man is certainly one of the guests who repeatedly came into the café with the Russians. All of them struck me as suspicious characters, because they all spoke in a foreign language, and because they all dropped their voices whenever anyone went past their table.[18]

Detective Walter Holzhäuser then showed Helmer a number of photographs, whereupon he readily picked out van der Lubbe's (which he had just seen in the evening paper). He went on to say: 'I am positive that this man came to the Bayernhof a number of times from the spring to the late summer of 1932.'

Since the police were being overrun with reports of this kind they merely asked Helmer to report back the moment the Russians appeared again.

Two days later – on 9 March – Helmer rang Holzhäuser.

'They are back,' he told them.

Holzhäuser and Detective Gast raced over to the Bayernhof, and sat down with such conspicuous indifference that the 'Russians' became suspicious and tried to leave. The whole scene was described by the Communist writer Ernst Fischer after the war:

> ... Round the table sat a big, broad-shouldered man with a dark, lion's mane, and two younger men, slighter in build and less striking in appearance.
> The detective asked them to come along. The big, broad-shouldered man produced his papers. His real name was Georgi Dimitrov.[19]

True, that was the man's real name, but not the name he gave to the detective, or which appeared in his passport. The second 'Russian' carried a passport made out in the name of Penev. The third 'Russian' tried to escape through the revolving door, but was caught by Detective Gast. He then gave his name as Popov. Popov, who had no passport on him, tried to escape again, but in the end he gave up the struggle, and all three were taken to headquarters in a taxi.

Once there, the passports were quickly recognized as forgeries from the Berlin Communist forgers' shop which had recently been raided and whose stamps had been confiscated.

On the way to headquarters Dimitrov had tried to squeeze a piece of paper behind the taxi seat. When Holzhäuser had delivered his three charges, he went back to the cab and pulled out a Comintern appeal dated 3 March 1933. Clearly the 'Russians' were dangerous Bolsheviks, and Helmer had been quite right to report them.

Dimitrov and his two compatriots had a wild political past. After fleeing from his native Bulgaria in 1924, Dimitrov had lived in Yugoslavia, Austria, Germany and Russia, constantly changing his name. Like an experienced confidence man, he had played on the German respect for academic titles, calling himself Dr Jan Schaafsma-Schmidt, Dr Rudolf Hediger, Dr Stein, Dr Steiner and Professor Dr Jahn. When he insisted that he had obtained his last passport from a Swiss friend, he merely increased suspicion against himself, for the police knew perfectly well where his passport had been 'issued'.

Popov and Tanev were exiled Bulgarian Communists as well, and had lived in Russia and Germany. Tanev was the only one of the three who had been amnestied and who had been back to his native Bulgaria.

Dimitrov tried to excuse his false papers and the fact that he had failed to report regularly to the police, by claiming that his political opponents in Bulgaria, where he had been sentenced to death, would not hesitate to take his life even abroad. For that reason he had simply had to 'disappear'. He had no connection whatsoever with either the Reichstag fire or with the German Communist Party. His sole concern was with Bulgaria, and the moment a political amnesty was proclaimed, he would be returning home.

Not love alone, but distrust as well, is blind. How else explain police readiness to listen to Helmer's allegations? One fact alone ought to have given them pause for reflection: so oddly dressed an individual as van der Lubbe was bound to have been noticed by everyone in the Bayernhof, not only by one waiter.

Nor did the police bother to check whether van der Lubbe had been in Berlin at the time Helmer alleged he had seen him. This very neglect led to the ridiculous trial of the three innocent Bulgarians, and earned the German police world-wide scorn. In fact, van der Lubbe had spent the time in question at home, signing for his weekly disability allowance in his own hand.

True, Helmer's avarice provided the Nazis with a deceptively welcome increase in the number of culprits, but they were the first to regret it later. For when the 'Russian' Dimitrov was attacked in Court, he did not lie down meekly but gave his accusers and judges at least as good as he got.

THE ENABLING LAWS

In the weeks following the fire, the Government's unfounded fear of possible Communist outrages became the excuse not only for police raids and vicious excesses by Hitler's brown henchmen, but also for a wave of new laws and regulations. The first and most notorious of these, the 'Decree for the Protection of the People and the State' was promulgated on 28 February 1933.

The fact that this decree was passed only one day after the fire, has suggested to many historians that it must have been drafted well in advance. To obtain the sweeping powers this decree conferred on him, they said, all Hitler had to do was to send the Reichstag up in flames.

Today it can be shown that the decree was not drafted in advance, 'merely to be fetched out of a drawer'. It was during the *ad hoc* conference in the Prussian Ministry of the Interior on the night of the fire that the then Under-Secretary and former Attorney-General, Ludwig Grauert, insisted on the obvious fact that the emergency measures demanded by Hitler in the blazing Reichstag, and endorsed by all those present, must be put on a sound legal footing.

For that reason an Extraordinary Meeting of the Cabinet was called for next morning. The only point on the agenda was the political situation. After Hitler had called for the 'ruthless suppression of the Communist Party' which 'was determined to go to any lengths', he 'submitted' the following five points to the Cabinet: (1) to thank the Reichstag officials, the police and the fire brigade for their magnificent work; (2) to start rebuilding the Reichstag at once; (3) to leave the date of the general election unchanged; (4) to transfer the new Reichstag to the Potsdam Palace; and (5) to adopt Grauert's suggestion and to pass a law for the protection of the nation against the Communist danger.

The Cabinet was so unanimous in its fear of a Communist 'counter-revolution' that Hitler had no need whatever of bludgeoning them into signing his odious decree.

6. Counter-Attack

REFUGEES FROM NAZI TERROR

THE 60,000 unfortunate refugees[1] who had to flee their native land when Hitler came to power could console themselves with the fact that all they left behind in the Third Reich was one great concentration camp. Few carried away more than bitter hatred, and none believed a single word the Nazis ever spoke or published. The Communists among them, knowing that the very idea of a 'red uprising' was sheer nonsense, declared that the whole Reichstag fire was a Nazi pre-election stunt.

Furious because what they thought was a Nazi bluff had paid off, and sorely discountenanced at the ignominious collapse of the great German workers' movement, they decided to hit back as best they could from abroad. To start with, they knew that Göring's 'official communiqué' on the night of the fire had been a tissue of lies or, at best, of gross exaggerations – the German press itself had been forced to retract the story that van der Lubbe had been caught with a Communist Party membership card and that he had been in close touch with Social Democratic leaders. And since Göring had been caught out in two whopping lies, there was little reason to think that the rest of his pronouncements were any better. In vain did the 'Führer' of the 'German Legal Front', Dr Hans Frank, appeal to the world:

> We have done no harm to you, nor do we mean you any harm. All we ask is that we – who want peace through justice – be treated with the respect due to a cultured people.

Thirteen years later, a completely broken Dr Frank had to confess that not even by atoning during a thousand years could he wipe out his share in the inexpressible horrors and bestialities by which Germany's name had become besmirched for all time.

Quite understandably, German refugees fell easy prey to the Communists: common persecution called for a united front, and

98

when Willi Münzenberg, Chief of the Communist 'Agitprop' in Paris, launched his 'anti-Fascist education campaign' he managed to ensnare a vast number of genuine democrats.

THE POT AND THE KETTLE

In fact, the Communists and the Nazis were like two brothers who had fallen out, swearing undying hatred to each other. Both were firmly convinced that the struggle for power would continue even after the Reichstag fire.

The Nazis were afraid, and rightly so, that if they failed to score immediate and spectacular economic successes, many of their unemployed and poverty-stricken converts would lose faith and desert *en masse*; the Communists, on the other hand, were counting on the Nazis' inability to steer Germany off the rocks – they still believed that Hitlerism was nothing but the brief death rattle of capitalism.

When news of the Reichstag fire struck both camps like a bolt from the blue, each immediately concluded that only the other was capable of so much malice and stupidity.

Not surprisingly therefore, each side was outraged when the other, in ringing tones of indignation, unscrupulously laid the crime at its door. While the Communists asked *cui bono?* and pointed out that only because of this dastardly plot had the Nazis been able to outlaw the otherwise 'unconquerable' Communist Party, the Nazis explained that the Communists, knowing their cause to be hopelessly lost unless they made some sort of spectacular show, burned the Reichstag as a last act of desperation.

In addition, brown and red alike claimed that blaming the fire on the other was a certain way of swinging votes in the forthcoming election.

The mirror symmetry between the two went further still. Thus, both Göring and the Communists claimed that the – red or brown – incendiaries had fled the Reichstag through the underground passage. Again, while the German press called van der Lubbe a Communist agitator, the Communist press called him a Nazi spy.

In short, even Solomon the Wise would have had great difficulty in deciding between the two, let alone the President of the Supreme Court, Dr Bünger, whose wisdom fell far short of the proverbial.

'ATROCITY PROPAGANDA' AND 'ANTI-ATROCITY DEFENCE'

This grotesque symmetry may perhaps explain why both sides became more and more ruthless as time went by. The Communists had the decided advantage over their opponents for they appeared before the world as the champions of freedom and democracy. Every sign of trouble, however slight, in the Third Reich was systematically blown up to gigantic proportions, and when there were no signs of trouble at all, the Communists would simply manufacture them.

Incensed and full of righteous indignation, the Nazis hit back. On 14 July 1933, they passed a law by which the Government was enabled to deprive 'disloyal' emigrants of their German citizenship and to confiscate their property.

However, it would be quite wrong to say that German refugees were the only detractors of Hitler's Third Reich, since a number of foreign journalists had also been privileged to watch the power-drunk brownshirts at work, and many of them – particularly those who looked Jewish – had felt the brown jackboot at even closer quarters. Thus it came about that even the most respected foreign papers lent their columns to what the Nazis called 'anti-German atrocity propaganda', and that Hitler and his henchmen came to be held in contempt by civilized men the world over.

Because Germany continued to be in the news, the world press sent its shrewdest and most capable reporters to Berlin. Meanwhile, German papers were growing more and more colourless, so that every German who could tried to get his news from abroad and particularly from Switzerland. The German circulation of foreign papers rose so steeply that Goebbels became exceedingly nervous and, as early as July 1933, he started to confiscate some of them and to arrest or expel their reporters.

Even before then, in March 1933, he had issued a warning against 'tendentious foreign reporting'. He claimed that, as a result, he had been promised better behaviour in the future, when no such promise was given by anyone.

Apart from press attacks, the German Government also had to brave military attacks, which did not help to soothe tempers in the Cabinet. Thus on 6 March 1933, Poland occupied the Westerplatte off Danzig – a fact that is generally forgotten – and encouraged the

French and the British to use force as well. Luckily for Hitler, the Western powers refused, in the mistaken belief that the collapse of the Nazi Government was only a matter of weeks away.

At the same time, anti-Nazi processions and demonstrations became a common sight in most European capitals. Demonstrators would gather outside the German Consulates or Embassies, shouting slogans, posting pickets, breaking windows, and disfiguring walls.

More unpleasant still for the Hitler Government were the anti-German boycotts and the constant attacks on Germany in the British Houses of Parliament. Time after time, members protested against acts of Nazi bestiality and political persecution, and the British Government had a hard time convincing a disgusted country that, short of going to war, there was little they could do about it.

Though the Nazis tried to refute the charges against them, in the end even Goebbels had to confess defeat.

MÜNZENBERG'S ANTI-SWASTIKA CRUSADE

It is mainly thanks to the recantations of ex-Communists that we know anything at all about the Communist 'Agitprop' (Agitation and Propaganda Department) in Paris, which spread anti-Fascist propaganda with so much skill. Arthur Koestler, in particular, has thrown much light on that charmed circle of Communist intellectuals, whose central star was Willi Münzenberg, or the Red Eminence as some have called him. According to Koestler, Münzenberg was '... a magnetic personality of immense driving power and a hard, seductive charm ...'[2]

Margarete Buber-Neumann, Münzenberg's sister-in-law, took much the same view:

> Probably no leading German Communist was anything like as sparkling as Münzenberg. ... Most [of his collaborators] were under the spell of his forceful personality, and admired his ability to subordinate everything to his central purpose, no matter whether it was collecting signatures from influential poets, artists and scientists, or the organization of a relief campaign.[3]

As a young artisan, Willi Münzenberg, who came of a very poor working-class family in Erfurt, had moved to Switzerland where he met a great many refugees from Tsarist Russia, including

Lenin, Trotsky and Zinoviev. After the end of World War I, Münzenberg, who had organized a number of successful strikes, was repatriated by the worried Swiss.

Back in Germany, he quickly came into his own. He was one of the founders of the German Young Communist League and was sent as their delegate to the 'Workers' Fatherland' in 1920. He was the brilliant organizer and leader of the 'International Workers' Aid Association', and the head of the huge Münzenberg Trust, which owned dailies and weeklies, illustrated journals, film companies and publishing houses. At the age of forty-four Münzenberg became one of the youngest Reichstag deputies.

On the evening of the Reichstag fire, chance threw Münzenberg near the Swiss frontier – luckily for him, because he was one of the Nazis' chief *bêtes noires*. He crossed into Switzerland where the police dug up his old file, and caused him so much trouble that he preferred to go on to Paris. In France, to which 25,000 of the 60,000 German refugees had fled, Münzenberg quickly established his Comintern propaganda headquarters and launched his world-wide anti-Fascist campaign, which, as Koestler put it, was 'a unique feat in the history of propaganda':

> This [World Committee] with its galaxy of international celebrities became the hub of the crusade. Great care was taken that no Communist – except for a few internationally known names such as Henri Barbusse and J. B. S. Haldane – should be connected in public with the Committee. But the Paris secretariat, which was running the Committee, was a purely Communist caucus, headed by Münzenberg and controlled by the Comintern. Its offices were at first in the Rue Mondétour near the Halles, and later at 83 Boulevard Montparnasse. Münzenberg himself worked in a large room within the World Committee's premises, but no outsider ever learned about this. It was as simple as that.[4]

Under the pretext of bringing relief to the victims of German Fascism, the Committee danced to Moscow's tune – and so did a great many other of Münzenberg's Communist front organizations:

> He [Münzenberg] produced International Committees, Congresses and Movements as a conjurer produces rabbits out of his hat: the Committee of Relief for the Victims of Fascism; Committees of Vigilance and Democratic Control; International Youth Congresses and so on. Each of these 'front organizations' had a panel of highly

respectable people, from English duchesses to American columnists and French savants, most of whom had never heard the name of Münzenberg and thought that the Comintern was a bogy invented by Goebbels.

Moreover:

He organized the Reichstag Counter-Trial – the public hearings in Paris and London in 1933, which first called the attention of the world to the monstrous happenings in the Third Reich. Then came the series of *Brown Books*, a flood of pamphlets and *emigré* newspapers which he financed and directed, though his name nowhere appeared.

Koestler goes on to tell how Münzenberg enterprises came to assume 'truly dazzling proportions':

He organized the Committee for Peace and against Fascism (the so-called Amsterdam-Pleyel movement) presided over by Barbusse; the Writers' Organization for the defence of Culture; the Committee of Inquiry into alleged Breaches of the Non-Intervention Agreement on Spain; and a series of other international mushroom growths.[5]

Across the Atlantic, Ruth Fischer added her voice:

During the depression years, 1929–1933, the Münzenberg Trust burgeoned with every variety of anti-Fascist propaganda, with ballyhoo for Russian culture, films, literature, science, scenery. Progressives and liberals the world over, who wanted to join the fight against Fascism, but were reluctant to join a political party, found a haven in one of the numerous organizations Münzenberg founded. Of these the most important was the League against War and Fascism (in the United States, it [the League] changed its name successively to the American League for Peace and Freedom; in September 1939, to American Peace Mobilization; in June 1941, to American People's Mobilization; in April 1946, to National Committee to Win the Peace) which had the enthusiastic support of such prominent figures as Edo Fimmen, the secretary of the International Transport Union, and Ellen Wilkinson, a leader of the British Labour Party.[6]

Münzenberg's Trojan horses proved so effective that his successors are still trying to copy his methods today. It was Münzenberg's Paris office that spawned that gigantic forgery, the Oberfohren Memorandum, which took in practically the whole world. The Memorandum proved clearly that even non-Communists could be fooled very easily as long as the foolery was directed against the common enemy – Hitler. 'It was as simple as that.'

7. The Oberfohren Memorandum*

THE OBERFOHREN CASE

THE first published reference to the Oberfohren Memorandum appeared in April 1933 in the first of two articles, in the *Manchester Guardian*, on the Reichstag fire:

> A confidential memorandum on the events leading up to the fire is circulating in Germany. It is in manuscript, and the Terror makes any mention or discussion of it impossible. But it is a serious attempt by one in touch with the Nationalist members of the Cabinet to give a balanced account of these events. In spite of one or two minor inaccuracies, it shows considerable inside knowledge. While not authoritative in an absolute and final manner it is at least a first and a weighty contribution towards solving the riddle of that fire.[1]

The *Manchester Guardian*'s two articles, clearly based on this 'confidential memorandum', and accusing the Nazis of firing the Reichstag, aroused the bitter indignation of the Nazis:

Disgusting defamation of the German Government by English paper.
Berlin, April 27th:
The English *Manchester Guardian* has been guilty of slandering the German Government in so shameless a way that a sharp protest has been lodged with the British Government.

In an article, entitled 'Germany in April', which dealt with the Reichstag fire in an extremely provocative and slanderous way, the paper's so-called special correspondent has suggested that the incendiaries must be sought in the ranks of the German Cabinet. The article further alleged that a confidential memorandum on the fire is being circulated in Germany. This brazen and baseless attack on the

* For full text of *Oberfohren Memorandum*, see Appendix C, p. 293.

Government of a neighbouring state is without equal in the history of any Western nation. The German Government considers the article an act of unwarranted vilification and has, as we have already mentioned, ordered the German Legation in London to lodge a sharp protest against this kind of publication.[2]

However, only one day later, Goebbels was presented with yet another 'slanderous' article in the *Manchester Guardian* (see Appendix B). That article, too, was based on the Oberfohren Memorandum, and Goebbels replied with mounting fury:

Manchester Guardian continues its provocation.
The Liberal English *Manchester Guardian* continues its campaign of slander against Germany's National Government, even though a previous article forced the German Government to lodge a sharp protest in London. Regarding the second article on the burning of the Reichstag, official German sources today expressed their amazement that a leading English paper should open its columns to so monstrous a vilification of a foreign power. It is known that a clandestine press of the German Communist Party has been printing and circulating deliberate lies about the Reichstag fire ever since the middle of April. Oddly enough, these lying reports agree essentially with the articles published in the *Manchester Guardian*.

Those of us who have followed the methods of the Communist Party during the past years in various parts of the world know that setting the Reichstag on fire is completely in their line of country. Naturally, they now wish to blame their crime on a Government that has proved their relentless enemy. The *Manchester Guardian* has openly proclaimed itself a tool of the Communist propaganda machine.

It is in fact surprising that the *Manchester Guardian* should have allowed itself to be taken in by the Memorandum.

Sefton Delmer, the London *Daily Express* correspondent, who failed to report the Oberfohren affair to his paper, has explained:

My editor immediately wanted to know why I had not done the same. So I pointed out that apart from other improbabilities contained in the alleged Oberfohren document, I was particularly doubtful concerning the validity of one of the ten points it put forward as proof of the Nazi guilt. This 'point' was not in the *Manchester Guardian* version. But it was contained in the copy of the document I had seen.

'I think you will agree with me that it rather undermines the credibility of Herr Oberfohren's alleged revelations – if indeed he was their author. Listen to this!' And then I read him the passage.

'Hitler's constant companion and friend, the English journalist Delmer,' it said, 'telegraphed full details of the fire to his newspaper before it was discovered, and the name of van der Lubbe as being the culprit.'

The Editor agreed that perhaps we had not been scooped after all.[3]

Nevertheless the Memorandum, soon to be published in English by the so-called 'German Information Office' in London and in various other languages elsewhere, was widely regarded at the time as important evidence of Nazi guilt. Even after the war, in his report on the fire, Dr Wolff was to call it 'The fullest and most reliable report about the circumstances of the fire.'[4]

The Memorandum gained credence in the first place because of its supposed author's name. At the time the Nationalists, under the leadership of Hugenberg, were still in uneasy coalition with the Nazis. As chairman of the Nationalist deputies in the Reichstag, and because of his supposed close contact with Hugenberg, Dr Oberfohren might well be assumed to know the true inner story.

We shall therefore have to consider whether Oberfohren was indeed the author of the Memorandum, and also whether he was in fact on such close terms with Hugenberg as he was supposed to be.

Then we shall have to consider the credibility of the Memorandum itself. Its allegations about the fire have never received factual corroboration from any other source, but it also purports to give the inner story of various events leading up to the fire and shortly after it. As we shall see, its account of these matters not only conflicts with a great deal of credible evidence, but also contains a number of significant inherent improbabilities. An examination of these parts of the Memorandum will show us how little credence can be given to its uncorroborated statements about the fire.

Dr Ernst Oberfohren was a doctor of political science who, at the age of forty-three, had decided to abandon his teaching post in Kiel and to devote himself instead to politics. At the end of 1929, when Hugenberg became the national leader of the German Nationalist Party, Oberfohren was appointed its Parliamentary leader.

According to the *Brown Book*, as a confidant of Hugenberg's, he was fully informed of all that went on in the Cabinet. He set down in a memorandum what he knew of the preparations for the burning of the Reichstag, and sent the memorandum to his friends.[5]

But did Oberfohren, in fact, continue to enjoy Hugenberg's confidence after Hitler became Chancellor?

At the end of March 1933, the news that Oberfohren had resigned his seat caused a great deal of public speculation. The Nazi press reported the matter with suspicious brevity. A number of reasons were put forward for his resignation. One historian has said that he differed with Hugenberg over the Party's relationship to the National Socialists; a newspaper article claimed that there was disagreement within the German Nationalist Party on the monarchist issue, while another paper said Oberfohren's reasons were purely personal.

During a Nationalist caucus meeting on 11 April 1933, the leader of the Party, Hugenberg, also dealt with the Oberfohren case. According to the communiqué issued by the German Nationalist Press Agency, he explained that 'as everyone present knows, Oberfohren was opposed to the policy the Party adopted on 30 January'.[6]

Needless to say, this communiqué by Hugenberg makes nonsense of the *Brown Book*'s claim that Oberfohren continued to enjoy Hugenberg's confidence even after Hitler came to power.

At the same caucus meeting Hugenberg gave the real reasons for his break with Oberfohren. This is how the press reported the matter:

He [Hugenberg] said he felt compelled to disclose a number of unpleasant facts to the caucus. The Prussian authorities had, without his knowledge, raided the house of Dr Oberfohren's Berlin secretary, who had made a formal declaration to the effect that two of the circulars which were found by the police and which attacked the Party Chairman [Hugenberg] had been composed by Dr Oberfohren and sent out on his orders. Dr Hugenberg was informed of this declaration, and made the contents of the circular known to the Parliamentary Party. . . . Immediately afterwards, Dr Oberfohren resigned his seat without any explanation. . . . [7]

There had obviously been a severe rift in the Nationalist Party. According to Dr Sack:

Oberfohren killed himself because he was unmasked as a traitor to his Party leader Hugenberg, and because he saw the game was up. All these facts, however, were kept from the outside world, and that is why the so-called Oberfohren Memorandum was accepted as an authoritative document, though only after Oberfohren himself was no longer there to disclaim it.[8]

Oberfohren's resignation caused a scandal, but the news of his suicide became a world sensation. One of the earliest reports was published in the *Hannoverscher Anzeiger* on 8 May 1933:

On Sunday, the fifty-three-year-old former German Nationalist Deputy, Dr Oberfohren, shot himself in his own home.

We learn that Oberfohren took his life at about twelve o'clock, before lunch, when his wife was not at home. The cause seems to be a conflict with his Party.

The very next day the German Nationalist Press Agency sent out the following correction:

The death of Dr Oberfohren, which has shocked everyone who had worked with him in the German Nationalist Party, has led a section of the press to publish speculations which are quite incorrect, inasmuch as they associate Dr Oberfohren's death with the treatment meted out to him by the German Nationalist Party. We are therefore forced to publish a letter which Dr Oberfohren addressed to Dr Hugenberg on April 12th:

Dear Dr Hugenberg,

I have been told that despite all the trouble between us you could still speak up for me at a caucus meeting. This forces me to admit quite freely how wrongly I have acted. I sincerely regret the great damage my actions have done the Party. I can only add that it is my firm conviction that the [circular] letters were badly misused. I myself have suffered almost superhuman agonies during the last few weeks. Even before then, the course of political events almost overwhelmed me. My nerves are completely frayed, and I cannot bear the thought of further disputes. I beg you to forget the whole business, if only for the sake of our common struggles in the past. Herr Stein [Adolf Stein, the journalist] was kind enough to assure me that you would lend a ready ear to so open a recantation.

Although that letter ought to have proved to even the most confirmed sceptic that Oberfohren killed himself because he was caught trying to alter the ominous course of Nationalist Party politics by intrigue, the Communist legend that his suicide was connected with the Reichstag fire has persisted to this day. In vain did his widow, Frau Eda Oberfohren, declare:

108

My husband was not killed by the Nazis. However, he felt he had become the object of a campaign of persecution, and realizing that the Nazi dictatorship was bound to lead to disaster for Germany and her people, he committed suicide in black despair.[9]

A similar view was expressed by a Social-Democratic journalist, who called on Oberfohren at his Kiel home on 3 May 1933, shortly after Oberfohren's return from a sanatorium:

Oberfohren was quite alone, for he wanted to keep his wife out of all the scandal.

'Everything is hopeless,' Oberfohren cried whenever I mentioned the possibility of his standing up to the dictatorship. He was, in fact, a completely broken man.

'Everything is hopeless,' he repeated.

He had pleaded with Hugenberg, he told me, but Hugenberg deluded himself that the Nazis could be taught better.

Then he told me about the embarrassing police raids on his homes in Kiel and Berlin, the interrogations and the countless threats he had received. He prophesied the complete victory of bestiality.

'If it were not for my wife, I should have killed myself long ago. Because ... we shan't see happy days again. What is happening now is merely the overture. Things are bound to get much worse.'

Three days later, Oberfohren was dead![10]

Oberfohren's real downfall had been his own weakness, his lack of courage when, instead of following the light of political reason and breaking openly with Hugenberg, he preferred the questionable method of sending out anonymous circulars.

THE REAL AUTHORS

Shortly after the fire, the exiled Central Committee of the German Communist Party published a pamphlet with the title: 'The Reichstag is in Flames! Who are the Incendiaries?' According to Dr Sack, Torgler's counsel,

... its approach, style and presentation were highly reminiscent of the so-called Oberfohren Memorandum. With some imagination and a great deal of ill will, this pamphlet became the basis of a crude forgery. All that was missing was a good author, and he was found on Oberfohren's death.[11]

Whereas the German edition of the resulting Memorandum called Oberfohren himself the author, the English edition explained:

So he [Dr Oberfohren] inspired a journalist to write a memorandum on the Reichstag fire, he himself supplying most of the necessary information. This is the now famous 'Oberfohren Memorandum'.

The reason for this difference was explained by Dr Sack, who attended the London Counter-Trial in September 1933 – just in time to hear Professor Georg Bernhard and Rudolf Breitscheid agree that '. . . while the so-called Oberfohren Memorandum might reflect Oberfohren's political views, he would never have used that particular style'.

In fact, the German text of the Memorandum was written by an uneducated hack, and could not possibly have stemmed from the pen of Dr Oberfohren, who had studied at the Universities of Berlin, Bonn and Kiel.

So much for the authorship; what about the contents?

One of the 'minor inaccuracies' referred to by the *Manchester Guardian* which was later incorporated into *Brown Book I*, p. 130, was the claim that the Nazi posse alleged to have burned the Reichstag was led by the notorious Storm Troop leader Heines. In fact, Heines spent the night of the fire at an election meeting in far-away Gleiwitz, as he was able to establish to the Supreme Court's entire satisfaction.[12]

Moreover the various editions of the Memorandum contain a number of major differences – a circumstance that does not speak highly for its authenticity. Nor are these differences due to improvements in style or corrections of linguistic errors, for all the changes have obvious political motives. Under the threadbare German Nationalist cloak, the red tunic blazes forth quite unmistakably.

If we analyse the Memorandum carefully, we discover the following main theses:

(1) The Nazis broke German Nationalist opposition in the Cabinet to the prohibition of the Communist Party by planting incriminating documents and arms in the Karl Liebknecht House, the Communist Party Headquarters;

(2) The Nazis burned the Reichstag as a pre-election stunt and as an excuse for a putsch.

Regarding the claim that the Nationalists in the Cabinet were opposed to Hitler's anti-Communist measures, Torgler's counsel, Dr Sack, had this to say:

The Cabinet had no differences whatever of the kind mentioned in the Memorandum. It was not the National Socialists who urged the prohibition of the Communist Party, but the German Nationalists themselves. . . . The further allegation that the German Nationalists were against the prohibition of the Communist Party in order to prevent an absolute Nazi majority, runs counter to the general view taken by most foreign observers, according to whom the election prospects of the Nazis were bad. In that case, the prohibition of the Communist Party could not possibly have benefited the Nazis, but would have strengthened the Social Democrats. In other words, the combined size of the opposition would have remained the same. . . . Had they wanted an absolute majority, the Nazis would have left the Communist voters severely alone, and later disqualified their deputies.[13]

Even more preposterous was the allegation that the Nazis had planted large quantities of incriminating material in the Karl Liebknecht House. First of all, they could only have done so with the active support of a large number of policemen, and particularly of Police President Admiral von Levetzow, a staunch Nationalist, when the idea was allegedly to deceive the Nationalist Party. Secondly, the raid was first mooted, not by the Nazis, but by Superintendent Reinhold Heller, a policeman of the old school. Thirdly, the material could only have been planted if the Karl Liebknecht House had been deserted or closed beforehand by the police. In fact, the place was full of people at the time of the raid as the following article in a Communist paper showed:

Karl Liebknecht House raided again
Yesterday the Karl Liebknecht House was raided by the police once again. All those present had to leave the building, and a number of comrades were arrested. The police also raided the Communist Press Agency and confiscated the edition of February 23rd.[14]

Now, this article gave the lie to the whole story, for even had the police managed to smuggle the material in under the vigilant eyes of the Communist officials, they could not possibly have hidden it away in special caches during a fairly short raid. Here is Sommerfeldt's description of the finds:

The first secret cache was discovered in the cellar, and, of all places, in the shower and washrooms. In one of the last cubicles on the courtyard side the police found a secret door, tiled over to look like the other walls. This cubicle was ostensibly used for keeping supplies of towels, etc., for which purpose the walls and the secret door had been fitted with screw-on shelves. Now, one of the screws was, in fact, part of a secret lock: by removing it and introducing a fairly long screw-driver into the hole, one could press against a secret spring mechanism and unlock the door. The back of the door was bricked over so that it would sound solid. The door led into a room, some 16 ft. by 6½ ft., without any windows but provided with an electric light. Here the police found a small number of weapons, whose presence fully corroborated the widespread belief that the Karl Liebknecht House was stocked with arms for warding off surprise attacks.

Criminologists wondered whether these weapons were intended purely for defensive purposes or for equipping Communist shock troops. In the ground floor windows the large display shelves had been replaced with boxes which, at first glance, looked like the original shelves. They were heavy, had been nailed expertly and hooped, and were stuffed with compressed newspapers. Any soldier would have considered this type of box a kind of sandbag, behind which one could easily cover the entire Bülow Platz with machine-guns. This view was corroborated by the caretaker of the Karl Liebknecht House, the Communist Vorpahl:

'The boxes were made by a carpenter at the end of January, working partly in the courtyard and partly in a garage behind the courtyard. A few days later, I saw the boxes in the windows of the Karl Lieb-knecht House bookshop. As far as I know, these boxes were intended as barricades. They were so placed in the display windows that one could just see across them. They were built a few weeks before the Reichstag fire.'

The proof that the boxes were not built before the end of January, was provided by another incontrovertible fact: the Communists had stuffed them full of newspapers dated late January. The Central Office in the Karl Leibknecht House could not have shown more clearly that they were considering an armed uprising at the beginning of 1933, with the Karl Liebknecht House as one of their military strongpoints.

A second cache was reached through the goods lift in the courtyard. In order to get to it, the lift had to be taken down to the cellar, where the rear wall of the lift could be opened by a mechanical device. It gave into a room in which a wooden boarding, some 8 ft. by 5 ft., had been fixed between two pillars to form a secret cupboard. The cupboard itself, which was locked, contained about twenty bundles of important documents, some dated 1933.

Further well-hidden caches were discovered on the fourth floor, in a suite of rooms previously used by the Central Committee. These caches were reached by the removal of window sills. They, too, contained important documents.

Similar caches were also discovered on the third floor, the former Berlin-Brandenburg district headquarters. These caches were intended for the sudden 'disappearance' of important Party documents during sudden police raids.[15]

Sommerfeldt's text was illustrated with a large number of photographs. In short, the claim that material was planted in the 'empty' Karl Liebknecht House seems to have just about as much substance in fact as the story about Nationalist opposition to the proscription of the Communist Party.

Now, who was interested in making these false claims? Surely not the Nationalist parliamentarian, Oberfohren, who, though appalled by his Party's alliance with Hitler, was as opposed to the Communists as he was to the Nazis! The very fact that the Communist Party was given so much prominence in the Memorandum shows clearly that neither Oberfohren nor any other German Nationalists could possibly have been its authors – German Nationalists were far too worried about other matters to give more than a fleeting thought to an anti-Communist raid.

THE ALLEGED NAZI PUTSCH

As for the thesis that the Nazis had planned a putsch for the night of 5–6 March (Oberfohren Memorandum, p. 9f.), it was so far-fetched that subsequent Communist accounts of the fire usually omitted it altogether. In fact the whole story, together with that of a Nationalist counter-putsch, came straight out of Münzenberg's head.

On 1 March 1933, the *Völkischer Beobachter* published the following story:

> We learn from official sources that, among the vast quantities of material discovered in the Karl Liebknecht House, the police also found orders with the forged signatures of high police officers and leaders of the S. A. and the S. S. . . . It is known that the evil genius behind these forgeries is the notorious Communist editor Münzenberg, who is still at large.

These sham S. A. orders were mentioned at length in Göring's radio address on 1 March:

In addition, numerous forged orders of the Storm Detachment and Stahlhelm leaders were found, in which the Storm Detachment were directed secretly to hold themselves in readiness for the night of March 6th in order to occupy Berlin, and they were to be prepared to use their arms and beat down all resistance, etc. These forged orders were then to be circulated to the authorities and among the citizens in order to create the fear of a National Socialist putsch.[16]

Göring returned to this question when he gave evidence to the Supreme Court on 4 November 1933:

These forged reports were sent first of all to President von Hindenburg with the polite comment that he, too, was to be removed on that occasion [the S.A. uprising on 5 March]. They were also sent to Minister Hugenberg, to the Stahlhelm and to the Reichswehr. They were even sent to me, with the impertinent suggestion that the Storm Troopers wanted to seize complete power, and that they intended to do away with the police and the Ministry of the Interior. Clearly these forgeries, though sometimes clumsy, were often devilishly clever. . . . One object was to incite the S. A. against their own leaders by suggesting to them, 'Why on earth don't you act on your own?' In other words, they [the orders] were an important and dangerous part of a well-planned propaganda campaign. . . .

Although we might be inclined to dismiss Göring's story as a simple attempt to whitewash himself after the event, there is, in fact, strong evidence that he was speaking the truth. This, for instance, is how Storm Troop Leader Karl Ernst described the forged orders in his inimitably stilted style:

As the official leader of S. A. Detachment Berlin-East, I was shown a yellow carbon copy by Herr Reichsminister Göring. It was alleged to be a copy of an order issued by me to the 8,000 men of my detachment.

Asked officially to swear on my honour whether or not I had ever issued that order, I was forced to say no, if only because such unmitigated rubbish could not possibly have been committed to paper by any S. A. leader; and secondly because the National-Socialist Party follows none but the orders of the Führer himself, who sets out all the steps to be taken to his corps of group leaders, in clear and unmistakable terms. Either the supreme S. A. leader gives the marching order and everyone obeys, or else there is no march at all, for no one in the German Freedom Movement ever marches out of step.

Again, from the purely tactical point of view, the order, logic, and sequence of the forgery attributed to me have been so incompetently botched that I would blush had I to sign such utter drivel. The heading of the 'order' is quite out of keeping with the usual S. A. procedure, so that it alone was bound to cause laughter. The same is true of the salutation.

Every order must be signed by the leader of the detachment, and not, as in this case, vouched for by someone with the name of Tetra, purloined from German mythology, and who was certainly never on my staff. The reference number has obviously been improvised, for my staff had never had a Division 22, a number which has been placed before the date.

If people forge documents, they ought at least to aim at making a credible impression. Now, even if we take the most favourable view of the work of these amateurs, we can adduce no evidence in their favour or in favour of their expert knowledge.

If I am further blamed because a Herr Wels from the Social Democratic Party has taken the trouble of blaming these ridiculous orders on an S. A. leader, all I can say is that Herr Wels, belonging as he does to a Party that is inimical to Germany's military honour, might be expected to come out with such allegations, though no one in good faith can tell me that Herr Wels himself believes in the validity of his claim. No doubt he took prior advice from a party comrade familiar with military matters, and then had the impertinence to dish up this 'alarming document' in feigned surprise and horror.

I accuse the Social Democratic Deputy Wels before German public opinion not only of belonging to a discredited party, but also of engaging in the vilest form of political struggle: the forgery of a political document in order to incriminate an opponent, to decry him before his compatriots and then to accuse him of incompetence in a sphere of which this rabble-rouser [Herr Wels] himself knows absolutely nothing. If Herr Wels wishes to refute this accusation (and nothing could be further from his mind!) all he has to do is to submit to the Reich President the original of this forged report, of which only a copy is at present available.[17]

With their story of dissension in the Nationalist camp, the Communists merely helped Hitler to re-arm while the foreign powers sat by, waiting confidently for an internecine massacre. But the Communist story had no substance in fact.

On 6 March 1933, for instance, when Sefton Delmer, the Berlin correspondent of the *Daily Express*, told Hitler that the wave of arrests in Germany had caused rumours to spread both in Berlin and abroad that he was planning a great slaughter of his enemies, Hitler replied:

I need no St Bartholomew's Night. Under the decrees for the Defence of the People and the State we have set up tribunals which will try enemies of the state and deal with them in a way which will put an end to conspiracies.

In any case there was little, if any, tension between Hitler and the Army. We have more than Hitler's own word for this – we know that General von Blomberg was anything but the anti-Nazi hero of the Oberfohren Memorandum: he was, in fact, one of Hitler's keenest admirers.[18]

Nor did Blomberg threaten to arrest Hitler, Göring, Goebbels and Frick, or to occupy public buildings, as the Oberfohren Memorandum claims. Moreover, in the spate of reminiscences published by officers of the Reichswehr since the war, there is not a single mention of any of the acts of resistance described in the Memorandum. It is amusing to learn from the alleged Nazi 'plan' in the Memorandum that Hitler would have been satisfied with the office of Reich President, leaving the far more important office of Chancellor to Göring. His later actions, particularly after Hindenburg's death, proved clearly how averse he was to sharing power with anyone else.

In short, the Oberfohren Memorandum was a tissue of Communist lies, and the most remarkable thing about it is that it managed – and continues even today – to take in eminent scholars when its sole and transparent purpose was to pave the way for Münzenberg's masterpiece: *The Brown Book of the Hitler Terror and the Burning of the Reichstag.*

8. The London Counter-trial

THE SIXTH DEFENDANT: THE *BROWN BOOK*

THE *Brown Book*'s very title was a brilliant stroke: it suggested the book was an official document, a kind of White Paper in disguise. To publish it and similar material, Münzenberg specially founded the 'Editions du Carrefour', in Paris.

In Alfred Kantorowicz's reminiscences about the preparation of the *Brown Book*, we read:

> The world at large learned of the history of this fire and of the true incendiaries from the *Brown Book of the Hitler Terror and the Burning of the Reichstag*, which contained a complete and irrefutable body of evidence, since then supplemented by captured Nazi documents, on this world-shaking criminal case.
> In Paris, all this evidence was ... carefully sifted, carefully checked, and put into order by a group of well-known writers and journalists, including André Simone, Alexander Abusch, Max Schroeder, Rudolf Furth, and the author of this report. The *Brown Book* is not a pamphlet, but a collection of documents.[1]

Just how carefully this 'collection of documents' was assembled is best gathered, not from Kantorowicz, but from Arthur Koestler:

> But how could we make the naïve West believe such a fantastic story? We had no direct proof, no access to witnesses, only underground communications to Germany. We had, in fact, not the faintest idea of the concrete circumstances. We had to rely on guesswork, on bluffing, and on the intuitive knowledge of the methods and minds of our opposite numbers in totalitarian conspiracy. The 'we' in this context refers to the Comintern's propaganda headquarters in Paris, camouflaged as the 'World Committee for the Relief of the Victims of German Fascism'.[2]

The real authors of the *Brown Book* preferred to hide behind the noble name of Lord Marley, whom no one could have called a suspicious Red. However, as the former Communist Reichstag Deputy Maria Reese, who knew both Münzenberg and Lord

Marley, has since explained, Lord Marley's real contribution was restricted to the loan of his title. 'It was as simple as that.'

Koestler continues his account as follows:

The book contained the first comprehensive report on the German concentration camps (including statistics and lists of victims), on the persecution of the Jews, the repression of literature, and other aspects of the terror. The documentation had been assembled by the Comintern's intelligence apparatus. The *Brown Book* further contained the 'complete inside story' of the fire, starting with a detailed biography of Lubbe, unearthed by the *Apparat* in Holland, his contacts with the homosexual circles around the leader of the Brownshirts, Captain Roehm, and ending with a convincing description of how the incendiaries penetrated into the Reichstag through the underground tunnel. Several direct participants in the action were named: Count Helldorff, S.A. Leaders Heines and Schultz. All this was based on isolated scraps of information, deduction, guesswork, and brazen bluff. The only certainty we had was that some Nazi circles had somehow contrived to burn down the building. Everything else was a shot in the dark.

According to a former confidant and political friend of Münzenberg, Erich Wollenberg, Münzenberg told him in Paris

... that in view of the panic which seized large masses of the German people after the Reichstag fire, he was forced to include a great deal of fantasy and invention which – like the alleged association between van der Lubbe and Ernst Roehm – were soon completely refuted.

Münzenberg also told him that '. . . all these inventions were sworn to by witnesses before the so-called London Counter-Trial . . .'[3]

Koestler describes his own share in the preparation of the *Brown Book* as follows:

My part in it was a subordinate one. I had to follow the repercussions of the trial and of our own propaganda in the British press and in the House of Commons, to study the current of British public opinion, and draw the appropriate tactical conclusions. For a while I also edited the daily bulletins which we distributed to the French and British press.

These daily bulletins were swallowed by most of the bourgeois press, with few exceptions. One such was the *Morning Post* which suggested that the real identity of the authors emerged during the reading of the very first chapter.

Somebody else, too, had reservations – a man who knew Münzenberg and his methods as well as anyone. When Ernst Torgler was handed the *Brown Book* in prison, he felt 'a little shaken':

> I had never thought the whole thing had been so simple. Van der Lubbe an old acquaintance of Roehm and on his list of catamites? Could Goebbels really have planned the fire, and could Göring, standing, as it were, at the entrance of the underground tunnel, really have supervised the whole thing?[4]

Unencumbered by bourgeois inhibitions, Münzenberg even proclaimed Einstein one of the book's sponsors. This immediately prompted Goebbels to wield his poison pen:

Einstein in Trouble
Berlin, September 6th.
    Under the presidency of the notorious hack-writer and Communist, Albert Einstein, a so-called *Brown Book against the Hitler Terror* has recently been published. Two days after this forgery appeared, Herr Einstein was forced to disown his own literary creation. There seems no doubt that Einstein's denial was prompted by sheer panic, for nothing can disguise his personal responsibility. Numerous foreign papers, as well as the anonymous authors of the book, continue to hide behind Einstein's authority. During earlier discussions by the so-called World Committee for the Victims of German Fascism it was unanimously claimed that the book was a publication by Einstein and his circle.

One of Einstein's recent biographers, Catherine Owens Peare, tells how Einstein tried in vain to protest that he had absolutely no connection with the book, and that he had not even been told about its impending publication.

In fact, Münzenberg used names very freely, and the Nazis, quite impotent in the face of this onslaught from abroad, vented their rage on what friends and dependents of their detractors they could lay their hands on. Impotent rage was the reason why they threw five relatives of ex-Chancellor Philipp Scheidemann into concentration camps, as 'just retribution' for a 'slanderous article' Scheidemann had published abroad (*Völkischer Beobachter*, 15 July 1933); impotent rage drove them into launching an anti-Jewish boycott on 1 April 1933; impotent rage dictated most of their press and radio communiqués.

Now this is precisely what Münzenberg wanted. The world came to believe that a Government capable of reacting in this way was also capable of committing the vilest crimes, even those invented in Münzenberg's Paris 'Agitprop' office.

THE LONDON COUNTER-TRIAL

After his great success in harnessing good liberals as 'Trojan horses' to the Bolshevik cart, Willi Münzenberg, the inventive Ulysses from Thuringia, hit upon another brilliant propaganda idea. He remembered the secret revolutionary courts of pre-war Russia, and decided to transplant them to London. The World Committee for the Victims of German Fascism was quickly turned into a 'Commission of Inquiry into the Burning of the Reichstag', presided over by an 'International Committee of Jurists and Technical Experts'. In practice, these experts were recruited on Comintern recommendation. The men in question – internationally famous lawyers of liberal opinion, one and all – would one day receive a flattering letter inviting them to serve as impartial members on a committee investigating Nazi atrocities. Those who agreed to serve and who were finally selected were:

Dr Betsy Bakker-Nort (Holland)
Maître Gaston Bergery (France)
Mr Georg Branting (Sweden)
Mr Arthur Garfield Hays (U.S.A.)
Mr Vald Hvidt (Denmark)
Maître de Moro-Giafferi (France)
Mr D. N. Pritt, K.C. (England)
Maître Pierre Vermeylen (Belgium)

None of the Committee members was a Communist; all were respectable citizens. To this day, some of these honourable men have still not understood with what devilish skill Münzenberg and his pupils diverted their willingness to serve humanity into purely Communist channels. This is particularly true of the Chairman, the then forty-six-year-old K.C., Denis Nowell Pritt. In 1957, at the age of seventy, Pritt was given the freedom of the city of Leipzig, as a 'prominent member of the World Peace Movement'.

Originally, the Münzenberg Trust had appealed to a number of leading American jurists, including the famous lawyer (later Judge), Samuel S. Leibowitz of New York, Leo Gallagher of Los Angeles, Edward Levenson of Philadelphia, and also Paul Gravath, Clarence Darrow, and Felix Frankfurter of New York. In England, they had appealed not only to Pritt but also to Neil Lawson and many others; in France they had turned to Maîtres Henri Torrés, César Campinchi, Marcel Villard, and Vincent de Moro-Giafferi. Further they had invited Dr van't Hoff-Stokk (Holland), Adolphe Jaeglé (Strasbourg) and the advocates Soudan, Graux, and Braffort (Belgium). Of all these, only Pritt and Moro-Giafferi ended up on the final list.

The American member, Arthur Garfield Hays, was to have the unique experience of seeing through both smoke screens – the red as well as the brown. In July 1933, Hays had just finished a dramatic case, and, as he tells us, had no plans for the immediate future, when to his utter surprise he received a telegram from Edward Levenson, an American lawyer. The telegram, which had been sent from Moscow, read:

GEORGI DIMITROV CHARGED WITH COMPLICITY IN REICHSTAG FIRE. HIS MOTHER REQUESTS YOU DEFEND SON AS WELL AS OTHER COMMUNIST DEFENDANTS BEFORE GERMAN REICHSGERICHT. CHARGE IS A VICIOUS FRAME-UP AGAINST INNOCENT MEN. YOUR HELP NEEDED. TRIAL SEPTEMBER.

Hays cabled back: 'I shall be glad to join in defence provided German Government permits. Please bear in mind I am a Jew.'

Today Hays admits honestly that he can no longer tell whether his acquiescent reply was due to his emotional reaction at the time, a desire for change, or perhaps a thirst for adventure.

Hays – who was born in 1881 in the State of New York – was a most successful lawyer of liberal views. He was legal adviser to the American Civil Liberties Union, and one of the defence lawyers in the Sacco-Vanzetti trial. He could well afford to forgo fees, when the need arose, and had done so on a number of occasions. All these reasons must have made him appear an excellent choice to Münzenberg.

How very difficult the role was which Münzenberg expected the various members of his Commission to play is shown by the example of Georg Branting of Sweden, to whom the German Public Prosecutor wrote the following letter on 10 August 1933:

Since – despite public appeals for information that might throw light on the matter and despite the offer of a very high reward for any information leading to the apprehension of the culprits – we have received no evidence beyond that set forth in the Indictment, and since the Court is extremely anxious to base its verdict on all the available facts, I should be most grateful to you if you would kindly let me know what documentary evidence the Commission has in its possession. I should be most obliged if you would reply at your earliest convenience, and if you could also let me have the names and addresses of any witnesses of the Reichstag fire, who might feel obliged, and who are willing, to appear before the Supreme Court.

Since even the worst lawyer must have realized that, compared with the boastful claims of the Committee, the evidence was extremely tenuous, Branting's reply to the Public Prosecutor (18 August 1933) was full of evasions:

The best and most convincing evidence is futile if it may not be used to exonerate the defendant.

I am not entitled to hand over documents at my own discretion, but I have no doubt that the Commission of Inquiry ... will hand them over to counsel for the defence as soon as adequate guarantees are given that the accused will enjoy unrestricted legal representation.

As a result, Drs Sack, Seuffert, and Teichert, all of whom felt completely 'unrestricted', turned to the Commission and requested a sight of the famous evidence, but all in vain. Dr Sack even flew to Paris and later to London so as to leave no stone unturned in the defence of his client Torgler. In Paris, he and his assistants, Dr Hans Jung and Dr Kurt Wersig had a conference lasting five hours with Branting, Leo Gallagher and an 'Austrian journalist' who called himself 'Breda' but who was none other than Otto Katz, Münzenberg's chief lieutenant. When Dr Sack asked to see what evidence there was exonerating his client Torgler, he was told by Branting and his colleagues that they were not entitled to disclose the address of the attorneys to whom the material had been handed for safe keeping.

Instead of 'entitled' they ought to have said 'able', for the material never existed. Why else should they have made such a mystery of the whole business? For even if the Commission did not trust the German Supreme Court or its advocates with the material itself, there was no reason why photostats should not have been handed over, or published in the foreign press. Why then did the Commission agree to a conference with Dr Sack? Dr Sack and his colleagues soon discovered the real reason – it was to get information out of *them*. Disappointed, Dr Sack returned to Berlin on 9 September.

On 11 September 1933, 15,000 people crowded into the Salle Wagram in response to an appeal which the Münzenberg Trust had plastered all over Paris. The chief speaker was the French advocate and deputy Maître Vincent de Moro-Giafferi, who referred to his exhaustive study of all the documents bearing on the Reichstag fire, and who roused the audience to near-frenzy when he shouted: 'It is you, Göring, who are the real assassin and the real incendiary!'

It was certainly not mere solidarity with Göring that prompted Dr Sack to make the following objection: 'He [Moro-Giafferi] had seen neither the result of the preliminary examination nor the indictment (which, in cases of high treason, must be kept secret according to German law), yet this did not seem to weigh heavily on his legal conscience.'

A few months later, on 4 November 1933, Göring, whom Moro-Giafferi had denounced with so much emotion, followed suit when he, too, anticipated the Supreme Court verdict with: 'My sixth sense tells me that the fire was started by the Communists.'

Meanwhile Arthur Garfield Hays, accompanied by his daughter Jane, had arrived in Paris. In the Hôtel Mirabeau he was met by 'a self-effacing, apparently bewildered little lawyer who introduced himself as "M. Stephan Detscheff, *avocat bulgare*" '. With the help of an interpreter, Hays managed to find out that the *avocat* represented a committee of Bulgarians for the defence of Dimitrov, Popov and Tanev.

> I tried to find out who constituted the committee and asked: 'Who is the committee?' Answer: 'We'. I made further inquiry: 'Who are we?' Answer: 'A group of people interested in defending these innocent men.' 'What group of people?' The answer came back: 'Our Committee.' I gave up.

We can sympathize with Detscheff's reserve. Such unwelcome, inquisitive questions were not wanted, and were, in any case, rarely asked, for their 'panel of brilliant names' usually protected the Committee against any awkward questions.

In Paris, Hays also met his French colleague, Maître de Moro-Giafferi. 'My conference with him was unsatisfactory... One could not confer with him; one just listened. His rapid-firing comments did not even permit interruption for translation by my secretary.'[5]

With how little real knowledge Hays was expected to serve on the Committee is best shown by the fact that he arrived in Europe just one day before the beginning of the Counter-Trial and without any detailed briefing. He ought to have suspected straightaway that the Committee was far less concerned with his legal ability, than with using his name.

On 14 September 1933, the London Counter-Trial was formally opened in the courtroom of the Law Society. The inaugural address was delivered by Sir Stafford Cripps, to an audience including such famous men as H. G. Wells. Shaw, too, had been invited but he had declined with the remark: 'Whenever a prisoner is used as a stick with which to beat a Government, his fate is sealed in advance.'[6]

The whole trial was carefully staged with the 'bench' ranged on one side of the room. One of the 'judges' was Moro-Giafferi of whom Dr Sack had this to say:

> Legally-trained observers were unpleasantly surprised when they saw Moro-Giafferi on the bench. Four days earlier, this French lawyer had told all Paris that Hermann Göring was the real instigator of the Reichstag fire, and now he, whom every court throughout the world would have deemed an interested party, sat here as judge. He was judge and prosecutor rolled into one.[7]

Hays's comments were different, though no less telling:

> On the third day of the hearing, I saw my colleague, Moro-Giafferi, of France, apparently engaged in deep thought. He scribbled a note and pushed it to Bergery who sat at my right. I wondered what I had missed that this eminent French lawyer had caught. I glanced at the note. It read (translated into English): 'There isn't a good-looking woman in the courtroom.'[8]

Nor was the French lawyer the only one to be dissatisfied with the atmosphere at the Counter-Trial; the original sense of great excitement soon gave way to a general sense of great boredom. The reason was simple: the wirepullers, Münzenberg and Katz, were able to set the stage, but they could not keep control of it. One difficulty – and source of boredom for the ever-decreasing number of journalists – was the multi-lingual composition of the bench. Thus when a French 'judge' wished to put a question to a German witness, his question had first to be translated into English and then into German, and the German's reply had to be translated back into French via English. Most of the interpreters were ordinary members of the public and there were constant arguments about the correct translation of a given phrase. In the end, but only after a great deal of unpleasantness, it was agreed that an English-speaking German would put English questions to German witnesses and that a German-speaking Englishman would translate the German's reply, on the assumption that an ordinary person can understand a foreign language better than he can express himself in it. How closely the courtroom resembled the Tower of Babel can best be gathered from Hays's wry remark that, on one occasion, his own American idiom had first to be turned into the King's English before it could be translated into German.

Oddly enough, the Nazi press reported the Commission's original deliberation with surprising fairness:

> The International Legal Commission into the Burning of the Reichstag today heard the evidence of Georg Bernhard on the political position at the beginning of the year and his claim that stories about Communist responsibility [for the fire] were so many fables. Only if all their leaders had gone absolutely mad, could the Communists have hatched out so idiotic a plot.
>
> Bernhard went on to state that he knew the Communist Torgler extremely well. In his opinion, it is quite inconceivable that Torgler did anything so preposterous as setting the Reichstag on fire.
>
> After the noon recess, the Commission heard the Social Democrat Breitscheid. He, too, stated that he had known Torgler for many years and that he thought it impossible for Torgler to have had any connection with the Reichstag fire.

Then there is the story of how Albert Norden – editor of the *Rote Fahne* and, according to many people, the real author of the Oberfohren Memorandum – appeared before the Commission with a masked face, pretending he was a Storm Trooper from Germany. The mask was ostensibly worn so as to enable the Storm Trooper to return to Germany, when in fact it served to disguise Norden's 'pronounced Jewish features'. Even before producing his mysterious witness, Münzenberg had prepared the ground so well that, as Hays tell us,

. . . one of the [London] papers reported that three of the fifteen witnesses whom we contemplated calling were on a 'Death List' posted on the bulletin of a London Nazi club. Under the names and photographs of those listed appeared the comment: 'If you meet one of them, kill him; if he is a Jew, break every bone in his body.'

Often the doors to the hearing room would be locked before a witness was called and remain so until five minutes after the witness had testified. This in order to enable the witness to get away. . . . Many of the names of witnesses were kept secret.

But cleverly though Otto Katz played this cloak-and-dagger game, some of his schemes proved too hard to swallow even for the Commission. An example was the evidence of the witness 'W. S.' that Bell had shown him a list of thirty well-known homosexuals whom he had introduced to Röhm. Among these names, the witness went on to say, he 'particularly remembered' the name of Marinus van der Subbe or Marinus van der Lubbe and beneath it the entry: 'Holland'. Herr W.S. made so bad an impression, that the Commission had to dismiss him as 'not very reliable'. Still, there were many others no better than Herr W. S. whose monstrous lies the Commission saw perfectly fit to believe.

By means of the careful sifting of witnesses, the secretariat – that is, Otto Katz – made sure of one thing at least: the systematic exclusion of any real friends of van der Lubbe. Thus, when a special committee consisting of Dr Bakker-Nort, Mr Georg Branting and Maître Pierre Vermeylen heard the evidence of sixteen witnesses in Holland, all of these witnesses 'happened to be' hostile to van der Lubbe. One of them, the 'poet' Freek van Leeuwen, played a particularly odious role, for it was largely thanks to him that the London Commission accepted the story of van der Lubbe's homosexual relationship with Röhm.

On the evening of 19 September, members of the Commission assembled in a hotel suite. Hays tells us how the stolid and dignified Pritt sat in the bathroom with a typewriter, while Dr Kurt Rosenfeld (Torgler's former counsel) and other members of the committee straightened out exhibits. Others again were wandering about the rooms. Having finished his job and finding the bed covered with papers, the exhausted Hays, 'forgetting the dignity of the American bar', crept into a corner and fell asleep on the floor.

Next day, the Commission published its 'preliminary' findings, and it was in the nature of things that these were the mirror-image of the subsequent verdict of the German Supreme Court: where the former blamed the Nazis, the latter blamed the Communists.

The Final Conclusion of the Committee (formulated by Bergery) was:

(1) That van der Lubbe is not a member but an opponent of the Communist Party; that no connection whatsoever can be traced between the Communist Party and the burning of the Reichstag; that the accused Torgler, Dimitrov, Popov and Tanev ought to be regarded not merely as innocent of the crime charged, but also as not having been concerned with or connected in any manner whatsoever, directly or indirectly, with the arson of the Reichstag.

(2) That the documents, the oral evidence, and the other material in its [the Commission's] possession tend to establish that van der Lubbe cannot have committed the crime alone;

(3) That the examination of all the possible means of ingress and egress to or from the Reichstag makes it highly probable that the incendiaries made use of the subterranean passage leading from the Reichstag to the house of the President [Speaker] of the Reichstag; that the happening of such a fire at the period in question was of great advantage to the National Socialist Party; that for these reasons, and others pointed out in the third part of the report, grave grounds exist for suspecting that the Reichstag was set on fire by, or on behalf of, leading personalities of the National Socialist Party.

The Commission considers that any judicial organization exercising jurisdiction in the matter should properly investigate these suspicions.

Many lawyers have rightly objected to the German Public Prosecutor's absurd plea that the Court need not consider '. . . in which particular way each of the accused carried out the crime.' The London conclusions are open to precisely the same objection, for like the German Court verdict later, they were based on so many unverified political speculations.

As a known member of the London Commission, Hays was understandably reluctant when he was asked to go to Leipzig as an observer:

I tried to persuade some of the other lawyers to go with me. Most of them were too busy to go. Said Bergery: 'I can't go, I am a French deputy; if anything happened to me in Germany, it would create an international incident.'

Said I: 'Bergery, that wouldn't bother me. What bothers me is that if anything happens to me – nobody will pay a damned bit of attention to it.'

Hays started for Germany with trepidation, but he soon discovered that his fears were groundless. No one took the slightest notice of him – so much so that he confessed he was a 'little disappointed'.

In general, much to my surprise, the trial was objective. Dr Sack was defending Torgler conscientiously and with ability. He made it clear that he had no sympathy for or with the Communist Party or with Torgler's political views, but that the man, not the party, was on trial. He left no doubt that he was sure of his client's innocence. Any lawyer, even though a non-Nazi, would in that atmosphere have taken the same position.

These remarks, which were published during the war, show not only that Hays was a man of outstanding honesty, but also why the Communists grew extremely chary of him. Thus he wrote:

My committee, with headquarters in Paris, continually criticized Sack for not trying to prove that the arson was committed by the Nazis. Preposterous! Not only was that not his job, but it would have been inexcusably stupid.

Hays made it clear that he, the American Jew, was invariably treated with professional courtesy by Sack, the German Nazi, who was ready for conference at any time.

The Communists kept in touch with Hays in their own conspiratorial manner:

Every few days I was visited by a Communist – usually a different individual – but always giving the name 'Mr Glueck'. I refused to go to out-of-the-way places, so Mr Glueck always came to my hotel.

The Paris Communists now thought it was high time to save poor Arthur G. Hays from the clutches of the Nazi devil, Dr Sack, and to lead him back to the straight and narrow path of anti-Fascism. To do so, they behaved with typical ruthlessness. After his return to Germany from a brief visit to Paris, where he had given an interview to a *Pravda* correspondent, Hays found that his words had been twisted out of recognition. Whereas he had told the reporter no more than

... that the Nazis were not on trial, that Sack had based his defence on the innocence of his client rather than on the guilt of others, and that the only reason the Nazis came into the picture at all was because the court had gone out of its way to disprove the charges in the *Brown Book....*[9]

Pravda had reported him as saying:

> ... I had charged the Court with ignoring evidence pointing to the guilt of the Nazis, and had charged Sack with betraying his client.

With that 'interview' the Communists nearly attained their object – Dr Sack was deeply offended with Hays.

It was at about the same time that four foreign lawyers and observers at the trial, viz. the Bulgarians Grigorev and Detscheff, the Frenchman Marcel Villard, and the American Leo Gallagher, caused an incident which led to their temporary arrest and subsequent expulsion from Germany. Grigorev had tried to approach Dimitrov at the beginning of a noon recess, but the guards had pulled Dimitrov away. Enraged, Grigorev and the other foreign lawyers came to Hays's hotel and insisted that a protest be made immediately to the Court. Hays objected, stating with good reason that he had more important things to do than to make mountains out of molehills. A few days later, the Paris Committee sent him clippings from the French press to the effect that Dimitrov had been brutally handled in Court, and asked why Hays had ignored the matter.

Meanwhile, the others had lodged a protest with the Presiding Judge who referred them to Dr Teichert, Dimitrov's counsel. When their protest remained unheard, they wrote a letter to Dr Teichert calling him a Nazi stooge and the whole trial a frame-up. As a result, Grigorev, Detscheff and Villard were whisked across the border, while Gallagher, an American citizen and hence not so easily got rid of, was barred from Court. He stayed on in Germany and continued to bombard the President of the Court with letters of complaint.

The upshot of all this was that the stage-directors in Paris were left with no one at the trial except Hays, who kept letting them down badly:

> ... I had continually expressed resentment at their continued insistence that I urge Dr Sack to play up the Nazi angle. I had pointed out that the defence of the innocent was a big enough job and that this would be jeopardized by making charges we could not sustain in Court. ... The correspondence had become so heated that I had threatened to leave Berlin if the committee presumed to give me

instructions. I had begun to feel that the committee might be controlled by 'leftists' who were more interested in anti-Nazi propaganda than in the fate of the defendants whom I was supposed to represent and that they were trying to use me as a pawn to further their political game.[10]

When all the factual evidence had been given at the trial, Hays felt that his job was ended, and he accordingly left Germany on 22 October 1933. Before his departure he wrote to Dr Sack:

After a month of observing the trial I have the fullest confidence in the objectivity of your defence, and if anyone should criticize you abroad, you can always rely on my support.[11]

But Hays had not yet heard the last of the business. On 13 December 1933 the Public Prosecutor, in the course of a sharp attack on the *Brown Book* and the London Counter-Trial, which he called grotesque, charged Hays with hypocrisy, claiming he had told Soederman, a Swedish criminologist, that though he was convinced the Nazis were not involved, he had not had the courage to say so openly. This, the Public Prosecutor added, was typical of the manner in which the London Commission had set to work, and showed how much attention should be paid to its findings.

Hays immediately sent the following cable:

DR KARL WERNER, REICHSGERICHT, LEIPZIG, GERMANY. ANSWERING NEWSPAPER REPORT YOUR SPEECH – I MADE THE SAME STATEMENT TO SOEDERMAN, TO LONDON COMMISSION, AND PUBLICLY, TO WIT – THERE IS NO DIRECT EVIDENCE THAT LUBBE HAD ACCOMPLICES BUT IF, AS YOU CLAIM, HE DID NOT ACT ALONE, THEN HIS ASSOCIATES MUST HAVE BEEN NAZIS. I HOPE YOU WILL MAKE THIS CORRECTION IN COURT BUT I DONT EXPECT IT.

ARTHUR GARFIELD HAYS[12]

In other words, Hays was one of the few to realize that van der Lubbe had fired the Reichstag by himself. Small wonder, therefore, that he was not invited to attend the final session of the International Legal Commission (Caxton Hall, 18–20 December 1933), at the conclusion of which the Chairman, D. N. Pritt, K.C., read the verdict – three days before the Leipzig judgement. Once again the date had been chosen skilfully – if all the accused were sentenced there would be an international outcry, and if they were acquitted, the whole world would know that it was thanks to the efforts of Münzenberg's Commission.

The 'verdict' was largely a rehash of the 'final conclusions' of 20 September. In other words, it was based on evidence that most lawyers would have considered extremely slender, at best, and it was, once again, the German High Court verdict in reverse:

(1) Marinus van der Lubbe could not have committed the crime alone.
(2) Grave grounds exist for suspecting that the Reichstag was set on fire by, or on behalf of, National Socialist circles.
(3) The Communist Party had no connection with the burning of the Reichstag.[13]

In addition the Commission found:

That the retrospective application of the penal law of March 29th imposing the death sentence in cases of arson or high treason would constitute a monstrous violation of one of the principles of justice most universally recognized among all civilized nations;

That the conviction of the accused Torgler, the accusation having been withdrawn against the three accused Bulgarians, will doubtless and rightly give rise to universal protest;

That, bound by its terms of legal reference, the Legal Commission is not in a position to give expression to that protest in this report;

BUT that it considers it its duty to proclaim that in these circumstances the sentencing to death of Torgler would constitute a judicial murder.[14]

In short, Münzenberg had made certain that the German Supreme Court always lagged one step behind the *Brown Book*, which Otto Katz correctly described as the 'sixth defendant' – the German Court sat for three months, most of which time it spent on desperate attempts to refute the *Brown Book* and the findings of the Counter-Trial.

As Koestler put it:

It was a unique event in criminal history that a Court – and a Supreme Court to boot – should concentrate its efforts on refuting accusations by a third, extraneous, party. Hence the parade of Cabinet Ministers on the witness-stand, hence the fantastic request of the court to the Head of the Potsdam police, to furnish an alibi for his movements at the time when the crime was committed. . . .[15]

A German observer summed up the Court's 'fight against the sixth defendant' as follows: 'Their propaganda . . . was so widely believed that any failure to discuss their lies, however stupid, would have been considered an evasion'.[16]

Or, to quote Koestler again: 'Both Heines and Schultz had

produced fairly convincing alibis, and in some other respects, too, the guesses of the *Brown Book* had been wide of the mark. But that did not diminish the effects. In totalitarian propaganda details do not matter.'

In order to brazen it out with those who had seen through the *Brown Book*, Otto Katz produced a further masterpiece called *The Fight for a Book*. Here is a specimen of its methods:

> The *Brown Book* has been taken to task for calling Heines, Helldorff and Schultz the real criminals, when all three have protested that they were not. Now, that is the only 'proof' of their innocence. The so-called 'alibis' these men submitted were accepted by the Supreme Court without question – and that is now called a refutation of the *Brown Book*!

In fact, the three S.A. leaders had alibis that any court would have accepted. Thus Arthur G. Hays wrote:

> Heines, the Silesian Storm Troop chieftain and Reichstag deputy who, in the *Brown Book* and by the Oberfohren Memorandum, was said to have been the leader of the Nazis who had assisted van der Lubbe and had then left him alone in the burning building, presented an unimpeachable alibi. Not only he, but his wife, a nurse who attended his children, and others, testified to his whereabouts on the night of the fire, in a distant city, Gleiwitz, Silesia.

But facts had never bothered the *Brown Book* compilers: 'The Court failed to determine whether Heines had time to fly to and from his near-by constituency to Berlin.'[17]

But Hays closed even this loophole:

> More convincing, however, were clippings from local newspapers showing that Heines had made a speech at a public meeting on February 27th. Thinking this might have been planted, I had one of our Mr 'Gluecks' check up on newspapers of the town. Personally, I have no doubt that Heines was not involved. The same was true for Schultz, von Helldorff, and others who had been mentioned as Nazi accomplices.[18]

9. Münzenberg's Striking Success

THE CASE AGAINST GOEBBELS

THOUGH Münzenberg failed to take in Hays, he took in almost everyone else, particularly when the German Supreme Court agreed that van der Lubbe must have had accomplices. If the accused Communists were innocent, what could be more obvious than to seek the real incendiaries in the National Socialist camp? Oddly enough, Hitler himself was not implicated, either in the *Brown Book* or in the Oberfohren Memorandum. Instead, the Communists fastened suspicion on all sorts of leading Nazis, and especially on Goebbels and Göring.

Dr Goebbels became their favourite target simply because he, of all the Nazis, was the only one clever enough to have hit on the idea of burning the Reichstag as a means of seizing power. The whole thing was started in the Oberfohren Memorandum, where we read: 'The ingenious Goebbels, handicapped by no scruple, soon devised a plan . . .'

The *Brown Book*, which elaborated this argument with more enthusiasm than good sense, claimed: 'It was he [Goebbels] who first thought of a *grand coup* which would at one blow change the political position of the National Socialists.'[1] And elsewhere, in unmistakable Communist Party jargon: 'Goebbels provided the plans for the most outrageous provocation which a ruling class has ever used against the insurgent working class.'[2]

Goebbels himself scoffed at these accusations, when he gave his evidence before the Supreme Court:

> It came as a great surprise to me when I read that the *Brown Book* considers me the author of this plan. That is just one more proof of the complete lack of imagination with which the Communists trump up their charges. Can anyone really believe that I have no better way of fighting the Communists than starting a fire?[3]

Now, Goebbels would, in fact, have had to be a political idiot, and not the shrewd schemer he was, had he really hit upon so dangerous a plot. Let us, for the sake of argument, assume that a fire would have been needed by the Nazis in order to squash the Communist Party or 'the insurgent working class'. Let us further assume that the best plan would have been to set the Reichstag on fire. Then this is how Goebbels might have planned it:

A posse of Storm Troopers is returning from a victorious street battle. Singing a rousing song with throats hoarse from cheering for Germany, they are just rounding the Reichstag, full of the joys of life, when they are alerted by passers-by. The Reichstag is on fire! With their usual sang-froid the Storm Troopers rush into the burning building and catch the incendiaries red-handed. They are ten well-known Communists, carrying detailed instructions for a putsch and Communist Party membership cards in their pockets, and all are killed on the spot by the enraged Storm Troopers. Later, the press is allowed to inspect the gutted building, and the well-known faces of the Communist criminals. There is no lengthy trial, there are no foreign suspicions – just perfect co-ordination. And yet even this plan would have been studded with difficulties. First of all it would have involved a fairly large number of accomplices and hence a grave risk of betrayal. Secondly, most Reichstag officials, porters, etc., would have had to be replaced beforehand with reliable Storm Troopers.

But in any case Goebbels would have made certain that his men discovered real Communists – albeit dead – rather than Marinus van der Lubbe, who insisted he had left the Communist Party and had burned the Reichstag all by himself.

Torgler's counsel, Dr Sack, dealt with this question at some length:

It is quite ridiculous to suggest that the National Socialists should have picked a tramp as the best person to carry out a plan whose discovery would threaten the whole nation. . . .

Only a fool would have allowed the intended arsonist to wander about alone, in rags and tatters, begging for food in the streets, and sleeping in the public shelters in Glindow, Berlin and Henningsdorf.

Only a fool would have instructed van der Lubbe to scale up the wall of the Reichstag, to break windows, and thus to expose the whole plan to so many risks of discovery. After all, the shot fired by Sgt Buwert might easily have hit van der Lubbe and might thus have thwarted the 'whole plan'. This plan, allegedly invented by Goebbels, the undisputed master of the art of propaganda, would therefore have been so full of flaws as to invite discovery deliberately. This suggestion alone shows that the Oberfohren Memorandum is a tissue of malicious lies. The Memorandum, which claims to know precisely what happened, is bound to be wrong, simply because its authors were, in fact, quite unaware of the real course of events. They did not know where van der Lubbe had spent the previous day, that he had climbed into the Reichstag instead of entering through the subterranean passage, or that a revolver was fired at him. They did not know all this because the records of the preliminary investigation had mercifully not been made public.[4]

All Dr Goebbels did do – and who would gainsay that he did it brilliantly? – was to exploit the *results* of the fire, the more so because he himself was fully convinced that the Communists were responsible.

Though neither Goebbels, Göring nor any other National Socialist had thought up the idea of burning the Reichstag as a pretext for starting an anti-Communist pogrom, Münzenberg's propaganda was so effective that the Nazi leaders themselves began to suspect one another. Thus one of Goebbels's collaborators, Werner Stephan, wrote after the war, when the burning of the Reichstag appeared a minor transgression in comparison with all the inhuman crimes the Nazis had committed, that Goebbels 'probably conceived the idea', and '. . . in any case, the burning of Parliament provided the main theme of his election campaign'.[5]

Dr Wolff's conclusion in his report on the fire was that

Goebbels must be considered the evil genius behind and, thanks to his tremendous intelligence, the real perpetrator of, this devilish plan.

Also there is Sommerfeldt's highly informative *Ich war dabei* ('I was there') which threw a great deal of light on the circumstances surrounding the fire. In 1933 Göring had 'promoted' Sommerfeldt to the rank of Oberregierungsrat, and like many of Göring's minions, Sommerfeldt felt acutely suspicious of Goebbels, Göring's chief rival in the Nazi hierarchy. In his book, Dr Wolff published a letter from Sommerfeldt, from which we quote the following significant passage:

From the night of the fire to this day, I have been convinced that the Reichstag was set on fire neither by the Communists nor at the instigation, let alone the participation, of Hermann Göring, but that the fire was the *pièce de résistance* of Dr Goebbels's election campaign, and that it was started by a handful of Storm Troopers all of whom were shot afterwards by an S. S. commando in the vicinity of Berlin. There was talk of ten men, and of the Gestapo investigating the crime. This was reported to me on the one hand by the chief of the Berlin Storm-Detachment, Gruppenführer Ernst, who was filled with poisonous hatred of Goebbels, and also by Dr Diels who, at the time – it was the spring of 1934 – gave me exact details about the scene and of the crime and the identification of the ten victims.[6]

If Sommerfeldt did, in fact, claim that he knew all this in the spring of 1934, it seems most odd that he failed to disclose it in his *Ich war dabei* which was published in 1949. Moreover, if Sommerfeldt claims that he heard details of the crime and the victims from Diels, why did he not think fit to mention any of their names, thus helping to turn mere suspicion into certainty? But once again, it is more than accident that no names were mentioned, and it is not surprising that Diels's *Lucifer ante portas* contains no single reference to what would certainly have been a most important aspect of the Reichstag fire story – had the murder of the ten Storm Troopers ever happened, that is.

All Sommerfeldt wrote in 1949 was:

> If we look back today across the ruins of Germany at the ruins of the Reichstag, we realize that that act of arson was no more than an act of malice and a 'masterpiece of agitation' of the kind for which Dr Goebbels was so well known. Today I am convinced of what I could only suspect at the time: that Goebbels administered this act of incendiarism as a shot in the arm of the floating or lazy voters. . . .
>
> With his alleged signal for a Communist uprising, Goebbels flung Hitler and Göring into a whirlpool of profound and irrevocable decisions. And this master-psychologist showed that he knew what he was doing.[7]

It was in 1933 that Sommerfeldt first discussed his suspicions with his friend, Storm Troop Leader Prince August Wilhelm, who told him that the S.A. was in a state of great agitation because '. . . a number of Storm Troopers had been arrested and had since disappeared. S.A. Leader Ernst was prepared to swear any oath that Dr Goebbels was behind it all, and asked that Goebbels be paid out for his treachery.'

Sommerfeldt immediately asked whether there was any connection between these arrests and the Reichstag fire which, foreign rumour had it, was started by Ernst's gang. To Sommerfeldt's great disappointment, the Prince who, as a close confidant of Röhm and Ernst, ought to have known the truth '... denied categorically that he had heard anything on the subject except wild rumours'.[8]

Sommerfeldt also discussed his suspicions with Röhm:

> I dropped a gentle hint that the Reichstag fire trial had led to personal differences between Göring and myself, and Röhm asked in surprise: 'What on earth did Göring have to do with the whole business?' When I replied: 'Who else?' he said furiously: 'Well, who but that devil, Jupp [Joseph Goebbels]?'
> I must have evinced too much curiosity, for he quickly changed the subject . . .[9]

Now, all that this proves is that the Nazi leaders thought one another capable of any piece of villainy – quite rightly so, as all of us have had to learn to our cost.

Unfortunately, Sommerfeldt was not able to draw the only reasonable conclusion from these mutual recriminations, even though that conclusion stared him in the face:

> I had written a pamphlet on Göring and I had conducted the German and foreign press to the scene of the crime – for that was my job. This very fact was enough to stamp me an incendiary as well. It is understandable, therefore, why this stupid charge suggested to me that the accusations against the others might be just as false.[10]

And yet Sommerfeldt went on to blame Goebbels without producing a shred of real evidence against him. To this day, no such evidence has been brought forward by anyone, despite the fact that so gigantic a plot as the one Goebbels is alleged to have hatched out, must have involved a large number of accomplices, and despite the fact that accomplices invariably talk. In 1933, the Nazis were not nearly as well entrenched as they were, for instance, in 1939 when they attacked the Gleiwitz radio-station, pretending they were Poles. Yet, despite all their efforts to wipe out the evidence on that occasion, the real facts could be established without much difficulty, and far beyond mere rumour and speculation.

THE CASE AGAINST GÖRING

While not a single one of the many survivors from Göring's immediate circle considered it even vaguely possible that Göring could have had anything to do with the Reichstag fire, there are

137

two men who claim to have heard Göring himself confess his guilt. These men are Hermann Rauschning and Franz Halder.

In 1940, Hermann Rauschning published a book in the United States which quickly became a best-seller and was translated into most European languages. The book was called *Voice of Destruction*.

Rauschning, who was elected President of the Danzig Senate in July 1933, left the Nazi bandwagon in the autumn of 1934. He stayed in Danzig for another two years, and then went abroad with his story of Hitler's intimate thoughts.

In his book Rauschning tells how, shortly after the Reichstag fire, Hitler asked him for a report on the Danzig situation, and how, while waiting in the lobby of the Chancellery, he got into conversation with some Nazi celebrities, including Göring, Himmler, Frick, and 'a number of Gauleiter from the western provinces':

> Göring was giving details of the Reichstag fire, the secret of which was still being closely guarded. I myself had unhesitatingly ascribed it to arson on the part of persons under Communist, or at any rate Comintern, influence. It was not until I heard this conversation that I discovered that the National Socialist leadership was solely responsible.
>
> The complacency with which this close circle of the initiated discussed the deed was shattering. . . . There is nothing more extraordinary than that this enormous crime, the perpetrators of which gradually became known in the widest circles, should not have been sharply condemned, even in middle-class quarters. Many people actually condoned this *coup*. Still more extraordinary is the fact that the incendiary himself has actually enjoyed a certain amount of sympathy in foreign countries, even till quite recently.

The incendiary Rauschning referred to was, not van der Lubbe, but Hermann Göring.

> Gratified laughter, cynical jokes, boasting – these were the sentiments expressed by the 'conspirators'. Göring described how 'the boys' had entered the Reichstag building by a subterranean passage from the President's Palace, and how they had only a few minutes at their disposal and were nearly discovered. He regretted that the 'whole shack' had not burnt down. They had been so hurried that they could not 'make a proper job of it'.

The many inverted commas round Göring's alleged phrases

suggest that Rauschning 'jotted them down under the immediate influence of what he had heard' – as he himself put it in the preface to his book. Hence it seems doubly surprising that, when asked to fill in some of the missing details, Rauschning was quite unable to do so. For instance, Rauschning was unable to identify the 'Gauleiter from the western provinces', though he continued to insist that '. . . after every such conversation he had made careful notes and that there was no doubt whatever about the general accuracy – though not necessarily the precise wording – of his reports.'

Rauschning added that the Reichstag fire discussion was dominated by Göring, who spoke 'very loudly and quite unashamedly'. However when he (Rauschning) approached the group, Gauleiter Forster (who had accompanied Rauschning from Danzig) gave a signal and the conversation stopped.

A few years later still, Rauschning described his experiences as follows:

> Göring did not describe these details to me or to Forster, but to a circle of confidants and friends in different sorts of uniforms, who surrounded him before we arrived. Forster and I heard no more than snatches of the conversation. When one of the group spotted me, the outsider, he gave Göring a sign and Göring stopped talking.

This version differs markedly from the one in Rauschning's book, in which Rauschning specifically stated that he 'got into conversation with the Nazi celebrities'. Also in the last version it was not Forster but one of the people round Göring who had signalled Göring to stop. Moreover, according to the book, Göring did not stop abruptly at all, but closed with the significant words: 'I have no conscience. My conscience is Adolf Hitler.'

True, Rauschning, when asked about these and other contradictions, insisted that his version of the conversation was the correct one, but it seems rather difficult to decide which of his versions he really meant. For in the end Rauschning himself had to admit that

> . . . detailed and careful investigations have shown certain contradictions in my evidence. . . . Indeed, I admit gladly that, as a result, I have grown less certain, not about my evidence, but in my previous attitude to the fire. . . . I declare with all emphasis that there had been no misunderstanding and that I vouch for the literal truth of Göring's closing words.[11]

And Rauschning went on to say:

Whether Göring himself was speaking the whole truth, or indeed the truth, is quite a different matter. I myself have never fully believed Göring's version . . .

A far cry from the allegations made in his book!

Göring himself had, of course, read Rauschning's book, so that when he was asked by Mr Justice Robert H. Jackson, Chief Prosecutor at the Nuremberg Trial, whether he himself had not admitted to setting the Reichstag on fire, he knew at once what it was all about, and protested angrily:

No. I know that Herr Rauschning said in the book which he wrote . . . that I discussed this with him. I saw Herr Rauschning only twice in my life and only for a short time on each occasion. Had I set fire to the Reichstag I would presumably have let that be known only to my closest circle of confidants, if at all. I would not have told it to a man whom I did not know and whose appearance I could not describe at all today. That is an absolute distortion of the truth.[12]

Now, Göring may have been too hard on Rauschning, for there is yet another possible explanation of the whole business: Rauschning might well have overheard, not a boastful outburst of Göring's, but one of Göring's frequent displays of his particular brand of twisted humour. For this is precisely what happened to the second 'star witness' against Göring, Franz Halder, the Chief of the General Staff:

Jackson: 'Do you remember a luncheon in 1942, on Hitler's birthday, in the officers' mess, at the Führer's Headquarters in East Prussia?'
Göring: 'No.'
Jackson: 'You do not remember that? I will ask that you be shown the affidavit of General Franz Halder, and I call your attention to his statements which may refresh your recollection:
' "On the occasion of a luncheon on the Führer's birthday in 1943, the people round the Führer turned the conversation to the Reichstag building and its artistic value. I heard with my own ears how Göring broke into the conversation and shouted: 'The only one who really knows the Reichstag is I, for I set fire to it.' And saying this, he slapped his thigh." '
Göring: 'This conversation did not take place, and I request that I be confronted with Herr Halder. First of all, I want to emphasize that what is written here is utter nonsense. It says: "The only one who really knows the Reichstag is I." The Reichstag was known to every

representative in the Reichstag. The fire took place in the general assembly room, and many hundreds of thousands of people knew this room as well as I did. A statement of this type is utter nonsense. How Herr Halder came to make that statement, I do not know. Apparently that bad memory, which let him down in military matters, is the only explanation.'

Göring had previously been examined on Halder's testimony by Dr Robert Kempner, Assistant Trial Counsel for the American Prosecution:

Kempner: 'A number of generals have alleged that you have boasted of your connection with the Reichstag fire.'

Göring: 'What the general says is not true. I should very much like to see him here, so that he can say it to my face. The whole thing is preposterous. Even had I started the fire, I would most certainly not have boasted about it. . . . These generals all talk utter nonsense. I object most strongly that people keep saying I did it. All I did was say, by way of a joke, that people will soon stop believing that Nero burned Rome, because the next thing they will say is that it was I who was fiddling in his toga.'

Now, even if Göring did make the remark Halder alleges he heard, the fact that he slapped his thigh suggests strongly that he must have been joking. Halder would certainly have missed the joke, for his lack of humour was proverbial.

The case against Göring also rested on the allegation by Diels and Gritzbach (Göring's Secretary of State) that their chief had told them about the Reichstag fire long before it started.

Kempner: 'Diels says that you knew exactly that the fire was to be started in some manner, and that he had prepared the arrest lists already previously, the lists of people that were to be arrested immediately the night after the fire.'

Göring: 'When did he say that?'

Kempner: 'He told that for the first time two days after the fire and he later repeated it.'

Göring: 'To whom did he say that two days after the fire?'

Kempner: 'To certain officials of the Ministry of the Interior'.

Göring: 'It is true that lists for the arrests of Communists quite independent of the Reichstag fire had already been prepared. The fire did not start for that. They would have been arrested anyway. If Diels said that I knew about the fire, then for some reason he must have spoken nonsense, and I can't explain it in any way, and it would be very interesting to me to be confronted with Diels so that he can tell it to my face.'

And elsewhere:

Göring: 'I cannot judge what people are saying now, but I should like to be confronted with Gritzbach so that he can tell it to my face that I knew about it. . . . I knew nothing about it and even they [Diels and Gritzbach] could have known nothing about it. Gritzbach, at the time, did not even belong to my personal staff. I never had such thoughts, and I must stress again that it would have been idiotic to deprive ourselves of the House, which was very important for us, and that afterwards I had great difficulties in finding a substitute for the Reichstag building.'

Kempner: 'You had nothing to do with it, and yet there were rumours that it was the Storm Troopers.'

Göring: 'No, I had nothing to do with it. I deny this absolutely, and am prepared to face anyone with whom you care to confront me. I can tell you in all honesty, that the Reichstag fire proved very inconvenient to us.'

Kempner: 'To whom?'

Göring: 'To the Führer and also to me as the President of the Reichstag. Had we given such a signal, we should have picked less essential buildings.'

Kempner: 'What buildings, for instance, would have been a better signal than the Reichstag? The Berlin Palace?'

Göring: 'Yes, the Palace or any other buildings. After the fire I had to use the Kroll Opera House as the new Reichstag. You must know that I took a keen interest in my state theatres, and that I found it bothersome, for the Kroll Opera was our opera number two, and the opera seemed to me much more important than the Reichstag.'

The International Military Tribunal apparently believed Göring rather than his accusers, for Diels's and Gritzbach's evidence was not pursued any further.

OR WAS IT KARL ERNST?

Before 30 June 1934 neither the *Brown Book* nor any other Communist publication contained even the slightest hint that Karl Ernst had played any active part during the fire. But when Hitler suddenly obliged them with three corpses: Gruppenführer Karl Ernst, and his associates Mohrenschild and Sander, the opportunity seemed far too good to be missed.

Immediately after the executions, in the summer of 1934, Münzenberg's Editions du Carrefour published a *White Book on the Shootings of June 30th 1934* (see Appendix D), containing a forged letter, ostensibly sent by Karl Ernst to Edmund Heines on 5 June 1934. The letter was written in what was assumed to be S.A. barrack-room style, and accompanied a signed confession to the effect that Ernst was 'Incendiary No. 1'.

Wisely the authors of the *White Book* refrained from telling their readers how they of all people had managed to get hold of this top secret Nazi document. Despite this omission, and despite the crude way in which they forged the letter, the Communists were, once again, able to take in a host of unsuspecting people.

Unfortunately for the forgers, two of the accomplices named by Ernst – S.A. Oberführer Richard Fiedler and Dr Ernst Hanfstaengl – survived 30 June 1934 and both men called the confession a complete fabrication.

Moreover, one of Münzenberg's former colleagues, Erich Wollenberg, published an article in Schulze-Wilde's *Echo der Woche* in which he stated that the Paris Communists forged documents so successfully that they managed to fool even the former Gestapo agent Gisevius. Among these documents was

... the so-called Ernst testament, which was concocted by a group of German Communists in Paris – including Bruno Frei and Konny Norden – after Ernst's murder on June 30th, 1934, and only published after Dimitrov himself had edited it in Moscow. ....[13]

Göring, who was in any case extremely sensitive about his alleged part in the Reichstag fire, was absolutely incensed when he heard that this forged document coupled his name with that of Karl Ernst. When Dr Robert Kempner asked him whether Ernst might have had a hand in the fire, he received the following reply:

Göring: 'Yes, he is the man who could have done it. But I think the letter I was recently shown is absolute nonsense. ...'
Kempner: 'One of your friends told me that Ernst's part was discussed in your circle and that other people were also present. Will you tell us what was said on that occasion? There was talk in your

house that Ernst and the S.A. were involved. Will you tell us about that conversation?'

Göring: 'The matter was mentioned very briefly. There was no proof at all. Marinus van der Lubbe had admitted that he had taken these things into the Reichstag, and therefore nothing more was said about it.'

Kempner: 'Why did you mention Ernst's name and the S.A. in connection with the fire?'

Göring: 'Ernst played a part in it, but I don't remember who told me. From the start, I thought that Ernst was a man who would love to give us trouble, for he was responsible for savaging people in concentration camps. He was also a real live-wire and at one stage very important to Hitler.'

Kempner: 'We have some evidence to show that Goebbels and Ernst got on very well together at the time, that Goebbels knew something about the Reichstag fire, and that he talked about it.'

Göring: 'I do not believe that. Ernst was the leader of the S.A. and Goebbels did not get on with him. Goebbels was always suspicious of the Berlin S.A., because they staged a putsch in 1930, as a result of which our situation became very, very difficult.'

Kempner: 'Is Diels right to claim that you gave express orders to dig up evidence against the Communists but not to follow any trail leading to the S.A. or to Ernst?'

Göring: 'That is untrue. Ernst was not mentioned at all at the time.'

Kempner: 'How do you explain the fact that the whole world says you did it?'

Göring: 'Yes, that was said quite suddenly. They "just knew" it. The entire foreign press claimed two days afterwards that I had burned the Reichstag.'

Kempner: 'Why didn't they say it was Ernst and his men?'

Göring: 'They were not so well known abroad. I was the President of the Reichstag, and so it seemed more fitting to involve me.'

Kempner: 'Who were Ernst's friends or who do you think belonged to his circle at the time?'

Göring: 'I don't know who was close to Ernst. I don't know these people. I liked neither Ernst nor his tendencies.'

Kempner: 'Are you referring to his homosexual tendencies?'

Göring: 'Yes, but for political reasons.'

Kempner: 'But as a politician and as Prussian Prime Minister did you not know that those who constantly caused you trouble were Ernst's people?'

Göring: 'That's true of Ernst himself. But the names of his people – well, there were quite a few S.A. leaders outside Berlin, for instance,

Heydebreck in Pomerania, who were also making trouble. Ernst provided me with a comical S.A. guard, which was supposed to arrest me one day and of which I got rid with some excuse or other. I simply disbanded them.'

Kempner: 'What was said about Ernst's role? If his men burned the Reichstag, what motive could they have had? In criminal cases we have to ask: *Cui bono?*'

Göring: 'It was only discussed once, not immediately after the fire, but later. When all those allegations against me were being made, we wondered whether the S.A. had had anything to do with it, simply because that came out during the investigation.'

Kempner: 'In other words, you yourself had nothing to do with it, and it was merely rumoured that the S.A. was involved?'

Göring: 'No, I had nothing to do with it. I say so categorically and I look forward to any confrontation whatsoever.'

Kempner: 'There are these alternatives: either van der Lubbe did it, or else the S.A. did it for political reasons.'

Göring: 'In either case van der Lubbe was involved, for he, after all, was caught.'

Kempner: 'But van der Lubbe was half crazy, is that not true? Do you agree?'

Göring: 'Yes.'

Kempner: 'Is it therefore not possible that van der Lubbe was used by the S.A.?'

Göring: 'Yes, well, I have read the letter [he was referring to Ernst's letter]. As far as I know, van der Lubbe could not speak a word of German.'

Kempner: 'Yes, but there were interpreters who could have spoken to him.'

Göring: 'How could they have met van der Lubbe? But anything is possible.'

Kempner: 'Anything is possible, indeed. Do you think that Goebbels and the S.A. might have been jointly involved?'

Göring: 'I really cannot imagine it.'

Kempner: 'You cannot imagine it?'

Göring: 'No, I really cannot.'

Now Kempner urged Göring once again to recall who could possibly have been interested in starting the fire. Göring took the opportunity to put forward certain conjectures, but no more:

Göring: 'I must repeat that no pretext was needed for taking measures against the Communists. I already had a number of perfectly good reasons in the form of murders, etc. The fire served – or was supposed to serve – or could . . . well . . . I'm really wondering what motive Ernst might have had. Perhaps he argued: "We'll start the fire and then give it out that it was the Communists." Perhaps the S.A. thought in that way they might gain a larger slice of our power.'

Kempner: 'Well, now we're getting somewhere.'

Göring's reasons for harbouring vague suspicions against Ernst were obvious. After the Reichstag Fire Trial he, too, must have begun to wonder whether van der Lubbe's accomplices could have been Communists. Moreover, the S.A. outrages, and his growing dislike of Ernst and Ernst's gang must have made even Göring receptive to foreign and local rumours.

However, Göring himself gave his word to Count Schwerin von Krosigk and also to Presidential Secretary Otto Meissner, who was interned with him and who asked him about his share in the Reichstag fire, that he (Göring) was completely innocent. All he did was grant the possibility that '. . . some "wild" National Socialist commando, and possibly even the Berlin S.A. leaders Count Helldorff and Karl Ernst, might have been responsible for the Reichstag fire, and might have used van der Lubbe as their tool'.[14]

And why, after all, should Göring have thought Karl Ernst, the man who, in his opinion, had prepared a putsch against Hitler in 1934, incapable of setting fire to the Reichstag? Or for that matter Count Helldorff, who had participated in the anti-Hitler revolt of 20 July 1944?

But that is all Göring did – admit that these men *might* have started the fire. Yet unlike most of his detractors, he left it at that, and refrained from whitewashing himself by making direct accusations against others.

Finally, let us listen to a witness whose evidence is more than speculation or surmise: the former S.A. Obersturmführer and subsequent Detective-Inspector, Dr Alfred Martin. This is what he had to say:

At the time of the Reichstag fire, I was an S.A. Obersturmführer on the personal staff of Gruppenführer Helldorff and Ernst, which made me a sort of general factotum. The reason for my promotion was simply that my doubts had caused me to keep clear of politics and also that – as one of the few trained men among a whole lot of rowdies – I was more presentable than such types as Schweinebacke. In my S.A. work I enjoyed the complete confidence of Ernst and of his lieutenants, and I am quite certain that I should have known, had Ernst, Schweinebacke, etc. – all those names were later mentioned by anti-Fascist circles as having been involved in the Reichstag fire – really had anything to do with it. In particular, I had highly confidential conversations with them – and also with Walter von Mohrenschild, a debonair young man of very good family and Ernst's second in command. At the time I had already joined the Resistance and whenever these men were in their cups I made a point of returning to the subject of the fire. Moreover, von Mohrenschild and I were both dragged by S.A. gendarmes before the summary court of that fine gentleman Herr Fritsch and sentenced to death [June 30th, 1934]. Until Mohrenschild's execution, we shared a cellar of the Lichterfelde Kaserne, and had many long and serious conversations, during which I referred to the part he was alleged to have played in the Reichstag fire. All these men steadfastly denied S.A. or Party responsibility for the fire. I, personally, have gained the conviction that the Party and the S.A. had absolutely nothing to do with it. Moreover, during my training with the criminal police in Berlin in autumn 1933, I had occasion to glance at the files and I also had long conversations with the man in charge of the investigations and above all of van der Lubbe's interrogation. . . . This man [Dr Zirpins], whom I knew very well, was anything but a Nazi. He told me that there was no doubt that van der Lubbe had burnt the Reichstag by himself.

The reliability of this witness is vouched for by Diels, who wrote:

This organization [Division Ic of the S.A.] also contained a number of decent young men, some of them students, who had joined the S.A. merely in order to fight Communism. But when all sorts of sordid desperadoes from the gutters of Berlin started flocking into Ic, the better elements left in horror. Among them was the group round young Dr Martin, who made contact with the 'anti-militarist machine', thus probably saving the lives of many intended Storm Troop victims.[15]

THE MASS ARRESTS

One weighty reason for blaming the Reichstag fire on the National Socialists was that they had ostensibly prepared a huge number of warrants, with only the date missing, against the night of the fire, when they hauled thousands of Communists out of bed and dragged them off to police-stations and S.A. barracks.

Now, there is no denying the arrests themselves, but they do not necessarily imply Nazi complicity in the Reichstag fire.

First of all, the large-scale arrests and raids involved the full co-operation of the Political Branch (Division IA) of the Prussian police and ready access to their documents. Hence the whole plan hinged on the silence of men, many of whom, as we saw, were still so filled with 'old-fashioned' notions that Göring was forced to create the more reliable Nazi 'auxiliary' police on 22 February 1933. These men kept silent, simply because there was nothing to reveal. This fact alone exonerates the Nazis even if we choose to ignore the statements by Diels, Dr Schneider, and other high-ranking officers of Division IA, that the Reichstag fire took them completely by surprise.

During his evidence to the Supreme Court on 4 November, Göring himself had this to say:

> Many people have wondered how it came about that my orders to arrest the ringleaders were carried out so promptly. Far from proving my prior knowledge of the fire, this merely shows how efficient our measures were. . . . Now, for the reason why: on the night of the fire, I knew all about the whereabouts of leading Communists because my predecessor had already prepared a full list of their addresses and hide-outs. On coming into office, I immediately checked and completed that list, and that is why I was able to arrest thousands of Communist officials immediately after the Reichstag fire.[16]

Göring's explanation was fully corroborated by Diels:[17] a list of the names and addresses of leading Communists had been prepared under Police President Severing, together, of course, with a similar list of Nazis and rightist extremists – a fact which Diels did not mention. In other words, the mass arrest of Communist officials could have been ordered any time the Minister saw fit to do so.

When Göring was asked about the matter in 1933 and again in 1945, he kept insisting:

> I very much regret – and I confess it openly before all the world – that the Reichstag fire saved certain Communist leaders from the gallows, when it had always been my intention to smash them completely the moment they gave the slightest hint of rebellion. . . .

There were many other 'regrettable' mistakes during Göring's action, including one which caused great amusement in Court, viz. the abortive attempt to arrest Ernst Torgler. This is how Torgler himself remembers the occasion:

Because I expected them to come for me next morning, if not that night, I decided to spend the night [of the fire] with our parliamentary secretary, Otto Kuehne, at his house in Berlin-Pankow. While he himself was arrested there next morning, I was left severely alone. This fact caused some amusement in the court-room because of the light it cast on the 'shrewdness' and 'intelligence' of the police officers. When a policeman opened the door to the room in which I had slept, I was just dressing and bade him good morning politely. He returned the greeting with equal politeness, and closed the door.[18]

Really though, there was no reason to laugh at dapper detective Franz Hohmann, for like so many of his colleagues, he had been summoned to police headquarters in the early hours of the morning, and ordered to bring in a whole lot of men. Naturally he realized that all of them were Communists, but he never even thought of arresting anyone for whom he had no warrant. After all, he was a policeman and not a politician.

Thus Hohmann is our best witness for the fact that 'outmoded' police methods were still being used at that time and, beyond that, that the black list had been compiled by Göring's predecessors. For Torgler's host for the night, Otto Kuehne, had moved house a year before, yet Hohmann had been sent to look for him at his old address, where he wasted hours trying to dig him up. In fact, Hohmann did not arrive at the correct address until seven o'clock in the morning.

But while the police were going about their business, the Storm Troopers were making another, quite independent, series of mass arrests which has often been confused with the police action. This wave of arrests was completely improvised, as many former Nazis have since testified. Dr Taube, for instance, an 'anti-Communist propaganda expert, spent the evening of the fire in the Berlin Nazi headquarters, from which the Reichstag blaze could be seen. Since no one thought the fire had any political implications, Dr Taube eventually went home to bed. An hour later, he was ordered back to headquarters, where he found everyone in a state of great agitation. He was told that the police had caught a Dutch Communist, that a Communist putsch might start at any moment. A senior S.S. officer – the S.S. was a branch of the S.A. until 30 June 1934 – was poring over a list of 'suspicious political elements' compiled by Nazi blockwardens and by Heydrich's intelligence

149

service. The S.S. officer then ticked off all 'dangerous' names, on the principle that members of the intelligentsia were particularly noxious. That is how it came about that such non-Communists as Ludwig Renn, Erich Mühsam, Carl von Ossietzky, Otto Lehmann-Russbüldt and many like them were hauled out of their beds in the middle of the night.

The Nazi lists, like those of the police, were out of date, and included names of people who had died some time earlier. Moreover, former Nazis have admitted that individual S.A. leaders and men made hay while the sun shone, and started settling personal scores with people who were not on the list. On 20 October 1933 the Supreme Court asked Count Wolf von Helldorff, Police Chief of Potsdam and Berlin S.A. Chief, to describe his movements on the night of the fire. He testified:

> On the day of the Reichstag fire, I worked in my office until about 7 p.m. Then I joined Professor von Arnim, the then Chief of Staff of the Berlin S.A., for dinner at Klinger's in the Rankestrasse. When we were at table, someone rang us up and told us about the Reichstag fire. I asked Herr von Arnim to get to the Reichstag as quickly as possible, and to ring me at home in case I was needed. At about 10 p.m. I was told that my presence in the Reichstag was not required. At about 11 p.m. I drove to my offices in Hedemannstrasse where I had a conference with my staff. The subject of the Reichstag fire was broached. Next day, I gave orders for the arrest of a large number of Communist and Social Democratic officials.[19]

(This statement was corroborated by Professor von Arnim and the owner of the restaurant.)

After his testimony, Helldorff was greatly embarrassed by Torgler, who asked him: 'Did you give the orders for the arrest of the Communist and Social Democratic leaders in your official capacity [as Chief of the Potsdam police] or in your capacity as S.A. leader?'

Helldorff started hedging; he was not quite sure what Torgler was getting at. The Public Prosecutor immediately rushed to his assistance, objecting that Torgler's question was irrelevant and immaterial inasmuch as it had no bearing on Helldorff's movements. However, the Presiding Judge overruled the objection, and Helldorff was compelled to answer. He preferred to sacrifice the truth and incriminate himself rather than throw the blame on Göring, the Minister of the Interior:

I gave the orders entirely on my own responsibility. As Gruppenführer of the Berlin S.A., I felt fully entitled to arrest enemies of the
state, particularly since the Reichstag had been set on fire and since
we all knew who the culprits were.

Fourteen days later Hermann Göring tried to correct Helldorff's damaging admission, and told the Court:

We threw in the entire police force. Because that was not enough, I
naturally deployed the S.A. and the S.S. as well. That is why I
summoned Count Helldorff. I know he has told the Court that he
acted entirely on his own initiative, but I must add the small proviso
that, though I left him a free hand in details, I gave him the clear order
to use his Storm Troops and arrest every Communist vagabond he
could lay his hands on. That was a measure which I supported one
hundred per cent. Without the praiseworthy help of our S.A. and
S.S., the colossal success of that night, during which 5,000 Communist
leaders were taken behind lock and bar, would not have been possible.

Clearly, either Göring or Helldorff had committed perjury. The
truth came out much later, when Göring was forced to admit,
under Dimitrov's piercing questions, that Helldorff had ordered
his S.A. henchmen out into the street before he (Göring) had a
chance to sanction the order, thus giving it a semblance of legality.
Unable to grasp that the only reason why the Communists made
no effort to hit back was that they had made no plans to do so,
Göring and Helldorff both boasted to the Court that it was the
Government's speedy measures which had thwarted a Communist
rebellion. Goebbels was under a similar misapprehension: 'No
resistance was shown anywhere; the enemy was apparently so
taken aback by our sudden and drastic measures that he lifted no
finger in his defence.'[20]
Diels has described the confusion resulting from Helldorff's ill-
prepared action: a large number of prisoners caught by the S.A.
could not be found on the blacklists – and had to be released, only
to be caught again by the Storm Troopers. This explains why the
figures varied so much: Göring spoke first of 4,000 prisoners and
then of 5,000; Diels mentioned 1,800 arrests in Prussia, when the
official figures gave 10,000.[21]

All in all, there is little doubt that, when Hitler ordered the
arrests on the night of the Reichstag fire, he did so on the spur of the

moment, and in genuine fear that a Communist rebellion was imminent. That is also the reason why Göring was able to complain that far too many Communist leaders had managed to elude his net.

THE PRE-ARRANGED DATE

A further Communist argument for Nazi responsibility is that all Nazi leaders kept 27 February suspiciously free of election engagements. Instead, they all seemed to have repaired to Berlin for a grandstand view of the fire.

This story saw the light of day in the Oberfohren Memorandum:

> 'All was prepared. On Monday 27th February, for some extraordinary reason, not one of the National-Socialist Propaganda General Staff was engaged in the election campaign. Herr Hitler, the indefatigable orator, Herr Goebbels, Herr Göring, all happened to be in Berlin. With them was the *Daily Express* correspondent Sefton Delmer. So, in a cosy family party, these gentlemen waited for the fire.'*

What happened in fact on the night of the fire was that Göring was at work in the Prussian Ministry of the Interior; Hitler and Goebbels were listening to music in the company of a group of people including Professor Hoffmann; von Papen was entertaining President von Hindenburg in the Herrenklub; the Foreign Office spokesman, Dr Hanfstaengl, was in bed with influenza; Count Helldorff was having supper in a restaurant in the Rankestrasse; and Himmler was in Munich. Seen thus, the evening of 27 February seems considerably less suspicious than the Oberfohren Memorandum made it out to be.

Moreover, there was no need, even had the Nazis planned the fire, for all the leaders to assemble in Berlin – suspiciously and quite pointlessly. True, in his testimony to the Supreme Court in November 1933, Goebbels did not produce the preceding explanation, but argued instead that the pause in the election campaign had been chosen at random in order to enable the Nazi leaders to attend a Cabinet Meeting.

And oddly enough, no one seems to have wondered why men who had ostensibly planned so gigantic a pre-election stunt as the fire should have spent the whole afternoon discussing such prosaic

* Delmer was not in fact 'with' the Nazi leaders, in this 'cosy family party'. He met them at the fire. See *Trail Sinister*, p. 185.

topics as changes in the milk law, the national insurance regulations, etc. Neither did anyone wonder why the Nazi leaders were so obviously astonished when they first heard of the fire: Goebbels slammed down the receiver on what he thought was one of Hanfstaengl's silly hoaxes; Hitler, too, refused to believe the news at first, and we know from Ludwig Grauert that Göring's surprise was not shammed. In any case, both Goebbels and Göring expressed the view that somebody's carelessness was to blame, and Göring repaired to the scene of the crime, where he wasted precious hours staring at the flames and speculating about their causes and consequences, instead of pulling his prepared plans out of his breast pocket, or issuing his prepared newspaper and radio communiqués.

Now, it is precisely the remarkable confusion and the many contradictions in the Nazi press after the fire, that ought to have suggested how little Hitler, Göring and Goebbels were expecting the fire. For if the Reichstag had really been burned by the highly organized Nazis, their press would have thrown the blame on the Communists from the start, instead of publishing a host of contradictory rumours, allegations and denials. Dr Goebbels proved often enough that he could order the entire German press to speak with one drab voice. It may be argued that at the time of the Reichstag fire Goebbels was not yet Minister of Propaganda and could therefore not yet order the non-Nazi press to dance to his tune. However, the Nazi press itself was completely under his thumb, so that there was no reason why the *Völkischer Beobachter*, for instance, should give the name of the incendiary as van Durgen, and why the man who left the Reichstag with Torgler was variously said to have been Wilhelm Pieck, Otto Kuehne and Wilhelm Koenen. The Nazi press even mentioned the presence in the burning Reichstag of a man who 'was identified as an American'.[22]

WAS THE FIRE BRIGADE CALLED IN TIME?

The suspicion that the Reichstag fire was started by mysterious criminals gave rise to a series of legends about the Berlin Fire Brigade and its chief, Fire Director Walter Gempp, particularly after Gempp was suddenly dismissed from his post. Once again, the real source of these legends was the Paris Agitprop office, and once again the German Supreme Court had to refute them. Still, we ought to be thankful since otherwise we should never have been able to discover what measures the fire brigade took on the night of the fire – all the brigade records were destroyed during the war.

Dr Wolff has repeated the legend that Gempp, during a meeting of fire brigade officers held in Berlin early in March, complained that the 'grand alarm' was given too late when, as the former Police President of Berlin, Albert Grzesinski, told the London Commission of Inquiry: '. . . any fire in the Government quarters of Berlin automatically calls for the highest-stage alarm, unless there is a specific order to the contrary.'

The *Brown Book* wondered who gave that order, and in whose interest it was that

> . . . the highest stage of alarm was not given to the fire brigade until half an hour too late . . . by which time the flames had attained considerable dimensions. . . . The delaying of . . . the highest alarm, coupled with the non-compliance with the fire regulations was responsible for the disastrous effects of the fire in the Session Chamber, the devastation in which was made good use of by the National Socialist propagandists.[23]

In fact, the existence of automatic regulations of the kind mentioned by Grzesinski has never been proved. Instead, Berlin, then as now, had a special Decree for the Alarm and Deployment of Fire Fighting Forces, according to which fire calls from public buildings, theatres, warehouses, factories, etc., were given various priorities. Thus the report that the Reichstag was on fire automatically set off the third-stage alarm. In other words, Grzesinski was quite wrong to claim that every fire in the Government quarters automatically called for the grand (fifteenth-stage) alarm. In any case, such automatic rules would have been quite preposterous, since even the smallest fire in the Government quarters would have left the rest of the gigantic city of Berlin denuded of fire engines. Even today, the highest-stage alarm sounded automatically for any public building in West Berlin is the fifth-stage.

If then the first report of the Reichstag fire called for 'no more than the third-stage alarm', the question still remains why the three sections of pumps associated with that stage were not automatically sent to the fire. Was there perhaps a deliberate plot to sabotage the fire-fighting arrangements?

As with so many historical events, here, too, the combination of a series of quite independent accidents led to the strangest consequences. However, the fact that there was no organized attempt to interfere with the work of the fire brigade is proved, not only by the evidence of firemen, but above all by the Court's reconstruction of the actual events:

First alarm, 9.05 p.m.

At 9.05 p.m., the police officer on duty outside the Reichstag, Sergeant Buwert, was told by two passers-by (Flöter and Thaler) that incendiaries had climbed into the Reichstag. After dithering for a few minutes (until 9.09 p.m.), Buwert requested another passers-by to alert the police at the Brandenburg Gate. One minute later – at 9.10 p.m. – he also requested the passers-by Kuhl and Freudenberg to call the fire brigade. These two sprinted to the Engineering Institute, whence Brigade Headquarters, Linienstrasse, were alerted at 9.13 p.m. Headquarters transmitted the call to the 'Stettin' Brigade, in the Lindenstrasse. A minute later, Section 6 pulled out, commanded by Chief Fire Officer Puhle. Puhle arrived at the Reichstag at 9.18 p.m. Passers-by directed him first to the northern front, whence he drove on to the restaurant (western front).

Second alarm, 9.15 p.m.

At 9.15 p.m., a patrolman pulled the fire alarm in the Moltkestrasse. Section 7, under the command of Fire Officer Klotz immediately left the 'Moabit' Brigade in the Turmstrasse, reaching the Reichstag four minutes later. When he saw the four vehicles of Section 6 outside the Western Entrance, Klotz drove on with three of his vehicles, leaving the fourth, commanded by Fire Officer Wald, at the south-western corner. Klotz stopped briefly outside Portal Two (south) which was locked, and then went on to Portal Five (north), the only entrance which was kept open at night. He arrived there at about 9.20 p.m.

Third alarm, 9.19 p.m.

At 9.17 p.m., immediately after his arrival at the Reichstag, Police Lieutenant Lateit ordered Sergeant Buwert not only to watch the windows and to fire at anything suspicious, but also to give the 'grand alarm'. Since Buwert could not possibly carry out both orders, he decided to remain where he was until a fellow policeman arrived on the scene. By that time the fire brigade had decided to sit tight, since two sections of pumps had already been sent out, and since, in any case, the 'grand alarm' had no precise technical significance. During the trial, Buwert was given a severe dressing down by the Public Prosecutor for having carried out the first part of his order first: 'Should you not have known that the last order always takes precedence?'[24]

Fourth alarm, 9.31 p.m.
Fire Officer Wald gave the tenth-stage alarm by telephone from Portal Five at 9.31 p.m.

Fifth alarm, 9.32 p.m.
Immediately afterwards – at 9.32 p.m. – the tenth-stage alarm was given, once again from Portal Five. Altogether eight sections of pumps were now on the way to the Reichstag, in addition to the two sections that had meanwhile arrived. With them came Chief Fire Director Gempp, Fire Directors Lange and Tamm, and Chief Government Surveyor Meusser.

Sixth alarm, 9.33 p.m.
Chief Fire Officer Puhle ordered Fireman Trappe to give the fifth-stage alarm from the Engineering Institute, but when Trappe did so he was told that the tenth-stage alarm had already been sounded.

Seventh alarm, 9.42 p.m.
Immediately after his arrival at the Reichstag, Chief Fire Director Gempp consulted Fire Director Lange and then gave orders for the fifteenth-stage alarm to be sounded. Chief Government Surveyor Meusser gave the same orders on his own authority.

Since every section consisted of four vehicles, no less than sixty fire-fighting vehicles were now drawn up round the Reichstag. At the same time a number of fire-boats had begun to fight the fire from the River Spree.

The time-table we have just drawn up shows why Dr Sack, Torgler's counsel, was able to speak with some justification of the 'exceptionally quick mobilization of the fire brigade'. Still, the question remains why the very first telephone call did not lead to the automatic and prompt dispatch of at least the three sections which the regulations demanded.

From the study of all the evidence given at the preliminary examination and at the trial, the following explanations emerge:

1. When the fire was reported to Brigade Headquarters from the Engineering Institute, the caller apparently said it was a minor fire. In order not to deplete the central brigade of all its pumps for the sake of a minor fire, only one section was sent out.

2. When the second alarm was sounded from the Moltke-strasse fire alarm, the call went automatically to Brigade Head-quarters, and hence to the 'Moabit' Brigade which sent out Section 7. Headquarters still felt that two sections were more than enough to deal with an insignificant fire.

3. From that moment – 9.15 p.m. – until the tenth-stage alarm was given at 9.31 or 9.32 p.m., no further alarm was received by Brigade Headquarters. It seemed reasonable to assume, therefore, that the two sections were quite adequate.

4. Brigade Headquarters also inferred that the fire was under control from the fact that none of the fire-alarms in the House itself had been pulled. Had that been done, three sections would undoubtedly have gone out straightaway.

Night porter Albert Wendt, whom Constable Poeschel had asked to pull the fire alarm in his lodge, had not done so for the following reasons: firstly he simply refused to believe Poeschel's story before he had checked it; then, when he saw the blazing restaurant, Lateit told him the fire brigade had already been called; finally, as he returned to his lodge, he could hear the jangle of the approaching fire brigade. Wendt could not have known that there was a difference between calling the brigade from inside and outside the House.

The time-table shows that the fire officers themselves gave the tenth-stage alarm thirty minutes after the arrival of the first section. During that interval, the fire in the Session Chamber had grown to unmanageable proportions. The alleged 'omission' of the fire officers to give the tenth-stage alarm sooner was due to the following reasons:

At 9.22 or 9.23 p.m., Section 6 under Chief Fire Officer Puhle, used ladders to enter the restaurant. There they found a burning window curtain draped over a table, a burning door, and another burning curtain.

All these fires were immediately put out. Then Puhle walked through the scorched door into the lobby where he met men from Section 7. The restaurant and the lobby were filled with smoke which he thought came from the restaurant. He therefore concluded that two sections were more than enough. When the remains of van der Lubbe's firelighters were discovered in the restaurant, Puhle ordered a search of all the neighbouring rooms. During the search Puhle himself entered the Session Chamber. Recently, he described his impression as follows:

> When I entered the Chamber, I saw much the same picture as on the other floors and rooms: a thin veil of smoke, but no sign of fire. . . . When I returned to the Chamber after a further inspection, I was suddenly faced with a large fire, and I immediately ordered Trappe to give the fifth-stage alarm.[25]

Meanwhile, many smaller fires – for instance bits of carpet that had caught fire when van der Lubbe's burning firelighters or burning rags had dropped on them – were quickly stamped out or extinguished. As a result, many of these minor fires were surrounded with moist spots, which gave many journalists and particularly Pablo Hesslein the wrong impression that they were so many 'pools of petrol'.

Douglas Reed, who followed all the evidence most carefully, came to the following conclusion:

> The firemen, ignorant of what was happening in the Session Chamber, devoted their attention to the small fire in the restaurant which they quickly extinguished, so that Thaler, looking back from the Victory Column, thought they were already packing up to go home. Firemen, then, were already in the Reichstag when the fire in the Session Chamber was in its first beginnings, but were busying themselves with the insignificant outbreak in the restaurant. By the time they reached the Session Chamber, it was too late.[26]

Reed's reference to Thaler is explained by the latter's testimony to the Supreme Court on 10 October 1933:

> I remained on the spot for a brief time, after which I and the other passers-by who had meanwhile gathered there were pushed back by officers of the flying squad. All the passers-by dispersed, and I crossed towards the Lehrter Bahnhof. . . . When I reached the end of the Victory Column, I turned round once again. Quite suddenly I noticed

a deep red glow in the dome of the Reichstag. I assumed that the fire
had grown to large proportions, ran back to the Reichstag building,
and reported my observation to the fire brigade.[27]

In a 'radio report from the desolate chamber', Fire Director
Gempp also explained that the fire brigade had at first thought the
fire was restricted to the restaurant alone: 'The first section from
the Linienstrasse found nothing except the two fires in the
restaurant. Only when they were ready to leave again, did they
hear of a third fire.'

Not only the fire officers, however, had the impression that the
fire was relatively harmless, for Police Officers Lateit and Losigkeit
were of precisely the same opinion. Lateit later told the Court that,
in his view, the Chamber could easily have been saved, had the fire
in it been discovered in time.

None of these factors – except the last one, of course – might
have been crucial by itself, but coming as they did on top of one
another, they led to the complete destruction of the Chamber.

Oddly enough, Douglas Reed was the only observer to have
considered the actual evidence – most other observers were completely taken in by the *Brown Book* allegations which, for their part,
rested on the flimsiest of speculations.

In short, the firemen did their best in difficult circumstances, and
there is not the slightest shred of evidence that anyone tried to
obstruct them in their work.

THE GEMPP AFFAIR

At about the same time that Dr Oberfohren made his exit from
the political stage, another prominent personality suddenly left his
job: the Chief of the Berlin Fire Brigade, Herr Walter Gempp.
He, too, was seized upon by the *Brown Book*, which turned him into
yet another poor victim of the Reichstag fire 'conspiracy'. However, the real facts of the Gempp case were far less flattering to the
Herr Direktor.

After the Reichstag fire, Chief Fire Director Gempp, an
extremely popular man, was hailed by the Berlin press for the
speed with which he had acted. No one blamed him for the loss of
the Chamber, for it was generally appreciated that, once the glass
dome had cracked, it acted as a giant chimney, spitting fire and heat
into the dark night. That was also the reason why the fire was

controlled so quickly once the flames had consumed everything combustible in the Chamber.

Hence the *Völkischer Beobachter* could speak of the 'quick and decisive intervention of the fire brigade' and add that its handling of this fire had been exemplary. On 1 March, the *Völkischer Beobachter* further published Hitler's motion in the Cabinet (28 February 1933), 'that this Cabinet expresses its gratitude to all Reichstag officials, the police and the fire brigade, for their unstinting efforts in subduing the flames.'

Next day, Hitler sent a special letter to Hermann Göring, the Minister responsible for the German fire-fighting services. That letter, which was published in all German papers, read as follows:

> The foul attack launched yesterday by Communist criminals against the Reichstag was thwarted within a few hours, thanks only to the swift action of the Berlin fire brigade, and the resolute leadership and personal courage of individual firemen.[28]

Though Gempp had received similar praises (and the Kronenorden) from Kaiser Wilhelm II, and from President Hindenburg, he was not allowed to bask in the favour of the new rulers for long – zealous brown rats began quickly to gnaw at his reputation. Göring's noisily promulgated 'Anti-Corruption Law' was encouraging a growing army of Nazi job-hunters to denounce their superiors. Every day the newspapers were full of sensational 'revelations' about the alleged misdeeds of the great – including such respectable and honourable men as, for instance, Dr Adenauer, and the former Prussian Ministers Braun and Severing, who were said to have embezzled millions of marks.

On 25 March 1933, the *Völkischer Beobachter* published the following laconic note:

> At the request of State Commissioner Dr Lippert, Chief Fire Director Gempp and Chief Clerk Drescher were given indefinite leave of absence. Gempp is succeeded by Fire Director Wagner, and Drescher by Inspector Feind. Other staff changes are expected.

Though sudden dismissals had become the order of the day, Gempp's case was bound to attract very special attention: unlike most of the other victims, he had never played the slightest part in politics so that there was no possible reason why he should have focused National Socialist resentment on himself. The *Vossische*

Zeitung expressed its dismay on 25 March 1933 in a brief report entitled 'Chief Fire Director Gempp Dismissed':

> It is still not known what motives swayed the State Commission to dismiss the tested leader of the Berlin Fire Brigade, a man who has devoted twenty-seven years to the service of the City of Berlin. This much alone we know: Gempp, who is fifty-five years old, helped to make the Berlin Fire Brigade the pride of all Berliners. The thousands of foreigners who come to us in order to study fire-fighting are full of admiration for Gempp's work.

Once this article was published, the authorities could no longer keep quiet, and published the following communiqué:

> Director Gempp, Chief of the Berlin Fire Brigade, who was provisionally granted leave of absence by State Commissioner Dr Lippert, was accused of having tolerated Communist intrigues in the service under his control. Gempp then requested that disciplinary proceedings should be started against him. This request was not granted at the time, in view of the fact that Gempp was suspected of other offences. Disciplinary proceedings have now been opened against him; he is charged with dereliction of duty under Section 266 of the Criminal Code in connection with the purchase of a motor car by an ex-official, the Social Democratic councillor Ahrens.

Needless to say, most people preferred to believe a different story. Thus ex-Reichspräsident Löbe explained that Gempp was hounded to death 'because he was the only one to look into the real causes of the Reichstag fire',[29] and according to Pablo Hesslein,[30] Gempp was punished for what he said at a press conference shortly after Hitler left the burning Reichstag:

> Chief Fire Director Gempp, who spoke first, was visibly excited. He stated quite openly that the fire was a well-planned affair involving a number of people, and that he had counted some 25–30 specially prepared areas which were meant to catch fire but did not. A Dutchman had been caught in the act, and had been described as the sole incendiary, but it was quite impossible for a single man to have started so many fires within so short a space of time. The last Reichstag officials had left the building some time after 8 p.m. and the first alarm was received at 8.45 p.m.; consequently van der Lubbe, who entered the building in a most mysterious way, would have had, at most, 20–35 minutes in which to do his work.

Now, even this brief report contains a series of errors which

161

Gempp was unlikely to have committed. Firstly, there were no specially 'prepared areas' that failed to catch fire, nor was the first alarm received at 8.45. Marinus van der Lubbe entered the Reichstag through a window in a most unmysterious manner, and the last Reichstag officials left the building well before and not 'some time after' 8 p.m.

Hesslein continues: 'Gempp was immediately suspended and placed under house arrest. A few months later, after he had sworn an oath of silence, he was finally dismissed.'

This allegation, too, is false, just as false as the many lies about Gempp which the *Brown Book* published at the time. Because of his alleged refusal to let the Nazis get away with it, Gempp was even elevated to the role of Resistance fighter by many misinformed observers:

> The Reichstag fire faced this man, who was respected at home and abroad as an outstanding engineer and a conscientious official, with a decision that was to cost him not only his job but also his life. Because his conscience was not for sale, Gempp felt impelled, during a conference with his inspectors and officers, to correct the official story.[31]

At this conference Gempp is alleged to have told his officers:

1. that the fire brigade had been summoned too late;
2. that he – Gempp – had met an S.A. detachment when he arrived at the scene of the fire;
3. that Göring had expressly forbidden him to circulate a general call and to summon stronger forces to fight the fire;
4. that undamaged parts of the building contained enough incendiary material to fill a lorry.

And, having made these 'corrections' which clearly refuted the Nazis' claim that the Reichstag had been burned by Communists, Gempp simply had to disappear.

As one historian, who believed the *Brown Book* story that Gempp was one of those people who knew too much and whom the Nazis had to get rid of, put it:

> Not even his dismissal was enough to satisfy the new rulers. They uttered the vilest slanders, persecuted him, and finally arrested him in September, 1937. At a put-up trial he was charged with misdemeanour, and duly convicted. Gempp appealed, but shortly before the appeal was heard, on May 2nd, 1939, he was found dead in his cell.

The *Brown Book* added that Councillor Ahrens was dismissed and arrested for exactly the same reasons. Now, had Gempp and Ahrens really been such dangerous witnesses, one wonders why the Nazis did not use their tested method of shooting them 'while trying to escape', why Ahrens was set free soon after his arrest so that he could survive Hitler's glorious Third Reich (he died in West Berlin in 1957), and why Gempp was given the chance of refuting the 'trumped-up' charges against him, and hence of exposing his detractors in open Court.

Gempp's alleged 'corrections' were first published on 21 April 1933 in *La République* and four days later in the *Saarbrückener Volksstimme*.

At the time, it was extremely risky to publish such dangerous stories abroad, for they were likely to jeopardize the lives of men who were completely at the mercy of a ruthless dictator. Luckily for Gempp and for Ahrens, they could easily prove that the whole article was a fabrication.

As a result, the *Brown Book* was forced to 'explain':

> Göring, who had not the courage himself to deny what the *Saarbrückener Volksstimme* reported, compelled Gempp to issue a *démenti*. Gempp seems to have refused to do so for a long time. It was only on June 18th, 1933, that a statement by him appeared in the German press, in which he declared that the report published in the *Volksstimme* was false.... Under the pressure of the charges made against him, and from fear of imprisonment with which he was threatened, Gempp gave way to Göring's threats.[32]

On the very day when Gempp was alleged to have held his staff conference and to have criticized the official story of the fire, he gave an interview to the *Berliner Lokalanzeiger*:

> The fire brigade came across two main fires and countless little fires. The fires had all been started with firelighters, paraffin and petrol. One fire was discovered in the immediate vicinity of the Chancellor's office. The carpet was charred. A large fire was also blazing in the restaurant. In the Session Chamber, the Speaker's Chair, the deputies' benches and the tribunes were almost completely destroyed. Fragments of the cracked wall had fallen down. The dome itself did not collapse, only the glass ceiling. Individual girders were melted by the heat.[33]

Moreover, a Swiss journalist, Ferdinand Kugler, wrote on the subject of the 'Gempp affair' during the Leipzig trial:

163

Of special interest is the evidence of Berlin's ex-Fire Chief Gempp, who was dismissed shortly after the Reichstag fire, and who was supposed to have been murdered.

First he declared with a broad smile that he was, of course, the same Herr Gempp who had directed the fire brigade on February 27th. . . . He was then questioned by the President of the Court:

Dr Bünger: 'You have been asked to appear before this Court because of certain newspaper articles and remarks in the *Brown Book.* The *Brown Book* alleges that, after the fire, you held a conference with inspectors and officers of the fire brigade during which you said that the fire brigade had been summoned too late, that 20 Storm Troopers were at the scene of the fire by the time the fire brigade finally appeared, that the Prussian Minister of the Interior, Göring, had expressly forbidden you to circulate a general call, and that those parts of the Reichstag building which were not destroyed were found to contain large quantities of unused incendiary material which would have completely filled a lorry. I request your comments on these points.'

Gempp: 'I have been heard on these points more than once, first by a representative from State Commissioner Dr Lippert's office, and again by the Secret State Police. In both cases I have declared that all these allegations are pure nonsense. I found no Storm Troopers on my arrival – at least not in large numbers, for one or two might have been there whom I cannot remember – neither did I find large quantities of incendiary material. As for my discussion, or rather meeting, with Minister Göring, this is what happened: roughly fifteen minutes after I arrived at the Reichstag, I spotted the Minister and some gentlemen in the southern wing. I immediately approached him in order to give him a full report, for he was my highest superior. The Minister walked with me towards Portal Two. I described the damage, the fire-fighting forces we had deployed, and soon. The Minister then asked me if I had seen the Director of the Reichstag, Herr Galle. That was the only question he put to me. When I asked if he had any instructions for me, the Minister replied: "Please don't let me detain you. You are in charge here." '

Gempp went on to say that the conference he held with his inspectors had been pure routine. Such conferences were convened after every large fire.

Gempp further declared that no pressure had been brought to bear on him to deny the *Brown Book* allegations, and that the *démenti* he had issued to the press on 18 June had been given quite freely. Neither had he ever been placed under arrest or in any way attacked in connection with the Reichstag fire.

In this connection we must now refer to the subsequent statement of Councillor Ahrens whom the *Brown Book* was forced to
turn into the 'real' source of the corrections once Gempp had let the
Communists down so badly. Ahrens not only repeated Gempp's
explanation of what had really happened at the official conference
on the morning after the fire, but added that he thought Gempp far
too intelligent to call Göring a liar before so large a crowd, even
had he believed that a correction was called for.

After the war, ex-Chief Fire Officer Emil Puhle, who had also
attended Gempp's conference, confirmed that only ordinary
routine questions were discussed. He added: 'It is nonsense to
suggest that Göring prohibited the circulation of a general call,
when, in fact, the tenth-stage alarm was given fairly early on.'[34]

In fact, though Gempp smiled when he told the Supreme Court
that he was the man who had extinguished the Reichstag fire, he
could not have been very happy. His vaunted conscience was anything but clear, and he would very much have liked not to be in the
limelight of public attention right then.

It is quite true that Gempp was originally charged with tolerating
Communist intrigues in the Berlin Fire Brigade, and later with a
dereliction of duty in connection with the purchase of a motor car.
However, the real charges against him were being kept secret at the
time, because they might have shaken public confidence in
Göring's great pet: the Prussian Civil Service.

In the summer of 1932, Dr Pitzschke, a former chief adviser to
Minimax, the internationally renowned makers of fire-ex-
tinguishers, started a legal action against his erstwhile employers.
Inter alia he alleged that Minimax were on the verge of bankruptcy
because they had spent 'vast sums of money on bribing public
servants'. Though the Court ruled that Dr Pitzschke had no case,
the Presiding Judge nevertheless informed the Public Prosecutor of
Dr Pitzschke's allegations. This happened on 24 January 1933, i.e.
before Hitler came to power.

The whole affair culminated four years later in a monster trial
which had far-reaching repercussions but not the slightest political
background. Gradually more and more leading fire officers were
inculpated, some of whom later took their lives. The trial, which
started on 29 September, was concluded on 1 July 1938, when
Judge Böhmer read the verdict: Friedrich Gunsenheimer, a
director of Minimax, was found guilty on sixteen charges of

bribery and sentenced to two-and-a-half years' imprisonment. Chief Fire Director Walter Gempp was sentenced to two years' hard labour, loss of civic rights for three years and confiscation of 15,600 marks. Because of repeated acceptance of bribes, seventeen of the eighteen accused fire directors, engineers, fire officers, etc., from Berlin, Cologne and Munich, were sentenced to hard labour or imprisonment.

Gempp himself cut rather a poor figure during his trial. It appeared that although he lived rent-free, and earned a monthly net salary of 1,000 marks, an annual bonus of 2,000 marks from the City of Berlin and of 1,200 marks from the Prussian Fire Department – not to mention his consultant's fees and royalties – he nevertheless allowed Gunsenheimer to press quite a number of envelopes containing from 1,500 to 1,800 marks into his greedy hands. Gunsenheimer had carefully and discreetly kept a record of all these sums, using the secret code:

1 2 3 4 5 6 7 8 9 0
u n i v e r s a l o

Though Gempp had learned of the charges against him well before the trial, he steadfastly refused to admit to his shady dealings with Minimax. Even after the police raided Gunsenheimer and discovered his meticulously kept records, Gempp merely admitted to having been Minimax's official adviser – for a fee of 300 marks a month.

However, all these evasions proved of no avail. The Court not only found against him but even refused to take his excellent record into consideration:

The accused Gempp was Head of the Berlin fire service which – thanks largely to him – was famed far beyond the boundaries of Berlin and the borders of the Reich. As Chief Fire Director, he held a respected and highly-paid position which together with his considerable other earnings – quite apart from his own and his wife's private incomes – guaranteed him so high a standard of living that he and his family went short of absolutely nothing. And yet Gempp saw fit to accept bribes from Minimax over the years, and to render to Minimax services incompatible with his office. By accepting sums amounting to 15,600 marks, Gempp received the third highest sum of money Minimax spent on bribery. The Court has not taken into account the many lavish presents he was given in addition to this. A chief of the Fire Brigade who, despite his excellent income, sees fit to lend himself to such corrupt practices, to set his subordinates so bad an example, and to sully the reputation of the Berlin Bire Frigade in the way he has done, must be punished with the full severity of the law.

The Court also takes a most serious view of the fact that the accused showed no signs of remorse, but tried to cover up his actions with all manner of stupid and mendacious excuses, as for example the fable that he was a bona fide consultant to W. G. [Managing Director of Minimax].

Others to be pilloried by the Court included such well-known 'patriots' as Fire Director P., who was sentenced to only one-and-a-half years' imprisonment because 'the Court took into account the part he played in Germany's rebirth', and Chief Engineer R., 'who had shown so much devotion to the national cause'.

All this explains why the Nazi press was so anxious to play this gigantic scandal down. None of the accused was a Jew, a Marxist, a Freemason – all were tested Prussian officials whose blood was as unobjectionable as their politics.

No more need be said about the 'mysterious' circumstances surrounding Gempp's death – like so many of his co-accused he committed suicide before the sentence became legally binding. The allegation that he was killed because he might have betrayed the Nazi Reichstag incendiaries is absurd: the Minimax trial lasted for a total of 123 days, during which time Gempp had ample opportunity to say what he liked. In fact, Gempp was turned into a martyr for purely political reasons, and it is sad – but unavoidable – that we have had to strip him of his halo. Gempp's suicide – and there is no doubt whatever that it was suicide – was the last act of a man who, though brilliant at his job, would not resist the temptation to which all successful public servants are continuously exposed.

THREE FURTHER *BROWN BOOK* SUSPECTS

In 1957, when the journalist Curt Riess tried to repeat one of the many *Brown Book* slanders, he was threatened with a libel action and withdrew the charge, viz. that:

Amongst Göring's confidential men was a certain Dr Lepsius, who later gave evidence at the trial. Although he occupied a high position in the Air Ministry, Dr Lepsius certainly had no official authority or competence, and it may be doubted whether he possessed the qualifications requisite to conduct the interrogation of a political incendiary [van der Lubbe]. . . . On the fourteenth day of the trial he told the Court how, afterwards, he had retraced with van der Lubbe the route which the latter had taken in firing the Reichstag. . . . What precise interest Dr Lepsius – not a police or judicial official – had in interrogating van der Lubbe, much more in retracing his path in the Reichstag, remained unexplained. Perhaps it was that Dr Lepsius was better acquainted with the geography of the Reichstag than van der Lubbe and so was able to assist him in the choice of route.[35]

Dr Lepsius, an internationally renowned chemist and one of a long line of scholars, could not possibly allow this libel to go unanswered. He had never even met Göring, and he held no position at all in the Air Ministry, let alone a high one. His only connection with flying – and this shows what mental acrobatics the *Brown Book* authors were capable of – was that, as a chemist, he had been coopted to the Air Defence League. On behalf of that body, he had requested Under-Secretary Schmid to admit him to the Reichstag on the day after the fire, so that he could pursue his studies of the effects of incendiary bombs on massive buildings.

The detectives – including Heisig and Dr Zirpins – who had just been going over van der Lubbe's route – were so impressed with Dr Lepsius's letter of introduction that they immediately acceded to his request and asked van der Lubbe to retrace his steps once again. Dr Lepsius then asked van der Lubbe a number of questions about each individual fire, and came away with the firm conviction that the fires had been started precisely in the way van der Lubbe had told him.

In particular,

. . . the witness [Dr Lepsius] took the occasion to ask van der Lubbe whether he had specially set fire to the curtains over the door in order to burn the Session Chamber. Van der Lubbe said no, and explained that the Session Chamber had probably caught fire because the flames from the curtains had leapt across to the panelling.[36]

Dr Lepsius thereupon examined the Reichstag curtains more closely and learned from the Director of the Reichstag, Geheimrat Galle, that they had been put up dozens of years earlier. He concluded correctly that they were extremely inflammable. We shall have to return to this point again.

.   .   .   .   .

It was Dimitrov's persistent questions which threw suspicion on Dr Herbert Albrecht, Nazi deputy and 'standard-bearer of Troop 33', as he proudly described himself in the Reichstag handbook.

On the night of the fire, Dr Albrecht, who was staying in a boarding-house some fifty yards from the Reichstag, had retired to bed with influenza. He was suddenly alerted when a maid shouted through the open door: 'The Reichstag is on fire.' Despite his illness, he immediately got up, for he remembered to his horror that important family papers including, of all things, the proof of his 'Aryan' descent were kept in the Reichstag offices of the National Socialist Party. He dressed quickly and, not bothering to put on a collar, a tie, or a hat, rushed across to the burning House. At Portal Five he was challenged by a police official, and allowed to pass when he showed his deputy's card. Dr Albrecht raced up the stairs, collected his papers and stormed out of the building 'as if in flight'. When he had just passed Portal Five, he was challenged and – because he did not obey at once – fetched back by a policeman. A Reichstag official then told the officer:

'He's all right. I know him.'

When Dr Albrecht tried to return to the Reichstag a little later, perhaps to salvage other valuables, he was turned back, for Göring had meanwhile given orders not to admit anyone.

This incident had already been discussed in the Police Court, when Albert Wendt, the porter who had been on duty at Portal Five on the night of the fire, told an attentive audience – including Douglas Reed – that a collarless and hatless deputy had rushed out of the Reichstag at 10 p.m., and that he, Wendt, could swear that he had not let him in through the only open Portal.

However, even while the fire had still been raging, detectives had checked Albrecht's alibi, and found that it was unshakeable. As a result, Judge Vogt decided quite rightly that there was no need to subpoena Dr Albrecht to the main trial.

.   .   .   .   .

Alexander Scranowitz, Reichstag House-Inspector from 1930 to 1945, was another favourite *Brown Book* suspect.

In 1904, Scranowitz, who held an honourable discharge from the German Navy, was given a job in the Reichstag. He slowly worked his way up the ladder: in 1927 he became Assistant House-Inspector, and in 1930 – on the death of his predecessor – he was promoted to the position he held at the time of the fire.

Scranowitz was a tall and powerfully-built man, who chose to wear his Kaiser moustache even under the Republic. Though he had served the Reichstag most faithfully for thirty years, the *Brown Book* saw fit to accuse him of dereliction of duty, and to stamp him a Nazi for good measure.

On February 27th, the National Socialist inspector of the building released the officials on duty at one o'clock in the afternoon. The staff told him that it was contrary to the terms of their employment to leave before the end of their spell of duty.

Crude though this slander was, it must nevertheless have caused Scranowitz a great deal of anguish. Thus the Presiding Judge asked Scranowitz on 14 October 1933:

I have seen a press report to the effect that you took the unusual step of dismissing all the officials before they had completed their duty, to be precise at 1 p.m., and that the staff lodged a protest with you. Is that really so?

Scranowitz replied that he had neither dismissed the staff nor had he had the power to do so. He added that, even if he had, it seemed most unlikely that the staff would have objected. In any case, it had by then been fully established that not a single one of Scranowitz's many subordinates had been sent home.

In answer to a question by Dr Sack, Scranowitz replied that most of the officials on duty at the time of the fire were old-timers, and that the Nazis had not sacked a single one of them.

Because Scranowitz had been called a National Socialist in the *Brown Book*, the Assistant Public Prosecutor, Dr Parrisius, asked him whether he would care to tell the Court what his political opinions were. Scranowitz replied:

When I came to the Reichstag in 1904, I met an old Reichstag official, Maas by name. He told me: 'Scranowitz, as Reichstag employees, we have to serve every party alike. Take my advice and don't join any of them.' And that is precisely what I have done. To this day I have not belonged to a party. Still, you may say I hold Rightist views.

Accordingly, the *Brown Book* changed its original account into:

The suspicions against this official, of decided National Socialist leanings (*sic!*) were shortly indicated in the *Brown Book*. Scranowitz's denial in Court cannot be regarded too seriously inasmuch as he stated that he himself had gone home at 3 p.m., which was not his usual hour.[37]

In fact, Scranowitz left the Reichstag at 2.45 p.m., for the simple reason that he had a doctor's appointment. Later, while he was sitting at dinner, he was alarmed by the noise of fire engines. He sprang to the window, and seeing that the fire brigade had stopped across the road, he immediately rang the porter's lodge to find out what was happening. The telephone was answered by Albert Wendt, who told Scranowitz that the restaurant was on fire. Whereupon Scranowitz roared at him:

> 'And why the dickens didn't you report it to me?', slammed down the receiver . . . dashed into the bathroom, grabbed my shoes and shouted to my wife and my son: 'Notify the Speaker and the Director,' slipped on my jacket and coat and rushed out of the house. I finished dressing as I ran.

Dr Wolff has attacked Scranowitz because

> . . . shortly before his death [1955] he published two newspaper articles in which he still asserted that van der Lubbe had no accomplices and burned the Reichstag alone. This self-confessed Rightist played a very strange role in the whole affair.

And Dr Wolff went on to mention the observations of firemen, according to whom Scranowitz's

> . . . only concern was to get the brigade to save a precious Gobelin tapestry. When a number of people asked the House-Inspector why he was less worried about the House than about the tapestry, he explained that this valuable piece was one of the articles that France had claimed as part of the German reparation payments after World War I.

What the firemen could not have known, but what Dr Wolff himself could have read in Dr Sack's book (op. cit., p. 20) would have made Scranowitz's 'only concern' far less suspicious than it looked:

> Göring knows that the House contains two irreplaceable treasures: the library and the Gobelin tapestries which were kept in a room behind the diplomats' box. 'The Gobelins must be saved,' the Minister cried. His first care was for these irreplaceable works of art.

Dr Wolff went on to quote from a truly astonishing article by his friend, the late Pablo Hesslein.[38] Apparently Hesslein heard of the fire as early as 8.30 p.m., and saw the fire from the Victory Column at 9 p.m. – before van der Lubbe had even entered the building! He then witnessed the arrival of the Cabinet, and heard Papen's indignant denunciation of the Communists. Hitler and the rest apparently left the building in complete silence.

Then Hesslein and other journalists were invited by a Reichstag official – obviously Scranowitz – to join a conducted tour of the building: 'In the lobby leading to the Reichstag restaurant, we noticed that the thick carpets had been soaked in petrol. In the restaurant, too, we found similar pools . . .'

In fact, the 'petrol pools' were pools of water, squirted on the carpets by the fire brigade. While this was a forgivable error, the rest of Hesslein's story is not. Thus, no one will believe his claim that he heard the Director of the Reichstag, Geheimrat Galle, assert that:

> Göring had ordered all Reichstag officials without exception to leave the House punctually at 8 p.m. This order applied to him, Galle, as well, so that . . . the Reichstag was completely deserted from 8 p.m. onwards.

Once again we have the assumption that the Speaker of the Reichstag – even had he wanted to set fire to the House – would have been stupid enough to give away his intentions by such blatant orders. Then we are asked to swallow the claim that Geheimrat Galle, the very prototype of a conservative official' (*Neue Zürcher Zeitung*, 21 October 1933), would have obeyed an order of that kind.

This sensational article by Hesslein caused Dr Wolff to write to Galle's widow, who quite naturally replied that she thought the whole story unlikely, and that '. . . although her husband had never discussed official business with her, he would certainly have dropped a hint about this particular matter during the long years of his retirement'.

In footnote 36 of his Reichstag fire report, Dr Wolff further mentions a letter by the former Director of the Reichstag library, Professor Fischer Baling, which included the following sentence: 'I was present at his [Scranowitz's] interrogation and did not gain the impression that he was telling everything he knew.'

Now that impression was absolutely correct, for at the time it would have been extremely dangerous for Alexander Scranowitz to tell what he knew or – rather – what he thought he knew. He came out with it long after the war, when he admitted 'quite openly' that he had said nothing about the ridiculous official theories to anyone except a small circle of close friends 'because he had believed that the truth would come out anyway, once all the stored-up bitterness gave way to quiet objectivity. Now, however, he felt he could keep quiet no longer'.[39]

And the old gentleman – he had recently turned seventy-two – added in broad Berlin dialect:

> It's not that I don't think Adolf and his gang couldn't have done it, it's just that they didn't happen to have anything to do with the Reichstag fire. And when your paper published all that stuff about a secret passage and about Storm Troopers blundering about in the burning building, I really did feel my gorge rise.

Scranowitz went on to call himself the 'chief witness' in the Fire Trial, and, in fact, that is precisely what he was, though only in a certain sense: he was responsible for the commonly held idea that the fire had spread with 'supernatural' speed, or as he himself put it at the trial:

> I looked into the Session Chamber for a mere fraction of a second. The whole top of the Speaker's Chair was blazing away. Behind the Speaker's Chair, three curtains were burning quite steadily. The individual flames were quite distinct. In addition, I saw flames on both the Government and the Federal Council benches, though I cannot state with certainty whether in the first or second row. These flames represented individual, completely independent, fires, bunched together into pyramids, each twelve to twenty inches at the base, and some twenty to twenty-five inches in height.
>
> I made out similar bundles of flames on the first rows of deputies' seats – fifteen of them in all. I also spotted a fire on the Orator's Table, flanked by the burning curtains of the stenographers' well below. I quickly slammed the door shut.

As a result of this evidence, based on observations during 'a fraction of a second', the judges and experts alike underplayed the testimony of the police officers who saw something far less dramatic:

> When Lateit pushed the door open, and looked across the downward sloping rows of benches, he saw a fire which he estimated at some ten feet wide by twelve feet high. The fire was topped by tongues of

173

flame so that it looked like a 'flaming church organ'. The flames themselves were extremely steady. Lateit saw no flames to the right or left of this 'organ', i.e. on the Government or Federal Council benches, nor could he detect any smoke. Poeschel and Losigkeit, who were looking over Lateit's shoulder, observed the same picture.[40]

Hence Lateit had every reason to think that the fire could be put out very quickly. Moreover, his testimony tallied with van der Lubbe's.

One Swiss correspondent had this to say on the difference between Scranowitz's and Lateit's evidence:

Not even the late Edgar Wallace could have hit upon a more intricate plot than the one that came out at this trial. Who is the magician? In this trial the great dénouement does not coincide with the dramatic climax. On the contrary, at 9.22 p.m., one minute after Police Lieutenant Lateit saw the lonely 'fire organ' on the Speaker's Chair [actually: behind the Speaker's Chair] a second witness looked into the Chamber, and saw a completely different picture: the first three rows of the semicircular deputies' seats were aglow with twenty to twenty-five small pyramid-shaped fires, each about twenty inches wide, all of equal height, and neatly placed at regular intervals of five feet from one another, just as if an assembly of fiery spirits were holding a meeting. Other flames of equal height and of the same bright-red colour were neatly distributed over the government benches to the right and the left of the Speaker's Chair. A similar fire was blazing on the Orator's Table. At its feet another flame had leapt across the solid oak 'Table of the House'. But the palm of this parliamentary Walpurgis Night went to a larger fire, some thirty inches high, above the Speaker's Chair; behind it three curtains were ablaze but the fire had not yet reached the panelling. In addition, the curtains on either side of the stenographers' places had caught light. And all this was stated on oath, not by a crystal-gazer, but by Herr Scranowitz, the tried, tested, and pensionable inspector of the Reichstag, a man who had gone on his nightly key-rattling rounds of the House, under the Kaiser, the Republic, and the Third Reich. This good man, who must consider appearing in court a welcome break in his otherwise unusually monotonous life, likes to hear the sound of his own voice.[41]

Unfortunately, nobody – not even the fire experts – suspected that Scranowitz, who, after all, knew the Reichstag better than anyone else, might have been wrong. Now if the fire had in fact changed from a minor into a major conflagration within the one minute that separated Scranowitz's and the police officers' inspection of the Chamber, then the flames could not possibly have spread spontaneously; then accomplices and plotters must indeed have been at work.

And yet there is no need to dismiss Scranowitz as a deceitful or extravagant witness, for there is a completely natural explanation for his mistake: in that 'fraction of a second' during which Scranowitz peered into the Chamber, all he did, in fact, see was the burning curtains – all the other 'flames' were reflections from the highly polished desks.

The police officers, on the other hand, who watched the fire for a much longer time, were able to distinguish clearly between the burning curtains and their flickering reflections.

In short, Scranowitz was sincere but – utterly confused.

Unfortunately the President of the Court chose to ignore this obvious fact, and adopted Scranowitz's erroneous story, simply because it fitted in much better with the accomplice theory. Scranowitz himself told the Public Prosecutor:

> I said one man couldn't possibly have started all the fires by himself; no less than six to eight people must have done it. That was my guess at the time, though I didn't actually see anybody. All I knew was that one person couldn't possibly have done it all in so short a time.

Luckily for Scranowitz, no one asked him to give any reasons for these guesses and assumptions. Later, when he realized the truth, he admitted publicly that van der Lubbe must have been the sole culprit. Since he is dead, he can no longer speak for himself.

III

THE TRIAL

10. The Preliminary Examination

THE EXAMINING MAGISTRATE

ONCE the police endorsed Hitler's 'inspiration' that the Reichstag fire was a call to Communist rebellion and hence to high treason, the case against van der Lubbe and 'accomplices' had to be referred to the Supreme Court.

One man who did not like these developments was Hermann Göring. On 2 March 1933, he told the Cabinet:

> The police will soon have to hand the case over to the Supreme Court. The examining magistrate is Dr Braune, who used to investigate charges against members of the National Socialist Party, and who has always been most ruthless with us. Even if he did his work objectively, he would hardly be the right man to handle so important a case. Thus he might restrict his investigations to the criminal alone, when all the experts agree that six to seven persons, *at the very least*, must have been involved. He might even give orders to set Deputy Torgler free. Any slips now would have extremely grave consequences later. Hence it is advisable to see if another, more suitable, magistrate could not be put in charge of the investigation of the Reichstag fire, considered not as an act of common arson but as one of high treason.

Hitler, too, objected to Dr Braune, so that Under-Secretary Schlegelberger had to hunt up an examining magistrate more to his liking. He found him in the person of Judge Paul Vogt, a man who responded with such alacrity and who set to work with such zeal that Torgler, for one, became convinced the Government had offered him a chance of 'rehabilitating' himself.

Vogt, who had investigated many other political cases, had joined the Supreme Court in 1931. By all accounts, he was the very model of a Prussian judge: conservative, correct, unrelenting once he had arrived at a decision, unwilling to temper justice with mercy, and self-assured to the point of arrogance. A Swiss correspondent described him as follows: 'His bearing is that of a typical Prussian reserve officer. His legal knowledge and loyalty are beyond question.'[1]

179

For simplicity's sake, Vogt ran the examination from the Reichstag itself. At his own request, Detective-Inspectors Heisig and Dr Braschwitz, and Detective-Sergeant Raben were allocated to him. His legal assistant – also appointed at his own request – was Dr Wernecke.

When most of the information supplied by willing members of the public proved completely useless, Vogt asked the entire German press to publish photographs of Marinus van der Lubbe together with a reward of 20,000 marks – a tremendous sum at that time – to anyone offering useful information. Similar photographs were pasted up on countless hoardings and walls.

The high reward helped to lend wings to the public's sporting instincts and fantasy. Of the many who came forward, a large number were eventually unmasked for what they were: petty crooks and informers out to feather their own nests or to blow their own trumpets.

But far-fetched though all their stories were, none of them produced any further accomplices, so that Judge Vogt felt he must hang on at any cost to the five suspects he already had.

Because of the official thesis that a Communist rebellion had been quashed at the last moment, Vogt asked police chiefs throughout Germany to supply him with information about Communist activities. The results were condensed and included in the Indictment, from which every unbiased person would have been forced to conclude that the Communists had been lying low. Yet Judge Vogt held fast to his Communist putsch theory, though – according to Diels – he did realize that, were he to arraign the leaders of the Communist Party on the basis of the 'documentary evidence' he had gathered, his whole case might collapse. Hence he decided to argue that, though there was insufficient direct evidence to show that there had been a central plan to fire the Reichstag as a signal for rebellion, the existence of such a plan could nevertheless be inferred from Communist acts of terror and arson in the past. When Göring heard of this development, he exploded. The Führer himself had blamed the Communist leaders directly – hence there just had to be an organized plot.

And indeed, at first the whole case had seemed quite cut and dried. Had a Communist not been caught red-handed? Was it likely that he had acted alone? Would not a thorough police investigation and the offer of a high reward bring the other culprits to book? And could van der Lubbe's accomplices be anything but Communists? Had not the Communist deputy, Ernst Torgler, been incriminated by a number of quite independent witnesses? And was there not weighty evidence against the three Bulgarian Communists?

Thus when Vogt set to work it was quite reasonable to assume that the Government thesis of a Communist putsch was the right one. But by the time he had heard more than five hundred witnesses, and had filled twenty-four volumes with depositions and documents, he ought to have realized that Göring's first press communiqué on the night of the fire had been quite wrong. Far from doing that, Vogt held fast to the spirit, if not to the letter, of the official thesis, and continues to do so to this day. Still, not even he could close his ears to the persistent rumours that the Nazis themselves had fired the Reichstag as an election stunt. Thus, on 3 March 1933, Walter Lassmann, a merchant from Apolda, petitioned the Court to investigate the rumour that the National Socialist Party had set the Reichstag on fire. He added:

> Those arrested so far are said to have been paid by the National Socialist Party, and to have been instructed to blame the crime on the Communist Party. . . . Only the National Socialist Party is in favour of governing without a Parliament and hence without a House.[2]

On 2 March 1933, one Baron von der Ropp humbly petitioned the President of the Supreme Court

> . . . to instruct the Public Prosecutor to put on record the names of the real incendiaries. At the moment, these men are still employed in Göring's Residence, whence they carried the incendiary material into the underground passage. It would be an irreparable loss if future German historians were kept in ignorance of the names of the real incendiaries.[3]

While Baron von der Ropp merely repeated a general rumour, the Communists themselves were careless enough to mention the actual names of the alleged Nazi accomplices. When all of these had supplied Vogt with perfectly good alibis, he quite understandably concluded that the Communists were merely trying to pass the buck. That, by the way, was also the view of the Public Prosecutor.

On the other hand, Vogt saw no reason to protest against the equally unsubstantiated Nazi claim that the Communist Party was implicated. He accordingly dismissed van der Lubbe's protestations that he had fired the Reichstag by himself as so many further Communist lies, all of which were meant to whitewash the real culprits. Hence the good magistrate was able to promise Dr Taubert, an emissary of the anxious Dr Goebbels, that he would somehow manage to get the Communists convicted.

Although Vogt was obliged to submit regular reports to the Minister of Justice, there is not the slightest evidence that he was under any direct political pressure. Vogt was allowed to fill his twenty-four volumes of records as he chose. Early in June 1933, he handed them over to the Public Prosecutor's office, whence they were returned to him briefly for a number of factual emendations. He completed the work at the end of June 1933.

THE NEUKÖLLN 'LINK'

As we saw, Vogt shared Dr Zirpins's view that van der Lubbe's real principals were the leaders of the Communist Party, and Torgler and Koenen in particular. However, when he tried to substantiate this thesis and the Government thesis that the Reichstag fire had been the signal for a Communist uprising, he came up against an insurmountable obstacle: how could van der Lubbe, the unknown Dutch tramp, have got hold of the leaders of the German Communist Party within so short a time of his arrival in Berlin? After all, these leaders were ostensibly planning a major civil war, and must have been terribly busy. All Vogt could say was that van der Lubbe must have managed it somehow.

Then, on 6 March 1933, he was apparently proved right when, duly encouraged by the reward of 20,000 marks, a worker by the name of Ernst Panknin reported from Neukölln. Panknin claimed that on the Wednesday before the fire he had seen van der Lubbe in 'conference' with the metalworker Paul Bienge, the labourer Paul Zachow, and the shoemaker Herbert Löwe – all three men with known Communist leanings – outside the Neukölln Welfare Office.

The Indictment devoted fifteen long pages to this 'conference', which was to have such tragic consequences: the three men were arrested, threatened, and subjected to torture when they refused to confess something of which they were completely innocent.

According to Panknin, this is what had happened:

Zachow began by complaining very bitterly that a horde of Storm Troopers had torn off 'Iron Front' badges from Socialist passers-by in the Sonnenallee. He, Zachow, had been forced to restrain his friend Bienge since otherwise there would have been a fight. Bienge then said:

'If all of us were like you, we shouldn't ever amount to anything.'

Marinus van der Lubbe, who was listening to all this, then asked the way to the Sonnenallee; he wanted to go there at once, and was very disappointed when he learned that the whole story had happened the day before. Van der Lubbe was very excited and said that the workers ought to be encouraged to hit back, and to start a revolution after the great Russian model; it was now or never. Zachow, for his part, suggested that the best way of shaking up the people and of inciting them to revolution was firing public buildings. To which Bienge had added: 'Well, let's start with the Reichstag and the Palace. For either we come to power and we shan't need the Reichstag, or else the others will come to power and won't let us in anyway.'[4]

Bienge went on to say that special groups would have to be formed, whose job it would be to catch single Storm Troopers, pour petrol over them, and then set fire to them.

Zachow argued in favour of burning 'the lot', and not just individual buildings. When Marinus van der Lubbe agreed with all their plans, Bienge gave Zachow a dig in the ribs and said:

'This lad is all right; we can use him.'

At that point, Marinus van der Lubbe confessed that he was an experienced and active Communist and pulled a red booklet out his pocket. This, according to Panknin, had to be a Communist Party membership card because it was red. Then van der Lubbe asked to be directed to Communist Party headquarters.

On 30 March 1933, when Panknin was confronted with van der Lubbe, he repeated the whole story, adding:

When the conversation was over, I mean their discussion about setting public buildings on fire, van der Lubbe asked if he could join in, and all the others agreed readily.[5]

With that the fate of the three men from Neukölln was sealed, and it did not help van der Lubbe to protest:

I can only repeat again and again that I heard no conversation whatsoever on the subject of burning public buildings. When I first decided to set public buildings on fire, I was thinking of the Neukölln Welfare

Office because it seemed the best place to me. If I am told it is unlikely that my actions should accidentally have agreed with what was allegedly discussed outside the Welfare Office, I can only reply that it was, in fact, a sheer coincidence. And if I am further alleged to have asked for the address of Communist Party headquarters, all I can say is that I did nothing of the kind. On the contrary, I insisted that the Communist Party was using the wrong kind of tactics. True, I asked whether the Communist Party was still active in Neukölln, and was told that it was very difficult to do anything at all these days.[6]

Of course, van der Lubbe's words went unheard. The Neukölln link, or rather the Neukölln fantasy, was something to which Juge Vogt had to cling like a leech, for that fantasy was the corner-stone of the Communist conspiracy theory, and hence of the whole trial. Thus when the President of the Court, Dr Bünger, asked Vogt later whether van der Lubbe had admitted inciting the others to arson, the following dialogue ensued:

Vogt: 'Yes, I believe he did at the beginning . . . no, to the best of my knowledge he denied it.'
President: 'He has kept repeating: "I did not say it; I merely heard it." '
Vogt: 'I believe the records will show the contrary. I think he merely denied that he himself was the one to say that public buildings must be burned. I seem to remember that it was Bienge who said that.'
President: 'Did you say that he admitted having asked the way to Communist Party headquarters?'
Vogt: 'Oddly enough, he denied everything that might constitute a link with Party headquarters. He was afraid of admitting that link.'[7]

The witness Ernst Panknin still dreams of the 20,000 marks which, despite his efforts, slipped through his fingers. The fate of his poor victims was less happy: Paul Zachow died soon afterwards from the treatment his captors meted out to him; Paul Bienge had all his teeth broken and was beaten mercilessly to confirm the fable of the Neukölln link – but in vain. The shoemaker Herbert Loewe, too, was 'imprisoned' for a whole year without obliging his tormentors with a confession. Bienge and Loewe are still alive.

Nor was Panknin the only pretender to the reward of 20,000 marks: a second claimant of the same sort appeared on the scene soon afterwards, and actually provided the grateful Judge Vogt 'direct evidence' against the Communist Party leaders. The name of that witness was Willi Hintze.

During those sad February days which Marinus van der Lubbe had spent in Neukölln, an unemployed man, Fikowsky by name, decided to put an end to the miserable life he had been forced to live.

When Fikowsky's sobbing widow was taken to Schlaffke's, a near-by bar, by her brother, Willi Hintze, she sobbed out that her husband had committed suicide because he could no longer bear to look on while his family starved. Thereupon Walter Jahnecke, a member of the Unemployeds' Executive, suggested a demonstration against the Welfare Office. Hintze went one step further and called for an armed attack, offering to supply the requisite arms himself. At first, everyone was enthusiastic, but soon Jahnecke and the rest of the unemployed grew suspicious. All of them knew that Hintze had been to prison, not for his political work, but because he was a member of a notorious gang of criminals. He was also said to be a police informer. In any case, instead of an armed attack on the Welfare Office there was a police raid on Schlaffke's. Jahnecke and some other 'ringleaders' were arrested – very luckily for them, as it later turned out, for otherwise they would most certainly have been implicated in the Reichstag fire.

The Director of the Welfare Office, Stadinspektor Frank, told the Supreme Court on 28 September 1933, that Hintze had warned him of an impending attack. He had immediately notified the police who, on Friday morning, sent him an officer and eight constables to guard the Welfare Office. At about 10 a.m., the police raided Schlaffke's, but found no arms – simply because Hintze had not brought any along.

Judge Vogt swallowed the whole story hook, line and sinker, particularly when Hintze, or 'Swindle-Hintze' as he was generally called, told him that the details of the attack on the Welfare Office had been planned by Communist Party headquarters in Neukölln, that he had seen van der Lubbe in Schlaffke's back room, and that Torgler's name had been mentioned in connection with the planned attack on the Welfare Office.

At the trial, it was this last, quite gratuitous, embellishment, which brought Torgler's counsel, Dr Sack, to the fore – much to Hintze's discomfiture. Referring to Hintze's many previous convictions, his well-deserved nickname, and the rest of the evidence, Dr Sack argued that it had been Hintze himself who had hatched

185

out the whole plan of attacking the Welfare Office. Hintze tried to deny everything at first but in the end he confessed that he 'had played along with the police'. A newspaper report on Hintze's court performance concluded with the observation: 'The character of this witness is such that even the Public Prosecutor ignored his evidence against Torgler.'[8]

VAN DER LUBBE'S 'UNTRUSTWORTHINESS'

One of the experts whom Judge Vogt consulted about the fire was the proud owner of the Halle 'Private Institute for Scientific Criminology', Dr Wilhelm Schatz. At the time, Dr Schatz was as little known to the public as he was to his fellow-scientists.

At the end of May 1933, the experts performed a series of tests on the curtains, tablecloths, and towels which van der Lubbe had used as additional firelighters. This is what they found:

The restaurant door-curtains burned with astonishing speed. Time: about thirty seconds.

The restaurant tablecloth burned quickly. Time: fifty-five seconds.

The towel lit with a firelighter burned quickly.

Then came the first surprise:

A piece of the curtain from the western corridor did not catch fire even when it was held in the flame of a firelighter for five minutes.[9]

This bit of curtain was immediately turned into a prize exhibit for, if the experts were right, van der Lubbe could only have set fire to it if it had been 'prepared' well in advance. It followed that the curtain had been '. . . soaked in a . . . petroleum derivate, i.e. benzine or gasoline.'[10]

To what extent Judge Vogt allowed himself to be blinded by science, and how badly he misjudged poor van der Lubbe as a result, can be seen from his own evidence to the Supreme Court on 27 September 1933 when he testified:

Finally, van der Lubbe was greatly embarrassed when I put it to him that we had tried in vain – the experts will describe all the details – to light the curtain over the exit to the western corridor with a fire-lighter. . . . I told him: 'Marinus van der Lubbe, there can no longer be any doubt that, at least as regards the complicity of other persons, you have not spoken the truth.' He replied: 'Well, the experts can say what they like, but I know that it caught fire all the same.' Then

I pointed to the curtain once again and said to him: 'You can see for yourself, if it can't even be lit with a firelighter, then you could not possibly have lit it by brushing against it with bits of material.' Then he thought hard and said: 'Yes, perhaps it wasn't me after all!' I persisted: 'But how did the curtain catch fire in that case?' Then he shrugged his shoulders and said: 'Well, perhaps I tried to burn it after all.'

I could get absolutely nothing definite out of him, and I became convinced that the more I drove it home to him that his statements did not tally with those of the experts, the more determined he became to say nothing further.[11]

With the last sentence, the ingenuous judge had hit the nail squarely on the head, for van der Lubbe, who had kept repeating the simple truth, gave up in despair when he realized that Judge Vogt was far less interested in the facts than in his own pet theory. In fact, Vogt believed that van der Lubbe lied 'at every opportunity':

Whenever it was a question of determining whether others had helped him, he invariably told deliberate lies. Only when it came to explaining that he – Lubbe – was the big hero who had started the fires all by himself, did he speak quite openly.[12]

Here we can see by what criterion Vogt judged van der Lubbe's trustworthiness: everything that did not fit in with the official views was dismissed as a lie. Since Marinus van der Lubbe knew perfectly well that he had set fire to the curtain, no amount of expert evidence could convince him of the contrary. All the experts did manage to do was to make him feel confused.

In contradistinction to Judge Vogt, Detective-Inspector Heisig told the Supreme Court that van der Lubbe had always struck the police as a reasonable man:

It was quite remarkable how much interest he showed in the investigation, and how he tried to explain every last detail. When he was asked to sign the statement we had taken from him, he insisted on making a number of corrections, and explained at length why he preferred particular turns of phrase.

And Heisig, who was only too familiar with Vogt's fatal bias, added: 'He remained interested for as long as he stayed with the police.'

Heisig also insisted that van der Lubbe's description of the path he had taken through the Reichstag had never changed, while Judge Vogt told the Supreme Court that van der Lubbe had made a number of contradictory statements about his movements. For once, the Supreme Court refused to listen to Vogt, finding instead that there was

> . . . no doubt that the accused took the path he described in the preliminary examination and which he was asked to retrace on a number of occasions during the trial. It would have been impossible for a man whose eyesight is as poor as van der Lubbe's to describe time and again the complicated trail he followed on the night of the fire, had he invented the whole story.

On the essential points, however, the Supreme Court agreed with Vogt rather than with Heisig. Thus, when van der Lubbe shook off his 'torpor' on 23 November 1933, to repeat that he had used his jacket to set fire to the curtains in the Session Chamber, the President reproached him, saying:

> 'All that is quite untrue, for the experts tell us that the curtain could not have been set on fire that way.'
> Van der Lubbe: 'But it did catch fire!'
> President: 'The Court does not believe you. The fire could not possibly have started in the way you have described.'[13]

The same attitude was also reflected in the Court's verdict:

> The Court holds that the curtains were not set on fire by van der Lubbe, the more so because his vagueness on that point is in marked contrast to his lucid and uniform description of the path he took through the Reichstag. At the preliminary examination he explained that he did not know whether, or precisely when, he had set fire to these curtains.

And yet van der Lubbe had spoken the truth, the whole truth, and nothing but the truth. Unfortunately for him, the Supreme Court chose to listen instead to the director of the 'Private Institute for Scientific Criminology'.

There were many other reasons why Vogt doubted van der Lubbe's truthfulness. First of all, van der Lubbe had been a Communist, and Communism was anathema to the Judge. Then van der Lubbe seemed to be a shiftless vagabond, one who preferred cadging his way through Europe to a respectable existence in his native Holland. Third, the Bulgarians' and Torgler's insistence that they had never met van der Lubbe was most suspicious, when so many witnesses had come forward to assert the contrary.

Vogt had strong private reasons for hating all Communists, for in 1928 an attractive Communist woman, Olga Benario, had persuaded him to send for her alleged fiancé, Otto Braun – whose real name was Karl Wagner and who was a leading Communist conspirator – in Moabit prison. While the two 'lovers' were reunited under Vogt's watchful eyes, a band of Communists carried Wagner off by force. There was a tremendous scandal, and poor Vogt was made to look an absolute fool.[14]

He must have been thinking of this when, on 27 September 1933, he told the Supreme Court: 'I believe I have some experience in interrogating and dealing with Communists.'

What made things particularly difficult for Vogt now was that the five Communist 'incendiaries' were so completely unlike one another. For one, there was van der Lubbe, who had been caught red-handed, and who confessed his crime quite freely; then there were the three Bulgarians who travelled with false papers and who thought it their duty to deceive the 'Fascist' police; and finally there was Torgler who could so easily have been mistaken for a gentleman. All Vogt knew was that he must not allow himself to be taken in by any of them.

He never guessed how little Dimitrov thought of him from the very start – as early as 3 April 1933, the Bulgarian scribbled the following entry in his diary: 'Vogt – small stature – Jesuitical. Good for petty crimes. Too small for historical trial, for world publicity. Petty; an idiot.' And Dimitrov added an observation which most observers of the trial came to share: 'Had he had even a modicum of intelligence, he would have fought tooth and nail to keep me out of the courtroom.'[15]

THE ACCUSED IN CHAINS

On the very first day of the preliminary examination, Judge Vogt ordered the accused to be put in chains. Torgler and the Bulgarians had to endure this torture for five long months, until 31 August 1933; van der Lubbe was forced to drag his chains into the courtroom as late as 25 September.

Dimitrov later described '. . . the agony of their fetters, the unbearable pain caused by the gashes on their ankles and wrists where the chains cut into them; the sleepless nights which they passed. What Vogt's intentions were in this respect passes almost beyond conjecture.'[16]

Torgler raised a similar outcry: 'It was left to the warders' discretion either to tighten our chains until the blood circulation was gravely impeded, and the skin broke, or else to take pity on us and to loosen the chains by one notch.'[17]

To make things worse, the summer of 1933 was exceptionally hot, so that the poor wretches had to drag their chains in an unbearably stifling atmosphere.

Vogt later told the Supreme Court that he had ordered fetters 'in accordance with the regulations'. He added:

When he [van der Lubbe] complained about the chains I told him – and, by the way, the other accused as well – that much as I regretted this step . . . I had to act in accordance with the regulations. I suggested that he petition the Supreme Court.

As Dimitrov was quick to point out, Vogt's 'regulations' (Article 116, Section 4 of the Criminal Procedure Code Act) had nothing to do with the case, for:

The Criminal Procedure Code prescribes circumstances in which accused persons may be put in fetters. This course should be taken only when they are specially dangerous to other persons or when they have attempted or have prepared to attempt suicide or escape.

In his testimony to the Supreme Court, Vogt claimed that he had told Dimitrov's counsel, Dr Werner Wille:

I cannot help myself; it is my bounden duty to put them in chains but I have no objection to your petitioning the Supreme Court, thus releasing me from a grave responsibility.

When the Presiding Judge asked why no such petition had been lodged, Vogt replied:

'Wasn't it? I really do not know. Wille told me that he fully appreciated the necessity of the step I had taken, and that he personally would never even dream of petitioning the Supreme Court.'

Whereupon the Presiding Judge said quite pointedly:

'In this connection, I should like to have it established that the chains were subsequently removed on the instructions of this Court.'

In short, Vogt's so-called 'regulations' should never have been applied.

What the Presiding Judge did not point out was that it had been Vogt's moral, if not his formal, duty to submit all petitions to the Supreme Court personally. In other words, there was no need to wait for Dr Wille to 'release him from this grave responsibility'. In fact, when the Supreme Court first heard about the chains from Dr Sack, the learned Judges not only ordered the chains to be removed forthwith, but instructed Judge Vogt to submit a written explanation of the reasons which had prompted him to take this unusual step. Vogt's answer, dated 18 August 1933, betrays his bias and his bad conscience: to him all the accused were dangerous criminals even before they were convicted, and had to be treated as such. In addition, van der Lubbe had attacked an official, Tanev had attempted suicide, and Dimitrov had once come towards him with clenched fists!

At the time, it was suggested that Vogt had been given orders to chain the prisoners lest they commit suicide in prison. (In fact, Tanev tried to kill himself precisely *because* of the fetters.) The *Manchester Guardian* had warned that any such suicide would be looked upon as deliberate murder and an admission of Nazi guilt in the Reichstag fire.

But when Paul Vogt was asked in January 1957 whether he had, in fact, been ordered to put the prisoners in fetters, he insisted that he had not. In fact, he could remember nothing about the whole episode. This gap in his memory is most surprising, for Dimitrov had made a great point of taunting him with the chains.

In particular he ought to have remembered the following clash in Court:

President (to Dimitrov): 'This is not the place to accuse the Examining Magistrate. This is no Court of Appeal, Dimitrov.'

Dimitrov: 'Of course not. . . . But isn't it true that I lodged at least ten oral and written protests, and that I asked to have the chains removed in accordance with the Criminal Code. Is that true or not?'

Vogt: 'Yes.'

Dimitrov: 'Were all these protests and requests summarily dismissed, without my receiving any explanation or reason?'

President: 'Did you examine his requests?'

Vogt: 'No. No written request was ever submitted to me.'

Dimitrov: 'I sent you three!'

Vogt: 'Just one minute! Quite possibly he did. He certainly kept referring to the matter, for at almost every interrogation Herr Dimitrov asked me to remove his shackles. It is also quite possible – I am ready to concede that – that he put it in a letter. I can't possibly remember any more.'

Vogt, who considered every lapse of memory on the part of the accused an admission of their guilt and dishonesty, quite obviously applied different standards of probity to himself.

'I AM A GERMAN JUDGE AND MY NAME IS VOGT'

The trial brought to light many of Judge Vogt's other exceedingly strange methods.

The reader will remember that the three Bulgarians were arrested and brought to trial on information lodged by the waiter, Johann Helmer. His evidence was one long fiasco for the Examining Magistrate and the prosecution; Helmer proved only one thing – his absolute untrustworthiness. Or as Counsel for the Bulgarians, Dr Teichert, put it:

Helmer's testimony is highly improbable. If we are to believe him, the Bulgarians met van der Lubbe in the Bayernhof at least four to six times from the summer to the winter of 1932. . . . They engaged in mysterious conversations and carried suspicious pamphlets on their persons. The clear implication of his evidence was that they and van der Lubbe were plotting an attack on the Reichstag, and perhaps other crimes as well. Now, the Reichstag did, in fact, go up in flames and Lubbe was caught. His picture was published in all the newspapers and pasted up on advertising pillars. In addition, a high reward was offered for further information. I ask the Court, does it seem likely that, after all this had happened, the Bulgarians would have gone back to the very place where they had formerly hatched their plots with a man who had meanwhile been arrested?

Torgler's Counsel added:

I should like to draw attention to some other blunders which have been allowed to come up during the trial; blunders which hinge on the allegation that the accused van der Lubbe was seen in the Bayernhof. One witness, Helmer, was suddenly turned into a star witness for the prosecution. And why? Simply because no one bothered to ask what sort of place the Bayernhof really was, and how van der Lubbe was dressed at the time he was supposed to have been in the place. Had I been asked to investigate the crime, I should surely have said: I do not know what sort of place the Bayernhof is, so I shall go and have a look. I shall find out whether they have a doorkeeper who bars shabbily-dressed customers. Only then will I be able to tell whether the accused van der Lubbe could have met Dimitrov and the others in that place.

And yet it was left until the trial for this point to be cleared up.[18]

Dr Teichert then pointed out that inquiries in Holland had shown beyond a shadow of doubt that van der Lubbe could not have been in Berlin at the times mentioned by Helmer. This fact, too, ought to have been established, not at the trial, but during the preliminary examination.

Though Dr Teichert generally left all the talking to Dimitrov, he simply could not contain himself when, on 7 November, Helmer came out with the further fable that he had seen the three Bulgarians with van der Lubbe on the day before the fire:

This is so improbable an allegation that I can only express my regret that the Examining Magistrate should have followed this witness who, I am convinced, is absolutely mistaken, on to a path that has proved so disastrous for the German people.

When the Public Prosecutor objected to this remark, Dr Teichert explained that it was his acceptance of Helmer's evidence which had made Judge Vogt, and hence German justice, an easy target for attacks from abroad. The acquittal of all three Bulgarians fully proved the justice of Dr Teichert's remark.

During the trial, it also came out that, although the three accused had repeatedly insisted on their right to be confronted with witnesses, Judge Vogt had just as insistently refused them. Hence the *Brown Book* was able to say:

Vogt declined to accede to the requests of Dimitrov, Popov and Tanev to be confronted with van der Lubbe. Popov and Tanev had stated, quite independently of each other, that at about 9 p.m. on the evening of February 27th they were in the UFA pavilion in the Nollendorfer Platz seeing a film. Popov stated that he had left his gloves behind, had gone back later to look for them and had searched with the help of an attendant. His request to be confronted with the attendant Vogt refused. Popov and Tanev gave detailed accounts of their movements on February 27th. They asked to be confronted with the waiters at the Aschinger Restaurant in the Bülowstrasse where they had dinner that evening. Vogt declined to do this. He

failed to confront Torgler with Karwahne, the most serious of the
witnesses against him. Had this been done, Torgler would have been
able at an early stage to demonstrate the falsity of Karwahne's statements. By refusing to hold any of these confrontations, Vogt deliberately deprived the accused men of the benefit of their legal rights.[19]

And Dr Sack added in his final address:

The Examining Magistrate, having first shown the witness photographs, ordered a confrontation, but not with the witness Karwahne,
because in the Magistrate's opinion Karwahne knew the accused
Torgler extremely well. I, however, as Counsel for the Defence, take
the view that it was quite irrelevant whether or not Karwahne was
previously acquainted with the accused Torgler. It was the Examining
Magistrate's duty to confront the two with each other.

By contrast, Vogt allowed repeated confrontations between the
witness Bogun and Popov, during each of which Bogun 'remembered' fresh details. Apparently Vogt made a clear distinction
between the needs of the prosecution and the defence, so much so
that Popov was forced to complain:

The Examining Magistrate refused to confront me with the waiters
at the [Aschinger] restaurant. When I repeated my request, he merely
told me that Tanev had already admitted he had been there with
me.[20]

Dr Sack rightly objected to Vogt's bluffing the witnesses with
the story that their alleged accomplices had already confessed.
When he cross-examined Vogt on that point, the Magistrate was
stung into quick fury and betrayed a highly exaggerated sense of his
own importance:

Dr Sack: 'Did you ever try, by alleging that Torgler had already
confessed, to get the other accused to admit that Torgler was an
accomplice in burning the Reichstag?'
Vogt: 'I should have hoped . . .'
Dr Sack: 'I am in duty bound to put that question to you. . . .'
Vogt: '. . . that I would have been spared that question. For first,
as I have already said, I am a German judge and second my name is
Vogt.'
Sack: 'Might I then ask you another question? The man who made
the allegation [that Vogt had bluffed the witnesses] is also a German
lawyer. Why did he accuse you?'
Vogt: 'I do not know. But since you insist, and so as to avoid any
misunderstanding, I hereby declare most emphatically that nowhere

and at no time did I ever do anything incompatible with the honour of a German judge.'[21]

The *Brown Book* added the following laconic comment: ' "First, I am a German judge; second my name is Vogt!" This is perhaps unique amongst Vogt's statements in that it cannot be contradicted.'[22]

The *Brown Book* also took up a number of other complaints by the defence. For instance, it stressed the importance of a list of Torgler's appointments, which had been found in the office of the Communist Party Parliamentary Group, and which Vogt claimed had 'disappeared'. This list, the defence had argued, was important evidence for Torgler's innocence: 'A man intending to burn the Reichstag so as to bring about a political upheaval would hardly go to the trouble of working out a complete list of ordinary engagements to follow the deed.'[23]

This is what Dr Sack had had to say on this subject:

'There is one thing that has made me sit up and think. I submit, Your Honours, that I, as Torgler's counsel, should have been in no position to adduce proof of Torgler's plans on and after February 27th, 1933, had I not hunted through the Court's dossiers. Is it counsel's job to go to such lengths, to say "I would rather see for myself" when he is told a document is missing? I ask you, Your Honours, what would have happened, had I been unable to find this list and to place it before you? Your Honours, I could mention many further oddities of this kind.'[24]

In view of the importance of the preliminary investigation and the keen interest the world press took in it, Judge Vogt saw fit to publish communiqués from time to time. Some of his press handouts proved rather premature – to put it very mildly. A typical example was the following, which appeared thirteen days after the Bulgarians were taken into custody:

The investigations so far have shown that the Dutch Communist incendiary who was arrested in the Reichstag at the time of the fire has been in touch not only with German Communists but also with foreign Communists, including some who have been condemned to death or to long terms of penal servitude in connection with the blowing up of Sofia cathedral in 1925. The men in question have been apprehended.[25]

What had happened was that Dr Ernst Dröscher, a Nazi press

officer, had 'identified' Dimitrov as the man who blew up the cathedral, and that Judge Vogt had not bothered to ask any questions. In fact, as Dr Teichert later found out from the German Legation in Sofia, the cathedral was blown up by one Stefan Dimitrov Todorov, a man who had no connection with, or any resemblance to, Georgi Dimitrov.

On 27 September 1933, when – very angrily – Dimitrov asked Vogt whether or not he had issued a press statement on 1 April, i.e. before the start of the preliminary investigation, to the effect that Dimitrov, Popov and Tanev had been in touch with van der Lubbe, Vogt was so taken aback that he stammered out the completely irrelevant, though highly revealing, answer:

> It is correct that a statement was issued to the press which implied that the three arrested Bulgarians had taken part in the setting on fire or blowing up of the Sofia cathedral. At a later date I told Dimitrov that this information was apparently incorrect. He himself, however, is responsible for the error, since he failed to correct me when I connected the commencement of the Bulgarian insurrection in 1923 [in which Georgi Dimitrov had participated] with the outrage in Sofia Cathedral which did not, in fact, take place until 1925.

This odd claim on the part of a judge that the accused is to blame for the Court's blunders, is all the more incomprehensible because Vogt went on to admit that Dimitrov had, in fact, tried to put him right. But then Judge Vogt was singularly deaf when it came to any protests on the part of the accused, no matter whether their protests were concerned with points of fact or with the wearing of chains.

In any case, Dimitrov's original question, which had so flustered Judge Vogt, had been about the Bulgarians' alleged meetings with van der Lubbe and not about his own part in the Sofia bombing. However, before Dimitrov had time to point that out, Vogt had gone on to make an even greater fool of himself. Having just agreed that Dimitrov did not take part in the bombing, he now went on to say: 'The accused Dimitrov *was* involved in the blowing up of Sofia Cathedral. Yes! Mr Dimitrov, we are a little confused. But you wait a while for there will be a witness who will swear that you had a part in that affair.'

(Vogt's witness was Dr Dröscher, who contradicted himself so much and so often that the Court had to dismiss his evidence.)

When Dimitrov finally managed to get a word in edgeways, he began very quietly:

'I did not ask about the Sofia cathedral, but I did ask, and I ask again about our alleged association with van der Lubbe. I shall prove that Judge Vogt has conducted the judicial investigation in a biased manner, and that he has deliberately misled public opinion.'

President: 'Hold your tongue! I cannot permit you to conduct your defence in this disgraceful manner!'

When Dimitrov thereupon pulled Vogt's 'premature' press release out of his pocket and passed it across to the President,[26] the President was forced to ask:

'I take it, this is the report which the Examining Magistrate issued at the time, and on which he has already testified?'

Vogt: 'Yes. That is quite correct. Not only did I have the right to issue this statement, but the statement was proved right by the subsequent investigation. After all, we only caught the three Bulgarians because we could prove they had been in touch with van der Lubbe. Otherwise we should never have been able to arrest them.'

During the trial, Dr Sack asked Vogt:

'What were you trying to establish when you interrogated van der Lubbe? Did you think he was the sole culprit? Or did you think he must have had other accomplices?'

Vogt: 'I never come to a case with preconceived ideas. I thought I have made that perfectly clear.'

Dr Sack returned to the problem of Judge Vogt in his final address:

'Even magistrates are in danger of becoming confused... particularly those who never have the slightest doubt that they are in the right.'

The very same judge who would not forgive the accused their most trivial lapses, himself perpetrated a number of terrible blunders. Torgler inferred from Vogt's great zeal that he was trying to ingratiate himself with the new masters. Heisig gained much the same impression, for, as he told von Papen during their common internment in Regensburg:

Those chiefly responsible for trying to turn this criminal offence into a political one were Göring and Goebbels. They found a useful ally in

Judge Vogt, whose chief purpose was to gain a position of influence in the National Socialist Party.[27]

Heisig was probably too hard on Vogt. True, Vogt had no sympathy for Socialists and Liberals, let alone for Communists, but he was not so much corrupt, as misguided in thinking that the Nazis were serving his country's best interests. This is borne out by his subsequent career. In June 1937, Vogt was appointed President of the Second Criminal Court of Appeal. Seven years later he was summoned to Berlin and censured for political misconduct. When he refused to go into voluntary retirement, he was forcibly placed on the retirement list.

Vogt's 'crimes' were that he had given a clergyman, Dr Jannasch, leave to appeal against a sentence of two months' imprisonment for 'misuse of the pulpit' (the clergyman had prayed for Dr Niemöller), and that he had allowed the appeal of a German Nationalist leader, Joachim von Rohr-Demmin, against a sentence of eight months' imprisonment. Von Rohr-Demmin's misdemeanour had been very grave indeed: he had refused to throw two dead Russian prisoners into a pit and had given them a decent funeral.

Six months later, the Americans marched into Leipzig. After weeks of contradictory rumours, they finally withdrew and left Saxony and Thuringia to the Russians. Within days, a Russian commission called on the Supreme Court and took the fifty-two volumes constituting the records of the preliminary examination. One day later, on a Sunday, the Commission called on Judge Paul Vogt and questioned him very politely about the trial.

Vogt was arrested a short while later and taken to Dresden together with Judges Brandis, Wernecke and Frölich. Wernecke had been Vogt's assistant during the preliminary investigation and Frölich an Assistant Judge at the trial itself.

When the arrested men were told that their help was needed at the Nuremberg Tribunal to discover the real culprits of the Reichstag fire, they recommended that the records be consulted, and that all those witnesses at the trial who were still alive be re-examined.

The Russian legal experts immediately took up this suggestion, only to return empty-handed: none of the witnesses they could discover was able or willing to change his original testimony, none had apparently given his evidence under Nazi pressure.

Now Vogt was asked to write a 'Memorandum on the Reichstag Fire', and he submitted a thirty-two-page summary of everything he could remember. Naturally, he produced no fresh evidence inculpating the Nazis.

This caused the Russians so much embarrassment that they proposed a face-saver: they asked the former judges to write an affidavit to the effect that, although the Nazis could not be directly incriminated, their other outrages made their complicity seem highly probable. The judges merely shrugged this suggestion off. Nor could they satisfy the Russians that they had really told all they knew. Time and again they referred their captors to the records, and though Russian legal experts must have gone through these with more than one fine-tooth comb, they were quite unable to pin anything fresh on the Nazis. No wonder then that no Third Brown Book has ever been published in Moscow or East Berlin.

The treatment of the arrested judges had been scrupulously correct, indeed polite and friendly, and their quarters and their food had been unexceptionable. All that was changed the moment the Russians realized that the judges could not or would not help them. Vogt, Wernecke, and Frölich were sent to internment camps in August 1945. Their treatment there would require a book in itself; suffice it to say that Dr Walter Frölich, whose bearing during the Reichstag fire trial had attracted a great deal of favourable attention abroad, died within a few months of his arrest. Judge Wernecke died of malnutrition in a hospital in 1946.

Paul Vogt, who was sent from camp to camp, remained unbroken, taciturn and unrepentant. To this day he is convinced that the Communists set the Reichstag on fire. For the rest he wants to be left alone.

Still the old gentleman, who now lives in West Germany, cannot really object when people criticize the part he played in the Reichstag fire trial. He, who drove innocent men to the depth of despair, who shackled prisoners without justification, and blustered his way through the trial, must not complain if he himself is now put in the dock by historians and found wanting.

TORGLER'S COUNSEL

Many people have wondered how it came about that Ernst Torgler, the Communist Deputy, was defended by an avowed National Socialist.

In early June 1933, after the preliminary examination, Judge Vogt told Torgler to obtain the services of a barrister. Dr Kurt Rosenfeld, who had been Torgler's lawyer for many years, and who had even accompanied him to police headquarters on the day after the fire, had decided to leave Germany, and such well-known advocates as Dr Puppe, Walter Bahn, and Count Pestalozza politely declined the brief. Torgler's wife ran from lawyer to lawyer, and finally discovered one whose courage had not entirely evaporated. He was Dr H. R. Habicht of Berlin, and he wanted to be paid handsomely: from a letter reproduced in the *Brown Book* it appears that he asked Frau Torgler (who was completely destitute) for an initial fee of fifteen thousand marks with an additional thousand marks a day if the trial lasted for more than ten days. Needless to say, that demand was as good as a refusal.

August was drawing near, and Torgler was still without a lawyer. At this point the Supreme Court stepped in and nominated a Dr Huber as his official counsel. Weeks later, a terrified old gentleman appeared in Torgler's cell and complained bitterly about his brief. In his opinion, things looked very black – at best Torgler would get a life sentence. No wonder that Torgler

... thanked him for his reassuring opinion and thought that, in these circumstances, I would rather do without his help. Rescue came a few days later, in the uniform of a prison warder:

'Do you know Dr Sack?' he asked me rather unexpectedly.

And then he told me that Sack was a well-known member of the criminal bar who had got 'quite a few people off in his time'. He advised me to fill in a printed card, and gave me Sack's address.[28]

On hearing Dr Sack's name, Torgler was vaguely reminded of 'patriotic' and other Nazi murder trials, but what choice did he have in the matter? He filled in the card and sent it off. As Dr Sack explained later, he was completely taken aback when he received it:

Knowing that the new laws forced Torgler to brief a Nationally-minded layer, I was concerned with only one question: is the man guilty or is he innocent? Only if I could be reasonably certain that Torgler had entered politics for idealistic reasons and not for selfish motives and that he had never made personal capital out of his political beliefs, would I find it within me to accept his defence. When my partner, Pelckmann, returned from his visit to Torgler, all he said was: 'You will have to go to him!'[29]

At the end of August, Dr Sack moved to Leipzig with eight juniors and began to plough through the thirty-two volumes of depositions. He also took the earliest opportunity to demand that Torgler's chains be removed. As a result, the Court ordered the unshackling of all the accused – except van der Lubbe.

Having once undertaken to stand by Torgler, Dr Sack kept faith with him through thick and thin. Not only did he stand up to the Public Prosecutor, but he mercilessly attacked National Socialist witnesses, no matter how prominent, once his client's interests were at stake. Thus he could say with perfect honesty:

> Thank God that all these underhand activities did not succeed in sowing mistrust between the Communist Torgler and myself, his National Socialist counsel. All they did do was to bring me closer to the accused. . . . And this trial has proved me right: I have gained the firm conviction that Torgler always told me the truth.

These brave words nearly cost Dr Sack his life:

> Dr Sack was unable to shake off the odium of having appeared for Torgler, and after the great purge of June 30th, 1934, he was kept behind bars for some considerable time, ostensibly so that he could 'adjust' his views.[30]

Dr Sack's dignified and noble bearing in Court was praised by all objective reporters. Douglas Reed, for instance, wrote:

> It was no enviable task that Dr Sack undertook, and his acceptance of it – at a fee which learned counsel, accustomed to enormous retainers and to subsequent payments not rare but eminently refreshing, would have regarded with the same feelings as a Savoy waiter a tip of two-pence – did him great credit. He was reproached from the bench with challenging the trustworthiness of official National Socialist wit-nesses; he was reproached in the press with the vigour of his final speech in Torgler's defence: and he was vilified abroad for his lack of activity in that same cause. Actually, he did all he could for his client.[31]

In his final speech, the courage of which was greatly praised by the *Neue Zürcher Zeitung*, Dr Sack exposed the lies that had been told by witnesses to whom common sense, logic, and reason meant little if anything. In particular, he exposed the Nazi deputy Karwahne and the methods of Judge Vogt, thus arousing the Nazi press to a high pitch of fury.

Nor did the Communists show any gratitude:

No thanks to Sack's defence, Torgler was acquitted. The transparent weakness of the case against him, his own courage and the bold defence of Dimitrov furnished the conditions for his acquittal. The moral pressure of world opinion secured it.

Yet, Dr Sack had been the only man to volunteer for the job, and the only German lawyer to protest against the *lex Lubbe*, i.e. the decree of 29 March 1933 which enabled the Government to impose the death sentence retrospectively. And had he not paid for two expensive trips to Paris and London out of his own pocket? According to Torgler:

> I once again made inquiries whether the Party had any objections to this lawyer. The reply was: 'Everything is in order.' And my wife added: 'They have even given me money for Dr Sack.'[32]

But soon after the main trial opened in Leipzig, the Communists changed their minds. One day, just after he had told foreign correspondents that he was fully satisfied with Dr Sack and therefore did not require the services of Arthur Garfield Hays,[33] Torgler noticed his ailing mother among the spectators: 'She was given permission to exchange a few words with me, and used the occasion to slip me a note from my comrades. We were nearly caught at it.'

That evening, when Torgler, who as we saw had just expressed his confidence in Dr Sack, read the note, he was utterly perplexed:

> I simply failed to understand. One moment they told me everything was in order, and now they wrote: 'The Central Committee asks you to take the first opportunity to disown Dr Sack as an agent of Hitler.' Added was a rather stilted paragraph instructing me to tell the Court that Goebbels and Göring had set the Reichstag on fire. The thing was signed by Wilhelm Pieck. I argued with myself for at least twenty-four hours. If I complied, I would cause a sensation, and that would make an extremely good headline. But what would happen to me...?

And, indeed, it does not require too much imagination to realize what would have happened to Torgler had he carried out the orders Pieck sent him from his safe refuge abroad. But then, the Communist Party, realizing that they could no longer use Torgler in Parliament, had only one use left for him: to let him be a martyr for the cause.

> I had fallen between two stools: Fascism and Bolshevism. . . . If I really told the Court that Göring and Goebbels had set the Reichstag

on fire – without being able to produce a shadow of a proof for this allegation – was I not simply signing my own death warrant . . .? I must frankly confess that these Party orders broke my spirit. I had resolved to throw myself into the struggle with enthusiasm, now I was paralysed, and without friends. . . .[34]

THE PUBLIC PROSECUTOR'S DILEMMA

After the lengthy preliminary investigation, the Public Prosecutor was handed thirty-two volumes of depositions, and the task of weeding this unwieldy mass of papers into a convincing indictment proved extremely onerous for even such experienced lawyers as Dr Werner and his assistant, Dr Parrisius.

Dr Karl Werner, who had come to the bar in 1926, was 'a zealous, somewhat dry official who had grown grey in the service of the law'.[35] Whereas Torgler still thinks that Werner was not at all cut out to play the part of Torquemada, Otto Braun, remembering his own bitter experiences, called him a reactionary with a blind eye to the errors of the Right, and with pitiless clear-sight when it came to those of the Left.[36]

Though Werner had previously acted as Public Prosecutor to the Supreme Court, the Reichstag fire trial was his most important – and most embarrassing – case by far. He might not have realized it at first, but as the trial proceeded he must often have wished most fervently that someone else were in his shoes. Here the sketchy witnesses for the prosecution stepped out of the dry pages of Judge Vogt's record, were made flesh, and – one and all – turned into miserable swindlers, psychopaths and hardened criminals. An old German saying has it that only a rogue can give more than he owns, and it did not take the Public Prosecutor long to realize that most of his witnesses owned nothing at all. Some were such transparent liars – for instance Anna Meyer and the chauffeur Theel, who had sworn they had seen Dimitrov near the Reichstag on the night of the fire – that they had to be dropped without further ado, and none of the others were very much better either. As a result, Dimitrov was able to keep jeering at Dr Werner and his 'classical indictment'. Indeed, the *Brown Book* was right to assert that the only remarkable thing about that legal document was its impressive size of 235 pages.

In any case, we can understand why Dimitrov wrote to his lawyer:

It is most regrettable that the indictment has not been published to this day, for its publication would be my best defence. I am certain that my position, as the accused, is incomparably sounder than that of the Public Prosecutor who must substantiate his indictment before the Court and before public opinion. I don't envy him at all.

No, the Public Prosecutor was in a truly unenviable position, for though Diels had warned Hitler and Göring repeatedly against trying to involve the Communist Party leaders, Göring had insisted on taking just that course.

Only because poor Dr Werner had to carry out the orders of his superiors, was Dimitrov able to proclaim that Göring and Goebbels had rendered yeoman service to Communism by pressing their ridiculous charges in the Supreme Court.

All these facts must be borne in mind by anyone wondering how so paltry a document as this indictment could ever have been presented in a court of law. Because he had to uphold Göring's and Hitler's thesis that the Reichstag fire was a desperate attempt on the part of the Communists to stop the irresistible march of National Socialism, Werner had to clutch at even the most fragile straws. No wonder that all the pieces of evidence assembled by Judge Vogt and the Prosecution collapsed like a house of cards under the merciless probing of the defence, and particularly of Torgler's lawyer, Dr Sack. It was largely thanks to him that all Judge Vogt's witnesses were unmasked as hardened criminals, pathetic liars, Nazi fanatics, police informers, Communist renegades, hysterical old women, and psychopaths.

It did not help Dr Werner that he fought a desperate struggle on behalf of every one of them – no single witness was able to establish that the Communists had, at the time in question, made any plans for an organized uprising, in which case the Reichstag fire could not have been a Communist 'signal' for anything. To save his case from utter collapse, Dr Werner himself was forced to ask for the acquittal of the three Bulgarians. His fiasco was complete when the Court acquitted Torgler as well. The Court's verdict was, at the same time, a verdict on Judge Vogt and his preliminary examination.

What the Court was left with was only one man who had done his utmost to incriminate himself without any prompting from the police, from the Examining Magistrate, or from the Public Prosecutor. That man was Marinus van der Lubbe.

11. The German Court and its Shadow

THE COURT

W HEN the case against 'Van der Lubbe and Accomplices' was duly sent for trial to the Fourth Criminal Chamber of the Supreme Court in Leipzig, the accused found themselves before the very same Bench which, in September 1930, had tried three army officers – Ludin, Scheringer and Wendt – for National-Socialist subversion in the army. One of the witnesses on that occasion was Adolf Hitler who stated on oath that he intended to come to power by legal means.

The President of the Court, since 1931, had been Dr Wilhelm Bünger. Before then, Dr Bünger was a well-known National Liberal politician who had served as Saxon Minister of Justice, and even as Prime Minister of Saxony. His appointment to the Supreme Court was frowned upon by his professional colleagues, most of whom considered him a political failure rather than a legal success – possibly out of jealousy.

Dr Bünger's associate judges were Dr Coenders, Dr Rusch, Dr Lersch and Dr Froelich. Coenders was described by Douglas Reed[1] as having 'a massive, finely carven head surmounted by masses of waving silver hair' and as having a voice 'with the vibrant resonance of a cathedral bell'. Another observer, however, disapproved of Coenders's behaviour during Göring's testimony on 4 November: 'The judges listened to [Göring's] deliberations quite expressionlessly; the only exception was Dr Coenders who kept nodding with satisfaction, and beaming all over his face.'[2] However, most permanent observers praised the strict impartiality of Dr Froelich.

The tensely awaited trial opened on 21 September 1933, in the presence of eighty-two foreign correspondents. So large was the rush for press tickets that a system of 'rationing' had to be instituted. Naturally, Dr Goebbels saw to it that his 'Marxist enemies' and the hated *Manchester Guardian*, were sent away empty-handed. However, two Soviet representatives of Tass and *Izvestia* were admitted later.

We owe the description of the strange procession in which the accused were led into the courtroom to Douglas Reed:

A being of almost imbecile appearance, with a shock of tousled hair hanging far over his eyes, clad in the hideous dungarees of the convicted criminal, with chains around his waist and wrists, shambling with sunken head between his custodians – the incendiary taken in the act. Four men in decent civilian clothes, with intelligence written on every line of their features, who gazed sombrely but levelly at their fellow men across the wooden railing which symbolized the great gulf fixed between captivity and freedom. . . . Torgler, last seen by many of those present railing at the Nazis from the tribune of the Reichstag, bore the marks of great suffering on his fine and sensitive face. Dimitrov, whose quality the Court had yet to learn, took his place as a free man among free men; there was nothing downcast in his bold and even defiant air. Little Tanev had not long since attempted suicide, and his appearance still showed what he had been through, Popov, as ever, was quiet and introspective.[3]

The general appearance of the incendiary-in-chief, van der Lubbe, caused a tremendous stir among the observers. Was this shadow of a man really so dangerous that he had to be put in chains like a common murderer? Sitting in the dock with downcast head, he looked far more like a terrified child than a terrorist:

According to the affidavit and also to the police witnesses, van der Lubbe was intelligent, mentally alert, and quick to respond. But the van der Lubbe whom we were now shown was a mental wreck, completely broken and dull-witted.[4]

The proceedings were opened by Dr Bünger promptly at 9.15 a.m., with a dignified speech which, with slight modifications, was reported in the *Völkischer Beobachter* of 22 September 1933, and also in *Brown Book II*:

The enormous repercussions of the event which constitutes the background of this trial have had the consequence of elevating the subject-matter of these proceedings to the rank of universal interest. It has formed the object of passionate discussion and speculation in the press of the whole world. Attempts have been made to anticipate the results of these proceedings. It does not, however, follow that this Court is entering upon its task with preconceived views or with its mind already made up. So far that has never been the custom either in Germany or abroad. Nor has prejudgment of the issues of a trial in the press been usual.

The struggle between these various conflicting theories has not affected the Court before which these issues come to be tried. This Court will pass sentence solely upon the results of the proceedings within its cognizance. For the purpose of this Court's decision only facts which are revealed in the course of the proceedings before it can have weight. Not only is this trial open to the public of all lands without restriction but the prisoners are represented by counsel without let, hindrance or condition. It has been said that no foreign lawyer has been permitted to appear for the defence. In this connection it must be observed that the law only permits such a course in exceptional circumstances. In the present case, the Court in the free exercise of its unfettered discretion has not seen fit to permit the admission of foreign lawyers. Not only has the Court seen no occasion for their admission but it holds the view that such applications as were made for this purpose were not directed to serve exclusively the interests of the prisoners, but were chiefly intended to cast doubt on the independence of German justice.

In this connection, it might be worth quoting Professor Friederich Grimm:

The question has been raised abroad why no foreign lawyers were admitted to this trial. In van der Lubbe's case, the answer was simple for he had expressly refused the services of a Dutch lawyer; in the case of the other accused, and particularly the Bulgarians, it was obvious that the briefing of foreign counsel could only serve the ends of propaganda.... No court in the world would have admitted foreign lawyers to a political trial once there was even the slightest risk that their admission might endanger the safety of the state.[5]

The generally objective Swiss correspondent, Kugler, however, had grave doubts: 'I am completely baffled. The renown of German jurisprudence would clearly have been enhanced had foreign lawyers been admitted.'[6]

Now, though Kugler had every right to be baffled, particularly as his native Switzerland had often admitted foreign lawyers, it seems doubtful whether anyone could have served his clients better than the German advocates. Arthur Garfield Hays, for instance, had nothing but praise for Torgler's counsel, Dr Sack, and van der Lubbe, though he steadfastly refused to accept legal assistance and though he would not exchange a single word with his state counsel, Dr Seuffert, was extremely well served by the latter – it was certainly not his fault that he failed. Nor is there any doubt that Dr Teichert, the Bulgarians' lawyer, defended his clients as best he could in the circumstances.

Moreover, most correspondents were agreed that Dr Bünger, the President of the Court, set to work with great patience and perfect courtesy to all. It was only as the trial proceeded that he gradually succumbed under the tremendous cross that had been placed on his somewhat too slender shoulders.

To begin with, the Nazis had begun to 'clear up' the Department of Justice and all 'politically unreliable officials' were in danger of instant dismissal. Now, Bünger had been made a judge under the Weimar Republic, and knew full well that the new Government expected him to atone for his 'evil' past. Needless to say, he became increasingly nervous as the trial failed to produce the expected results. To make things worse, Associate Judge Coenders thought very little of his forensic gifts and made many caustic comments on Dr Bünger's clumsiness, absent-mindedness, and frequent mistakes.

In fact, as the trial ran its difficult course, Bünger got more and more out of his depth. Nothing seemed to make any sense or to hang together in any way. All the evidence was contradictory; van der Lubbe refused to play by the rules, and the other accused kept holding the Court in contempt. Worst of all, two of the accused needed interpreters who muddled things further still.

On the very first day of the trial, Bünger earned Coenders's understandable strictures when he asked van der Lubbe: 'Have you ever been an active National Socialist, I mean have you ever pretended to be one except in Sörnewitz?'

As Coenders noted laconically, van der Lubbe had not even been active as a National Socialist in Sörnewitz. Moreover, that whole business had already been cleared up when Bünger asked his leading question.

A typical sample of the President's bungling was his examination of Constable Poeschel:

> Bünger: 'You started giving your evidence yesterday during the inspection.'
> Poeschel: 'No, not yet.'
> President: 'Not yet?'
> Poeschel: 'No.'
> President: 'How is that?'
> Poeschel: 'I merely took the oath.'
> President: 'You took the oath? Well, that's splendid. When I asked

you last night I thought you said that you had not taken the oath.'
Poeschel: 'On the contrary, I said that I had taken the oath.'

Bünger's time-consuming excursions into irrelevant issues are
best appreciated from the following sample:

Bünger: 'You said that there were four officers. Who were they?'
Poeschel: 'Lieutenant Lateit, Constable Losigkeit, another officer
and myself.'
Bünger: 'But that only makes three. Who was the fourth officer?'
Poeschel: 'I don't know him by name.'
Bünger: 'Ah, so there was another one!'

With this and other clumsy interrogations, Bünger kept leading
the Court into one blind alley after another, wasting not only hours
and days, but weeks and months.

A tragi-comical scene was enacted on 18 October 1933, when
the Court examined the evidence of the Reichstag official Robert
Kohls. Kohls had alleged that, on the night of the fire, Torgler
failed to answer his telephone. When Krueger, a telephone expert,
testified that the ringing tone recurred every ten seconds, Bünger
remarked:

'In that case, Herr Kohls must have misinformed us. He said the sound
was ss – ss – ss.'
Dr Sack: 'May I remind the Court that it was I who made that
sound. I said "Was it sss?" and the Public Prosecutor said: "Wasn't
it mmm?" It was you, Mr President, who suggested "sss" and the
witness Düsterhoeft who suggested "rrrrrr".'

These edifying reflections on possible ringing tones covered
many pages of the Court's records. Another illustration of Dr
Bünger's legal prowess was given on 6 December, when the Court
rose to consider a motion by Dimitrov, and returned after a brief
recess.

Bünger: 'Please be seated. The Court refuses the request of the
accused Dimitrov that the sentence passed on the leaders of the
uprising on November 9th 1923 [the Hitler putsch] be read out here.
Or was that a motion of yours, Mr Public Prosecutor?'
Dr Werner: 'I have submitted no such motion.'

Clearly Dr Bünger's memory was such that it did not even last
him from his chambers to the courtroom.

    .   .   .   .   .

In his address to the Court, the Public Prosecutor, Dr Werner, expressed his thanks to all those 'thousands of fellow-Germans' who felt obliged to report what observations they thought might have been relevant to the case, first to the police, then to the investigating magistrate and finally to the Public Prosecutor's office or the Court.

The combined chance of attracting world attention as a witness, of currying favour with the new German masters, and of carrying off the rich reward of 20,000 marks, proved quite irresistible to a host of shady and self-seeking characters. All of them felt that even if their evidence did no good it certainly could do no harm. Naturally, no one volunteered to appear as a witness for the defence; in fact those defence witnesses who were subpoenaed proved rather reluctant and – sometimes – rather untruthful. One of these was Ernst Torgler's 'friend', the journalist Walther Oehme, who lied about the time he had visited Torgler on the day of the fire.

In contrast to the hesitant and vague witnesses for the defence, the witnesses for the prosecution all took the stand with amazing self-confidence. What they had to say, they said with perfect assurance. Thus the star witness Helmer, who swore that he had seen van der Lubbe in the Bulgarians' company, identified van der Lubbe with an emphatic: 'I would sooner mistake my own wife than the accused van der Lubbe.'

So definite were the witnesses for the prosecution, and so unsure those for the defence that foreign journalists kept remarking on the striking distinction between the two categories. In every other trial, this very distinction would have made the Court sit up and take notice, particularly when the general quality of the prosecution witnesses was as poor as it proved to be here. Yet Dr Werner, the Public Prosecutor, could not afford to be very discriminating since, as he confessed, he had been unable to dig up '. . . a single person who had direct evidence that the four accused [Torgler and the Bulgarians] had participated in the crime'.[7]

Clearly, in a totalitarian state, justice stands on feet of clay.

And so the trial dragged on under the critical eyes of Nazis and Communists alike. Like a blind man in a maze, Dr Bünger followed every possible trail, clinging to every possible clue as Theseus did to Ariadne's thread. Yet the more he tried, the more he became engulfed in a yawning abyss of boredom, and the more he revealed the absolute aimlessness of the whole trial.

To make things worse, Bünger adopted quite a different manner to the two classes of witnesses, so much so that it was easy to tell from his tone alone whether a given witness appeared for the prosecution or the defence. Understandably enough, Bünger, who must have come to realize that he was making no headway whatever, vented his spleen on the 'obdurate' and persistent causes of his failure, the accused and their witnesses. On the other hand, all those witnesses for the prosecution who obviously tried so hard to help the 'truth' to victory, naturally needed every kind of encouragement and sympathy.

As a result, witnesses for the defence, who in any case were afraid to open their mouths, had their slightest slips treated with utmost scorn and severity, while witnesses for the prosecution were encouraged to come out with the wildest feats of fantasy. Time and again the Public Prosecutor and the President intervened to help witnesses for the prosecution out of their difficulties.

A Dutch newspaper summed it all up as follows:

> National Socialist witnesses quite especially, are protected against every kind of reprimand. All of them are handled like unboiled eggs, indeed with every consideration and politeness. This distinction has become so blatant that the tone in which the Court addresses a witness is a clear indication of the latter's political colour.[8]

Douglas Reed took much the same view. Thus he tells us that, when Dr Sack wished to lay bare the discrepancies in the witness Karwahne's testimony, Dr Bünger intervened with: 'There will always be discrepancies in such statements, and I must protect the witness against the suggestion that he intentionally, or through negligence, concealed anything.'[9]

THE 'SUBSTITUTE INCENDIARY'

Douglas Reed – undoubtedly one of the shrewdest and best-informed observers of the Leipzig trial – has described the court appearance of Georgi Dimitrov:

> His exchanges with Dr Bünger – who told him sharply at the start that he came into Court with the reputation of indiscipline during the preliminary examination and had better comport himself differently now – were the beginning of a duel which lasted fifty-seven days. In

vain did the little judge . . . seek to subdue Dimitrov, to compel him by admonition, by threat of expulsion, by repeated expulsion itself, to be meek, to behave himself as a disreputable Bulgarian Communist should who is under grave suspicion of tampering with the edifice of the Reich. Dimitrov felt himself not only innocent, but as good as any man in Court, and was not prepared to have an inferiority thrust on him which he did not feel. Nothing could stop him. At the end, the Court itself had a certain rueful affection for the disarming and dauntless man.

The great pomp with which the trial was conducted did not impress Dimitrov for a single moment. His intelligence was razor-sharp and, unlike his two compatriots, he had a good command of the German language, and was therefore able to expose the prosecution's case for the sham it was.

When he was first arrested, Dimitrov had been afraid that the 'Fascist police' might have recognized him as the leader of the West European Branch of the Comintern. Imagine his surprise when instead he discovered that they were seriously trying to blame him for a crime that had been committed at a time when he had a perfect alibi! No wonder that he refused to believe his enemies would be stupid enough to make him stand trial before the Supreme Court.

When Dimitrov presented his alibi to Judge Vogt, the Examining Magistrate neatly countered that in that case Dimitrov must certainly have prepared the fire and then gone off to Munich for the sake of the alibi, leaving van der Lubbe to take the blame. That was also the view adopted by the Public Prosecutor.

Now, Dimitrov had an inestimable advantage over his judges: he knew that the Communist Party was completely innocent of the Reichstag fire. Only in one respect was there complete agreement between him and the prosecution: both were absolutely convinced that van der Lubbe must have had accomplices.

Once Dimitrov recognized the shallowness of the case for the prosecution, he used his quick wit with unerring skill. A man whose name few people had heard when the trial opened, had become an international celebrity, and a godsend to the Communists, by the time the trial was over.

To Dr Bünger, on the other hand, Dimitrov's behaviour proved a constant provocation, and a test beyond endurance. As Dimitrov continued flinging veiled insults at the Court, Bünger increasingly lost his original composure. In the end, he looked for poisonous barbs in even the most innocent remarks and repeatedly excluded Dimitrov from the trial. The only result was an increase in Dimitrov's popularity with the press.

Bünger was, in fact, treating Dimitrov much as Judge Paul Vogt had done before him. The Bulgarian's very bearing was an affront to both, for he would miss no opportunity of exposing his judges.

After every expulsion Dimitrov came back into the courtroom with renewed vigour. He was always most careful to behave with formal courtesy; what made him so insufferable, indeed so terrifying, was the biting irony with which he attacked his accusers, often to the great amusement of the public gallery.

A typical example of how tense Dr Bünger became every time Dimitrov opened his mouth, is the following incident. Dimitrov was recalling his previous request that Detective-Inspector Heisig be cross-examined on the evidence of a witness, and added:

'As I remember, I was completely taken aback when the Public Prosecutor agreed to this request.'

President: 'You were taken aback! You really must omit these gratuitous remarks which, almost without exception, are affronts to this Court. I am telling you so for the last time.'

After further skirmishes, during all of which Dimitrov remained completely unruffled, while the President could barely control his temper, Dimitrov said quite unexpectedly and very quietly:

'And furthermore, Herr President, please allow me to say so – you are extremely nervous today, I don't know . . .'

President: 'I am not at all nervous; it is just that your constant repetitions and impertinent interjections force me to cut you short. In fact, I never get nervous, I should like to reassure you on that point, but I cannot possibly let you go on. I cannot and I will not. You simply do not respond when you are spoken to in civil tones. That is the simple truth of the whole matter. Well, let us proceed.'

Dimitrov: 'You can, of course, throw me out, Herr President, I know you have the right to do so, but please allow me, the accused, to say a word or two about the documents presented today . . .'

President: 'Provided you are not just taking another liberty. If that is the case, I shall simply refuse to hear you.'

Dimitrov: 'I merely call a spade a spade.'

President: 'It's for me to decide that.'

Dimitrov: 'Of course, it's sheer bad luck for the prosecution that a whole series of important witnesses are psychopaths, opium addicts and thieves.'

President: 'I object to the expression "bad luck", and therefore will not hear you further.'

Dimitrov: 'That would be quite wrong of you, Herr President.'

Once again things had come to a head. The Court retired, and returned with the warning that Dimitrov would be automatically ejected if he were guilty of the least impropriety. It added that he would have been expelled even earlier, had this not been the last day of the trial.

After the luncheon recess, the remorseless Dimitrov started plaguing the harassed Court with yet another petition.

Dimitrov: 'May I request, Herr President, that, for the sake of completing the judgment you have just read out, you also read out the verdict on the Rightist putsch in Munich on the 8th and 9th November, 1923. If it should be necessary to give reasons for this request, I ask for permission to do so.'

President: 'No. We shall decide about this and the other petitions afterwards.'

Dimitrov: 'A National Socialist putsch.'

President: 'I heard you. I am not deaf.'

Dr Werner: 'I object to the petition, for clearly it has no bearing on the question of who burned the Reichstag.'

Here we have another perfect illustration of the double standard applied by a Court which saw fit to admit as evidence Communist outrages that had no earthly connection with the Reichstag fire, but refused point-blank to allow Dimitrov to introduce evidence about similar National Socialist acts of subversion.

On the last day of the trial, Dimitrov also settled his score with House-Inspector Alexander Scranowitz, who had originally alleged that he had seen the three Bulgarians in the Reichstag but who later recanted. Dimitrov's reference to the matter once again brought out the incompetent worst in Dr Bünger:

President (to Scranowitz): 'You can no longer say so with any certainty?'

Scranowitz: 'No, not with the same certainty.'

Dimitrov: 'With what certainty?'

President: 'You say you can no longer say so with the requisite degree of certainty?'

Scranowitz: 'Not with enough certainty to state on oath: "It was him." '

President: 'You cannot do that?'

Scranowitz: 'No, I cannot.'

Dimitrov: 'Herr President, I should like to point out that when I saw Herr Scranowitz in the courtroom for the first time I immediately said to myself, this must be the Macedonian terrorist who murdered ten Communists. But as I could not believe my eyes, I did not tell the Court that Herr Scranowitz was this Macedonian terrorist, and even less that . . .'

The rest of Dimitrov's sentence was drowned in laughter.

From all these dialogues and arguments, one thing emerges quite clearly: the greater Dimitrov's composure, the greater Dr Bünger's discomfiture. Dimitrov's very presence gave the President palpitations. In this connection a Swiss journalist reported the following characteristic incident:

> Someone made an interjection in an undertone, and the President . . . turned irately to Dimitrov: 'Be silent! Hold your tongue!' It turned out that Dimitrov had not so much as opened his mouth. . . .[10]

THE FIRST FOUR EXPULSIONS

Dimitrov's first expulsion from the courtroom occurred on 6 October 1933, when, according to the foreign press, he was ejected for 'quite inexplicable reasons'[11] or 'on a ridiculous pretext'.[12]

On that day, the President put it to Dimitrov that the documents which the police had removed from his briefcase and from his suitcase seemed to belie his protestations that he was exclusively concerned with Bulgarian affairs. Afraid that if his real position in the Comintern were ever discovered all would be up with him, Dimitrov kept insisting that all these documents had been planted by the police. For instance, when Dr Bünger produced a pamphlet issued by the Central Committee of the German Communist Party dated 3 March 1933, and entitled: 'The Burning of the Reichstag', Dimitrov simply claimed that he had 'neither seen, possessed, nor read such a document' and that he had certainly never been asked about it by the police. Thereupon Dr Bünger read Dimitrov's own statement of 9 March 1933, the day of his arrest, in which Dimitrov admitted having obtained this pamphlet from 'Inprecorr' (International Press Correspondence) for which he had allegedly been

215

working. Now Dimitrov became excited: 'Impossible! This statement is not the one that was read out to me at the time.' (Dimitrov had consistently refused to sign any statements.)

The President now called Detective Officer Kynast to tell the Court about a 'Pharus' map of Berlin found among Dimitrov's effects. Kynast stated that he had found crosses on this map and corresponding crosses on the street index. The crosses referred to the Palace, the Reichstag and the Dutch Embassy.

Dimitrov immediately asked to see the map, looked at it, and exploded with: 'At the time of the police investigation these crosses were very thick. Now they are very thin!'[13]

Somewhat taken aback, the President then asked him for what reason he thought the crosses might have been altered, to which Dimitrov replied mysteriously that he would come back to the matter.

When the Public Prosecutor, who had introduced the map as a possible link between Dimitrov and van der Lubbe, asked whether Dimitrov admitted that it was his own, Dimitrov replied: 'I admit that I bought a map. Whether it is this particular one, I cannot say.'[14]

He added that, in any case, he himself had certainly not made the crosses; the whole thing was a police fraud.

When the President warned him not to make offensive remarks about police officers, Dimitrov, disgusted at the stupid manner in which the police were trying to manufacture a link between him and van der Lubbe, burst out with: 'I can't give any guarantees for the police.'

Half incensed and half amused, the President replied: 'We shall just have to make do without your guarantees.'

Whereupon Dimitrov

... took it upon himself to deliver an elementary lesson on deciphering code to the ignorant police officers. What he had learned during his illegal stay in Berlin, might be of great use to those Nazis who, at this very moment, were carrying on their nefarious activities in Czechoslovakia and in Austria, using false names and codes.[15]

When he added: 'The police have shown great incompetence and incomprehension,' the President sprang to his feet and the Court filed out in solemn procession. On their return, Dr Bünger announced that Dimitrov would be removed 'for disobeying repeated admonitions to desist from insulting police officers'.[17]

Furiously, Dimitrov snatched up his briefcase, shouting: 'Monstrous! Monstrous!'

And while two policemen hustled him out he added: 'My sentence has already been pronounced in another place.'[11]

Dimitrov had been somewhat impertinent, but when all was said and done, his head was hanging by these idiotic and, to say the least, suspicious pencil crosses on the map. Moreover, Dimitrov's remark that he could not give any guarantees for the police had a very serious, indeed a highly embarrassing, background, for when they searched his room the over-zealous police officers had quite clearly exceeded their powers: they had not produced independent witnesses (Article 105, Crim. Code); they had not carried out the search in the presence of the suspect or of his representative (Article 106); they had not handed the suspect a list of all confiscated articles (Article 107); they had not placed all confiscated documents in sealed envelopes or asked the suspect or his representative to seal them (Article 110).

It was only because of these undeniable errors and omissions, that Dimitrov could stand up in Court and allege that the police had tampered with his papers and the 'Pharus' map. This embarrassing fact was quite specifically referred to in the verdict where we read that 'it is impossible to establish the truth [about the crosses on the map, etc.] since no inventory of the confiscated documents was made.'

On 11 October Dr Bünger announced that the Court would move from Leipzig to the Reichstag for an on-the-spot inspection. Dimitrov immediately requested permission to put a question to the Court.

Dr Bünger: 'No, Dimitrov, it's no use at all. I have told you more than once that the Criminal Code does not allow you to keep asking questions or making long statements and you can hardly expect that I should allow you, of all people, who – to put it very mildly – have repeatedly tried to abuse the Court's indulgence, at least with respect to the putting of questions and the making of statements, to do something to which the Rules of Procedure do not entitle even you. Please calm yourself.'

From a purely formal point of view, the President was completely in the right. Dimitrov's persistent refusal to allow his

217

Government-nominated counsel, Dr Teichert, to act on his behalf, was, in fact, a technical breach of the Rules of Court. But Dimitrov was not dismayed by such trifles.

Dimitrov: 'Herr President . . .'
Dr Bünger: 'No, I don't want to hear another word. Please don't bother me, it's no use at all. Sit down.'
Dimitrov: 'I should like to . . .'
President: 'I cannot allow you to speak!'
Dimitrov: 'I am here not only as Dimitrov the accused but also as the defender of Dimitrov.'

Once again the Court rose in a flurry and, on its return, made known that Dimitrov was expelled from Court until further notice (and hence barred from attending the reconstruction of the fire which was to be enacted on the following night).

Before he was led out of the courtroom, Dimitrov quickly handed a note to Dr Teichert, saying: 'I had wanted to ask these questions, ask them for me!'

After his second expulsion, Dimitrov sent a letter of protest to Dr Bünger which deserves to be quoted in full:

Berlin, October 12th, 1933.
To the President
Fourth Criminal Chamber of the Supreme Court.
Mr President,
    When the Supreme Court rejected every one of the eight lawyers chosen by me, I had no option but to defend myself as best I could. As a result I have been compelled to appear in Court in a double capacity: first as Dimitrov, the accused, and second as the defender of the accused Dimitrov.
    I grant you that both as the accused and also as my own defender, I may have proved annoying and awkward to my accusers and their principals. However, I cannot help that. Once the Prosecution has been careless enough to put me, a completely innocent man, in the dock as a substitute incendiary, they must also be prepared to accept the resulting annoyance. They have called the tune, now they must dance to it. Whether they like it or not is neither my affair, nor is it my problem. I am a political suspect appearing before a Supreme Court, and not a soldier in barracks or a prisoner-of-war in an internment camp.
    I am firmly convinced that, in this trial, van der Lubbe is no more than what one may call the Reichstag-fire Faust, manipulated by the Reichstag-fire Mephistopheles. The miserable Faust now stands

218

before the bar of the Supreme Court, but Mephistopheles has disappeared.

As an innocent suspect, and particularly as a Communist and as a member of the Communist International, I have the utmost interest in discovering every last detail of the Reichstag-fire complex, and in bringing the vanished Mephistopheles to justice. My questions serve this one object and nothing else. I have no need to make Communist propaganda before the Supreme Court, the more so since the best propaganda for Communism has already been made, not by me, but by the mere fact that Dr Parrisius' classical indictment accuses innocent Communists of burning the Reichstag.

I have the natural right to defend myself and to participate in the trial both as the accused and my own defender. Expulsions from sessions of the Court or from inspections of the scene of the crime are quite incapable of intimidating me. These expulsions from what are the most important sessions and reconstructions are not only an open violation of my right to defend myself, but also serve to show the world that my accusers are not at all sure of their own case. The expulsions thus only serve to add further substance to existing Communist allegations about this trial.

If this insupportable treatment of myself is continued, I confess quite openly that I shall feel compelled to reconsider whether there is any purpose at all in my reappearing before the Court, irrespective of the consequences.

Dimitrov's brilliant use of a foreign language, his controlled tone, particularly in the last paragraph, his natural dignity – all these did not miss their effect on Dr Bünger. Dimitrov was henceforth given access to (at least some of) the Court files, and was allowed to petition the Court, albeit to have most of his petitions rejected. In other words, the Court gave him tacit permission to perform his double act of accused and defender. In addition, Dimitrov was explicitly granted the right to deliver a final address.

On 31 October 1933, one of the least reliable witnesses of all, the glazier Gustav Lebermann, was put on the stand.

When Dimitrov tried to discover why this witness had been fetched out of prison at such short notice, Dr Bünger told him that Lebermann had only come forward on 13 October. Dimitrov insisted on being told who had called Lebermann as a witness.

Dr Bünger: 'The Public Prosecutor. But I must order you straight away not to enter into completely pointless arguments. After all, you

219

cannot stop the Public Prosecutor or the Court from hearing any witnesses or any kind of material evidence.'

Dimitrov: 'I merely wished to point out that the chain of witnesses is now closed. After giving us National Socialist deputies and journalists, the Public Prosecutor now gives us criminals and thieves.'

When Dimitrov ignored Dr Werner's objection, and started again on the 'chain of witnesses', the irate Dr Bünger snapped at him:

'Dimitrov, I have told you on more than one occasion that though you may put questions to witnesses, you cannot address the Court on all sorts of subjects. There is a time and a place for doing that. You may ask questions now, but nothing else. Do you wish to put any questions? To the witness, mind, and not to the Public Prosecutor!'

Dimitrov: 'I should like to put a question to the witness of Dr Parrisius' [Dimitrov obstinately refused to address the Assistant Public Prosecutor by his full title].

President: 'No! Anyway, what question do you want to put to the witness?'

Dimitrov: 'I should like to ask the following question, Herr President . . .'

President: 'You have no questions, then?'

Dimitrov: 'I have the following question . . .'

President: 'Then for goodness' sake ask your question.'

Dimitrov: 'He made a statement on October 13th, that much is clear, after he had read the newspaper reports on the Reichstag fire trial. He has said that much here. He was in prison, he was not at large. He was given the third degree. He had hopes of being discharged on the basis of the lies he has told. I ask who influenced him to utter these shameless and disgraceful . . .'

Dr Bünger: 'Keep quiet! I will not have you insult witnesses.'

Even so, Dr Bünger, to whom Lebermann's character was no more of a mystery than it was to anyone else in Court, turned to the witness with: 'Has anyone at all influenced you?' Naturally Lebermann replied: 'No one at all!' and Dr Bünger was able to tell Dimitrov: 'Your question has been answered.' But Dimitrov had the last word: 'May I congratulate you on this witness, *Herr Reichsanwalt?*' he asked Dr Parrisius. And this time he used the full title.

This skirmish was to have grave outside repercussions on Dr Bünger. On 1 November 1933 the *Völkischer Beobachter* objected that neither the President nor the Public Prosecutor saw fit to rebuke Dimitrov for his malicious remark that the chain of National Socialist witnesses was now closed. The paper concluded with a massive threat:

> We National Socialists hope that even Dr Bünger's Court will find some means of preventing such unseemly and insulting attacks by a Communist criminal on National Socialist witnesses.

One can understand why Dr Bünger got cold feet immediately, and why, the very next day, he emphasized that, had he fully understood Dimitrov's unseemly remarks, he would most certainly have intervened at the time. He added that the accused would in future be kept under even stricter control, whereupon Dimitrov quipped back:

'The *Völkischer Beobachter* has every reason to be satisfied now.'

And with this he cut Bünger to the quick. Once again he ordered the police to take Dimitrov out of the courtroom, and once again Dimitrov cried:

'Monstrous! And this is supposed to be a fair trial!'

In the general uproar, the rest of his unflattering remarks were lost.

On 3 November, Dimitrov was back again, as aggressive as ever. A number of witnesses from the Soviet Union were testifying that they had met Popov and Tanev in Russia. One of the witnesses was a Frau Weiss, whom the Public Prosecutor treated with great suspicion, suggesting, *inter alia*, that Weiss was not her real name.

Dimitrov, who had obviously been spoiled by success, intervened to remark that, in the Soviet Union, anyone could choose any name he liked. He added: 'I am extremely surprised to see how ignorant the Public Prosecutor is of Soviet law.'

Dr Werner whispered something into the ear of Dr Bünger, who immediately rebuked Dimitrov for his impertinence. Dr Bünger then apologized to Dr Werner, saying that he had not understood what Dimitrov had been saying.

Dimitrov, for his part, objected to Dr Werner's whispers and exclaimed: 'You still have a lot to learn, Herr Oberreichsanwalt!'

Once again the Court filed out, and once again it decreed that Dimitrov, the incorrigible, be excluded from the trial – this time for two days.

This last expulsion was particularly annoying to Dimitrov, since next day a very special witness – Hermann Göring – was to appear in Court. For most observers of the trial, it had been a great sensation when, on 17 October 1933, Dr Werner had asked for leave to call the Storm Troop leaders and Police Chiefs Helldorff and Heines, together with Ministerpräsident Göring and Reichsminister Dr Goebbels. The reason for this unusual step was that

> . . . the *Brown Book* had made the monstrous allegation – without trying to produce a shred of evidence – that Minister Goebbels was the indirect, and the Prussian Ministerpräsident Göring the direct, instigator of the plan [to burn the Reichstag]. Once such impudent and unsubstantiated slanders were put abroad, the victims must be given the opportunity of clearing their names.[18]

Now, any other Court would, of course, have dismissed Dr Werner's request out of hand, since what the Court had to establish was not the guilt or innocence of Göring or Goebbels, but that of the five accused. Moreover, by acceding to this request, the Court helped not only to introduce the noisy atmosphere of the hustings into the hushed solemnity of the courtroom, but also to drag out the trial quite unnecessarily. As if to revenge this outrage on her dignity, Justice dealt the Nazi ministers, who had hoped to use the courtroom as a forum for cleansing their sullied names, a resounding blow. As her tool she chose a man whose courage more than stood up to the bullying of even his mightiest enemies.

THE FIFTH EXPULSION

Next day, on 4 November 1933, to everybody's surprise, a nonchalant Dimitrov took his place in the Court from which he had only just been banished for two days. Since it seemed unlikely that Dr Bünger had reversed his own decision by himself, the general feeling was that he had been given a 'hint' from above. Obviously Göring did not wish to give the impression that he had deliberately avoided a meeting with the wily Bulgarian.

A Swiss correspondent has described the dramatic climax of the trial as follows:

> Whole swarms of policemen, armed with carbines, surrounded the Reichstag building [where the Court was meeting at this stage], checking every visitor with unusual vigilance.
> The improvised courtroom was completely packed long before the judges arrived. People kept craning their necks to catch a glimpse of such well-known personalities as the American Ambassador, Minister

1. The Burning Reichstag.

2. The Nazi Leaders at the scene of the fire. Hitler talking to Prince August Wilhelm, Göring (second from left) and Goebbels (second from right).

3. The Burnt-out Sessions Chamber.

4. Marinus van der Lubbe
before the fire.

5. Dimitrov, Popov and Tanev

6. Van der Lubbe giving evidence.

7. Göring giving evidence.

8. Van der Lubbe and Torgler in court.

of Trade Schmidt, the two Prussian Ministers, Russ and Kerrl, Minister of Justice Frank, and Under-Secretary Koerner. The tension was tremendous.

And the tension mounted the longer Göring kept his expectant audience waiting. At 10.30 a.m. – over an hour late, and thereby expressing his contempt for the highest German court—

... Göring entered the room in the brown uniform, leather belt and top boots of an S.A. leader. Everyone jumped up as if electrified, and all Germans, including the judges, raised their arms to give the Hitler salute.

When all the arms had dropped again, the President addressed the following harangue to Göring:

'Herr Prime Minister, in naming you and Herr Reichsminister Dr Goebbels as witnesses whom he desired to summon before the Court, the Public Prosecutor stated that you could not be deprived of the right to express yourselves under oath concerning accusations and slanders which have been directed against your Excellencies from certain quarters, particularly in the so-called *Brown Book*, regarding the subject matter of this trial. The Supreme Court desires to express its concurrence in this statement.'[19]

Bünger's view of Göring's role did not suit the latter in the least. In a completely 'unministerial' tone, he explained his own views of the matter:

'Herr President, you have just said that I was summoned as a witness in order to clear my name of accusations and slanders made by the *Brown Book*. I should like to emphasize that I consider my evidence important in two quite other respects . . .'

And the President of a German Supreme Court meekly allowed a witness not only to instruct him in court procedure, but also to launch an election address lasting for over three hours. After every jibe at his enemies, Göring's fans roared out their approval while the President who, at the beginning of the trial had expressly forbidden 'all expressions of approval, of disapproval, or even of astonishment', sat by without a murmur.

The great clash between Göring and Dimitrov began with Dimitrov's rising from his seat '. . . with as much unconcern as if he were about to cross-examine an insignificant grocer or publican from Neukölln and not the Prussian Prime Minister'.[20]

As Dimitrov faced Göring, it became apparent that neither would give way. At the time, the Bulgarian was a hounded alien and in the hands of his political opponents; twelve years later the tables were turned – as Göring's political star reached its nadir, Dimitrov's rose towards its zenith: by the time Göring had to answer for his war crimes to the victors' tribunal at Nuremberg, Dimitrov had become premier of Bulgaria. Though no one could have predicted these developments in 1933, Dimitrov behaved all along as if there were not the least doubt about the final outcome.

Dimitrov started by trying to rattle Göring with a host of minor questions. Then, quite suddenly, he brought out his big guns:

Dimitrov: 'On February 28th, the morning papers published a statement or an interview by Ministerpräsident Göring on the Reichstag fire. This report alleged – I remember its general sense very clearly – that the fire had been started by the Communist Party, that Torgler was one of the culprits, and that the arrested "Dutch Communist" van der Lubbe carried his passport and a membership card of the Communist Party on his person. I should like to know how Ministerpräsident Göring could have known at the time that van der Lubbe had a Communist Party membership card on him?'

Göring: 'I must admit that, so far, I have not bothered unduly about this trial, that is, I haven't read all the reports. I did gather, however, that you are an exceptionally bright fellow and hence I should have expected even you to know the correct answer to this question, which was given long ago. I have already testified that I don't rush round pulling things out of people's pockets. In case you don't know, I have a police force to do that sort of thing and – in case you don't know that either – the police search every criminal and – in case you don't know even that – they report their findings to me. The whole thing is really quite simple.'

Dimitrov: 'Herr Ministerpräsident . . . ' (President: 'Dimitrov!') 'If I may speak quite freely . . .'

President: 'First listen to what I have to say. I should like to draw your attention to the fact that this question has been fully answered.' (Dimitrov: 'If I may speak quite freely . . .') 'The question has been answered I tell you. If you want to ask a further question then please do so, but in such a way as to make its purport quite clear from the start.'

Dimitrov: 'Yes, quite clear. I should like to put it to the Herr Ministerpräsident that the three police officers who arrested and searched van der Lubbe all agreed that no Communist Party member-

224

ship card was found on him. I should like to know where the report that such a card was found came from.'

Göring: 'I can tell you that very easily.' (Dimitrov: 'Please do!') 'I was told by an officer. Things which were reported to me on the night of the fire, particularly those which cropped up in the course of explanations by officials, could not all be tested and proved. The report was made to me by a responsible official and was accepted as a fact. As it could not be immediately tested, it was announced as a fact. When I issued the first report to the press on the morning after the fire, the interrogation of van der Lubbe was not concluded. In any case, I do not see that anyone has anything to complain of, because it seems to have been proved in the trial that van der Lubbe had no such card on him.'

Dimitrov: 'As Prussian Ministerpräsident and Minister of the Interior, did you order an immediate police investigation?'

President: 'I could not understand a word of what you were saying, so please repeat the last sentence.'

Dimitrov: 'I was saying, did Herr Göring, as Prussian Ministerpräsident, as Minister of the Interior and as Speaker of the Reichstag, give immediate orders for the apprehension of van der Lubbe's accomplices?' (Göring: 'Yes, of course.') 'After all, he is the one – and he has said so himself – who bears the full responsibility for his department and for his police. Is that not so?' (Göring: 'Quite so!') 'I would like to ask the Minister of the Interior what steps he took on February 28th and 29th or on the following days to make sure that van der Lubbe's route to Henningsdorf, and his stay and meetings with other people there, were investigated by the police in order to assist them in tracking down van der Lubbe's accomplices?'

President: 'Your question is quite long enough!'

Dimitrov: 'Quite clear enough!'

Göring: 'I have already acknowledged my responsibility. You didn't even have to ask your question. If you had only paid attention, you would have heard me say that, as a Minister, I don't have to track criminals like a detective, and that I leave it to the police to make detailed investigations. . . . I merely gave orders to carry out the investigation with the utmost speed and with the utmost care. Of course, I, too, was fully aware that van der Lubbe must have had accomplices' (Dimitrov: 'Quite true!') 'and I ordered their speedy arrest.'

Dimitrov: 'When you, as Prussian Ministerpräsident and Minister of the Interior, let it be known in Germany and abroad that the Communists burned the Reichstag' (Göring: 'Exactly!') 'that the Communist Party' (Göring: 'Quite so!') 'was responsible, that the

225

Communist Party of Germany conspired with van der Lubbe and other alleged foreign Communists, did you not, in fact, influence the police and judicial investigations in a particular direction, thus preventing the apprehension of the real incendiaries?'

Göring: 'I know what you are getting at, but there is really no problem at all. The police were from the start given orders to pursue their investigations in every possible direction, no matter where these investigations led them. But as I am not a detective myself but a responsible Minister, it was not important that I should trouble myself with trifling details. It was my business to point out the Party and the mentality which were responsible for the crime. All I had to determine was: is this a civil offence, or is it a political offence? Now it was clearly a political offence and at the same time it became clear to me, and it remains just as clear today, that your Party were the criminals.'

President (to Dimitrov): 'Regarding your reference to influencing the judges . . . you did refer to that, didn't you? To influencing the judges?'

Dimitrov: 'No. What I said, Herr President, was that the police inquiry and later the preliminary examination could have been influenced by these political directives, and mainly in one direction. That is why I am asking my question.'

Göring: 'Herr Dimitrov, that, too, is admitted. If the police were allowed to be influenced in a particular direction, then, in any case, they were only influenced in the proper direction.'

Dimitrov: 'That is your opinion. My opinion is quite different.'

Göring: 'But mine is the one that counts.'

Dimitrov: 'I am only the accused, of course.'

President: 'You may only ask questions.'

Dimitrov: 'I am doing that, Herr President. Does Herr Ministerpräsident Göring realize that those who possess this alleged criminal mentality are today controlling the destinies of a sixth part of the world, namely the Soviet Union?' (Göring: 'Unfortunately.') 'The Soviet Union has diplomatic, political and economic contacts with Germany. Her orders provide work for hundreds of thousands of German workers. Does the Minister know that?'

Göring: 'Yes, I do.' (Dimitrov: 'Good!') 'I also know that the Russians pay with bills and I should prefer to know their bills are met. In that case Russia's orders would really provide work for our workers. But that is not the point here. I don't care what happens in Russia. Here, I am only concerned with the Communist Party of Germany and with the foreign Communist crooks who come here to set the Reichstag on fire.'

(Loud 'bravos' from the public.)

Dimitrov: 'Yes of course, bravo, bravo, bravo! They have the right to fight against the Communist Party, but the Communist Party of Germany has the right to go underground and to fight against your Government; and how we fight back is a matter of our respective forces and not a matter of law.'

President: 'Dimitrov, I will not have you making Communist propaganda here.' (Dimitrov: 'But he is making National Socialist propaganda!') 'I most emphatically order you to desist. I will not have Communist propaganda in this courtroom!'

Dimitrov: 'Herr President, arising out of my last question, there is just one further question that needs explaining in any case: the question of party and philosophy. Herr Ministerpräsident Göring has stated that he is not concerned with what happens in the Soviet Union, but only with the criminal mentality of the Communist Party. Is the Minister aware that this criminal mentality rules the Soviet Union, the greatest and best land in the world?'

Göring: 'Look here, I will tell you what the German people know. They know that you are behaving in a disgraceful fashion. They know that you are a Communist crook who came to Germany to set the Reichstag on fire, and who now behave yourself with sheer impudence in the face of the German people. I did not come here to be accused by you.' (Dimitrov: 'You are a witness.') 'In my eyes you are nothing but a scoundrel, a crook who belongs to the gallows.' (Dimitrov: 'Very well, I'm most satisfied. . . .')

President: 'I have repeatedly warned you not to make Communist propaganda . . .' (Dimitrov tries to speak on.) 'If you continue in this vein I shall have you put outside. I have told you not to make Communist propaganda, and you cannot wonder that the witness gets angry when you continue to do so. I order you most emphatically to desist from doing so. If you have any questions, then let them be purely factual and nothing more.'

Dimitrov: 'I am highly satisfied with Herr Göring's explanation . . .'

President: 'Whether or not you are satisfied is a matter of complete indifference to me.' (Dimitrov: 'Most satisfied. I am merely asking questions.') 'After your last comment, I must ask you to sit down.' (Dimitrov: 'I'm asking questions.') 'I am asking you to sit down. Do so!'

Dimitrov: 'I am asking a purely factual question.'

President: 'I have asked you to sit down.'

Dimitrov: 'You are greatly afraid of my questions, are you not, Herr Minister?'

Göring: 'You will be afraid when I catch you. You wait till I get you out of the power of this Court, you crook!'
President: 'Dimitrov is expelled for three days. Out with him!' (Dimitrov is hustled out.)

A Swiss comment was:

The public applauded enthusiastically. They did not appreciate the full significance of what had just been happening: the whole trial had been turned into a farce. For the world had been told that, no matter whether the accused was sentenced or acquitted by the Court, his fate had already been sealed.[21]

GOEBBELS

Dimitrov's meeting with Goebbels promised to produce another highlight of the trial. It took place four days later, on 8 November.

Unlike Göring, Goebbels arrived in Court very punctually, and declared his willingness to answer all questions. After a preliminary skirmish, Dimitrov dropped his bombshell: he asked whether or not Goebbels had made a broadcast in which he had blamed the Reichstag fire not only on the Communists but also on the Social Democrats. Dimitrov's purpose in asking this question was quite plain: if Goebbels now admitted he had been wrong about the Social Democrats, might he not have been equally wrong about the Communists? The following dialogue then ensued:

Goebbels: 'I shall gladly answer this question. I have the impression that Dimitrov is using this Court as a platform for making propaganda for the Communist or the Social Democratic Party. Now I know what propaganda means, and he is quite wrong to think that he can trip me up with such questions. If we accuse the Communists, we do not forget their close relationship with the Social Democrats...'
Dimitrov: 'In the autumn of 1932, under the Papen and Schleicher government, a series of bomb attacks took place in Germany. As a result, there were trials and a number of death sentences were passed on National Socialists. I should like to know if these terrorist acts in 1932 were not committed by National Socialists?'
Goebbels: 'It is possible that *agents provocateurs* might have been planted in the National Socialist Party to commit such acts. The National Socialist Party has always used legal means; that is why it preferred running the risk of an internal crisis to coming to terms with its violent Stennes wing.' [This part of the evidence was not published by the German press.]

Dimitrov: 'Is the witness aware that National Socialists, who were condemned to death for the murder of an opponent, were released and demonstratively greeted by Chancellor Hitler?'

Goebbels: 'I know that Dimitrov is referring to the Potempa case [where five Nazis were sentenced to death for killing a man in his bedroom]. The National Socialists involved felt they were right to do away with a Polish insurgent who had betrayed Germany under the guise of being a Communist official. They were condemned for this. The Führer felt he could not desert these men, who thought they acted in the interest of the Fatherland, on the foot of the scaffold, and sent them telegraphic greetings.'

Dimitrov: 'Does the witness realize that many political murders were committed in Germany? That the Communist leaders Karl Liebknecht and Rosa Luxemburg were murdered . . .'

President: 'Silence! We are trying to find out who set the Reichstag on fire. We can't possible delve back so far into the past.'

Goebbels: 'We might as well talk about Adam and Eve. When these murders you complain of were committed, our movement had not even been born.'

Dimitrov: 'Were not the assassins of German statesmen like Erzberger and Rathenau the associates of the National Socialist Party. . . ?'

President: 'I cannot allow this question unless the Minister wishes to answer it specifically.'

Goebbels: 'I do not wish to evade this question. The murders of Erzberger and Rathenau were not committed by associates of the National Socialist Party. At the time, our movement was still very small and restricted to Munich. I am a National Socialist, and I am ready to answer for everything the National Socialist movement has done and omitted to do. At the time, Hitler was in the military hospital in Pasewalk, suffering from war-blindness. I cannot tell who the culprits were. Some fled abroad, some were shot by the Prussian police or committed suicide. Most of these people are no longer alive, and I am not particularly interested in them.'

Dr Werner: 'I consider it extremely courteous of the Minister to answer this question, but I submit that it would be far better not to allow such questions to be answered at all, for they are only asked for propaganda purposes.'

Goebbels: 'I am merely answering Dimitrov's questions in order that the world press shall not be able to say that, in the face of his questions, I remained downcast and silent. I have given reason and answer to greater men than this little Communist agitator.'

Dimitrov: 'All these questions arise out of the political case against

229

me. My accusers allege that the Reichstag fire was meant to overthrow the German constitution. I now ask what sort of constitution was in force on January 30th and which on February 27th?'

Goebbels: 'The Weimar Constitution–for better or for worse. It was legal and we recognized it as such. What changes in it had to be made we did not wish to leave to the Communists but reserved for ourselves. I consider that constitutional changes are necessary.'

Dimitrov: 'That is clear proof that you have no respect for the German Constitution.'

President: 'Leave the Constitution alone!'

Dimitrov: 'Are you aware, Herr Minister, that your spiritual brothers, the National Socialists in Austria and Czechoslovakia, have also to work with illegal methods, with false addresses and false signatures?'

Goebbels: 'It seems to me that you are trying to insult the National Socialist movement. I will answer you with Schopenhauer: Every man deserves to be looked at but not to be spoken to.'

There followed a brief duel between Goebbels and Torgler, who reminded the Court that strikes and not violence had always been the chosen weapons of the German working class. He himself had always tried to keep the political struggle to one of intellectual weapons.

Then Dr Goebbels turned, ostensibly to the Court, but in reality to the world press, and revealed the true reason for his and Göring's performances in Court:

'Herr President, I have been at the greatest pains to contradict the accusations which are made against the German Government and the National Socialists with minute scrupulosity. That is the reason why I have gone to such lengths in describing all the circumstances surrounding the crime, and all the known facts. On behalf of the German Government I express regret that the lying accusations made in the *Brown Book* are still being circulated abroad and that the foreign press has done nothing to remedy this state of affairs. I expect the foreign press to be decent enough to report the facts I have given, and to cease publishing vile slanders about a decent, diligent and honourable people.'

Goebbels's attempt to administer an antidote to the *Brown Book* misfired altogether, not least thanks to Dimitrov's refusal to put the 'right' kind of questions. *Le Temps*, for instance, wrote on 10 November 1933:

In his evidence yesterday, in the trial against the alleged incendiaries of the Reichstag, Dr Goebbels seems to have addressed himself to the foreign press. He requested that his statements should be fully reported. The Minister of Propaganda is deceiving himself if he imagines that he has contributed anything new to the content of the trial.[22]

And the *Brown Book* concluded gleefully:

For the most part, the foreign press was not satisfied with Goebbels's 'real' account of the facts. His appearance before the Court was received with as little favour as his colleague's had been. In his foreword to Dr Sack's book on the trial (*Reichstagsbrandprozess*, p. 12) Professor Grimm openly expresses regrets that despite Goebbels's appeal the results in the foreign press were and remain unfavourable. He particularly pointed to the treatment of Göring's evidence by the foreign press and complained that instead of being accepted as contradicting the accusations of the *Brown Book* it was largely taken as confirming them![23]

Clearly Dr Goebbels, too, had lost his battle against Münzenberg and Dimitrov.

When it became clear that neither Göring's heavy broadsword nor Goebbels's nimble foil had succeeded in subduing the irrepressible Dimitrov, the atmosphere in the courtroom changed perceptibly. Foreign observers like Douglas Reed suggested that the Court felt it could obviously not be expected to succeed where such great men as Göring and Goebbels had so signally failed. The lawyers, and particularly Dr Sack who had continually asked Dimitrov to refrain from making remarks behind his back, were suddenly on smiling terms with him: 'Dr Bünger at times became almost paternal in his altercations with Dimitrov; Dimitrov was occasionally seen roaring with laughter at some joke he shared with his police custodians.'[24]

This relaxation of the courtroom atmosphere was greatly helped by Dimitrov's correct manner. Thus, on 25 November 1933, he had the following brief exchange with Dr Bünger:

President: 'Dimitrov, a foreign newspaper has said that it is you who are really conducting this trial. I must gainsay this, but you will see that your manner makes this impression on public opinion. You must submit yourself to my authority and I desire that in future you restrict yourself to asking questions.'

Dimitrov: 'As defendant, I recognize only one superior, and that is

231

the President of the Court. But I beg my superior to give me the possibility of defending myself and elucidating the truth.'

He had the last word once again.

DIMITROV'S 'SATANIC CIRCLE'

Just as famous as Dimitrov's description of van der Lubbe as the 'Faust of the Reichstag fire' who danced to the tune of an unknown Mephistopheles (an unmistakable allusion to Dr Goebbels with his club foot) was his reference to a 'satanic circle of prosecution witnesses'.

The whole thing was based on a ring Dimitrov had drawn to illustrate the roles played in the Reichstag fire by:

1. Berthold Karwahne
2. Kurt Frey
3. Dr Ernst Dröscher
4. Major Hans Weberstedt.

Berthold Karwahne, who was born in Silesia on 3 October 1877, and whom nature had underendowed with scruples and over-endowed with a love of brutality, threw himself into politics at an early age. At first, he joined the Social Democrats, but at the end of World War I he moved further and further to the Left, ending up with the Communist Party in 1920. In 1927, he made a complete volte-face and went over to the National Socialists, who always received reinforcements from that quarter with open arms.

That same year Karwahne was appointed an alderman; shortly afterwards he was elected a Member of the Diet, and in 1930 a Member of Parliament. The Reichstag Handbook wisely refrained from mentioning anything other than his date and place of birth – clearly a full *curriculum vitae* would have proved extremely embarrassing to himself and to his political friends.

Over the years Karwahne managed to climb higher and higher up the Nazi ladder. In 1933, he was made Head of the State Chemical Syndicate in which capacity he persecuted his political opponents with such atrocity that his name still makes his former colleagues wince today.

After the collapse of the Third Reich, which had helped Karwahne to amass a small fortune, a well-known Hanover lawyer said of him: 'He is the most despicable and infamous man I have ever met – and I have met many despicable characters in my job! He is a bully lacking any sense of fairness, decency or morality.'

Others have called him a 'petty but sadistic man' and 'a spineless, brutal fellow'. To Torgler's Counsel, Dr Sack, Karwahne must have been anathema, not only because of his political past but also because of his bearing in Court. Thus while Dr Sack never disguised his personal respect for the Communist Ernst Torgler, no one in Court was left in any doubt about the contempt in which he held his fellow National Socialist Karwahne.

On one occasion, Dr Sack asked Karwahne why, on allegedly seeing van der Lubbe in the company of Torgler, he had immediately said to himself: 'That is one of the typical criminals Torgler always has round him.'

Karwahne, taken unawares, denied the whole thing, and Dr Bünger intervened at once to say that he, too, could not remember having heard the witness say anything of the sort. When the record proved Dr Sack right and the President wrong, Karwahne conceded quite nonchalantly: 'If it's in the record and if the stenographers have put it down like that, then I might easily have said it. No doubt it's slipped out of my mind.'

In the verdict, the evidence of Karwahne (and of his two companions) was described as being of little value, 'the more so because they might have been involuntarily influenced by the [police] remark: "That one [van der Lubbe] is the incendiary", and because they were already convinced the man they had seen in the Reichstag must be the culprit.' Moreover, whereas they had described van der Lubbe's features (which they had had every opportunity of studying at police headquarters) in exact detail, they were unable to say anything at all about the most unusual clothes van der Lubbe had worn – no wonder, for when they saw him in the police station he was wearing a rug over his shoulders! And yet, Karwahne and his companions were no more to blame than the police, who had quite unlawfully allowed them to take a good look at the criminal and then to 'identify' him later.

It was this very police misdemeanour which probably saved Torgler's life, for Karwahne would have been quite capable of 'identifying' van der Lubbe as Torgler's companion without ever having seen him anywhere. In that case, however, Dr Sack might not have been able to call Karwahne's bluff.

The Austrian Nazi, Stefan Kroyer, fared no better in Court than his friend Berthold Karwahne. The Court had this to say of his alleged identification of van der Lubbe:

> Kroyer was and remains under the spell of his original statement, for he himself admits that any retraction of his statement to the police is hardly possible inasmuch as – for better or for worse – he wrote an article about it three days after his return to Austria.

All that can be said in favour of this witness is that he was a simpleton, one whom Dimitrov found particularly good bait:

> Dimitrov: 'The witness lives in Austria. We all know that the National Socialist Party is illegal in Austria, and that the members live and work illegally.'
> President: 'These remarks are uncalled for.'
> Dimitrov: 'Does the witness know that National Socialists are living in Austria using false names and failing to report to the police?'
> President: 'I cannot allow this question.'
> Dimitrov: 'Does the witness know that National Socialist refugees live in Germany with false passports?'
> President: 'I cannot allow this question.'
> Dimitrov: 'Do not Austrian National Socialists print newspapers and leaflets abroad and send them to Austria?'
> President: 'What has all that to do with the Reichstag fire?'
> Dimitrov: 'In the indictment, Herr Parrisius has accused me, a Bulgarian Communist, of living in Germany illegally on a false passport and working illegally for the Bulgarian Communist Party.'

When Kroyer objected that there is a great difference between a Bulgarian meddling in German affairs and an Austrian working in the Fatherland, Dimitrov retorted:

> 'Of course, there is a difference between my Communism and your National Socialism. It is the difference between heaven and hell.'

    ·   ·   ·   ·   ·

The Nazi Deputy, Kurt Frey, from Munich, came off slightly better in the verdict.

Frey, too, had alleged that, when showing Kroyer over the Reichstag, he had noticed Torgler in the company of a badly dressed individual with a 'curly shock of hair and a coarse, common face'.[25] But when Frey was first confronted with van der Lubbe, he was unable to maintain his original identification, and he was accordingly commended on his honesty in the verdict.

Now, though Frey corrected one error, he persisted in a second, viz. that he had seen Popov and Torgler huddled together on a sofa outside the Communist Party rooms in the Reichstag.

In the verdict, the Court agreed with Torgler that he had shared the sofa not with Popov but with the Communist Deputy, Dr Neubauer, who, from a distance, could easily be mistaken for Popov. Frey's evidence in that respect lacked 'inner probability'. Unfortunately, the Court forgot this question of probability when, in the absence of any tangible evidence, it nevertheless insisted that van der Lubbe must have had accomplices.

The testimony of the National Socialist Press Officer, Major Hans Weberstedt, proved to be a most unseemly mixture of sheer fantasy and parade-ground swagger.

It was he who had 'immediately identified' two men waiting outside Judge Vogt's chambers – van der Lubbe and Tanev – as the two men he had seen together on the day of the fire. This fable was seized upon by Vogt, who at once issued a press communiqué to the effect that van der Lubbe's 'association with foreign Communists was an established fact'.

When the major repeated this fable in Court, Tanev protested that Weberstedt was either mistaken or telling an untruth, whereupon Weberstedt roared at him in his most solemn parade-ground voice: 'I wish to declare that a German officer neither lies nor makes mistakes.'

Tanev then pointed to the many contradictions in the major's evidence, and stressed the fact that, since he (Tanev) did not speak a word of German, let alone Dutch, he could not possibly have carried on a conversation with van der Lubbe.

When Tanev sat down, Dimitrov put the following question to the major:

'Did you discuss these things with Dr Dröscher?'

Weberstedt: 'Of course.'

Dimitrov: 'Very well, then. Weberstedt and Dröscher talked the thing over. Weberstedt saw Tanev, Dröscher saw Dimitrov. At the risk of being expelled from the Court again, I should like to ask the following question. I am my own defender. Did these two witnesses divide the parts between them? Is that how German officers behave?'

Though Dimitrov was strongly rebuked by the President, the verdict nevertheless dispelled the myth that a German officer does not lie or err, for it stated that Weberstedt probably fell victim to an unwitting act of self-deception when he identified Tanev after he had had a good look at him first. 'His belief that Tanev was the right man was not spontaneous, but the result of long reflection. . . . Weberstedt probably confused Tanev with the witness Bernstein, especially as he claimed to have seen Tanev in the Reichstag frequently when, in fact, Tanev had only entered Germany on 24 February.'

Torgler was able to refute another of the major's allegations, namely that Communists – including a striking number of foreigners – were always congregating in the Communist Party rooms in the Reichstag. As Torgler explained, any such meetings could only have taken place with the express permission of the Speaker. That was particularly true of one meeting which Weberstedt had considered 'most suspicious'. In fact,

> Göring, the Speaker of the Reichstag, gave us permission to hold this meeting; Göring, the Minister of the Interior, later prohibited the meeting by special decree. I then lodged a complaint against Göring the Minister of the Interior with Göring the Speaker of the Reichstag.

The verdict also dismissed the evidence of the journalist, Dr Ernst Dröscher, the man who had first spread the rumour that Georgi Dimitrov had been responsible for the bombing of Sofia cathedral – a rumour which Judge Vogt had handed on to the press without bothering to check its accuracy.

Dröscher had also alleged that he had seen Torgler in the company of a man whom he had 'recognized' as the Sofia assassin from a photograph, adding: 'The man had so typical and expressive a face that I could not possibly have mistaken him.'[26]

Now, as we saw, the photograph was not of Georgi Dimitrov, who had had to flee Bulgaria after the abortive uprising of 1923, but of the lawyer Stefan Dimitrov Todorov, who wore a beard while Georgi Dimitrov was clean-shaven.

With such witnesses the Public Prosecutor and the National Socialists were quite unable to make an impression on the Court, let alone on world opinion. The zeal with which, according to the Court, these witnesses tried to 'contribute to the elucidation of the truth' was rightly considered by most observers to be zeal in quite a different direction.

236

THE 'RED' SATANIC CIRCLE

On 27 February 1934 – the anniversary of the Reichstag fire –
Dimitrov held a press conference in Moscow. In it he said:

> ... in prison and in Court we were heartened by the knowledge that
> the great German Communist Party continued to stand firm. Loyalty
> and devotion to their Party could be read on the faces of the working-
> class witnesses who had been dragged into the Court from the
> concentration camps . . .

In a subsequent interview, Dimitrov paid similar compliments
to the 'indomitable' Communist witnesses, and the *Brown Book*,
too, eulogized their heroic stand in Court.

All these praises were meant to hide the awkward truth – the
'bankruptcy of Communist solidarity' as the *Neue Zürcher Zeitung*
called it on 23 October 1933.

True, there were quite a few witnesses from the concentration
camps who, to the utter dismay of the Presiding Judge, insisted on
speaking the truth now that their oppressors were no longer
standing over them. Bünger blustered and interrupted them at
every conceivable opportunity, for they proved a source of extreme
embarrassment to the Court.

But it was, in any case, not by prisoners dragged from concentration camps against their will, but by ex-Communist volunteers
that the moral bankruptcy of the Communist Party was laid bare.
These men formed a circle no less repulsive than Dimitrov's circle
of Nazi witnesses.

In October 1933, the glazier Gustav Lebermann from Hamburg,
who was serving a prison sentence for theft and fraud, told the
Court that he had been a secret Communist courier before resigning
from the Party.

He went on to tell a hair-raising story made up of odd pieces of
information which he had obviously gleaned from reading reports
of the trial. Thus he alleged that he had met Torgler in Hamburg on
25 October 1931, and again in January 1932, when Torgler had told
him to keep himself in readiness for a 'big job'. Torgler would meet
him in Berlin on 6 March and take him to the Reichstag where
Lebermann would receive detailed instructions. All Lebermann
was told at the time was that he would be expected to rush about
the Reichstag like a lunatic in order to focus attention on himself, to

allow himself to be caught, and to 'admit' that he was a National Socialist incendiary. Meanwhile the two real incendiaries – 'Arthur' and 'Black Willy ' – would quickly make their getaway.

When Lebermann refused to have anything to do with so 'mean' a trick, Torgler promised him a reward of 14,000 marks. In July 1932, Torgler visited Lebermann again, and when Lebermann persisted in his refusal, Torgler punched him in the abdomen. He had suffered from abdominal haemorrhages ever since.

While in prison in Lübeck, Lebermann tried to smuggle a letter to his wife. In it he told her he was pretending to be mad in order to be released. He also referred to his chronic stomach disorder. Clearly Torgler's 'punch' had had nothing to do with his haemorrhages.

Lebermann's evidence was so preposterous that even Torgler could not help smiling at it. He told the Court:

> All I can say regarding this evidence is how astonished I am that anyone should utter such lies before the highest Court of the land. I have never seen this man in my life. I have never been in Hamburg for any length of time, and when I did go to Hamburg it was merely to attend meetings of the Union of Post Office Workers, of the Union of Municipal Officials and to address public meetings. Not a single word the witness has spoken is true. Everything he says is a lie, from start to finish.

The impression Lebermann made on the Court was so bad that the President expressed his reluctance to put him under oath.

Even the journalist Adolf Stein, who was highly prejudiced against Torgler, was forced to admit that

> . . . the witness Lebermann really does not look as if he would allow himself to be ill-treated by so slightly built a man as Torgler. Moreover, Lebermann, good anarchist that he is, only remembered the whole business on October 13th, 1933, after he had been reading reports of the Reichstag trial in prison.

Yet so catastrophic was the lack of honest witnesses for the prosecution that the Public Prosecutor could not afford to dispense with even the most disreputable of them. He therefore argued rather lamely:

> 'Admittedly this witness has many previous convictions, and he is

certainly not what the Prosecution could have wished him to be. But that is no reason for doubting his credibility . . . Lebermann's testimony belongs to that category of statements of which I have said that, though they point strongly to Torgler's guilt, they are not in my opinion sufficient by themselves to establish that guilt conclusively.'[27]

Acquitting Torgler, the Court itself found that

. . . no credence whatsoever can be given to the evidence of the witness Lebermann . . . whom the Hamburg County Court has previously described as being of weak character and a morally inferior person . . .

And that was the man whose credibility the Public Prosecutor saw no reason for doubting!

Popov had insisted all along that he had only come to Germany on 3 November 1932. It was to refute this claim that the Public Prosecutor 'found' the locksmith Oscar Kämpfer in a concentration camp. Kämpfer, too, was an old convict whose previous convictions added up to six and a half years' hard labour and one and a half years' preventive detention. He admitted that he had been a member of the Communist Party and a Berlin district leader of the 'Red Aid' organization.

Kämpfer alleged that he had put up Popov at his home, albeit under a false name, from May to July and again in November 1932, both times on Communist Party instructions. One day someone brought Popov a case of bottles, and on one occasion Popov poured a glass of brown fluid down the kitchen sink. The sink smelt of benzol for hours afterwards. Another foreigner, whom Kämpfer identified as Tanev, had also called on Popov.

These allegations brought Popov, who had remained composed throughout the trial, to his feet:

'Even my patience can be exhausted. I have proved with official documents and with witnesses from Russia that I could not have been in Germany at that time. The witness Kämpfer, who has four previous convictions, is trying to buy his release from the concentration camp. His whole testimony is one barefaced lie.'[28]

The Public Prosecutor, however, thought otherwise:

'Kämpfer used to be a well-known member of the Communist Party. A number of witnesses have testified that, whenever the Communists made trouble in his district, he was one of the ringleaders – not that he often went out in front, for he generally preferred to egg others on from the rear. But he is certainly not one to level false accusations against a fellow Communist. In short, there can be no doubt that Popov came to Germany in 1932 and that he tried to conceal his stay.'[29]

The Court produced a still less flattering picture of Kämpfer:

Kämpfer, who has many previous convictions and who is a very un-trustworthy witness, has identified the foreigner who allegedly stayed with him from May onwards as Popov. Now the fact that he also alleged that Tanev asked him for Popov, makes his entire testimony suspect. Tanev did not even have a smattering of German. Kämpfer's fantastic story about a brown fluid . . . merely suggests that he must have read newspaper reports of Dr. Schatz's evidence . . .

To the same category of witnesses as Lebermann and Kämpfer there also belonged the bricklayer, Otto Grothe, a former leader of the Red ex-Servicemen's Union, and since 1921 a member of the Communist Party. He was also Agitprop leader of the 'Red Aid' in the Wedding district of Berlin.

Grothe, who remained a Communist Party member until May 1933, became one of the prosecution's star witnesses, so much so that the indictment devoted no less than eleven pages to his preliminary examination. The crux of his testimony was that, during a meeting on 23 February 1933, a fellow Communist by the name of Kempner had told him that Torgler was planning to burn the Reichstag, with the help of foreigners. Grothe further alleged that Torgler, Thälmann, Popov and other Communists had met on 27 February for a dress rehearsal. This secret meeting had taken place on 'a small bench in the Tiergarten'.

Though Grothe kept changing the names of those who had allegedly attended this secret meeting, Judge Vogt saw no reason at all to distrust him. As a result, Grothe was allowed to take the stand in the Supreme Court, and much time and effort was wasted on what turned out to be a 'psychopathic case, subject to hysteria and psychological disturbances'.[30]

Judge Vogt's credulity is the more surprising in that Grothe had alleged that the meeting at which he was told about Torgler's plans took place in the Karl Liebknecht House on 23 February, a day on which, as Judge Vogt must have known perfectly well, the

Karl Liebknecht House had already been closed by the police.

Characteristically, Grothe had made his first 'confidential reports' to the police while he was still a self-confessed member of the Communist Party.

The Communists, of course, could not swallow the fact that one of their own number should have behaved so despicably, and they accordingly disowned Grothe by claiming he had joined the 'Red Aid' organization as a police spy 'before Hitler came to power'. And indeed he had joined the Communists before that time, – in 1921, to be precise.

When two days of the Supreme Court's deliberations had been wasted on Grothe, Dr Sack's junior, Horst Pelckmann, caused a sensation by charging Grothe with perjury. The Public Prosecutor tried to avert disaster, and argued that Grothe, far from committing perjury, had merely been guilty of an understandable confusion of dates. Even so, the President could not simply ignore Pelckmann's request, and agreed to look into Grothe's evidence.

So weak was the Public Prosecutor's case that he put forward the following, absolutely ridiculous, argument:

> Grothe's testimony has now been checked, above all against that of Kempner from whom Grothe claimed he had received his information. Now, Kempner's outright denial of Grothe's story does not really convince me. Kempner, who is in prison on suspicion of having played a part in the events which form the substance of this trial, has very good reason to deny these allegations; they might easily incriminate Kempner himself.

The Court once again dealt a severe blow to the Public Prosecutor when it dismissed Grothe's testimony as utterly unreliable. In particular, Grothe's story of the meeting in the Tiergarten was called improbable in the highest degree.

In short, Grothe had utterly discredited the Examining Magistrate, the Public Prosecutor, and the Communist Party to which he had belonged.

The miner, Otto Kunzack, another important prosecution witness, had a record of sentences for crimes of violence and sexual offences. At the time of the trial he was in Naumburg Penitentiary.

Kunzack testified that he had been a member of the Communist

Party until March 1932. From 1921 to 1927 he was a secret Communist courier, in which capacity he had attended a secret conference in Düsseldorf in 1925. The conference was presided over by the well-known Communist Heinz Neumann, and attended by no less a person than van der Lubbe. He could remember the latter's name so clearly because it reminded him of the town of Lübben. The young Dutchman had taken part in the discussion and had been so violent that Kunzack had gained the impression he was quite capable of committing any kind of outrage.

Van der Lubbe had further declared his willingness '. . . to go out in front bearing the banner of the revolutionary proletariat'.[31]

Later, Kunzack was forced to admit that van der Lubbe had not delivered his 'fiery speech' in German, as he had originally alleged, but in Dutch. A Swiss reporter mused: 'How fortunate for Kunzack that the Court decided not to put him on oath. For this witness tells the most brazen lies in the most incredibly transparent manner.'[32]

Kunzack stuck to his story even when he was told that, had van der Lubbe really been present at the conference, he would only have been sixteen years old at the time.

When Kunzack, who had boasted that he had been a secret courier, *inter alia* to Heinz Neumann, was asked by Associate-Judge Coenders to identify a photograph, Kunzack looked at it for a long time, and then shook his head. He had fallen into a trap, for the photograph was of Heinz Neumann.[33]

Kunzack's honesty as well as the gullibility of the Examining Magistrate are best appreciated from the fact that Kunzack wrote to Judge Vogt from prison on 24 May 1933, offering to root out the Communist terrorists with the help of their 'female associates', and adding: 'And once I have proved myself, the rest of my sentence will be remitted. And moreover I ask that what time I lose during my interrogation be made good.'[34]

Kunzack's further fantasies included the claims that he had met Torgler in the latter's 'office in the Karl Liebknecht House', when Torgler had no office in that building, and that Torgler and the Deputy Wilhelm Kasper had attended dynamite tests outside Berlin. Torgler's retort that he had never even met Kunzack was dismissed by the Public Prosecutor with: 'Though the accused Torgler denies his part in the events described by the witness Kunzack . . . the Court must accept the latter's testimony.'[35]

Once again, the Court was forced to take a different view – it described the witness Kunzack as a completely untrustworthy person who had tried to gain financial and other advantages from his testimony.

Tanev, too, was falsely accused by two ex-Communists: the merchant Bruno Bannert and the blacksmith Adolf Kratzert.

Bannert alleged that in 1927 and 1928 he had met Tanev every month or so in the 'Red Aid' offices where he (Bannert) had worked as Agitprop leader for the Brandenburg region; and Kratzert alleged he had met Tanev in the Karl Liebknecht House.

All these ex-Communist witnesses proved to be completely consistent in one respect: they all refused to withdraw any part of their baseless denunciations. The collapse of Communist solidarity would therefore have been quite devastating, had Dimitrov and Torgler not helped so much to redress the balance.

FALSE FRIENDS AND BABBLERS

On 28 October, the Supreme Court heard the evidence of the journalist Walther Oehme. It was Oehme who had been mainly responsible for convincing Judge Vogt that Ernst Torgler was a liar, for whereas Torgler had explained that Oehme had called on him in the Reichstag shortly after 3 p.m., and that it was Oehme with whom Karwahne, Kroyer and Frey must have seen him, Oehme insisted that he had not met Torgler before 4 p.m. at the earliest.

Since Torgler had no reasons for believing that Oehme was lying, he desperately searched his memory for another visitor in whose company the three Nazis might have seen him, and suggested that it could have been Communist Deputies Florin or Dr Neubauer. The Public Prosecutor then accused him of trying to change horses in midstream.

In the end, however, Oehme was forced to admit the real truth: he had, in fact, been with Torgler at the time Torgler had originally stated. The incensed Public Prosecutor, who felt Torgler slipping from between his fingers, vented his disappointment in Court: 'Oehme's alleged reason for withdrawing his previous testimony is that he lied in order to protect his own valuable person and therefore betrayed Torgler, whom he is proud to call his friend.'[36]

243

This might have been the right moment for the Public Prosecutor to ask himself whether the 'liar' Torgler might not have been speaking the truth all along.

When Torgler's counsel, Dr Sack, addressed the Court on the Oehme incident, he said:

> I refrain from telling the Court what I think of the witness Oehme, a man who has said he considers it an honour to be called a friend of the accused, Torgler . . . I could sympathize with Torgler if he lost faith in mankind now, if he completely despaired of humanity. But perhaps the accused Torgler must bear his cross, perhaps he will have to drain his cup of bitterness to the last drop.[37]

When Dr Sack spoke these words, he was also thinking of another of Torgler's 'friends' – the Communist deputy Erich Birkenhauer – who, for much the same reasons as Oehme, had lied about Torgler during the preliminary examination, thus enabling the Public Prosecutor to say:

> At the preliminary examination, Birkenhauer testified that he had tried to get in touch with the accused Torgler on the day of the fire and that – as the accused Torgler admits himself – he managed to reach him over the telephone at about 4 p.m. It was arranged that Birkenhauer would ring later in the evening. According to Birkenhauer: 'When I rang again at about 7 p.m., I was told by a woman that Torgler was not available for the moment . . .' Now, it seems most unlikely that a Party secretary should say her chief is not available, had he been next door, in the antechamber, or anywhere near by. In my opinion, it follows that the accused Torgler was not anywhere near the telephone, that the witness Rehme had no idea where he was, or that she did know but did not care to tell. I therefore conclude that Torgler was away from his Party offices at about 7 p.m., i.e. at just about the time that the preparations for setting the Reichstag Session Chamber on fire would have been made.[38]

Torgler kept insisting that Birkenhauer's story about the second telephone call could not possibly be true. However, Birkenhauer had meanwhile fled Germany, and Torgler's counsel could not challenge his testimony in Court. As a result, Judge Vogt became even more convinced that Torgler was a brazen liar.

The Communists tried to cover up Birkenhauer's betrayal by alleging that the Public Prosecutor had deliberately falsified his testimony. Birkenhauer testified before the London Commission that, far from telling him that Torgler was not available, the woman had merely informed him that Torgler was not yet ready to fix the time for a meeting and had asked him to ring again at 8 p.m.

In that case, however, Birkenhauer must have told yet another lie, for the record shows that he declared before Judge Vogt on 17 May that:

> I remember that I rang the Reichstag once before, an hour or so earlier, say at about 7 p.m. . . . . The telephone was answered by a woman. . . . She told me – as far as I can remember – that Herr Torgler was at a conference or at a meeting. I then told her that I would ring again . . . [39]

Birkenhauer's story that he had rung Torgler, not at 4 p.m., as Torgler alleged he had, but at 7 p.m., was denied outright by Fräulein Anna Rehme, Torgler's secretary. The Court found:

> Finally no proof has been adduced that Fräulein Rehme told Deputy Birkenhauer at 7 p.m. that Torgler was at a meeting. In fact, there is no evidence that any call was made at that time. Birkenhauer has fled the country and did not testify before the Supreme Court; his deposition at the preliminary examination is not considered admissible evidence. The witness Rehme does not remember the call, but does remember that Torgler was expecting Birkenhauer's call and that she would certainly have called Torgler to the telephone.

In fact, Birkenhauer made his second call shortly after 8 p.m. Since the telephone exchange had closed down by then, Torgler had to run down to Portal Five where he arranged a meeting with Birkenhauer at Aschinger's. Obviously, Birkenhauer, too, had tried to clear himself of suspicion at the expense of his 'friend'.

The newspaper report that Torgler was suspected of complicity in the fire produced a spate of 'witnesses' who felt they had some helpful contribution to make. Among them were Frau Helene Pretzsch and her stepson Kurt Moeller, both of whom suddenly remembered that they had seen Torgler carrying two large brief-cases on the morning of the fire.

Both witnesses testified that Torgler looked as if he were carrying an exceptionally heavy load. They also noticed that Torgler had a 'shifty' look. Next day, when Frau Pretzsch learned about the Reichstag fire, she immediately said to her stepson: 'Now I know what Torgler was doing with those heavy brief-cases last night!'[40]

Torgler explained that, far from carrying incendiary material, he had filled his brief-cases with large quantities of newspapers, which he had intended reading over the week-end. One of these brief-cases was, in fact, found in his Reichstag rooms, but when it was first shown to the witnesses, they insisted that it was not one that Torgler had been carrying on 27 February. At the trial Moeller was allowed to inspect the ominous brief-case and admitted: 'Well, now that I have seen the brief-case packed with newspapers and have felt its weight, I must admit that there was nothing extra-ordinary in the way Torgler carried it.'[41]

What strikes us as odd today is that such 'classical witnesses', as Dr Sack called them, or such 'slight evidence', as the verdict had it, should have been admitted in the first place.

The palm, however, went to the daytime porter Wilhelm Hornemann, whose evidence earned him a roar of laughter from the public. Hornemann tried to throw suspicion on Torgler by alleging that he had noticed Herr Koenen, Torgler's subsequent companion, 'sneaking' into the Reichstag on the day of the fire at about 6.30 p.m., with his coat-collar turned up and with his glance averted to the left.

The whole thing was, of course, utterly absurd. What well-known deputy of long standing would have thought of sneaking into the Reichstag past the porter, when he knew that the porter had instructions to challenge all strangers?

Nor did Hornemann leave it at that, for he also alleged that on the same afternoon he had seen three men leaving the Reichstag, one of whom – later 'identified' by Hornemann as Dimitrov – had said in broken German: 'The Reichstag is going up in the air in fifteen to twenty minutes.'

Quite obviously Hornemann had not been told of Dimitrov's unshakeable alibi. No wonder that Dimitrov's face was wreathed in smiles through most of Hornemann's evidence.

But who knows what would have happened to Dimitrov had he not, by pure chance, been away from Berlin on 26 and 27 February, had he not returned in a sleeper, whose attendant Otto Wudtke remembered him clearly, and had he not started a mild flirtation with Frau Irmgard Rössler, who was returning from a ski-ing holiday, and to whom Dimitrov had introduced himself as Dr Hediger?

.   .   .   .   .

Another to take pride of place among the 'show-offs and confirmed liars', as Dr Sack called them, was the drunkard Leon
Organistka. Organistka went to the police with the 'important'
news that he and a friend, Oskar Müller by name, had met van der
Lubbe and another Dutchman on 15 October 1932, in the vicinity
of Constance. They had talked, Organistka alleged, of many things,
and he particularly remembered van der Lubbe saying: 'There will
soon be no more Reichstag in Germany,' and: 'If we Communists
don't soon have a turn there's going to be fire and brimstone in
Germany.' He greatly impressed the public by turning to van der
Lubbe during their confrontation with: 'Come on, van der Lubbe,
old mate, surely you haven't forgotten me?'

His friend Müller confirmed Organistka's testimony and basked
in the latter's glory – until an official report from Leyden established
that van der Lubbe had spent the entire October of 1932 in Holland
and that he had regularly fetched his weekly allowance at the
Leyden Post Office in person. The same report also invalidated the
testimony of Helmer who claimed he had frequently seen van der
Lubbe and the two Bulgarians in the Bayernhof.

As moths are attracted to the light, so the witnesses for the
prosecution were attracted by the dazzle of publicity, and by the
glitter of silver. And, like moths, most of them got singed in the
process.

During the appearance of this weird procession of witnesses,
there was much hearty laughter in Court. This laughter must not,
however, let one forget the frightful reality: all these fawning and
servile men were falling over one another in their eagerness to send
innocent men to their death. Sober workmen, good mothers,
chauffeurs, waiters, locksmiths and housewives, babblers and fools,
no less than professional criminals, were doing their utmost to
make their fantasies, lies, or delusions stick at any cost.

DIMITROV'S FINAL SPEECH

On 16 December 1933, one week before judgement was given,
Dimitrov was granted the right to address the Court on his own
behalf.

At last the moment had come for which Dimitrov had worked
throughout the long months of his imprisonment, and though Dr

247

Bünger interrupted him from time to time, Dimitrov proved more than a match for him. After one such interruption, Dimitrov said:

'I admit that my tone is hard and sharp. But my life has been hard and sharp. However, my tone is frank and open. I seek to call things by their correct names. I am not a lawyer appearing before this Court defending just another client. . . .

'I can say with an easy conscience that everything which I have said to this Court is the truth. I have refused to testify on my illegal party. I have always spoken with seriousness and from my deep convictions. . . .'

President: 'I shall not permit you to indulge in Communist propaganda in this Court. You have persisted in it. If you do not refrain, I shall have to prevent you from speaking.'

Dimitrov: 'I must deny absolutely the suggestion that I have pursued propagandist aims. It may be that my defence before this Court has had a certain propagandist effect. . . . If the question of propaganda is to be raised, then I may fairly say that many utterances made in this Court were of a propagandist character. The appearance here of Goebbels and Göring had an indirect propagandist effect favourable to Communism, but no one can hold them responsible because their conduct produced such results (laughter in Court). I have not only been roundly abused by the press – something to which I am completely indifferent – but my people have also, through me, been characterized as savage and barbarous. I have been called a suspicious character from the Balkans and a wild Bulgarian. I cannot allow such things to pass in silence. . . . Only Fascism in Bulgaria is savage and barbarous. But I ask you, Mr President, in what country does not Fascism bear these qualities?'

President: 'Are you attempting to refer to the situation in Germany?'

Dimitrov: 'Of course not, Mr President. At a period of history when the "German" Emperor Karl V vowed that he would talk German only to his horse, at a time when the nobility and intellectual circles of Germany wrote only Latin and were ashamed of their mother tongue, Saint Cyril and Saint Methodius invented and spread the use of old Bulgarian script in my "barbarous" country. . . . During the preliminary inquiries I spoke with officials, members of the investigating authority, concerning the Reichstag fire. Those officials assured me that we Bulgarians were not to be charged with complicity in that crime. We were to be charged solely in connection with our false passports, our adopted names, and our incorrect addresses.'

President: 'This is new matter. It has not been mentioned in the

248

proceedings hitherto and you have no right to raise it at this stage.'

Dimitrov: 'Mr President, during that time every circumstance could have been investigated in order to clear us promptly of any charge in relation to the fire. The indictment declares . . .' (Dimitrov began to quote from the indictment at some length.)

President: 'You must not read the whole of the indictment here. In any case, the Court is quite familiar with it.'

Dimitrov: 'As far as that goes, I must state that three-quarters of what the counsel for the prosecution and defence have said here was generally notorious long ago. But that fact did not prevent them from bringing it forward again (laughter in Court). Helmer stated that Dimitrov and van der Lubbe were together in the Bayernhof restaurant. Now permit me again to refer to the indictment, which says: "Although Dimitrov was not caught red-handed on the scene of the crime, he nevertheless took part in the preparations for the burning of the Reichstag. He went to Munich in order to supply himself with an alibi. . . ." That is the basis of this precipitate, this aborted indictment.'

[Here the President intervened again and warned Dimitrov not to refer disrespectfully to the indictment.]

Dimitrov: 'Very well, Mr President, I shall choose other expressions.'

President: 'In any case you must not use such disrespectful terms.'

Dimitrov: 'Göring declared before the Court that the German Communist Party was compelled to incite the masses and to undertake some violent adventure when Hitler came to power. . . . He stated that the Communist Party had for years been appealing to the masses against the National Socialist Party and that when the latter attained power the Communists had no alternative but to do something immediately or not at all. The Public Prosecutor attempted more clearly and ingeniously to formulate this hypothesis.'

President: 'I cannot permit you to insult the Supreme Court.'

Dimitrov: 'The statement which Göring as chief prosecutor made, was developed by the Public Prosecutor in this Court . . .'

And now Dimitrov really set to work. In particular, he developed the view that the Communist Party could confidently look forward to the speedy collapse of the Hitler Government, and that the glorious example of the Russian revolution was an example to be followed by all mankind.

'. . . What is the Communist International? Permit me to quote from its programme:

' "The Communist International, an international association of workers, is the association of the Communist Parties of individual lands; it is a united world Communist Party . . ."

'. . . A copy of the appeal of the Executive Committee of the Communist International was found in my possession, I take it that I may read from it.'

Dimitrov then read the appeal, and stressed that it made no mention of any immediate struggle for power. He went on to argue:

'The point is simply this: was an armed insurrection aimed at the seizure of power actually planned to take place on February 27th, 1933, in connection with the Reichstag fire?

'What, Your Honours, have been the results of the legal investigation? The legend that the Reichstag fire was a Communist act has been completely shattered. Unlike some counsel here, I shall not quote much of the evidence. To any person of normal intelligence at least this point is now made completely clear, that the Reichstag fire had nothing whatever to do with any activity of the German Communist Party, not only nothing to do with an insurrection, but nothing to do with a strike, a demonstration, or anything of that nature. The Reichstag fire was not regarded by anybody – I exclude criminals and the mentally deranged – as the signal for insurrection. No one observed any deed, act, or attempt at insurrection in connection with the Reichstag fire. The very stories of such things expressly appertain to a much later date . . . But it was shown that the Reichstag fire furnished the occasion and the signal for unleashing the most terrific campaign of suppression against the German working class.'

When Dr Bünger interrupted: 'Not the German working class but the Communist Party,' Dimitrov quickly retorted that Social Democratic and Christian Democratic workmen had been arrested as well, and went on to say:

'The law which was necessary for the proclamation of the state of emergency was directed against all the other political parties and groups. It stands in direct organic connection with the Reichstag fire.'

President: 'If you attack the German Government, I shall deprive you of the right to address the Court.'

Dimitrov: '. . . One question has not been in the least elucidated either by the prosecution or the defending counsel. This omission does not surprise me. For it is a question which must have given them some anxiety. I refer to the question of the political situation in Germany in February, 1933 – a matter which I must perforce deal with now. The political situation towards the end of February, 1933, was such that a bitter struggle was taking place within the camp of the "National Front".'

President: 'You are again raising matters which I have repeatedly forbidden you to mention.'

Dimitrov: 'I should like to remind the Court of my application that Schleicher, Brüning, von Papen, Hugenberg and Duesterburg should be summoned as witnesses.'

President: 'The Court rejected the application and you have no right to refer to it again.'

Dimitrov: 'I know that, and more, I know why!'

President: 'It is unpleasant for me continually to have to interrupt your closing speech, but you must respect my directions. . . . You have always implied that your sole interest was the Bulgarian political situation. Your present remarks, however, show that you were also keenly interested in the political situation in Germany.'

Dimitrov: 'Mr President, you are making an accusation against me. I can only make this reply: that as a Bulgarian revolutionary I am interested in the revolutionary movement all over the world. I am, for instance, interested in the political situation in South America, and although I have never been there, I know as much about it as I do of German politics. That does not mean that when a Government building in South America is burned down, I am the culprit.'

He then proffered his own theory of the part played by van der Lubbe, which was merely a copy of the Nazi theory, but with the 'link' shifted from Neukölln to Henningsdorf and with a change of principals:

'Is it not probable that van der Lubbe met someone in Henningsdorf on February 26th and told him of his attempts to set fire to the Town Hall and the Palace? Whereupon the person in question replied that things such as those were mere child's play, that the burning down of the Reichstag during the elections would be something real? Is that not probably the manner in which, through an alliance between political provocation and political insanity, the Reichstag fire was conceived? While the representative of political insanity sits today in the dock, the representative of political provocation has disappeared. Whilst this tool, van der Lubbe, was carrying out his clumsy attempts at arson in the corridors and cloakrooms, were not other unknown persons preparing the conflagration in the Session Chamber and making use of the secret inflammable liquid of which Dr Schatz has spoken?

'The unknown accomplices made all the preparations for the conflagration and then disappeared without a trace. Now this stupid fool, this miserable Faust, is here in the dock, but Mephistopheles has disappeared. The link between van der Lubbe and the representatives of political provocation, the enemies of the working class, was forged in Henningsdorf.'

Dimitrov went on to complain that no attempt whatever had been made to trace the man with whom van der Lubbe passed the night in Henningsdorf. He further complained that the identity of the civilian who first reported the fire to the Brandenburg Gate police station had never been revealed:

'The incendiaries were sought where they were not to be found. . . . As the real incendiaries could not and must not be found, other persons were taken in their stead.'

President: 'I forbid you to make such statements and I give you another ten minutes only.'

Dimitrov: 'I have the right to lay my own reasoned proposals for the verdict of the Court. The Public Prosecutor stated that all the evidence given by Communists was not worthy of credence. I shall not adopt the contrary view. Thus I shall not declare that all the evidence given by National Socialist witnesses is unreliable. I shall not say they are all liars, for I believe that amongst the millions of National Socialists there are some honest people.'

President: 'I forbid you to make such ill-intentioned remarks.'

Ordered by the President to conclude, Dimitrov finally proposed the following verdict:

'1. That Torgler, Popov, Tanev and myself be pronounced innocent and that the indictment be quashed as ill-founded;

'2. That van der Lubbe be declared to be the misused tool of the enemies of the working classes;

'3. That those responsible for the false charges against us be made criminally liable for them;

'4. That we be compensated for the losses which we have sustained through this trial, for our wasted time, our damaged health, and for the sufferings which we have undergone.

'. . . The elucidation of the Reichstag fire, and the identification of the real incendiaries is a task which will fall to the People's Court of the future proletarian dictatorship . . .'

Since Dimitrov gave no sign that he had any intention of concluding – the notes which he published subsequently indicate that he would have gone on for a very long time – the President, whose patience was completely exhausted, adjourned the Court, and Dimitrov had to be removed by force.

When the Court returned, Popov and Tanev delivered lengthy addresses which had to be translated sentence by sentence. Then it was Torgler's turn, whose final speech was as brief as it was to the point. Before he rose at 9 p.m. to adjourn the Court for a week, Dr Bünger had this to say:

> 'When I opened the proceedings nearly three months ago, I said that it was the custom, not only of the German press, but of newspapers the world over, not to prejudge the issues which this Court has been called upon to decide. . . .
> 'Unfortunately my remarks have not been fully heeded. The foreign press has not been alone in attempting to anticipate these proceedings in a manner which does no credit to its noble calling. I can only repeat, once again, that the clash of opinions cannot influence this Court.'

When Dr Bünger admonished 'not only the foreign press' he was clearly alluding to a recent interview Göring had given to the *Berliner Nachtausgabe*. In it Göring had complained that the Supreme Court trial was a great disappointment to the German people. When it came to dealing with vile political criminals, it was simply not good enough to keep to the letter of the law. Göring had added that the authority of the state and the safety of Germany would be undermined if this lengthy trial were allowed to continue much longer.[42]

Göring's outburst presented the judges with a terrible dilemma. How could they possibly satisfy the irate new rulers of Germany, and yet let it appear that justice was not being flouted too flagrantly? After nine long months of collecting depositions and testimonies, could they now admit that they had been quite unable to form any kind of reasonable picture of the real course of events on that icy night of 27 February?

The result was a blatant compromise, so blatant, in fact, that only because no one at the time was interested in the plain truth, could it be put forward at all.

12. The Experts

TWO FIRE EXPERTS

ONCE the Court had made up its mind to disbelieve van der Lubbe, it was willy-nilly driven into the arms of the so-called 'fire-experts'.

When the Public Prosecutor began to bore his way through the mountain of papers which the Examining Magistrate had bequeathed to him, he discovered to his dismay that no two of Dr Vogt's experts had agreed on the origins or the development of the Reichstag fire. To make things worse, each of the experts had tried to reconcile his particular opinion with the incompatible statements of various prosecution witnesses.

When Professor Emil Josse, a lecturer on thermodynamics at the Berlin Technical College, produced his opinion in May, he became the first of a series of experts who hid their profound ignorance of the facts behind a barrage of words. What had 'struck him so particularly' was the 'explosive disintegration of the Session Chamber', from which he concluded:

> Had there been no explosion or rather had the Session Chamber not been filled with an explosive mixture of gases, the small fires could quickly have been extinguished by the fire brigade – just as they were in the restaurant – so that the damage would have remained relatively small.

One week later, Fire Director Wagner, Chief of the Berlin Fire Brigade, came out with quite a different view when he said:

> If we bear in mind the special conditions prevailing in the Chamber, we shall find that the development of the fire, as the witnesses have described it, fits in perfectly with our experience of the development of fires in general. During the three minutes under discussion, from 9.18 to 9.21 p.m. that is, there was still quite enough oxygen in the large chamber to allow for complete and smokeless combustion ...

Professor Josse, who remained firmly convinced that the whole fire had been carefully planned, kept cudgelling his brain as to why the incendiaries should have bothered to set fire to the restaurant, thus 'giving the whole game away'. He concluded that there were two possibilities:

1. The restaurant was set on fire at random, which seems unlikely in view of there having been a complete plan, and which could only have happened had van der Lubbe started the fire by himself, or
2. The incendiaries hoped that, by starting the fire in the restaurant, they would obtain particularly quick results and wreak maximum havoc, so much so that they decided to run the risk of being discovered.

Professor Josse thought the key to this mystery was an 'extra' ventilator, However:

'If we postulate that, by starting the fire in the restaurant, the incendiaries hoped to take advantage of the fanning effects of the additional ventilator, then we must also postulate that an unforeseen circumstance led to a change in the plan since . . . the additional ventilator was apparently not working . . .'

Only Lewis Carroll could have thought up a more preposterous argument than that, or, for that matter, than the one with which Dr Josse came out on 23 October 1933: 'The main purpose of starting the fire outside the Session Chamber was to divert attention from the latter.'

This was too much even for the Public Prosecutor who pointed out that had the restaurant not been fired, the fire in the Session Chamber might not have been discovered until very much later.

Professor Josse was also the first to propound the theory that the incendiary material had been smuggled into the Reichstag long before the fire, and that it had been stored in the stenographers' well. That was also the view of Dr Schatz.

Imagine, then, the surprise of these two great experts and the disappointment of all those others who believed in their simple theories, when it appeared that the suspected well had been cleaned from top to bottom on the afternoon of the fire, that it had been personally inspected by Scranowitz, and that the liftman Fraedrich, who had wound up the clock there at 4 p.m. had seen nothing suspicious.[1]

After Professor Josse had finished giving his evidence, the President addressed the following remarks to van der Lubbe:

'Raise your head, van der Lubbe. Did you understand what has been said here? The expert, who is a learned professor, has told us that you could not have fired the Reichstag all by yourself. Who helped you? Answer me that!'

But Marinus van der Lubbe had long ago decided not to enter into any further useless and senseless discussions. He kept silent.

Afraid that van der Lubbe might have had no Nazi accomplices after all, Dimitrov put the following question to Professor Josse:

'Is it at all possible that van der Lubbe could have laid the fire trail within a quarter of an hour, or that he himself could have started the fire in the Session Chamber?'

To Dimitrov's disappointment, Professor Josse replied without any hesitation:

'I have reflected on this question at length. For a time I believed that he could not have done so; but when, during the on-site inspection, I saw the speed with which Lubbe crashed through the windows and was told that he was in a lather of sweat when he was arrested, I came to the conclusion that he might have done it with adequate preparation.'[2]

When Dr Teichert, the Bulgarians' counsel, next asked Josse what van der Lubbe had done with the containers of the 50 lbs of liquid fuel with which, according to the Professor, he had started the fire (the debris had been searched immediately after the fire and no traces of any such containers had been found), Dr Josse was at a loss for an answer. Nor, as Professor Urbain of the Sorbonne rightly objected, could he tell on what scientific data he had based his estimate of 50 lbs. Professor Urbain also attacked Josse and particularly Dr Schatz for putting forward the view that

... the Session Chamber was set on fire by means of a liquid hydrocarbon. .... Tables and chairs were covered with rags soaked in petrol or paraffin. .... The rags were then sprinkled with a self-igniting fluid or joined to one another by means of fuses or celluloid strips, probably the latter.

As Professor Urbain pointed out, petrol and paraffin do not produce the kind of flames all the witnesses had described. Fire Director Wagner added the view that no volatile liquids could have been used, since otherwise all the rags would have flared up simultaneously. In that case, no separate bundles of flames would have been produced or observed. According to Wagner, experiments in the Reichstag had shown that a large number of separate

THE TRIAL

fires could not have been started with reels of celluloid film, or with petrol and paraffin.

Dr Ritter, a Government technical officer, agreed with Wagner:

It seems unlikely that mineral oils, for instance petrol, were used to start the fire. During the lengthy preparations a large part of the petrol would have evaporated, later to be precipitated as heavy vapour. Had the incendiary tried to run a fuse through that vapour, flames would quickly have spread over the entire incendiary system, possibly with explosive effects.

With commendable honesty Dr Ritter concluded:

On the available evidence it is quite impossible to decide how the fire in the Session Chamber was started.

No wonder he was dropped out of the experts' and the Court's further deliberation.

On 23 October 1933, when Professor Josse, Dr Wagner and Dr Schatz were cross-examined in open Court, the public was astonished to learn how radically they differed on even the most elementary questions. As a Dutch newspaper put it at the time:

This has been a very important day, for it has shown how shaky are the foundations which these experts have erected.

Being poets and dreamers, they do not try to justify their respective theories with facts, but simply produce the theories and leave it to the Court and the prosecution to do the rest. They keep shooting arrows into the blue, and if mistakes occur – well, van der Lubbe must have made them, for compared with these gentlemen, he is a mere tyro when it comes to starting fires. They are all agreed that he could not have done it by himself. For the rest they beg to differ. But that is their privilege – they are the experts, after all.[3]

DR SCHATZ

Chemical discussions in Court paved the way for the appearance of that remarkable chemical expert, Dr Wilhelm Schatz, the man whose astonishing performance, mental acrobatics, and sleights of hand, left an indelible impression on all who watched him.

At the time, Dr Schatz was Head of the 'Private Institute for Scientific Criminology'. He was an extremely busy and versatile man: a court-expert on chemistry, fingerprints, type, a graphologist, a pharmacist, a food expert, a botanist, a toxicologist, and a scientific criminologist – in short, a Jack-of-all-trades. Another remarkable thing about him was that he usually wrote his opinions on the inside of used envelopes or on the backs of old letters, all of which he hid from his assistants and collaborators with a great show of secretiveness.

Despite – or perhaps because of – his great versatility, Dr Schatz did not enjoy a particularly good name in chemical and scientific circles. For one thing, his manner was most unprepossessing, for another he was generally considered to be a pompous and disputatious ass. The highly-respected chemist Dr Brüning called him a fantasy-monger, and the *Neue Zürcher Zeitung* a 'malicious expert'. Berlin chemical circles wondered why on earth the Court should have called in a dubious provincial chemist in the first place, and there were rumours that he was not a disinterested party. There certainly was no doubt that Judge Vogt had 'briefed' Dr Schatz carefully on van der Lubbe's so-called accomplices.

Now, by that time even Judge Vogt had come to appreciate that Torgler could not have been in the Reichstag at the time of the fire. However, he had apparently been out of his rooms between 7 and 8 p.m., during which time he might have been 'preparing' the fire, that is sprinkling petrol or some other inflammable fluid over curtains, carpets, chairs, etc.

Unfortunately, no one at all could be found who was willing or able to testify that Torgler had smelt of any of these pungent substances, nor was Professor Brüning able to detect any signs of such substances having been used. To help Judge Vogt out of the resulting impasse, Dr Schatz obligingly invented a mysterious igniting fluid, which Torgler might easily have sprinkled about between 7 and 8 p.m.

At the request of Dr Sack, Schatz, who had previously told the Court that he would not mention the name of that mysterious fluid lest other incendiaries came to hear of it, now described one of its properties: it smelt strongly of chloroform.

But, alas, no one had noticed Torgler smelling of chloroform either; hence Dr Schatz was forced to ask all sorts of silly questions. On 14 October, for example, he asked Chief Fire Director Gempp whether the liquid which Gempp alleged he had detected in the Bismarck Hall, had not smelt like rotten cabbage. Gempp, who had previously 'smelt' petrol, said he could not remember.

One day before, on 13 October, Dr Schatz had put the following question to Lieutenant Lateit: 'You have stated that you saw no smoke, but that you smelt smoke. Did you notice a peculiar smell or taste in your mouth or throat?'

When Lateit said no, Dr Schatz coaxed him with: 'Not at all?' Again the witness said no, but Dr Schatz refused to give up:

> Dr. Schatz: 'Do you know the smell given off by a smoky lamp – for instance by an old-fashioned oil lamp? Was the smell like that?'
>
> Lateit: 'No.'
>
> Dr. Schatz: 'You testified that your eyes were smarting.'
>
> Lateit: 'That was downstairs, when we came in through Portal Two, and were met by thick smoke. My men were completely blinded; our eyes were smarting and streaming so much that we had to cover our faces with handkerchiefs.'
>
> Dr. Schatz: 'Do you know the smell of the old kind of matches, you know the ones with phosphorus and sulphur? When you struck them, you got a strange prickling sensation in the nose and a taste resembling the one you get when you eat eggs with a silver spoon. Did you have that sensation?'
>
> Lateit: 'No.'

When Patrolman Losigkeit and House-Inspector Scranowitz corroborated Lateit's evidence, it became obvious that no one at all had smelt anything in support of Dr Schatz's theory. On the contrary, Dr Brüning's analysis had established that the trail which Gempp had described was not due to any inflammable or self-igniting fluid. Only one witness swore to the theory of the great expert Dr Schatz. That witness was the expert Dr Schatz himself.

But even he was left with the problem of why Torgler had not smelt of the miracle-fluid whose odour was supposed to stick to one for hours. He accordingly had a new inspiration and performed a secret experiment. The result was quite astounding:

> He explained that though he had rubbed his hands with the self-inflammatory fluid, two policemen and two Reichstag officials were quite unable to detect any smell even when he held his hands very close to their faces.[4]

Suddenly the strong and persistent smell was no longer; suddenly the smell of chloroform and rotten cabbage had evaporated, and – Torgler could remain a suspect.

Then Dr Schatz produced his second bombshell: van der Lubbe had never even set foot in the Session Chamber; the Chamber was fired by his accomplices. Asked by Dr Sack how these accomplices had managed to get in and out of the Reichstag, the great expert replied that he preferred to keep his own counsel on that subject since, after all, he was merely a scientific expert.

When Torgler thereupon implored Dr Schatz to forgo his scientific modesty for the sake of four innocent men, Dr Schatz could do no better than rehash an old theory: van der Lubbe's conspicuous behaviour in the restaurant could only have meant that he was trying to divert attention from his accomplices in the Chamber.

Douglas Reed has described the conclusion of Dr Schatz's testimony:

'If I have understood this interesting address aright,' said Dimitrov gravely, addressing himself to Dr. Schatz, 'a certain technical knowledge must be assumed on the part of persons employing this method of incendiarism?'

'The people who deal in these things know what they are about,' answered Dr. Schatz.

'And if they are not acquainted with the interior of the Reichstag?' asked Dimitrov.

'Some knowledge of the place is necessary,' Dr. Schatz replied.

'And when must this self-igniting liquid have been distributed?'

'At most an hour or two before the fire,' said Dr. Schatz.[5]

And Dr Schatz went on to say that van der Lubbe's accomplices had

'... the kind of knowledge which is found only among employees of chemical concerns and laboratories, pharmacists or pharmaceutical assistants.'[6]

It seems incredible that Dr Schatz should have been allowed to develop his unsubstantiated theories without anyone seriously challenging him. Not only did these theories imply the utter incompetence of all the police officers who had checked van der Lubbe's movements, but they also ran counter to all the other evidence.

On 15 October 1933, for instance, the upholsterer Otto Borchardt had testified that a piece of material adhering to van der Lubbe's coat came from a curtain behind the stenographers' table.

But why should Dr Schatz have worried about such trifles when he was not only helping the German authorities, but was also attracting the attention of the rest of the world? For the international press, too, was humming with the name of Dr Schatz and his mysterious 'self-igniting liquid'.

On 23 October 1933, Dr Schatz demonstrated his liquid to the Court during a special session from which the public was excluded. And lo! the liquid did burst into flames, though not after an hour, as Dr Schatz had predicted in order to 'explain' Torgler's absence between 7 and 8 p.m., but after eight minutes. However, the mere fact that the mixture had burst into flames at all so impressed the Court that it took the rest on trust.

Only one voice protested – that of Georges Urbain, the irrepressible Professor of Chemistry at the Sorbonne:

'What are we to think of someone who postulates that the accused, none of whom are chemists or trained in laboratory techniques, should have succeeded in performing an experiment in the Session Chamber where they were pressed for time, and probably afraid of being caught, which he, the acknowledged chemical expert, could not perform successfully under far more favourable conditions?'

Luckily for Torgler, no amount of juggling with the facts helped Schatz to pin the blame on him, for Dr Sack had established Torgler's innocence beyond the shadow of a doubt. What Schatz did succeed in doing was to seal van der Lubbe's fate. For since van der Lubbe could not describe the mysterious ingredients for the secret fluid, it 'followed' that these were handed to him by his principals and that he was one of a highly organized gang of insurrectionists.

No other Court would have listened to an expert whose every statement was so blatantly refuted by the facts.* Moreover, if van der Lubbe had, in fact, had Communist accomplices who carried the liquid into the Reichstag, why did he refuse to do an essential part of his job, i.e. blame the fire on the Nazis? Was not van der Lubbe's obstinate insistence that he started all the fires by himself proof positive of his complete veracity?

As Dr Seuffert, Douglas Reed and Mr Justice de Jongh among others realized at the time, van der Lubbe failed to confess anything simply because he had nothing to confess. Moreover, had a self-igniting liquid been used, van der Lubbe would not have been

* Dr Schatz was also called to give evidence as a graphological 'expert'. He made no better an impression in that role.

needed at all – why divert attention from accomplices who had finished their work long before?

Douglas Reed expressed his complete bewilderment in the following words:

> Van der Lubbe's part, then, was, at the most, to touch off the fire; possibly not even that. What function remained for this enigmatic figure with the sunken head than that of a scapegoat, a dupe, a cat's-paw, a tool, a whipping boy for others? Why the spectacular entrance from outside, the crashing glass, the waving fire-brands, the crazy dash through the rooms beneath the restaurant, with their windows facing the Königsplatz? ... How was van der Lubbe brought, or prompted, or induced to enter the Reichstag at the vital moment, and to remain there to be taken? Did he know who prompted him and why did he not say? As far as this, the fundamental issue, was concerned, the evidence brought no enlightenment whatever; the world was confirmed in its opinion that van der Lubbe was the tool of others, but was further than ever from the truth about them.[7]

WAS THE REICHSTAG FIRE REALLY MYSTERIOUS?

When Dimitrov, in the course of his final speech, said:

> Whilst this fool, van der Lubbe, was carrying out his clumsy attempts at arson in the corridors and cloakrooms, were not other unknown persons preparing the conflagration in the Session Chamber and making use of the secret inflammable liquid of which Dr Schatz here spoke?

van der Lubbe could no longer contain himself. He suddenly burst into laughter.

> He laughed almost soundlessly but with such lack of self-control that his whole body was shaking and he almost fell off the bench. Once again everybody gaped at him. His whole face was distorted into a grin.
>
> One wonders what sort of a man he really is, and if he will still be laughing up his sleeve when they lead him and his secret to the scaffold.[6]

In fact, Marinus van der Lubbe was not laughing up his sleeve at all; he was laughing because he could not help himself. He must have used a great deal of self-control during Dimitrov's wild speculations, starting with the unknown man in Hennigsdorf who allegedly asked van der Lubbe: 'Why such a small fire? I'll be able to put you on to something really big,' and ending with this ridiculous self-igniting liquid, and it was only a question of time before he would erupt into helpless laughter.

As early as 9 March 1933, Dr August Brüning, the highly respected director of the Prussian Institute for Food, Drugs and Forensic Chemistry, had corroborated van der Lubbe's testimony. At the request of the police, i.e. long before the whole business was turned into a political issue, Dr Brüning had gone to the scene of the crime, where he carried out a most careful examination and found '. . . no evidence that such substances as petrol, paraffin or methylated spirits had been used.'

The Professor had gone on to say that what traces of extraneous combustible substances he could discover, were all explicable in terms of firelighters or drippings from firemen's torches.

Having identified the mysterious 'incendiary substance' with van der Lubbe's humble firelighters, Dr Brüning – like Dr Ritter – was, of course, dropped by Judge Vogt.

Now these firelighters did, in fact, have a considerable power of destruction. Thus van der Lubbe used them to set the snow-covered roof of the Neukölln Welfare Office ablaze, to cause a fire in the Town Hall and another one on the roof of the Palace, where – as Dr Bünger confirmed – a massive window frame was set alight by half a packet of firelighters.

Moreover, the same lighters could easily have set fire to that crucial bit of evidence – the curtain in the western corridor whose alleged flame-resistance Dr Schatz had 'proved'. This proof, which was an essential link in the accomplice theory, shows better than anything else what manner of scientist the Director of the 'Private Institute for Scientific Criminology' really was. It took a quarter of a century – to be precise until 26 January 1957 – before the mystery of this curtain which was flame-resistant and yet burst into flames was solved: during a conversation Judge Vogt let it slip out that Dr Schatz had performed his experiments not with the actual curtains, but with remnants that had been stored away in heavy chests.

Now, if one could not expect Judge Vogt to know that fire-resistant treatment by impregnation wears off after years, let alone after decades, of use, one could certainly have expected this know-ledge from a fire expert. In particular, Dr Schatz ought to have known that if pieces of curtain, which had been kept in practically air-tight chests where their original impregnation was preserved, did not burn, that did not mean the actual curtains would behave in the same way. For Dr Schatz ought to have been familiar with the decree passed by the Berlin Police President on 5 June 1928, stipulating that the impregnations of all theatre curtains must be checked yearly and, if necessary, renewed. The reason for this decree was quite simple: experience had shown that such materials as velvet, velour, baize, or plush, in particular, gradually lose their fire-resistance through the unavoidable accumulation of dust, constant changes of temperature and humidity, and finally through natural deterioration. Now, the Reichstag curtains, as the Director of the Reichstag, Geheimrat Galle, told the chemist Dr Lepsius on the day after the fire, had been hanging undisturbed for decades. No wonder, therefore, that they caught fire so quickly and so easily.

On 4 October 1933, Dr Sack – a lone voice in the wilderness – objected that the expert opinions '. . . are faulted because the experiments were not carried out under the original conditions.'[9]

Needless to say, this objection was overruled.

We shake our heads when we read to what lengths Fire Director Wagner went in his vain attempts to set fire to massive chairs and desks with firelighters, petrol and filmstrips, while forgetting that only a full reconstruction of the original conditions could produce conclusive results. We know that van der Lubbe did not start the fire in the Chamber by burning an odd chair or an odd desk; what he did was to set fire to the curtains over the tribune, whence the fire leapt across to the tapestries and panelling behind. As a result, so much heat was generated that the glass ceiling cracked in a number of places, and a tremendous updraught was created. Moreover, the wooden walls needed no special preparation to catch fire, for, as Chief Fire Director Walter Gempp stated on the morning after the fire: 'The desiccated old panelling offered the fire excellent food, and that is the reason why the fire spread so quickly in the Session Chamber.'[10]

But it was not only the relative fire-resistance of the chairs in the Session Chamber which confused Professor Josse and Dr Schatz; what misled them even more was the difference between the development of the fire in the restaurant and the one in the Chamber. From the fact that the former was easily extinguished, and the latter was not, they concluded that the two could not have been started in the same way.

This thesis seemed highly plausible to Dimitrov and the Public Prosecutor, both of whom were looking for accomplices, albeit of different shades of political opinion. And yet the main difference between the two fires was the difference in updraught, as anyone who knew anything about fires ought to have realized at once.

We need only recall the fire which destroyed the imposing Vienna Stock Exchange on Friday, 13 April 1956:

> The fire which, for unexplained reasons, started in the cellar shortly after midnight, spread like lightning over the rest of the building, despite desperate attempts by the fire brigade to confine it . . . The flames shot very high into the air and turned the night sky an uncanny red. Thousands had gathered to witness this horrifying but impressive spectacle.[11]

In *Brandschutz*, the official journal of the Vienna Fire Brigade, Engineer Priesnitz explained the catastrophic development of the fire as follows:

> The great hall with its inflammable contents [panelling and furniture] could be compared to a huge oven. Once a fire had started in it and was not extinguished immediately, the fire was bound to spread with such speed that every attempt to extinguish it was doomed to utter failure.

The Reichstag, too, blazed up quite suddenly – the moment the glass ceiling of the Chamber burst. This set up so tremendous an updraught that one of the firemen – Fire Officer Klotz – had to cling to the door for fear of being sucked in.

As early as 1 March 1933, Dr Goebbels gave his own impression of the fire:

> The great Session Chamber is about to cave in. With every bit of debris, an ocean of fire and sparks shoots 250 ft to the dome, which has turned into a chimney.[12]

Engineer Foth of the Berlin Fire Brigade also referred to the updraught phenomenon at the time:

> The glass of the 250 ft dome had burst in places so that the flames could shoot through the cracks. The result was a considerable updraught which . . . caused the air to be sucked through all the passages into the burning Chamber.[13]

Since no such updraught was created in the restaurant and in other parts of the Reichstag, it is not surprising that they escaped the fate of the Chamber.

The ventilation expert, M. J. Reaney, has pointed out that it was one small spark that destroyed the General Motors factory in Lavonia, Michigan, a building that was almost exclusively constructed of fire-resisting materials. Reaney also explained that it was a spark from a neighbouring building which completely destroyed India House in London, a steel and concrete structure, in 1940. The reason was simple: India House contained enough paper, curtains, and furniture to superheat the air. Now superheated air surrounds the fire and dries out everything in its path. Even at small temperature differences, air may circulate with a speed of 1,000 ft per minute, but when air is superheated that speed is greatly increased. That is the reason why a tiny spark may cause even the largest fires – the concrete shell of a building does not, of course, burn, but will collapse under the pressure.[14]

Ever since Prometheus brought us fire, flames have been mankind's most faithful friends and bitterest enemies. With the rise of cities, fire damage has grown to gigantic proportions, yet the cause of most fires is usually a mere trifle – a stupid accident, a tiny omission, one spark, one cigarette end, and a forest, a skyscraper or an ocean liner is destroyed.

For example, a 1913 survey showed that of 1,200 theatre fires, thirty-seven per cent were caused by naked flames, twenty-one per cent by faulty lights, sixteen per cent by faulty heaters, twenty-three per cent by fireworks, firearms and similar explosive matter, and three per cent by arson. In no case were highly inflammable fluids involved, and in most cases, once the fire had started, the theatres were completely destroyed.

Or take another historical example:

On October 16th, 1834, between six and seven o'clock in the evening, the sky over Westminster turned an exceptionally bright colour. Fire alarms echoed throughout the south-east of London, while thick red smoke poured out of the front windows of the House of Lords.

Archivists had been burning old records when, quite suddenly, the Debating Chamber was on fire. Before help could come, the Lords' resplendent Hall with all its glorious furniture, was ablaze. Even the House of Commons was seized by the flames, which spread as far as Westminster Hall.[15]

Another historic fire, in the Tower of London, was discovered in much the same way as the Reichstag fire:

> On October 30th, 1841, at about 10.30 p.m., a passer-by noticed a strong glow in the Tower. He notified a policeman who fired a shot, as a result of which the whole garrison was alerted and 500 people came to the rescue. Pumps proved quite useless, partly because of the lack of water, and partly because the Tower was full of fabrics.[16]

In the case of Parliament, it was ordinary paper which had caused the conflagration, and no one so much as suggested that self-igniting liquids, petrol, paraffin, or, for that matter, pitch or resin had been used. Paper was quite enough to burn the fire-resisting furniture, and that was that. But then no one was trying to make political capital out of the London fire.

The Reichstag Session Chamber was set ablaze, not by paper, but by the old, heavy velvet curtains behind the tribune. From these musty curtains the fire quickly spread to the richly hung wooden panelling near it.

As every fireman knows, large fires radiate heat over fairly large distances, and this fact partially explains why the Court 'experts' failed to set light to the same kind of furniture that the actual fire consumed so quickly.

Firemen also know that the most dangerous fires are those which start in such vaulted buildings as cinemas, theatres, and – the Reichstag. Hence the Reichstag fire did not puzzle them at first:

> According to the fire office, a ventilation shaft in the Session Chamber acted as a chimney, sucking the fire upwards and impeding its lateral development. The roof girders suffered little damage since the panes burst very quickly, leaving the air free access and the flames free escape.[17]

Had the fire not broken out at a critical point in Germany's history, the experts would not have been expected to propound any of their far-fetched theories, or to perform any of their point-less experiments. They would have simply told the Court – what every housewife knows in any case – that once you light a fire in a stove with an unobstructed chimney, it will blaze away until all the fuel has been consumed. And that is precisely what happened in the Reichstag Session Chamber.

13. The Verdict

THE VERDICT

ON 23 December 1933, Dr Bünger solemnly read the judgement of the Supreme Court:

> The accused Torgler, Dimitrov, Popov and Tanev are acquitted. The accused van der Lubbe is found guilty of high treason, insurrectionary arson and attempted common arson. He is sentenced to death and to perpetual loss of civic rights.

This verdict was received with satisfaction abroad. The fact that four of the five accused had been acquitted, not because of their innocence but merely for lack of evidence against them, was considered a minor flaw, and van der Lubbe's death sentence caused only a flicker of revulsion. For there had never been any question about his guilt; what was in doubt was his sanity.

The National Socialist press, on the other hand, foamed with rage:

> The acquittal of Torgler and the three Bulgarian Communists for purely formal reasons is, in the popular view, a complete miscarriage of justice. Had the verdict been rooted in that true law on which the new Germany is being founded and in the true feeling of the German people, it would surely have been quite different. But then the entire manner in which the trial was conducted, and which the nation has followed with increasing displeasure, would have been quite different too.[1]

A less prejudiced German paper wrote:

> The highest German court has spoken. It has . . . shown the qualities which the new Germany expects of a 'royal' judge: an unflinching will to justice, the utmost objectivity in the discovery and assessment of the facts, complete independence.[2]

That view was no less objectionable for, as Erich Kuttner has rightly pointed out:

> The verdict is an abuse of logic and of reasonable thought. It is not by the acquittal of four innocent men, but by its specious attempt to

268

prove, despite the acquittal, what could only have been proven by a verdict of guilty, that we must judge this Court and assess its subservience to the political rulers of the Third Reich.[3]

In fact, the judges were paralysed from the moment Hitler made his fateful pronouncement in the blazing Reichstag. In addition, most German judges were Nationalists, and inclined to side with the Nazis against the Communists and Social Democrats as a matter of course. Thus, in 1923, when Adolf Hitler made a seditious attempt to overthrow the elected Government, and caused the death of many people, he was merely confined in Landsberg fortress, from which he was released soon afterwards.

Dr Bünger's Court, too, was no exception to the general rule; it openly paid homage to the Nazi masters when it declared:

On January 30th, 1933, the Reichspräsident expressed his confidence in Adolf Hitler, the leader of the National Socialist Party, by appointing him Chancellor . . . thus paving the path for the building of the Third Reich and for our political rebirth. . . . A wave of confidence met our Führer Adolf Hitler and held out the promise that the new elections, set down for March 5th, would ensure the overwhelming success of the National Socialist Party. . . . [Hence there was] not the slightest reason why the National Socialists should have burned the Reichstag and blamed the fire on others as a pre-election stunt. Every German realizes full well that the men to whom the German nation owes its salvation from Bolshevik anarchy and who are now leading Germany towards her rebirth and recuperation, would never have been capable of such criminal folly. The Court therefore deems it beneath its dignity to enter into these vile allegations, all of which have been spread by expatriated rogues, who stand condemned by their own words. It is sufficient to state that all these lies have been completely refuted in the course of the trial . . .

Inasmuch as the Court acquitted the accused Communists, it proved that it still enjoyed a measure of independence, but inasmuch as it upheld the absurd thesis of Communist complicity, it showed how small that measure really was – dazzled by the national firework display, the judges turned a blind eye to the most basic principles of jurisprudence. It was their subservience to Hitler which constantly forced them to shelter behind such evasions as 'possibly', 'apparently', 'probably', 'presumably', and so on. A summary of the verdict might have read: Somehow and somewhere, some unknown – but certainly Communist – criminals entered the Reichstag with some substance that somehow served to prepare the Chamber for the fire. Somehow, somewhere, and at some time, these Communist criminals made contact with van der Lubbe, and somehow, somewhere and at some time, they disappeared again after the crime was committed.

Though not a single accomplice was run to earth despite all the efforts of the famous German police, and despite the offer of a large reward, the Court nevertheless found that there could be

> ... no doubt about the objects which van der Lubbe and his accomplices were pursuing, or about the camp in which the criminal's accomplices and principals must be sought. Their intention was clearly to give the signal for a Communist rebellion.

And on what evidence did the Court base this conclusion, when it could not even establish how these accomplices got in and out of the building? It seems quite incredible but the answer is: On evidence which the Court itself found hard to swallow, viz. on Paul Bogun's claim that he saw one of the accomplices leave the Reichstag shortly before or just after 9 p.m. This is what the verdict said on the subject:

> ... While the Court has no reason to distrust the witness Bogun, and while the Court does not doubt that what Bogun saw outside Portal Two was the escape of one of the accomplices, the Court was able to satisfy itself that light conditions outside Portal Two were such that no positive identification of the clothing and appearance of the accomplice was possible from where the witness Bogun stood.

Bogun, who had become the star witness after most of the others had proved such transparent liars, came out rather poorly himself when the defence had finished with him. This is how the *Neue Zürcher Zeitung* described his appearance in Court:

> A barrage of questions fired at the witness by Dr Teichert and Dr Sack, counsel for the defence, revealed that his evidence is full of loopholes and contradictions. His times differ by quarter-hours; minutes are changed into seconds, and vice versa. The witness, who is short-sighted and wears thick glasses, had originally stated that it was too dark to tell the colour of the stranger's hair. Later he alleged that the stranger had dark hair, just like Popov. Bogun also gave five different descriptions of the stranger's headgear. The stranger's shoes changed colour; his face and eyebrows only assumed definite shape after Bogun had been confronted with Popov.

The witness has begun to twist and turn so much that, in his own interest, one would wish that the floor would swallow him up. Yet all Bogun can say is that details do not matter. He even swore on oath that he had spoken the whole truth.[4]

Dimitrov, too, turned his full scorn on Bogun:

German engineers are usually as precise as mathematics. Why, then, are Bogun's powers of observation so much better three months after the fire than they were at the time? How does he explain that Popov's light trousers have become blue? Bogun is not an engineer, he is a romancer.[5]

Another witness, Frau Elfriede Kuesner, who also alleged that she had seen the 'accomplice' escape from Portal Two, was known to have entered the National Club at 9 p.m. She therefore had to time her 'observation' at 8.55 p.m., i.e. a few minutes before Bogun did. On top of that, she had watched the 'getaway' from an extremely poor vantage point, at least 165 feet away from Portal Two, and against the light.

Now we know that Portal Two had been duly locked by Wocköck, an old and trusted Reichstag servant, because House-Inspector Scranowitz had to unlock it for the fire brigade. Moreover, the police had established that the lock had not been tampered with in any way, and that there were only two keys: the one Wocköck had handed to Wendt in Portal Five, and the other which was kept in a locked cupboard in Scranowitz's (locked) office.

In other words, some of the accomplices would have had to steal Wendt's key, race from Portal Five to Portal Two, unlock and lock the door to allow their friends to escape, race back to Portal Five to return the key, thus wasting much time and risking discovery, when all of them could have escaped by the mysterious and undetectable route by which they had allegedly come in.

All these strange facts did not apparently worry the Court, nor, for that matter, did the discrepancy between the evidence of the witnesses Bogun and Kuesner, or the internal contradictions in Bogun's own evidence. For Bogun had presented the Court with a much-needed accomplice, and the Court was determined to hang on to his gift through thick and thin. All that remained to be done was to link the accomplice to van der Lubbe, and linked to him he was:

The very fact that he [van der Lubbe] betook himself to Neukölln, the Communist stronghold, is extremely suggestive. His conversations outside the Welfare Office, at Schlaffke's and at Starker's are equally suspicious. . . . Even though his demand to be shown to Communist headquarters was refused, he was nevertheless taken to Neukölln Communist haunts. . . . In the view of the Court, it was here that van der Lubbe made contact with Communist circles. The precise nature of these contacts, their subsequent effects, and their precise relevance to van der Lubbe's participation in the crime could not be established. However, that the crime was preceded by other actions than lonely walks through the streets of Berlin, sudden unmotivated decisions, and the purchase of a few firelighters, is proved by the obstinate silence which the accused van der Lubbe maintained, even during the preliminary examination, on the subject of his movements on February 23rd and 24th, and from February 27th until the time of the fire. Undoubtedly it was during these times that the preparations were made. . . . Although the details of these preparations remain unknown, all the evidence points to the fact that van der Lubbe's accomplices are to be found in the ranks of the German Communist Party. In this respect it is not without interest that Hennigsdorf. . . was an industrial town with a Communist majority, and that it was here that van der Lubbe was seen in the company of known Communists and with the sister of a Communist leader . . .

And this compilation of idle speculations and bad logic was the basis on which the highest German Court decided the fate of van der Lubbe! But then the Court needed these crutches, for without them it could never have sentenced van der Lubbe to death – not even as a favour to Hitler.

The Court's remarkable arguments about van der Lubbe's movements were followed by no less remarkable arguments about the fire itself. When all was said and done, the allegation that van der Lubbe could not have started the gigantic fire with mere firelighters stood and fell by the fire-resistance of the curtains in the Session Chamber. Now the verdict declared all Reichstag curtains fire-resistant, even those which had caught fire easily during the experiments. The reason was simple: the idea that the curtains were fire-resistant had been so widely adopted that Dr Schatz thought it best not to confuse the issue with fine academic distinctions. Hence, when the witnesses, Thaler, Buwert, Freudenberg and Kuhl all testified how quickly the restaurant curtains had burned, Dr Schatz alleged that these curtains, too, must have been soaked in his famous liquid. Now, since the Court had established that van der Lubbe was the only person who could have 'prepared' the restaurant, he must somehow have procured a bottle or can of the mysterious substance between 2 p.m., when the witness Schmal saw him without a container, and 9 p.m., when he was seen breaking into the Reichstag. Moreover, he must have carried the large container (Dr Schatz spoke of one gallon of liquid) on his person while scaling the Reichstag wall, jumping over the parapet, kicking in the thick panes, lighting the first firelighters in the wind – the first five matches were blown out – and then climbing in through the broken window. Even Dr Schatz realized that to do all this van der Lubbe had to have both hands free, and he accordingly 'invented' a large container that could fit into an overcoat pocket. Needless to say, no traces of such a container were ever discovered. Even so, the Court found that

> Dr. Schatz's examination of van der Lubbe's charred coat has proved conclusively that the accused van der Lubbe carried the inflammable liquid on his person. The coat pocket had a clear burn-mark running inwards, and chemical investigations of the pocket revealed the presence of phosphorus and carbon sulphide in different stages of oxidization together with traces of hydrated phosphoric acid and hydrated sulphuric acid.

Moreover, whereas Lateit had testified that he saw the curtains burning from the bottom to the top, as they would have done had they been lit with firelighters, the Court preferred Dr Schatz's speculations on the subject:

> Both curtains burned diagonally from the inside top to the outside bottom. This fact is further evidence in favour of Dr Schatz's opinion that the curtains had been sprinkled with liquid.

According to the verdict, therefore, van der Lubbe not only sprinted through the Reichstag in record time, lighting firelighters, tablecloths, papers, shirts, and other pieces of clothing, but he also spent much additional time sprinkling curtains, carpets, etc.

> It seems reasonable to assume that van der Lubbe shed his clothes . . . not, as he alleged, in order to supplement his supply of lighters, but simply because, as a result of contact with the self-igniting liquid, they had themselves caught fire.

Yet this dangerous liquid, which had allegedly consumed massive oak furniture in a matter of seconds, was unable to destroy van der Lubbe's poor coat, remnants of which Dr Schatz had therefore been able to submit to his far-reaching examinations. In any case, it seems odd that neither van der Lubbe's hands nor his trousers and shoes showed the slightest burn-marks.

At first, Dr Schatz had argued that the inflammable liquid had been smuggled into the Reichstag well in advance. However, the trial soon showed that this view could not be maintained. The time available for preparing the fire kept shrinking until the Court had to face the remarkable fact that even the Session Chamber must have been 'prepared' immediately before the fire. For a brief moment, it looked very much as if the Court would have to believe van der Lubbe's story after all, and it was at this point that Dr Schatz came to the rescue with his self-igniting substance. He explained that it was merely in order to give this substance time to work that van der Lubbe had drawn attention to himself in the restaurant.

The Court offered no explanation of how the container or containers of the liquid had disappeared without trace. Moreover, whereas the Public Prosecutor admitted that there was no evidence to show that such inflammable liquids as paraffin, petrol, benzol or ether had ever been used, the Court preferred to listen to Dr Schatz once again:

> Since the soot in the ventilators and underneath both the Speaker's Chair and also the Table of the House contained simultaneously residual naphthalene and mineral oil, it seems likely that the [self-igniting] liquid and the sawdust-and-naphthalene firelighters were used in conjunction with petrol or benzol.

Again, whereas the Indictment had stressed that Professor Brüning's examination of the alleged 'fluid trail' in the Bismarck Hall had revealed no trace of an inflammable liquid, the Court (and Dr Schatz) believed that:

> It seems likely that the accomplice or the accomplices, having performed their allotted task in the Session Chamber, used the remaining liquid for firing the curtains in the western corridor, the southern corridor and the Bismarck Hall, on the carpet of which the incendiaries left a clear trail of fluid which, according to the chemical examination by the expert, Dr Schatz, consisted not only of mineral oil, but also of self-igniting liquid.

In other words, the Court saw no need for having the contradictory opinions of two of its experts checked by a third one. It sided with a provincial chemist against a scientist of international renown.

Now, had a highly inflammable liquid been used in fact, the fire would have spread like lightning over the entire liquid-soaked area, leaving a great deal of soot, when all the eyewitnesses were agreed that the flames looked steady and that there was no inordinate amount of soot.

How blindly the judges followed Dr Schatz is best shown by their argument that the self-igniting fluid caught fire at a predetermined moment. The reader will remember that even the great Dr Schatz was quite unable to fix that interval under laboratory conditions; how likely is it, then, that van der Lubbe's alleged accomplices should have been able to compound the mixture with so much greater precision?

Moreover, while agreeing that van der Lubbe himself was carrying the fatal liquid on him, the Court nevertheless found that he could not possibly have burned the Chamber:

Fully refuted is van der Lubbe's allegation that he himself started the fire in the Chamber . . .

In any case, there was no need for van der Lubbe to have fired the Chamber with firebrands, etc., when the Chamber had been prepared beforehand with the self-igniting substance . . .

The part which the accused van der Lubbe was apparently expected to play was to deflect attention from his accomplices. . . . In the opinion of the Court, this is borne out by his conspicuous waving of a firebrand outside the restaurant window, for such behaviour is quite incompatible with common arson. . . . In fact, van der Lubbe's accomplices or principals did achieve their object, for though they ran the risk of discovery, they did manage to divert the fire brigade from the main fire. . . . It was also in order to divert the fire brigade from the main fire that van der Lubbe laid a blazing trail through the corridors. . . .

And the only basis for all these 'findings' was the rich fantasy of Dr Schatz. For if, as the Court claimed, van der Lubbe did not even set foot in the Chamber, how was it that he was able to lead the detectives straight there on the very next day? And what must we think of a Court which finds that 'the detectives were *originally* convinced that van der Lubbe fired the Reichstag by himself' when neither (Heisig or Zirpins) had changed their original views in the slightest?

Even the fact that van der Lubbe chose 9 p.m. as the best time to climb into the Reichstag was twisted into an argument supporting the accomplice theory, for at that time the Reichstag was ostensibly deserted. In fact, had the Reichstag postman not accidentally started on his round a few minutes before his normal time, he would certainly have spotted any 'accomplices' that might have been at work.

Having made the most of Dr Schatz's fantastic gifts, and having twisted the facts to exhaustion, the Court easily arrived at the truly amazing conclusion that:

> It has been established that van der Lubbe's accomplices must be sought in the ranks of the Communist Party, that Communism is therefore guilty of the Reichstag fire, that the German people stood in the early part of the year 1933 on the brink of chaos into which the Communists sought to lead them, and that the German people were saved at the last moment.

In sentencing van der Lubbe to death for insurrectionary arson, the Leipzig Court ignored two legal maxims, without either of which justice becomes a mere sham: *in dubio pro reo* (the accused has the benefit of the doubt) and *nulla poena sine lege* (no punishment without law). To put it more plainly, when the Court convicted van der Lubbe of complicity in a non-existing plot and sentenced him to death for a non-capital offence, it chose political expediency and deliberately jettisoned the law.

THE MYSTERY OF VAN DER LUBBE

According to the French Ambassador, François-Poncet, van der Lubbe was 'the feeble-minded, mentally deficient, and probably drugged tool of the real criminals'.

In fact, drugging van der Lubbe would only have made sense had he, in fact, provided the Nazis with what they needed: the confession that he had acted on behalf of the German Communist Party. This he steadfastly refused to do.

But if not drugged, why did van der Lubbe, whom Inspector Heisig had described as being so alert after the fire, appear in Court speechless, bowed, slavering, with a running nose and, in general, wretched-looking?

Part of the answer was given by Kugler who wrote: 'It is quite possible that, having been kept in shackles for seven long months, the twenty-four-year-old van der Lubbe . . . was so exhausted that he had a nervous breakdown.'[6]

And it should not require too much imagination to realize the effects of a form of inhuman torture which had driven tough Tanev to attempt suicide and Dimitrov to the limits of his endurance. Van der Lubbe, unlike the other accused, had not a single friend, and was thus a singularly defenceless butt of Judge Vogt's sadistic attacks. To make things worse, his intended protest against the enemies of the working class had helped those very enemies to power, and his former associates were now calling him a Nazi stooge.

All these facts were mentioned in a medical opinion which two well-known authorities, Professor Karl Bonhoeffer, of the Psychiatric Clinic of the University of Berlin, and Professor Jurg Zutt, now Director of the Neurological Clinic in Frankfurt, submitted to the Court at the time.

What had caused Judge Vogt to call in the two psychiatrists as early as March 1933, was van der Lubbe's decision to go on hunger-strike. When asked about this, van der Lubbe told the doctors quite simply that, though he had been held for three weeks and though he had done his best to help the authorities, the trial was dragging on and on and he was trying to hurry things up, not only for his own sake but also for the sake of his innocent fellow-sufferers, Torgler and the Bulgarians. He also volunteered the information that he had found hunger-strikes most effective with the Dutch authorities.

Now, if three weeks was too long for him, how must he have felt after another forty-four weeks, for twenty-nine of which he was kept in chains day and night? In any case, the two psychiatrists, far from considering him an imbecile, found him

> . . . an individual who knows what he wants and who tries to say what has to be said and no more. . . . [Because of his eye injury] he gives the impression of staring into space at times; in reality, however, he pays careful attention to what goes on around him. Little seems to escape his attention.

It did not take van der Lubbe long to find out why the two psychiatrists had been called in:

> He laughed quite naturally, perhaps somewhat arrogantly, though not impudently. So that was what it was all about! He had burned the

Reichstag and now he had gone on hunger-strike, so, obviously, they all thought he was mad!

When the doctors tried to assess his intelligence with general knowledge and mathematical questions, he told them that

> ... he was far more interested in things he had experienced by himself. ... He considered religion just one branch of knowledge among many. ... When asked what he thought about life after death, he replied that it was a bourgeois mistake to expect an answer to that question. Either life continues after death or it does not, and that's that. Death and the beyond were, after all, no more than concepts, and all concepts are lodged in our heads; they only exist when we think about them ...
>
> He was inclined to burst into youthful laughter, especially when he was asked questions that seemed to be paradoxical, or others which, in his opinion, complicated simple things quite unnecessarily.

Van der Lubbe's youthful laughter repeatedly caused observers to shake their heads at what they could only assume were the antics of a lunatic. On the very first day of the trial, for instance, van der Lubbe started shaking with laughter after the pointless Sörnewitz-Brockwitz discussion had been going on for what seemed an eternity. In great perplexity, Dr Bünger asked him:

'Are you feeling ill or is something the matter with you? You must not laugh here.'

Dr Werner: 'He is shaking with laughter.'

President: 'Lubbe, will you stand up! What is the meaning of this? Why are you suddenly laughing when you are normally so serious? Is it because you find the subject matter of this trial amusing, or is there any other reason? Do you think our deliberations are ridiculous?'

Van der Lubbe: 'No.'

President: 'Do you understand everything? Do you understand this trial?'

Van der Lubbe: 'No.'

President: 'So it is not the subject matter of this trial which makes you laugh. What is it then? Why do you laugh? Out with it!'

Van der Lubbe: 'Because of the trial.'

President: 'Do you think the trial is a joke?'

Van der Lubbe: 'No.'

President: 'If it is not a joke, then please don't laugh!'

But how could van der Lubbe help laughing when so much pomp and circumstance was being wasted by the highest Court in the land to establish who said what to whom in Sörnewitz, a little backwater that had absolutely nothing whatever to do with the Reichstag fire?

Next day, Sörnewitz was still on the agenda, and van der Lubbe was told once again not to laugh.

President: 'Why do you laugh? These matters are of extreme gravity. I am warning you, van der Lubbe!'

A few days later, van der Lubbe burst into laughter once more, when Tanev replied to the question whether he had known van der Lubbe: 'Where should I have met him? I don't understand a single word of German. What should I have wanted with him?'

In short, van der Lubbe laughed whenever he was given cause for laughter. His was a special kind of morbid humour which grew as he watched the Court's blustering attempts to obscure the simple truth and to manufacture accomplices out of thin air.

In any case, Professors Bonhoeffer and Zutt found that '. . . during all our visits we never saw him laugh unless he saw something funny in the situation.'

But as the trial dragged on, van der Lubbe's humour began to wilt visibly. In the end, when he came to realize that these hopeless old fools in their fine robes were not in the least interested in what he had to tell them, he stopped smiling and wasting his breath.

When the two doctors asked van der Lubbe why he had set fire to the Reichstag, he replied that, as the German working class had done nothing to protest against the Nazis, he had felt it his duty to make an individual protest on their behalf.

The learned gentlemen confirmed that van der Lubbe could express himself in reasonably good German, and that he needed no Dutch interpreter. Moreover, the Court interpreter, J. Meyer-Collings, told Judge Coenders who had asked him about van der Lubbe's Dutch: 'It is an odd fact, but van der Lubbe does not talk like an ordinary Dutch worker; he uses the idiom of educated people.'

In March 1933, the two medical experts concluded: 'We found no indications of mental unbalance. Marinus van der Lubbe strikes us as a most intelligent, strong-willed and self-confident person . . .', but when they saw him again at the beginning of the

Leipzig trial, they found him a broken man. They described the results in purely medical terms, and wisely kept their own counsel on the causes: van der Lubbe's strength had been sapped by his fetters, and his morale undermined by the realization that nothing he might say to these pompous judges would make the slightest difference.

In order to kill the story that his transformation was due to drugs, the Court asked Professor Karl Soedermann, Lecturer in Criminology at the University of Stockholm, to examine van der Lubbe. On 28 September 1933, Soedermann reported:

> I can only say that they treat him better than they do the other prisoners, for instance as regards food. The moment he saw me, Marinus van der Lubbe asked: 'Why are you examining me?' I said: 'Because foreign papers allege that you are being badly treated here.'
>
> Van der Lubbe laughed and shook his head. I gained the impression that we could have conversed for hours, and that I would invariably have received intelligent and logical answers. . . . I also asked him if he had at any time felt anything strange after eating or drinking and he told me emphatically that he had not.[7]

Professor Soedermann also examined van der Lubbe's body, but found no marks of ill-usage (e.g. injections) of any kind.

The two German psychiatrists, too, felt compelled to refer to the drug rumours:

> . . . Then there are the many strange 'diagnoses' which no doctor would accept, but which are repeated by the public and above all by the suspicious foreign press, viz. that Marinus van der Lubbe has been hypnotized in prison, and that his odd behaviour is the result of his having been drugged with scopolamine.
>
> Even if it were feasible that medical men should lend themselves to such criminal practices, and even if someone could be kept under hypnosis for weeks and months on end, van der Lubbe's attitude, behaviour, and intransigence are by no means those of a hypnotized or drugged subject.

On 20 October 1933, the Court heard the evidence of S. A. Gruppenführer Wolf von Helldorff. When van der Lubbe was asked to step forward for the usual confrontation, the President, the interpreter and counsel tried in vain to make him look up at the Nazi. It was only when Helldorff yelled at him: 'Put your head up, you! And jump to it!' that van der Lubbe slowly did as he was told.

Helldorff and his applauding cohorts in the public gallery now felt that firmness was all van der Lubbe had needed, and that his downcast mien had been sham all along. In fact, van der Lubbe had merely been shaken out of his resigned boredom by the parade-ground voice of a professional bully.

Helldorff himself must have regretted his courtroom success the next day, when he read in the foreign press that van der Lubbe had obviously obeyed the voice of his master, or as the *Brown Book* put it: 'Had the shrill command penetrated through the mists of van der Lubbe's memory: had it cleaved the fog in his brain for one transient second?'[8]

The *Brown Book* even offered a 'scientific explanation' based on the findings of an 'eminent toxicologist': 'There is one poisonous drug with such qualities that comparatively minute doses will produce symptoms exactly similar to those produced in van der Lubbe.'[9]

In fact, as Professor Zutt had already pointed out, 'there is no drug that can completely silence a man'. Moreover: 'His behaviour is a natural reaction to his external circumstances. . . . True, he has grown apathetic, but he often glances up and round, though without appearing to move his head.'

Then, on 13 November 1933, van der Lubbe suddenly 'woke up' once again, sat upright, and looked attentively at everyone in Court. More miraculously still, he broke his long silence and answered all questions that were put to him.

One of his answers caused a sensation in Court, for when the President asked him whom he had gone to see in Spandau, he burst out with: 'The Nazis!' However, the excitement quickly subsided when it appeared that he had merely gone to watch a Nazi demonstration.

Van der Lubbe caused an even greater sensation on 23 November, the forty-third day of the trial, when he rose to his feet, raised his head, and faced the Court.

The judges, startled, gazed across at him. Defending counsel turned in their seats and hung on his words. His fellow-prisoners shed the weariness of two months like a garment and sat forward, straining their ears to hear what he should say. The public craned its neck. The few newspaper correspondents who had both followed the trial to Leipzig and risen early enough to be present at van der Lubbe's awakening – a brief awakening it was to be – congratulated themselves on their own perseverance and thought without compassion of their absent colleagues.[10]

Van der Lubbe explained that he had risen in order to ask a question. When Dr Bünger said he might, the following discussion ensued:

Van der Lubbe: 'We have had three trials now, the first in Leipzig, the second in Berlin, and the third in Leipzig again. I should like to know when the verdict will be pronounced and executed.'

President: 'I can't tell you that yet. It all depends on you, on your naming your accomplices.'

Van der Lubbe: 'But that has all been cleared up. I fired the Reichstag by myself, and there must be a verdict. The thing has gone on for eight months and I cannot agree with this at all.'

President: 'Then tell us who your accomplices were!'

Van der Lubbe: 'My fellow defendants have all admitted that they had nothing to do with the fire, were not even in the Reichstag, and did not fire it.'

President: 'I have told you repeatedly that the Court cannot accept your statement that you were alone. You simply must tell us with whom you did it and who helped you.'

Van der Lubbe: 'I can only repeat that I set fire to the Reichstag all by myself. After all, it has been shown during this trial that Dimitrov and the others were not there. They are in the trial, that is quite true, but they were not in the Reichstag.'

Dr Seuffert: 'And what about Herr Torgler?'

Van der Lubbe: 'He wasn't there either. You (turning to Torgler) have had to admit yourself that you weren't there. I am the accused and I want to know the verdict, no matter if it is twenty years in prison or the death penalty. Something simply has to happen. The whole trial has gone wrong because of all this symbolism and I am sick of it.'

Dr Werner: 'What does the accused mean by the term "symbolism"?'

Dr Seuffert: 'He objects to the Reichstag fire being called a signal.'

Van der Lubbe: 'What sort of deed was it anyway, this Reichstag fire? It was a matter of ten minutes, or at most, a quarter of an hour. I did it all by myself.'

And then he poured out his own feelings: what had troubled him so sorely was the fact that his dignified inquisitors were apparently determined to spin out their comedy of errors for as long as they could. He, for one, would rather die than have this sordid farce continue. How could they blame him for delaying the proceedings by not betraying accomplices he had never had? Though he knew that arguing with these senile old fools was a sheer waste of time, he tried once again:

Van der Lubbe: 'The Court does not believe me, but it's true all the same.'

President: 'Have you read the opinions of the experts who say one man could not have started the fire?'

Van der Lubbe: 'Yes, I know that is the personal opinion of the experts. But then, I was there and they were not. I know that I set fire to the Session Chamber with my jacket.'

What followed merely shows how right van der Lubbe had been to save his breath.

President: 'You have confessed to the crime and there is therefore no argument on that point. But it remains a fact that other persons have been accused and that the Court must now decide whether or not these person are guilty. It would help us greatly if you now admit with whom you committed the crime.'

Van der Lubbe: 'I can only admit that I started the fire by myself; for the rest I cannot agree with what this Court is trying to do. I now demand a verdict. What you are doing is a betrayal of humanity, of the police, and of the Communist and the National Socialist Party. All I ask for is a verdict.'

And when Dimitrov, too, said: 'In my opinion no one person could have started this complicated fire . . .' Van der Lubbe interrupted him with: 'There is nothing complicated about this fire. It has quite a simple explanation. What was made of it may be complicated, but the fire itself was very simple . . .'

When the President thereupon suggested that his poor fire-lighters could not have caused a major conflagration, van der Lubbe replied: 'In that case, the Session Chamber must have been far more inflammable than the experts believe.'

The Court's persistent blindness was referred to by Mr Justice de Jongh:

Why does it not enter anyone's head that both the National Socialists and the Communists might be innocent, and that the unhappy Marinus van der Lubbe committed the crime by himself, or, for that matter, with antisocial elements belonging to neither of the two parties?[11]

283

Another foreign observer to voice his doubts at the time was Douglas Reed, who wrote:

> Attempts from all sides of the court to wrest from van der Lubbe the secret of his accomplices, however, were parried in a manner that indicated either great cunning or the sincere conviction that he had none. ... There remained only two possibilities – that van der Lubbe had no accomplices or that he did not himself know who they were. The one man from whom, it had been thought, the secret might yet be wrested, either would not yield it or had none to yield.[12]

When the death sentence on van der Lubbe was finally pronounced on 23 December 1933, the Dutch Ambassador in Berlin appealed for clemency, and countless petitions poured into Germany from all over the world. Mr Justice de Jongh, in adding his voice, pointed out that with van der Lubbe's execution there would disappear the last chance of ever solving the mystery of the Reichstag fire.

On 9 January 1934, when the Public Prosecutor informed van der Lubbe that his appeal for clemency had been rejected, and that he was to be beheaded the following morning, van der Lubbe answered with great composure:

'Thank you for telling me; I shall see you tomorrow.'

Marinus van der Lubbe wrote no farewell letters to relatives or friends. On 10 January 1934, when he was led out of his cell, he looked calm and peaceful. A large company had assembled to witness the last act of an apalling tragedy. President Bünger and three of his assistant judges had come, and so had Dr Werner, Dr Parrisius, Dr Seuffert, the Court interpreter, the prison chaplain, the governor of the prison, two doctors, and twelve selected Leipzig citizens. The executioner was dressed in tails, top hat and white gloves.

The Public Prosecutor explained that the Herr Reichspräsident had decided not to exercise his prerogative of clemency, and then ordered the executioner to do his duty. There were no complications, no tears, no belated confession. A few moments later Marinus van der Lubbe was dead.

Appendix A

THE MANCHESTER GUARDIAN
26 April 1933
THE REICHSTAG FIRE
I. *Who was Guilty?*
THE CASE AGAINST THE NAZIS
Germany, April.

WHEN Hitler became Chancellor – with von Papen as Vice-Chancellor – at the end of January, the Nazis and their partners in office, the Nationalists, had antagonistic ambitions. The Nazis, above all Captain Göring and Dr Goebbels, wanted absolute and undivided power. Von Papen, as well as the Nationalist leader, Dr Hugenberg, and the President, von Hindenburg, wanted the Nazis, with their enormous following, to provide a 'National' Government with the popular support which was denied to the Nationalists themselves. The Nazis, in other words, were to share power with the Nationalists while being denied that preponderance which, by virtue of being by far the biggest party in the Reich, they considered their due.

The Nationalists, though a very small party, had certain sources of strength. They represent all that is left of Imperial Germany; they, and not the Nazis, incarnate old Prussian traditions. They were supported by a large part of the higher bureaucracy, by the higher ranks of the Reichswehr, by the Stahlhelm, a powerful conservative league of ex-servicemen, and by President von Hindenburg, whose personal authority was still considerable. Nor were they, in case of need, disinclined to negotiate for the support of the trade unions and even of the Reichsbanner, a strong militant force (made up chiefly of workmen) whose leaders had developed certain militarist and nationalist tendencies.

The Nazis were showing signs of disintegration. The Brown Shirts were growing mutinous in different parts of the Reich; several units had to be disbanded, and in the electorate there were symptoms of waning enthusiasm. Another election might (if sufficient time were allowed to lapse) mean a heavy loss of votes. And would not a movement that had arisen so rapidly and so high suffer a correspondingly precipitous decline?

NAZIS AND NATIONALISTS

Thus the Nazis were under a strong compulsion to take a share of power, lest the time might come when even a share would be denied to them. Hitler had become Chancellor of the 'Government of National Concentration' only on condition that there would be no changes in the Cabinet without the sanction of President Hindenburg. Thus the Nazis, although in a position of great influence, achieved nothing comparable with that complete transformation of the whole economic and social order to which they and the millions of their enthusiastic followers had aspired. Had they respected the terms imposed on Hitler, the disappearance of those millions would only have been a matter of time. They were indeed in a trap.

The Nationalists had no particular faith in Hitler's word, which had been broken more than once before. But they were vigilant, and on the slightest sign of bad faith they were ready, with the sanction of the President and the army, to proclaim a military dictatorship (in which case they could have counted on the support not only of the Stahlhelm but also of the police, amongst whom Socialist influences were still strong). How were the Nazis to get out of the trap? If there were a general election without loss of time they might still increase their vote, for Hitler's Chancellorship had the appearance of almost absolute power without the substance, and new hope had revived the ardour of his followers, though, with the inevitable emergence of the reality, it was bound to cool in a very short time. He therefore demanded a general election at the earliest possible date. His promise to the President was, it is true, binding, irrespective of the result of that election. At the same time, an increase of his already heavy vote could only be welcome. Indeed, if he obtained an absolute majority, could his promise be considered binding against the manifest 'will of the people'? Or would not Hindenburg give way before that 'will'?

But the chances that he would get such a majority were small, and as the election campaign developed it seemed probable that revived enthusiasm was ebbing once again and that the elections would show a loss in the Hitlerite vote. This would have bound

Appendix A

Hitler to his promise and the Nazis permanently to the Nationalists. It was clear to their more adventurous and ambitious leaders, Captain Göring and Dr Goebbels, that 'something' must be done to keep Nazi enthusiasm at its height, indeed to drive it still higher, and to precipitate a new situation in which Hitler could either be freed from his promise or that promise would lose its meaning. The election campaign promised to be violent, there was a tense atmosphere, extravagant rumours were abroad. The moment was favourable to men of imaginative daring and unscrupulous ambition.

NOT A SURPRISE

Everyone – including the correspondents of British, French, and American newspapers in Berlin – expected 'something' – a staged Communist uprising, a fictitious attempt to murder Hitler, or a fire. The Reichswehr warned the Communists, through an intermediary, that they must not allow themselves to be provoked into any rash action. On no account must they provide an excuse for raising an anti-Bolshevik scare.

When on 27 February the Reichstag burst into flames no serious observer of German affairs was at all surprised. Nevertheless, there was widespread horror and panic. Many understood the signal well and fled the country forthwith, fearing to wait until they should be arrested or until the frontiers should be closed. There were workmen who, with shrewd foresight, at once buried their 'Marxist' literature. It was the Reichstag fire, not the Chancellorship of Hitler nor his electoral victory on 5 March, that began the Brown Terror.

The fire was instantaneously attributed to the Communists by the Government, which at once began to manufacture false evidence, thereby not inculpating but rather exculpating the Communists and deepening the suspicion felt by all objective observers that the real incendiaries were to be found within the Cabinet itself. Before the tribunal of history it is not the Communists, not the wretched van der Lubbe (their alleged instrument, whose public execution Hitler has threatened before his guilt has been proved, before he has even been tried), but the German Government that is arraigned.

A confidential memorandum on the events leading up to the fire is circulating in Germany. It is in manuscript, and the Terror makes any open mention or discussion of it impossible. But it is a serious attempt by one in touch with the Nationalist members of the Cabinet to give a balanced account of these events. In spite of one or two minor inaccuracies it shows considerable inside knowledge. While not authoritative in an absolute and final manner, it is at least a first and a weighty contribution towards solving the riddle of that fire. The memorandum contains certain allegations of high interest that will be discussed in the next article.

Appendix B

THE MANCHESTER GUARDIAN
27 April 1933

THE REICHSTAG FIRE
II. *Nazis Guilty?*
A NATIONALIST VERSION
Storm Troopers Accused

Germany, April.

THE 'Karl Liebknecht Haus', the headquarters of the Communist Party, and editorial office of the 'Rote Fahne', had been searched again and again by the police, but no incriminating matter had been found. The Nationalists were opposed to the suppression of the Communists, for without the Communist members the Nazis would have had an absolute majority in the Reichstag. This the Nationalists wished to avoid at any cost.

But the chief of the Berlin Police, Melcher, a Nationalist, resigned under Nazi pressure. He was replaced by Admiral von Levetzow, a Nazi. On 24 February the Karl Liebknecht Haus was again searched. On the 26th the 'Conti', a Government news agency, issued a report on the sinister and momentous finds that were supposed to have been made 'in subterranean vaults' and 'catacombs' that had long been cleared of everything by the forewarned Communists. The report also hinted darkly at plans for a Bolshevik revolution. The confidential Nationalist memorandum mentioned in the first article describes the annoyance of the Nationalist members of the Cabinet over the clumsiness and transparent untruthfulness of this report. They refused to allow the suppression of the Communist Party.

On 25 February a fire started in the old Imperial Palace. It was quickly extinguished. The incendiary escaped, leaving a box of matches and some inflammable matter behind. From various parts of the country came news – all of it untrue – of arson and outrage perpetrated by Communists. On the 27th, according to the memorandum, the chief Nazi agitators, Hitler, Göring, and

Goebbels, all three of whom are members of the present German Government, were, 'strangely enough', not touring the country to address election meetings, although the campaign was at its height, but were assembled in Berlin 'waiting for their fire'.

THE ACCUSATION

The Reichstag is connected with the Speaker's residence by a subterranean passage. Through this passage, according to the memorandum, 'the emissaries of Herr Göring (the Speaker) entered the Reichstag'. Each of these emissaries – they wore civilian clothes – 'went to his assigned place, and in a few minutes sufficient inflammable matter was distributed throughout the building' (after the fire had been quenched several heaps of rags and shavings soaked in petrol were found unburnt or half-burnt).

The Storm Troopers then, so the memorandum continues, withdrew through the passage to the Speaker's residence, put on their brown uniforms, and made off. They left behind them in the Reichstag building Van der Lubbe, who, so as to make sure that the Communists could be incriminated, had taken the precaution to have on his person his Dutch passport, a Communist leaflet, several photographs of himself, and what seems to have been the membership card of some Dutch Communist group.

THE OFFICIAL STORY

On the following day, the 28th, the fire was announced by the official 'Preussische Pressedienst' as intended to begin the Bolshevik revolution in Germany, the plans for this revolution having been discovered amongst 'the hundreds of hundredweights of seditious matter' found in the 'vaults and catacombs' of the Karl Liebknecht Haus. According to these plans 'Government buildings, museums, palaces, and essential plant were to be fired', disorders were to be provoked, terrorist groups were to advance behind screens of 'women and children, if possible the women and children of police officers', there were to be terrorist attacks on private property, and a 'general civil war' was to commence.

It is peculiar that no preparations for this civil war had been made by the German Government – there had been time enough, for the alleged plans had been discovered on the 24th. Whenever there has been the slightest reason to suspect violent action against the State, carbines are served out to the police, Government buildings are specially guarded, and the Wilhelmstrasse is patrolled night and day. No precautions of this kind were taken against the 'general civil war', not even after the fire in the Imperial Palace.

The 'Angriff', of which Dr Goebbels is editor, announced that the documents found in the Karl Liebknecht Haus would be 'placed before the public with all speed'. Eight weeks have passed and this has not been done.

FALSE REPORTS

The full political effects of the Reichstag fire could not be achieved merely by the presence of a Communist (with leaflet and membership card) in the Reichstag building. The Nazis have all along been bent on the destruction of 'Marxism' as a whole – that is to say, of Social Democracy as well as Communism. The communiqué of the 'Preussische Pressedienst' therefore added that 'the Reichstag incendiary has in his confession admitted that he is connected with the Socialist Party. Through this confession the united Communist-Socialist front has become a palpable fact.' Since then the Nazi press has repeatedly published false reports that arms and ammunition have been found hidden in rooms owned by the Socialist trade unions.

So as to incriminate the Communists still further, it was announced (in the 'Deutsche Allgemeine Zeitung') that their leaders Torgler and Koenen had spent several hours in the Reichstag on the evening of the 27th, and had been seen not only with van der Lubbe but also with several other persons who were carrying torches, these persons having eluded arrest by escaping through the passage to the Speaker's residence. Why did no one telephone to the Speaker's residence to have them arrested there? The question remains unanswered.

Two persons happened to get into the Reichstag almost immediately after the fire broke out. One of them rang up the 'Vorwärts' with the news. He was promptly cut off at the exchange, and was, together with his companion, arrested. Neither has been heard of since – the memorandum describes the one as a member of the staff (*Redakteur*) of the 'Vorwärts', but this is an error. The arrest of Stampfer, the editor, was at once ordered, and the editorial office was occupied by police within an hour (Stampfer eluded arrest by flight). The entire Socialist press throughout Prussia was suppressed on the night of the fire. The first edition of the 'Vorwärts' was already out, but all copies were confiscated by the police. On the morning of the 28th, Torgler gave himself up to the police of his own free will, accompanied by his solicitor, Dr Rosenfeld, and prepared to face and answer any charges that might be brought against him. This was most inconvenient – 'his flight', according to the memorandum, 'would have been much more desirable'.

A SCARE CREATED

But the fire made a deep impression on the electorate. The elimination of the Socialist press in Prussia and the rigorous censorship on all other papers allowed hardly a suspicion to get into print. The Nationalists could not speak up, for even if they did not want the Nazis to have the mastery they could not afford to see them collapse – and the truth about the fire, if publicly known, would have meant the collapse of the Nazi movement. The scaremongering story of the impending Bolshevik revolution was supplemented by others – an alleged plot to assassinate Hitler, the alleged discovery of Communist arsenals and munition dumps, and so on. Such stories are still being invented and appear in the Nazi papers almost every day.

A Bolshevik scare was created, especially in the country districts (stories of burning villages were calculated to impress the imagination of the peasantry). Hitler seemed the one saviour from anarchy and red revolution. That scare not only gave the Nazis and Nationalists a joint majority, it also unleashed that inhuman persecution of Communists, Socialists, Liberals, pacifists, and Jews which is still going on. It made the complete suppression of the Communist Party possible, thus eliminating its members from the Reichstag and giving the Nazis the absolute and overwhelming majority which the elections alone had not given them.

Despite the clumsiness with which it was staged, and despite the grossness of the falsehoods with which facts and motives were concealed, the fire turned out to be a big success. The legend that it was the work of Communists and Social Democrats is the main foundation of the Hitlerite Dictatorship and of the Brown Terror.

Appendix C

THE OBERFOHREN MEMORANDUM

As published by the German Information Office, London, in 1933, except for minor alterations where the original English translation made poor sense. A. J. P.

INTRODUCTION

GERMAN Conservatives had for years encouraged and supported the Nazis. They did not think much of Hitler – he was too big a demagogue for them, besides being a foreigner (it was only later on that he exchanged his Austrian nationality for German). But the impoverished, demoralized middle-class was rallying round him and, in the villages and smaller towns, he was not only pushing back the local Socialists and Communists but was creating a movement that would, in time, challenge Socialism and Communism in their strongholds, the big industrial cities.

The Nazis, with immense propagandist skill, an instinctive sense of what would work on the German imagination, and with a new colourful romanticism and glittering martial display, roused long-dormant emotions and fired the youth of middle-class Germany into a revivalist mass-activity against organized labour.

To the German Conservatives – notably the German-National People's Party which is (or rather was, for it has gone down in the storm it helped to raise) roughly what right-wing Tories are in England – the new movement was more than welcome. At last, they thought, there was hope of achieving what years of vain effort by the gentry, the bankers, the industrial leaders, the judiciary, and the army, had failed to achieve, namely to thrust organized labour back to where it had been before the war.

And so they helped the Nazis where they could – they openly admired their martial spirit, applauded their idealism, and helped to fill the capacious and insatiable Nazi purse.

The Conservative calculation was not only accurate – it was too accurate. The Nazis did all that was expected of them – and much more. They developed a contagious fervour that swept the nation. They claimed to represent a new generation, they preached a kind of romantic, middle-class Socialism, and adopted the phraseology of revolution. They became by far the biggest of the political parties, thus ousting the Socialists from a position they had held for years.

Though financed by the same people and representing, as their decrees since gaining power have clearly shown, the same interests as the Conservatives, the Nazis had no intention of being the docile agents of the Conservatives – if they were victorious, then victory was to be theirs and theirs only.

Even in 1932, the Conservatives were getting alarmed. They still hoped that, together with the Nazis, they would have a majority in the Reichstag, they themselves just making up the difference between majority and minority, and so holding the balance of power. But the Nazis were not submitting to tame partnership in a conventional coalition.

So with incomparable audacity and imaginative cunning, they set fire to the German Parliament, the Reichstag, and, by putting the blame on the Communists and Socialists, they raised a Bolshevik scare and started an anti-Labour drive, creating an entirely new situation in which they could set their Terror going. They had long been training their militants, the Brown Shirts and Black Shirts, for this Terror. While winning a great electoral victory on the 5th March, they carried out arrests, beatings, and shootings, thus laying the foundations of the dictatorship that is still in power.

The Parliamentary leader of the German-National People's Party was Dr Oberfohren. He had been a hater of Socialism and Communism. The Nazis had filled him, too, with hope that they would stem its progress. But he was a man of decency. He could honour an honest opponent, like the Communist leader, Ernst Torgler, even when he fought him ruthlessly.

To him the triumph of the Nazis soon came to mean the triumph of barbaric violence and the end, not only of Socialism and Communism, but of law, order, and morality.

The burning of the Reichstag was to him an abomination. The world, he thought, should know about it and should be told what the Nazis really are. Only thus, he believed, could their influence be counteracted and, perhaps, their sweeping advance held up.

So he inspired a journalist to write a memorandum on the Reichstag fire, he himself supplying most of the necessary information (being in touch with the Cabinet in which his own Party was represented, he knew more than most). This is the now famous 'Oberfohren Memorandum', which contains the fullest existing account of circumstances surrounding the fire. Every newspaper being in Nazi hands, it was impossible to secure its publication in the ordinary way. Typewritten copies were secretly circulated in Germany towards the end of March.

One of these copies was brought out of Germany by an English journalist in April and so it reached the outside world, the first extracts being published in the *Manchester Guardian* on 27 April.

The genesis of the Memorandum was kept a secret, but one day a detachment of Brown Shirts raided Dr Oberfohren's house (he was growing more and more suspect). A copy of the Memorandum was found there. He was given a brief period to take the only course left open to him. After writing a heart-broken letter to his friend, Dr Hugenberg, the chairman of the German-National People's Party, he committed suicide.

HITLER'S HANDS TIED

The conditions under which the General Field Marshal (Hindenburg) conferred the Chancellorship on Adolf Hitler were very hard for the N.S.D.A.P. (the Nazi Party). They had to agree that the German-Nationalist Ministers were given a clear majority in the National Coalition Cabinet. They were also forced to agree to the appointment of a Vice-Chancellor with equal rights in the person of Herr von Papen. The very day after their accession to office, the N.S.D.A.P. were obliged to accept the transfer of the powers of the Commissioner for Prussia, conferred upon the Chancellor by the emergency decree of 20 July 1932, to the Vice-Chancellor Herr von Papen. The Prussian Executive had been deprived of all authority. It retained purely advisory functions.

Another thorn in Hitler's flesh was the promise he had been forced to make to Hindenburg that without the latter's consent no changes whatever would be made in the National Coalition Cabinet, no matter what the results of the elections demanded by the N.S.D.A.P.

Hindenburg had already had unpleasant experiences with a similar undertaking. At the time of Herr von Papen's nomination to the Chancellorship – in summer, 1932 – Hitler had tried to break his promise following his electoral victory in August, 1932, and had demanded the leadership of the Cabinet. His demand, as is well known, was met by a sharp refusal on the part of the General Field Marshal.

On 30 January Hitler had had to give a specific promise in the presence of all the other members of the Cabinet. During the election campaign that followed, individual members of the Cabinet, especially the Stahlhelm* leaders repeatedly referred to this pledge, and assured their supporters that the leader of the N.S.D.A.P. was bound to keep his word of honour.

GÖRING AND GOEBBELS TRY TO FREE HITLER

National-Socialist circles round Göring and Goebbels tried desperately to find a way out of this impasse. This section of the N.S.D.A.P., particularly the ambitious Dr Goebbels, had not the smallest intention of playing second fiddle to anyone. They regarded the hegemony of the N.S.D.A.P. as absolutely indispensable. A situation in which the relationship of forces within the Cabinet was distributed was intolerable to them. Further, Goebbels and his friends recognized that the authority of the General Field Marshal had grown enormously throughout the Nationalist ranks. They were also conscious of the fact that the greater part of the Stahlhelm and the Reichswehr† stood solidly behind the General Field Marshal and his Nationalist friends. Nor could Göring and Goebbels count on the police in the German States. In the largest State, Prussia, the police force was honeycombed with Social Democratic sympathizers.

Goebbels and his circle paid special attention to recent trends among the working classes. They could not help noticing, and fearing, the emergence of a Social Democrat-Communist United Front among the workers, in spite of all the resistance of the Social Democratic leaders, and in spite of many mistakes on the part of the Communist leadership.

The National-Socialist minority in the Cabinet had already tried in vain to force the prohibition of the Communist Party at one of the very first Cabinet meetings. But Herr Hugenberg had pointed

* Ex-Servicemen's organization; paramilitary and German-Nationalist in sympathy.
† The regular army.

out the likelihood of public disorder by uncontrolled and un-controllable acts of terror on the part of the Communists or Left Radical elements once the restraints imposed by preserving the legality of the Party had been removed.

The Police President,* Melcher, had made repeated raids on the Karl Liebknecht Haus. † At the beginning of February, yet another of these thorough searches was made. The result of this search showed that the building was as good as abandoned by the Communist Party. All documents, typewriters and stationery had been cleared out of the office, and all that was left in the bookshop and storerooms was a small number of pamphlets. Only the so-called City Press was still functioning and producing election material. All that was left in the former Party Secretariat was a man to answer the telephone.

GÖRING AND GOEBBELS CONCOCT A PLAN

Göring and Goebbels, the two most active champions in the fight for the hegemony of the N.S.D.A.P., took counsel. The ingenious Goebbels, handicapped by no scruple, soon devised a plan, the realization of which would not only overcome the resistance of the German-Nationalists to the demands of the N.S.D.A.P. for suppression of Social Democratic and Communist agitation, but, in case of its complete success, also force the actual prohibition of the Communist Party.

Goebbels considered it essential to plant such material in the Karl Liebknecht Haus as would establish the criminal intention of the Communists, the impending threat of Communist insurrection, and the grave danger of delaying. Since Melcher's police could find nothing in the Karl Liebknecht Haus, a new Police President had perforce to be appointed, and from the ranks of the National-Socialists. Only reluctantly did Herr von Papen let his henchman Melcher go from the Police Presidium. The proposal of the N.S.D.A.P. to nominate as Police President the leader of the Berlin S.A., ‡ Count Helldorff, was rejected. Agreement was finally reached on the more moderate Admiral von Levetzow, who certainly belonged to the N.S.D.A.P., but who had preserved certain connections with German-Nationalist circles. The

---

* Of Berlin.
† Communist Party Headquarters.
‡ *Sturmabteilung*, the private army of the Nazis.

smuggling of material into the vacant Liebknecht Haus was simplicity itself. The police had blueprints of the building, and the necessary documents could easily be brought in.

Goebbels had been perfectly aware from the first that it would be necessary to emphasize the seriousness and the credibility of the documents he had forged by some incident or other, even if only an indirectly suggestive one. This question, too, was not neglected.

THE PLAN PUT INTO EXECUTION

On 24 February the police entered the Karl Liebknecht Haus, which had now been standing empty for weeks, searched it and sealed it.* On the same day the discovery of a mass of treasonable material was officially announced.

On 26 February, 'Conti', a Government news agency, issued an exhaustive report of the results of the search. There is no point in reproducing this report word for word; the blood-and-thunder style of the announcement must have struck every impartial reader of it. Secret corridors, secret trapdoors and passages, catacombs, underground vaults, and similar mysteries were all listed in detail. The whole make-up of the report appeared the more ridiculous, in that, for example, the cellars of an ordinary building were described, literally, in such fantastic terms as 'underground vaults' and 'catacombs'. People must have wondered how it was that many tons of the most exact instructions for carrying out the supposed revolution had ostensibly been hidden in well-concealed annexes to the cellars. Particularly ridiculous was the announcement that these hidden discoveries provided clear proof 'that the Communist Party and its subsidiaries maintained a second, illegal, underground existence'!

Within the Coalition Cabinet the results of the search of the Karl Liebknecht Haus gave rise to the most lively controversy. Papen, Hugenberg and Seldte reproached Herr Göring in the sharpest possible manner for making use of such a common swindle. They pointed out that the documents supposed to have been found were so crudely forged that in no circumstances must they be made public.† They held that much more care should have been taken,

---

* The only search of the Karl Liebknecht Haus ever carried out at which the Secretary of the Communist Party was not present and at which receipts were not given for material taken away; see evidence London Commission of Inquiry.

† Today, seven months later, they have not yet been made public.

after the fashion of the English Conservatives at the time of the Zinoviev-letter forgery. The clumsiness of the communiqué issued to the Conti agency was attacked. German-Nationalists and the Stahlhelm both maintained that no one could be expected to believe that the Communists would have chosen, of all places, the Karl Liebknecht Haus as their illegal headquarters. The forgeries would have looked far more convincing had the illegal head-quarters been 'unearthed' in some other district.

However, once the whole affair had been made public, the German-Nationalists had no alternative but to agree to the anti-Communist decrees. They had never been motivated by any regard for the Communists; what they criticized was the clumsiness of the whole proceedings. And, moreover, they were particularly anxious that, come what may, the Communist Party should be allowed to contest the forthcoming elections, lest the National-Socialists obtain a clear majority in the Reichstag.*

The German-Nationalist paper *Montagszeitung* did in fact publish an announcement to the effect that the Government had been forced, in view of the material found, to take stern defensive measures. Among the proposed measures to be discussed on Tuesday, 28 February, one of the most striking was the prohibition of the printing† of foreign press reports injurious to the Government.

GOEBBELS AND GÖRING TAKE FURTHER COUNSEL

Goebbels and Göring were furious at the obstinacy of their German-Nationalist ally. They wanted at all costs to force the pro-hibition of the Communist Party. In order to increase the plausibility of the material found, they had already organized, with the help of devoted confidants, acts of arson in various parts of the city. On 25 February, for example, No. 43 of the Berlin evening paper *Tempo* announced in gigantic four-column headlines the discovery of a fire in the former Imperial Palace. In the course of their controversy with their German-Nationalist ally, the National-Socialists had come to understand that obtaining the prohibition of

* Reichstag election, November 1932 (before the fire) : Nazis 196, Nationalists 51, total 247; all others 337, less 100 Communists, 237. New election, March 1933 (after the fire): Nazis 288, Nationalists 52, total 340; all others 307, less 81 Communists, 226.

† In Germany.

the Communist Party was no easy task. Consequently a more prominent building had to be set on fire. A blow could then be dealt to the Communists and Social-Democrats and the German-Nationalist ally faced with a *fait accompli*.

All was prepared. On Monday, 27 February, for some extraordinary reason, not one of the National-Socialist Propaganda General Staff was engaged in the election campaign. Herr Hitler, the indefatigable orator, Herr Goebbels, Herr Göring, all happened to be in Berlin. With them was the *Daily Express* correspondent, Sefton Delmer.* So, in a cosy family party, these gentlemen waited for their fire.

THE FIRE

Meanwhile the agents of Herr Göring, led by the Silesian S.A. leader, Reichstag-deputy Heines,† entered the Reichstag through the heating-pipe passage leading from the palace of the President of the Reichstag, Göring. Every S.A. and S.S.‡ leader was carefully selected and had a special station assigned to him. As soon as the outposts in the Reichstag signalled that the Communist deputies Torgler and Koenen had left the building, the S.A. troop set to work. There was plenty of incendiary material, and in a few minutes it was prepared. All the men withdrew into the President's Palace, where they resumed their S.A. uniforms and whence they could disappear unhampered. The only one to be left behind was their creature, van der Lubbe, whom they had thoughtfully provided with a Communist leaflet on the United Front, a few odd photographs of himself, and even, it appears, a membership carrd of some Dutch Communist splinter group.

CONFUSION

The incendiaries, Goebbels and Göring, had thought out everything very cleverly, but they had none the less made far too many mistakes, mistakes that are very difficult to understand considering

---

* *Sic.* But Mr Delmer was not in Hitler's company *before the fire*. He learnt of its outbreak from a colleague who lived near the scene and arrived within a few minutes. Accordingly, the imputation in the memorandum is clearly unjustified. It is, however, easy to see how Oberfohren became mistaken. Mr Delmer in his account relates that, while hastening to the Reichstag, he was overtaken by Hitler's car and passed through the police cordon in his company. Thus he arrived with Hitler *just after the fire*.

† A self-confessed and convicted murde_er, now Chief of Police of Breslau.

‡ *Schutzstaffeln*, another section of the N.S.D.A.P. private army.

the skill and ingenuity of the present Minister of Propaganda. Let us look at some of them. In the official announcement of 28 February (Prussian Press Service) we can read, *inter alia*: 'This fire is the most monstrous act of terror yet committed by Bolshevism in Germany. Among the many tons of subversive material that the police discovered in their raid on the Karl Liebknecht Haus were instructions for running a Communist terror campaign on the Bolshevik model. According to these documents, Government buildings, museums, palaces and essential buildings were to be set on fire. Further, instructions were given to place women and children, if possible those of police officials, at the head of terrorist groups in cases of conflict or disorder. The burning of the Reichstag was to have been the signal for bloody insurrection and civil war. Widespread looting was to have broken out in Berlin as early as 4 a.m. on Tuesday. It has been established that for today (28 February) acts of terror were planned against certain individuals, against private property, against the life and safety of the population.'

The astonished reader may well ask how it was that the police authorities and the Minister of the Interior waited until after the burning of the Reichstag on 27 February to take their anti-Bolshevik steps, when they had 'discovered' the plans for the insurrection as early as the 24th. Further, as early as Saturday, 25 February, an act of arson was discovered in the former Imperial Palace. But Herr Göring and Herr Levetzow did nothing at all to guard Government buildings, palaces or museums. That was one of the mistakes they made in their hurry.

But it was certainly not the only one. Who in his right senses can believe the fairy tale they have spread about the incendiary van Lubbe? A hiker arrives from Holland. He spends the night of 17-18 February in Glindow near Potsdam. In the 'Green Tree Inn' he produces his Dutch passport and signs the visitors' book with his full name, birthplace, and place of usual residence. He is poorly dressed in a grey coat and soft hat, and in no way distinguishable from any of the other hikers that throng the roads. On 18 February, he leaves Glindow in the direction of Werder-Berlin. On the 19 February or so, he reaches Berlin, and lo and behold, he immediately succeeds in joining the Action Committee of the plotters and is assigned a most important part in helping to fire the Reichstag barely ten days later. Whereupon this fine revolutionary sticks a Dutch passport, a United Front leaflet and so on in his pocket, stays behind in the Reichstag and is the only one to get himself arrested by the police. 'Look, everybody, here's the Communist who set fire to the Reichstag.' Herr Goebbels and Herr Göring have badly overestimated the credulity of world public opinion. It is an even happier chance that this van Lubbe also volunteered the information that he was in touch with the S.P.D.* In the Press Service† report mentioned above we read: 'The Reichstag incendiary has admitted his contacts with the S.P.D. By this admission, the Communist-Social Democrat United Front has been implicated.' Goebbels and Göring went further still, although, on the whole, perhaps a little too far. For they also produced three scoundrels who had allegedly seen Deputies Torgler and Koenen in the Reichstag with van Lubbe. The *Deutsche Allgemeine Zeitung* declared that Herr Torgler had spent several hours before the fire in the company of the incendiary who was later arrested, and also with a number of other individuals, some of whom were seen carrying torches. The only reason why these individuals were not caught was because they managed to escape through the subterranean heating passage leading to the palace of the Reichstag President.

The astonished reader may well wonder once again why Herr Torgler was allowed to run about the Reichstag with several persons, all equipped with torches, for several hours. And he may also marvel at the smartness of Herr Göring, or at least of his police, who discovered, even before the fire was extinguished, that the incendiaries must have got away through the subterranean heating passage.

It may, perhaps, be worth mentioning further that two reporters from the *Vorwärts* managed to slip through the cordon round the Reichstag, to get into a telephone booth in the Reichstag and to ring up the *Vorwärts* with the news that Herr Göring had set the Reichstag on fire. Naturally, they were both caught in the telephone booth, if only as 'proof' that it was the Social Democrats who had started the rumour that Göring had set fire to the Reichstag. Again, Mr Sefton Delmer of the *Daily Express*, who had waited with Göring, Hitler and Goebbels for the conflagration to break

* Social Democratic Party.

† Official Prussian Press Service, under the direct control of Göring.

out,* wired to his newspaper that shortly after the news of the fire became known, he met his friends in the Reichstag. When Hitler saw von Papen there, he said to Papen: 'If this fire, as I believe, turns out to be the handiwork of Communists, then nothing can now stop us crushing this murder pest with an iron fist.' A little later, Göring joined them as well and said to Herr Hitler: 'This is undoubtedly the work of Communists. A number of Communist deputies were in the Reichstag twenty minutes before the fire broke out. We have succeeded in arresting one of the incendiaries.' Alas, how obvious this dispatch of Mr Sefton Delmer makes it why the Reichstag was burned!

How beautifully, too, they had prepared the lists of people to be arrested by the police! Hundreds of addresses had been got together, not only of Communists, but also of bourgeois journalists who might have added their voices to the protest. . . .†

THE GERMAN-NATIONALISTS AND THE FIRE

Though the German-Nationalist Party was in full agreement with the severe measures against the Communists, it was as fully opposed to the act of arson carried out by its partner in the Coalition. Thus the Cabinet endorsed the severest measures against the Communists and also against the Social-Democrats, but voiced the opinion that the fire would seriously damage the reputation of the National Front‡ abroad. So outraged were the Nationalists that the National-Socialist ministers failed to obtain the prohibition of the Communist Party. They§ needed the Communist deputies to prevent the National-Socialists securing a clear majority in Parliament. The Cabinet also told Herr Göring not to publish the forgeries he had 'found' in the Karl Liebknecht Haus. It was pointed out to him that the publication of these clumsy forgeries would damage the Government even further. Particularly embarrassing to the Government was the fact that the Communist deputy Torgler, Chairman of the Communist fraction in the Reichstag, had surrendered to the police on the Tuesday morning. It would have been far preferable had he fled abroad. The mere fact

* *Sic.* But Mr Delmer was not with Hitler before the fire. (In fact, Delmer won a libel action against one retailer of this completely unsubstantiated rumour. A. J. P.)
† This sentence was incomplete in the original.
‡ The coalition of the Nationalist groups.
§ *Sic.* 'They' refers to the German-Nationalist Ministers.

that, accused though he was of so grave a crime, after the arrest of thousands of Communist officials, and in peril of execution under martial law, he yet placed himself at the disposal of the police, was in the highest degree annoying to the Government. Herr Göring was instructed to deny that Torgler had surrendered voluntarily. The world press was, however, so unanimous in ascribing the fire to leading members of the Government, that the National Government's reputation was seriously undermined.

GÖRING AND GOEBBELS TAKE FURTHER COUNSEL

Much as Göring and Goebbels welcomed the paralysis of the Communist and Social Democratic election machinery, though they knew that broad masses of the petty bourgeoisie, white-collar workers, and peasants would believe their tales about the burning of the Reichstag and consequently vote for the N.S.D.A.P. as the vanguard against Bolshevism, they were not at all pleased with the position taken up by the German-Nationalist Ministers in the Cabinet. Approval continued to be withheld from the prohibition of the Communist Party. With increasing bitterness they felt that their boundless ambition was hemmed in by German-Nationalists, Stahlhelm and Reichswehr. It was obvious to them that they must break this grip as soon as possible. They plotted and schemed.

At last, this group decided on a bid for power during the night of 5–6 March. The plan was to occupy the Government buildings and to force Hindenburg to reconstruct the Cabinet. Should he refuse, his abdication was to be demanded. In that case, Hindenburg was to hand the Reich Presidency over to Hitler, and Hitler would appoint Göring as Chancellor. There was some talk that this might perhaps be effected on the occasion of the great propaganda march of the S.A. and the S.S. through Berlin, combined with the ceremonial paying of homage to Hitler, which had been fixed for Friday, 3 March. This great propaganda march was now being prepared with every possible dispatch. Already numerous battalions of S.A. men from districts outside Berlin were camped within the city, the streets along the route of the procession were cordoned off by the police, traffic was diverted, and thousands waited in the Wilhelmstrasse* for the demonstration.

As rumours were spreading that this march was to lead to seizure of the Government buildings, the German-Nationalist Ministers

* The quarter in which the Government buildings are situated.

managed, at the eleventh hour, to obtain Hitler's agreement to abandon the route through the Wilhelmstrasse. The thousands in the Wilhelmstrasse were suddenly informed, to their astonishment, that the S.A. procession was to take another route not touching the Wilhelmstrasse, but going west through the Prinz-Albrechtstrasse. The German-Nationalists had to bind themselves in return to renounce the march of the Stahlhelm through the Government quarter. The Stahlhelm march had been proposed as a march of homage to Hindenburg. To this change, the Stahlhelm leaders agreed.

A GERMAN-NATIONALIST COUNTER-MARCH

The German-Nationalist Ministers were in a very serious position. The election results in Lippe-Detmold had shown how real was the danger of the German-Nationalist voters going over bag and baggage to the Nazis. Their propaganda was no match at all for the Nazis'. The Herrenklub,* the Stahlhelm groups and the German-Nationalist leaders consulted together. Nazi occupation of the Government buildings having only just been averted on Friday afternoon, reliance could not be placed on the Stahlhelm and Reichswehr alone keeping the Nazis at bay on the night of 5–6 March. It was clear that the masses stood, not behind Hindenburg, but behind their idol Hitler. It would have been futile to fight alone against these masses and their mass enthusiasm. The only thing left was to act as unscrupulously as Göring and Goebbels had acted when they set fire to the Reichstag. The following plan was devised. The public would be told officially about the results of the investigation into the Reichstag fire, but the announcement would be so worded that, in case of need, it could be used against the Nazis. An official announcement of this kind could be used to exert pressure on the Nazi Ministers, if they really persisted in their plan to occupy Government buildings. In that way it was intended to fill the Nazi masses with doubt and to win them over for the National Front under the leadership of the German-Nationalists and Hindenburg. An appeal was prepared to nationalist Germany, in which Hindenburg would reveal the plot for the violent seizure of power,† accuse Göring, Goebbels and Hitler of arson, referring to the earlier, ambiguous communiqué, and summon the Nazi

* A group of *Junkers*, landowners and militarists – the Papen circle.
† By the National-Socialists.

masses to rally behind Hindenburg as the only effective answer to
Marxism. Hindenburg himself was not to be present at the
Stahlhelm's ceremony of homage to him, but was to spend the
night of the 5th-6th outside Berlin under the protection of the
Reichswehr. The Reichswehr itself would be put on the alert.

THE OFFICIAL ANNOUNCEMENT OF FRIDAY, 3 MARCH

The chief of the political police, Dr Diels, a man who, in spite of
his membership of the N.S.D.A.P., was very close to the German-
Nationalists, summoned, in the late evening hours of Friday, a
press conference to receive and make public the results of the
investigation, as far as it had gone, into the burning of the Reichstag. The Nazis were told that this communiqué was being issued
to support their election campaign. Besides the communiqué, Diels
gave out photographs of the incendiary, of his passport, of a Communist leaflet found on him, and of the gutted Session Chamber.
At the same time a reward of 20,000 marks was promised for
information leading to the discovery of those implicated in the
burning. The significant passages in the official announcement ran
as follows:

> 'There can be no question of van der Lubbe's having been in contact
> with the K.P.D.* Van der Lubbe is known to the police as a Com-
> munist agitator.'

Exact consideration of these two sentences reveals their ambiguity, indeed, rather, their single significance. Van der Lubbe's
contact with the K.P.D. is said not to be in 'question'; now, this can
mean that such contact has been proven; but it can also mean the
exact opposite. Now, this very ambiguity could – if the need arose –
be used to exonerate the K.P.D. Or take the following sentences:

> 'Van der Lubbe admits his own participation in the crime. How far the
> investigations have proved the complicity of other persons cannot at
> the moment be revealed in the interests of the pending proceedings
> and the safety of the State.'

It is perfectly obvious that the security of the State could be no
ground for concealment of serious evidence against Communists.
For election purposes, it would have been far better to say: 'The
investigations have shown cause for serious suspicions against
persons either belonging to or closely associated with the K.P.D.'

* German Communist Party.

306

But had the K.P.D. been accused straight out, the purpose of this press conference and of this communiqué as means of pressure against the Nazi Ministers would have been defeated. Further, one must not forget Diels's evasive answer – again in the interests of security – to an inquisitive journalist, who asked *how far* grounds existed for serious suspicions that there had been contacts between van der Lubbe and other Communists. How could the safety of the State have been endangered if Diels had merely declared that grounds *existed* for such suspicions?

Diels also refused to say anything about the discovery of seditious instructions in the Karl Liebknecht Haus, 'lest their content be made known to Communists throughout the Reich'. (This although Göring had already published the most essential part of this 'incriminating' material in an official announcement on the night of the fire.) At this moment, declared the ingenious Dr Diels, he would rather not make any statement about the assertion that van der Lubbe had been seen in the Reichstag with the Communist deputy Torgler or else with Koenen. (Why not?)

THE 5TH OF MARCH

Election day had come, and the police had taken a multitude of precautions. In particular, public buildings were guarded, far more carefully even than had been decreed after the fire. The authorities gave out that preparations had been made for every possible eventuality. None the less, it was said that demonstrations of some kind must be expected as soon as the definite results of the election became known.

With streets strongly guarded by police patrols on horseback, on foot and in motor vans, election day passed off unusually quietly in the capital. The Stahlhelm demonstration in honour of Hindenburg took place in Hindenburg's absence. In Hindenburg's message to the Stahlhelm we find the following remarkable passage: 'Your wish to convey to me the greetings of former Front soldiers cannot, unfortunately, be gratified for reasons which I have given verbally.' On the advice of his friends, Hindenburg was spending the day in Doeberitz with the Reichswehr, and not in the Government quarters. Hitler, however, had been told that Hindenburg was ill and unable to leave his palace. The Nazis thought that the President was in the Wilhelmstrasse on the night of 5 March. The Stahlhelm had already announced that its country contingents would move into Berlin for the night of the 5th–6th. In a Stahl-helm communiqué dated 12 March ('Die junge Front', No. 11) it is stated that after the demonstration, the field-grey Stahl-helm companies waited in readiness for further orders until mid-night before they were dismissed.

Shortly after the close of the ballot, between 6.30 and 8.30, picked S.A. troops poured into Berlin in squadrons of brand-new motor vans. One of these detachments, consisting of six vans, each carrying about thirty to forty men, drove from the Heerstrasse across the Reichskanzlerplatz and down the Neue Kantstrasse and Tauentzienstrasse at about 6.45 p.m. The occupants of the vans were newly equipped, wore dark breeches and dark S.S. caps, and brown shirts with brassards. Silently, without cheers, without slogans, these detachments rushed with extreme speed into the city, behind a special car carrying the leaders.

The Reichswehr, too, was not idle. The Reichskanzlerplatz was patrolled by an armoured radio car, and so were all roads leading into the city. In that way the Reichswehr command was given an exact picture of the forces pouring in as well as of their subsequent movements.

Midnight was the hour fixed for seizing the Government buildings. The Nazi leaders, including Hitler, Göring, Goebbels and Frick, waited in the Reich Chancellory. Shortly before eleven a strong detachment of Reichswehr officers, led by General von Blomberg, called on Hitler. They requested Hitler to order the immediate withdrawal of his private army. Hitler was also informed that Hindenburg was in Doeberitz with the Reichswehr and that the Reichswehr would quash any attempt at a violent seizure of power on the part of the Nazis.

For this purpose the Stahlhelm was stationed ready for action in a ring round the centre of the city and at other strategic points. In addition, the most important public buildings were occupied by the Reichswehr. Hitler was required further to announce to the press that, in spite of the great electoral victory of the Nazis, which even at this hour was already certain, no change would be made in the composition of the Government. In case of refusal, General Blom-berg declared, shortly and firmly, that Hitler, Göring, Goebbels and Frick would be arrested on suspicion of arson. Hindenburg would then issue an appeal to all Nationalists, and especially to the millions of Nazi voters, to stand firm behind him. The fight against Bolshevism called for the greatest determination, but the national cause must not be allowed to be soiled by such criminal acts as those committed by a number of the Nazi leaders. General Blomberg referred briefly to the equivocal communiqué of the political police issued on Friday night, which made it possible now for the Cabinet to denounce the Nazis as the true Reichstag incendiaries.

The gamble for power, which Hitler, Göring and Goebbels had imagined to be so easy, was lost. The torches they had lit had been snatched away by the German-Nationalists and their military allies. No time for reflection was granted. Motor cars bearing the adjutants of the Reichswehr and the S.A. and S.S. leaders accompanying them left the Wilhelmstrasse *en route* to all the action stations of the S.A. and S.S. The detachments of S.A. and S.S. men from outside the city which had been intended to occupy the Wilhelmstrasse left the city forthwith and returned to their camp in the Mark.* The Stahlhelm was told about midnight that no special orders were likely to be issued and that the men in field-grey could at last turn in.

NEW PLANS BY GÖRING AND GOEBBELS

Furious at being outwitted by their allies, Göring, Goebbels, and their cronies considered what next might be done. Should so gigantic an electoral success still bring them no nearer sole hegemony? They had 288 deputies and the German-Nationalist ally only fifty-two – a clear majority; yet the Cabinet still remained in the hands of the German-Nationalists.† This was really a bit too much for the pride of those who had already seen themselves as sole dictators of Germany. All that had taken place during this week in the way of illegal acts, private arrests by S.A. and S.S. men, private killings, bestial treatment of captured political opponents in the private prisons of the S.A.‡ – all had been organized by the Nazi leadership to create further disturbances and to provide the excuse for stealing further slices of power. Quick action was needed. In a

* Brandenburg.

† Before the Communist Party was prohibited, the Reichstag stood: National Front 340, Opponents 307; without the Communists: Nazis 288, all others (including Nationalists) 280.

‡ This is not the first protest by a German Conservative against Nazi brutality. See letter of Count Reventlow (an N.S.D.A.P. member) reprinted in the *Manchester Guardian*.

speech at Stettin, Göring expressly declared that he assumed full responsibility for every illegal act that might be committed during the week. The seizure of the newspaper offices of the Centre Party,* interference in administrative and judicial matters by S.A. troops, destruction of trade union buildings, in short everything that happened, all happened because the Leader so wished it. Goebbels busied himself with attacks on department stores and one-price shops.† Forgeries, like the letter from Messrs Hermann Tietz (a large department store) to the Central Committee of the Communist Party, were published to inflame the masses, and particularly the petty bourgeoisie. A deputation of S.A. men appeared outside the Stock Exchange, and as a climax to the disorder, Göring delivered the famous incitement speech of Essen, in the course of which he said: 'Go, rob and plunder far and wide. Break into houses, shoot – never mind if you shoot too far or too short – the main thing is, shoot! and don't come back to me without any booty.' This in short was the context of his infamous speech. A brigand chief could not have urged his bandits on more eloquently. During the night following this speech the S.A. seized the printing works of the Centre Party's newspaper and forced the editors, at gun point, to print Göring's speech verbatim on the front page. Two hundred thousand copies of the Centre Party newspaper were printed on the Friday morning and rushed by car for distribution to all towns and villages.

But the echoes of the speech had scarcely died away, when the Leader issued a new decree directly opposed to Göring's incitement.

Hitler, driven into a corner by the far more powerful and stronger forces of the German-Nationalists and Reichswehr, demanded, only a few hours after Göring's speech, in an appeal to his Party comrades of the S.A. and S.S., the strictest possible discipline, immediate cessation of all individual action, particularly the molestation of foreigners, the dislocation of motor traffic and the disturbance of business. Whoever promoted such acts was irresponsible and malicious. It was well-known that Communist spies were trying to incite Germans to such action. The further course of the national uprising must henceforth be directed from above. The effect of this appeal was like a thunderclap. A moment

* Catholic Centre Party.
† Shops like our Woolworths.

previously Göring had said: 'I refuse to regard the police as watchmen for Jewish department stores. There must be an end to the nuisance of every swindler detected in his swindles calling the police. The police will protect anyone in Germany who earns an honest living; they are not here to protect swindlers, bandits, usurers and traitors. To all those who say, that somewhere, some time, somebody has been seized and ill-treated, we can only reply: "You can't plane a board without shaving splinters." We live in exceptional times. For years we have been promising to settle accounts with these traitors.'

And a few hours later, Herr Hitler: 'Only unscrupulous individuals, and especially Communist spies, will seek to compromise the Party by individual action.' It was all too obvious.

GOEBBELS AND GÖRING STILL UNSATISFIED

Once more a shackled Hitler had been forced to call off the masses. Goebbels and Göring were frustrated. They now proposed to make a last attempt on Sunday 12 March. S.A. and S.S. men were equipped with cars and arms, ready to strike. They waited in vain – as they had waited in vain after the first Presidential election of 1932, as they had waited in vain in August 1932, and as they had waited in vain through the night of 5th–6th March.

As early as 10 a.m. the radio announced that the Reich Chancellor would make an important appeal at 2 p.m. And at two o'clock Adolf Hitler announced nothing more revolutionary than the Reich President's 'flag decree'* and added an energetic and extremely sharp appeal to his Party comrades for blind obedience to his orders. Every individual action must be suppressed. He, as Leader, appealed to them, the German people, in the name of the National Revolution. The economy must be put on a sound footing. Interference with the administration and with business must stop forthwith. All paltry desire for revenge must be checked. Hitler's appeal was repeated over the wireless almost hour by hour. S.A. and S.S. men all over the Reich listened to the impressive voice of the man they idolized. Goebbels, Göring and their cronies were powerless.

THE FIGHT GOES ON

Goebbels and Göring must postpone the realization of their dreams to some distant day. Goebbels is Reich Propaganda

* Making the Swastika Germany's new flag.

Minister. He keeps trying to undermine the Reichswehr, and to detach the Stahlhelm as well as the Reichswehr from the German-Nationalists. The Reichswehr is still exempt from hoisting the swastika flag, it still salutes the black-white-and-red banner with the iron cross. For how long? And who will prove stronger in the struggle? When will Hitler be unshackled?

This is the full text of the memorandum. The [original] translator has thought it better to preserve the irregularities and unclarities of what was obviously a very hastily typed sheet. Oberfohren has not had to wait long for the answers to his questions. Within three months the German-Nationalist Party had dissolved, the Stahlhelm had been incorporated into the ranks of the S.A., the Cabinet had been reconstructed and, as a climax, Göring has been promoted from Captain to General by Hindenburg! But rapid as has been this march of events, it has been too slow for Oberfohren, who was found dead on May 7th.

Had he lived, he would have seen Hitler still bound, as he and his Party must always be bound within the framework of its determination to preserve the national interests which the old German-Nationalists represent. But the mock-struggle he described has been resolved – the Nazis have bought power by endorsing in practice the substance, e.g. the whole social programme and decrees of the German-Nationalist landowning, military and big business interests; and the remaining German-Nationalists have bought tolerance by endorsing in silence the form, e.g. the brutalities of Göring, the demagogic falsehoods of Goebbels and what, as we see here, they know well to be the crowning infamy of tyranny of all time – the Leipzig trial.

Appendix D

EXTRACTS FROM THE WHITE BOOK ON THE
EXECUTIONS OF 30 JUNE 1934

(Editions du Carrefour, Paris, 1935.)

THE REICHSTAG INCENDIARIES

THE spectre of the Reichstag fire cannot be exorcized. In vain did
the Hitler Government try to clear its name before the whole world
at a trial lasting three months. In vain is Ernst Torgler being kept
imprisoned even after his acquittal, lest he raise his voice against the
true incendiaries. In vain did the Nazis hope that van der Lubbe's
secret would die with him. The accusing voices cannot be silenced.

Whenever Göring raises his voice, he is answered with an echo
of: 'Incendiary!' Whenever Goebbels addresses the world, the
reply resounds: 'Incendiary!' The flames of the Reichstag fire
continue to scorch the guilty.

In the Nazi camp itself, the fire has become a blackmail weapon.
The names of the incendiaries were known to eleven people. Three
of the incendiaries – Ernst, Fiedler and Mohrenschild were murdered on 30 June, and the accessories to the crime – Röhm, Heines
and Sander – were also sent to their death. All of them paid with
their lives for their knowledge of the Reichstag fire, and for the
great service they had rendered to National Socialism.

Fear of persecution and murder are rife as never before inside the
leading Nazi clique. Whenever we are shown pictures of Nazi
leaders, we invariably see them flanked by huge men, right hands
bulging in coat pocket, in the manner of American gangsters. But
not even these bodyguards are thought adequate, for, in addition,
every Nazi leader has thought fit to compile a dossier inculpating
all the others: Göring against Himmler; Himmler against Göring;
Goebbels against Göring; Ley against Goebbels – and all against
Hitler.

The S.A. Gruppenführer Karl Ernst was another to compile a
dossier and to deposit it in a safe place. In it, Ernst dealt with the
Reichstag fire and gave a full account of the actual events. He

named the incendiaries and their accomplices. Ernst was counting on the fact that, in case of his arrest or dismissal, the mere threat of publishing the document abroad would persuade Göring and Goebbels to rescind any measures they might have decided to take against him. Another reason why he compiled his dossier was that he needed a safeguard against his own assassination, or a means of revenge against his murderers. Ernst laid it down that the dossier was to be made public only in the event that he died an unnatural death or if Fiedler or von Mohrenschild authorized the publication. He deposited the document with a lawyer – probably the same Advocate Voss to whom Gregor Strasser, too, had entrusted his papers. Voss was murdered on 30 June, before he had a chance of taking the document abroad.

Ernst also sent a signed copy of his document and a covering letter of explanation to Heines, whom he advised to put his own knowledge about the Reichstag fire on record as well.

We cannot tell whether Heines followed Ernst's advice, but we do know that Heines sent Ernst's letter and confession, together with some other papers, to a friend in Breslau. It is this man, who still lives in Germany, who has sent us Ernst's confession. That confession explains the course of the Reichstag fire and bears out what was stated in the two *Brown Books* and the entire world press, and what was proved at the London Counter-Trial, viz. that the Reichstag was burned by the National Socialists.

We are now publishing Ernst's confession, in the hope that the National Socialist leaders may feel compelled to contest our case against them before an unprejudiced Court. We accuse the Prussian Prime Minister, Hermann Göring, Reichsminister Joseph Goebbels, the Saxon Prime Minister, Manfred von Killinger, and Potsdam Police President Graf Wolf Heinrich von Helldorff of having played a part in planning or in staging the Reichstag fire. We accuse the Nazi press attaché, Ernst Hanfstaengl, of being an accessory. We accuse the assassins of 30 June, of the murder of the S.A. leaders Ernst, Fiedler, von Mohrenschildt and Sander, all four of them men who had dangerous knowledge of the Reichstag fire.

The following were murdered:

Karl Ernst, S.A. Gruppenführer, Berlin-Brandenburg, Member of the Reichstag, Member of the Prussian State Council, Reichstag incendiary; Fiedler, S.A. Oberführer, Berlin-Brandenburg, Reichstag incendiary; Von Mohrenschild, S.A. Führer, Berlin-Brandenburg,

Reichstag incendiary; Sander, Standartenführer, Berlin-Brandenburg, accessory to the Reichstag fire.

With their deaths the Nazi leaders hoped to remove all traces of
National Socialist guilt in the Reichstag fire.

We now publish two documents, viz. Ernst's covering letter to
Heines, and his account of the Reichstag fire. These documents
prove conclusively that the National Socialist leaders stand for
everything that is vile and treacherous in political life.

On 5 June, when the battle for the S.A. had already been lost,
Ernst wrote the following letter to Heines:

June 5th, 1934.

Dear E,

The Chief has been round at last. Long discussion. The Chief told
me they were at it for hours. 'He' set up his usual howl and implored the Chief to believe that He would much rather see the Chief
at the head than an old geezer from Neudecker. But it didn't work.
General difficulties, fear of foreign opinion, a meeting in Venice
and the like. But you will meet the Chief yourself and will hear all
about it from him. The upshot of it all was a mutual promise to do
nothing until the old chap croaks. Then we shall see.

But that means getting down to brass-tacks. Anyone can see that,
if we wait until the Egyptian bastard makes common cause with the
cripple and the tailor's dummy, the three of them are going to do us
in. So we must act first. Hermann is out to skin us alive, and though
he can't stand the cripple, when it comes to fighting us he would
even make friends with Black Boy. We shall have to explode a
bomb right up their backsides. I would do anything to get hold of
the cripple alone. A pity R. stopped me smashing his skull that time
when he spread that muck about my marriage. I've told the Chief
about your letter. You know I'm usually not much of a speaker and
writer. He agrees with you that we must be prepared for the worst.
The cripple will stop at nothing. The Chief has sent all the most
important documents to a place of safe keeping. After my chat with
him, I, too, signed an account of the events in February which M
had typed out for me. It is now in safe hands. If anything nasty
should happen to me, the whole balloon will go up. I'm enclosing a
signed copy just in case. Look after it carefully, and put your own
things in a safe place, as well. Read it through. It is the strongest

weapon we have and our last resort. Perhaps it will help, but perhaps it won't. You know that the cripple can outwit us any time. Our strength lies elsewhere, and we are determined to use it.

But this time you'll have to stick with us through thick and thin. I have thought up a plan to smash the cripple once and for all, but we must lie low until everything is settled. The main thing is to hit the cripple where it hurts him most. That is my own aim but the Chief is more concerned with skinning Hermann alive. But then why not do them both in? Still, the first thing is to drive a wedge between the two bastards. If only we can get 'Him' on our side for a while, everything will be fine. Fi will tell you more about my plan. You can rely on him blindly. It's a pity that I'm not with you while you two are fixing things up. I agree with everything the Chief says but I insist on having the cripple to myself, nobody can rob me of that pleasure. He is the bastard who got me into this mess, and then laughed up his sleeve at me.

The Chief thinks we must not start before the Party Conference. He has news that the old boy will live for another ten years. I don't believe that, but since everybody agrees with the Chief, I can't do a thing about it. But after the Party Conference, we simply must get cracking. I'm going on leave within the next few weeks. I've just got to get away with her for a bit. Get Fi to send me a copy of your documents, don't put the thing off, and be careful with Sch. People are talking. Don't be seen with him so often. The Chief tells me 'He' has dropped a remark about it.

Clear up your den. Our friend from the Albrechtstrasse informs me that Black Boy is thinking of looking us all up; I myself am looking forward to the visit because I've prepared a lovely surprise for him.

> Keep your chin up,
> Yours,
> Carlos.

[KEY: 'He' = Hitler; the Chief = Röhm; the Cripple = Goebbels; the tailor's dummy and Hermann = Göring; the Egyptian = Hess; Black Boy = Himmler; Fi is probably Fiedler; 'M' is probably von Mohrenschild; the 'friend from the Albrechtstrasse' is a Gestapo official (the headquarters of the Gestapo are in the Prinz Albrecht-strasse); 'Sch' is probably another adjutant of Heines.]

ERNST'S CONFESSION

'I, the undersigned, Karl Ernst, S.A. Gruppenführer, Berlin-Brandenburg, Prussian State Councillor, born on September 1st 1904 in Berlin-Wilmersdorf, herewith put on record a full account of my part in the Reichstag fire. I am doing so on the advice of friends who have told me that Göring and Goebbels are planning to betray me. If I am arrested, Göring and Goebbels must be told at once that this document has been sent abroad. The document itself may only be published on the orders of myself or of the two friends who are named in the enclosure, or if I die a violent death.

I hereby declare that, on February 27th, 1933, I and two *Unterführer* named in the enclosure, set fire to the German Reichstag. We did so in the belief that we should be serving the Führer and our movement. We hoped that we might enable the Führer to deliver a shattering blow against Marxism, the worst enemy of the German people. Before this pestilence is completely smashed, Germany cannot recover. I do not regret what I have done, and I should do the same thing all over again. What I do regret deeply is that our action helped scum like Göring and Goebbels to rise to the top, men who have betrayed the S.A., who betray our Führer every day, and who use lies and slander to destroy the Chief of Staff and the S.A. The S.A. is the strongest weapon our movement has.

I am a National Socialist. I am convinced that National Socialism stands and falls with the S.A.

A few days after we seized power, Helldorff asked me to go with him to Göring's that evening. On the way, Helldorff told me that the idea was to find ways and means of smashing the Marxists once and for all. When we got there, I was surprised to see that Goebbels, too, had turned up, and that he had worked out a plan: when the Führer's plane touched down in Breslau, where he was to address an election meeting, two 'Communists' would attack him, thus providing the pretext for a campaign of retribution. Heines had been summoned to Berlin to discuss all the details. The Berlin-Brandenburg group of the S.A. was to stand ready. Helldorff would be told all the details within the next two days.

Two days later, we met again at Göring's, but this time without Goebbels. Göring had decided against the whole plan; he felt it might give undesirable elements the wrong ideas. He added that Goebbels disagreed with him, and implored us to do our best to talk him round. He had advised Heines to postpone his trip to Berlin for a few days.

Next day, I was ordered to report to Goebbels. I arrived last, and found that the others had all agreed to drop the original plan. Göring suggested a number of alternatives including the firing of the Palace and the bombing of the Ministry of the Interior. It was then that Goebbels said with a smile that it would be far better to set the Reichstag on fire, and then to stand up as the champions of parliamentarianism. Göring agreed at once. Helldorff and I were against the plan because we thought the practical difficulties involved were far too great. We pointed out that starting a fire in the Palace was much easier, because there was hardly anyone on guard there. But in the end, we were won over by Göring and Goebbels. We spent hours settling all the details. Heines, Helldorff and I would start the fire on the 25th February, eight days before the election. Göring promised to supply incendiary material of a kind that would be extremely effective yet take up very little space. On February 25th, we would all hide in the Reichstag Party rooms until everyone had left, and then set to work. The technical arrangements were left to me. When I called on Göring next day, he had suddenly grown less confident. He was afraid that our hanging about was bound to be noticed on a Saturday, when the Reichstag closed earlier than usual. He also felt that it would be wrong to let known S.A. leaders do the actual work. If one of us were caught, everything would be lost. He telephoned Goebbels, who turned up soon afterwards. Göring mentioned his objections, but Goebbels pooh-poohed them all.

Even so, we had to give up our plan in the end, when we realized that the Communists, whose Party rooms were opposite ours, kept very late hours. There was every reason to fear that they might spot us.

In the meantime Röhm had come to Berlin, and Heines, Killinger, Helldorff and I discussed the whole question with him over a meal. It was decided that none of us must take any part in the fire because the danger to the Party was far too great. Killinger recommended leaving all the dirty work to a few S.A. men who could later be got out of the way. Röhm felt he must make absolutely sure he was appointed State-Security Commissar before the fire.

At the next discussion which, I believe, took place in Göring's

318

house, Helldorff was absent because he was addressing an election meeting. I suggested to Göring that we use the subterranean passage leading from his residence to the Reichstag, because that would minimize the risk of discovery. I was ordered to pick my men. Goebbels insisted on postponing the fire from February 25th to February 27th, because February 26th was a Sunday, a day on which no evening papers appeared so that the fire could not be played up sufficiently for propaganda purposes. We decided to start the fire at about 9 p.m., in time for quite a number of radio bulletins. Göring and Goebbels agreed on how to throw suspicion on the Communists.

Helldorff and I paced out the subterranean passage three times in order to get our precise bearings. In addition, Göring had given us a section plan and also a precise time table of when the officials made their rounds of inspection. During one inspection of the subterranean passage we were almost caught – the watchman, who probably heard our footsteps, made an unscheduled round. We hid ourselves in a dead-end branch of the passage which the watchman fortunately overlooked – else he would not be alive today. Two days before the fire, we stowed the incendiary material which Göring had procured for us in the same dead-end branch. The material consisted of small canisters of a self-igniting phosphorus mixture together with a few litres of paraffin. During all our visits to the passage we always went in through the boiler-house to which we had been given keys. Whenever we went in and out, Göring would call the watchman so that we could come and go unnoticed.

I wondered for a long time whom I could trust with the execution of the plan and came to the conclusion that I would have to join in after all, and that I could only rely on men from my closest circle. I convinced Göring and Goebbels and they both agreed. I now think that they merely agreed because they thought they would get me more firmly under their thumb that way. My choice fell on two men in whom I had complete confidence, and to whom I am most grateful. I made them swear an oath of personal loyalty, and they kept it. I knew that I could rely on them. They themselves must decide whether or not their names, which are indicated in the covering letter, should be made public.

During our discussion, Göring told us that he had confided our plan to Hanfstaengl. Hanfstaengl, who lived in Göring's residence, would, on the 27th, divert the watchman's attention while we slipped in through the residence. We had keys to all the doors. Göring himself was going to be away – in the Ministry of the Interior.

A few days before the fixed date, Helldorff told us that a young fellow had turned up in Berlin of whom we should be able to make good use. This fellow was the Dutch Communist van der Lubbe. I did not meet him before the action. Helldorff and I fixed all the details. The Dutchman would climb into the Reichstag and blunder about conspicuously in the corridor. Meanwhile I and my men would set fire to the Session Chamber and part of the lobby. The Dutchman was supposed to start at 9 o'clock – half an hour later than we did.

The main difficulty was keeping to a precise timetable. The Dutchman had to climb into the Reichstag after we had left, and after the fire had already started. In order to familiarize him with the place, Helldorff sent him on a tour of inspection into the Reichstag. Apart from that he was made to learn the plan of the whole Reichstag by heart with the help of a very accurate map and with Sander's constant prodding. We decided that van der Lubbe must climb into the Reichstag restaurant, not only because that was the simplest way in, but also because, if he were caught, we should still have plenty of time to get away. To make perfectly certain that van der Lubbe would not take fright or change his mind at the last moment, Sander would not leave his side all afternoon. He would escort him to the Reichstag and watch him climb in from a safe distance. As soon as he was sure that van der Lubbe was in, he was to telephone Hanfstaengl and Göring. Van der Lubbe was to be left in the belief that he was working by himself.

I met my two helpers at eight o'clock precisely on the corner of Neue Wilhelmstrasse and Dorotheenstrasse. We synchronized our watches with Sander's. We were all dressed in civilian clothes. A few minutes later we were at the entrance to Göring's residence. We slipped into the passage unnoticed. Hanfstaengl had diverted the watchman. At about 8 o'clock we reached the dead-end branch. Here we had to wait until 8.40 p.m., i.e. until the guard had finished his round. Then we pulled galoshes over our shoes and walked on as silently as we could. We entered the Session Chamber at 8.45 p.m. One of my helpers went back to the dead-end branch to fetch the rest of the incendiary material. We started with the

Kaiser Wilhelm Memorial Hall and the Session Chamber, where we prepared a number of fires by smearing chairs and tables with the phosphorus mixture and by soaking curtains and carpets in paraffin. At exactly 9.5 p.m. we had finished, and started on our way back. It was high time – the phosphorus was fixed to go off within 30 minutes. At 9.12 we were back in the boiler-house and at 9.15 we climbed across the wall.

The allegations published abroad against any others are false. We three did the work entirely by ourselves. Apart from Göring, Goebbels, Röhm, Heines, Killinger, Hanfstaengl and Sander, no one knew about our plan.

The Führer, too, is said not to have known until later that the S.A. set the Reichstag on fire. I do not know about that. I have served the Führer for eleven years, and I shall remain faithful to him unto death. What I have done every other S.A. man would gladly have done for his Führer. But I cannot bear the thought that the S.A. was betrayed by those it helped to bring to power. I confidently believe that the Führer will destroy the dark plotters against the S.A. I am writing this confession as my only insurance against the evil plans of Göring and Goebbels. I shall destroy it the moment these traitors have been paid out.

Berlin, June 3rd, 1934
Signed Karl Ernst
S.A. Gruppenführer

The confession had the following addendum:

'This document may only be published on my orders, on the orders of my comrades Fiedler and von Mohrenschild, or if I die a violent death. My comrades Fiedler and Mohrenschild who have helped to set fire to the Reichstag must themselves decide whether their names can be made public or not. By our deed, the three of us have rendered yeoman service to National Socialism.'

Sources Consulted

OFFICIAL DOCUMENTS:

The case against van der Lubbe and accomplices (15 J 86.33).

Notes of Evidence, dated Sept. 21, 27 and 29, Oct. 10, Dec. 6 and 23; 1933.

Copy of Verdict (2P Aufh. 473.55; Public Prosecutor's Office, Berlin).

The Chancellory Records: 'Reichstag Fire' (Federal Archives, Koblenz R 43 II/294); 'Jews and the National Movement' (Public Records Office, London, Series E 611 913 – 612 666); 'Cabinet and Foreign Office Decisions' (Public Records Office, London, Series No. 3598, 4620, 8510, 2339, 2860, 8593, 8539, 8542, 9140, K 1052, 9094).

Records of the Berlin Fire Brigade (Institute of Contemporary History, Munich).

The Case against Gunsenheimer *et al.* (503) 77 KLs 16/37 (165.36); Public Prosecutor's Office, Berlin.

Dr Sack's extracts from the 32 volumes of Records of the Preliminary Examination.

Trial of the Major War Criminals before the International Military Tribunal, Nuremberg, 1947–1949.

WRITTEN AND VERBAL STATEMENTS TO THE AUTHOR BY:

Former members of the Berlin Fire Brigade;

Former officers of the Berlin Police;

Judge Paul Vogt, Cadenberger-Niederelbe;

Ernst Torgler, Hanover;

Paul Bienge, West Berlin;

Former S.A. staff-officers under the command of Karl Ernst;

Former Under-Secretary Ludwig Glauert, Hubbelrath-Mettmann;

Police officers, Leyden, Holland;

Ferdinand Kugler, Basle;

Dr Eberhard Taubert, Bonn;

Otto Schmidt, Hanover;

Dr Horst Pelckmann, now German Consul in Philadelphia;

Dr Hermann Rauschning, Portland, Oregon;

Dr Richard Lepsius, Baden-Baden;

Various ex-associates of Willi Münzenberg;

Prof. Dr Grimm;
Former Chief Clerk of the Reichstag, Ludwig Krieger, Bonn;
Prof. Robert M. W. Kempner, Lansdowne, Philadelphia, Pennsylvania;
et al.

BOOKS AND ARTICLES:

Abusch, Alexander: 'Das Braunbuch über den Reichstagbrand'. *Die Weltbühne*, Berlin, 1947.

Bergsträsser, Ludwig: *Geschichte der politischen Parteien in Deutschland.* (Isar) Munich, 1952.

Blagojewa, S.: *Georgi Dimitroff.* (Dietz) Berlin, 1954.

Bley, Wulf: Text of broadcast from the gutted Session Chamber as published in *Völkischer Beobachter* on 3rd March 1933.

Bonhoeffer, Karl and Zutt, Jürg: 'Über den Geisteszustand des Reichstagsbrand-stifters Marinus van der Lubbe'. *Monatsschrift für Psychiatrie und Neurologie*, Berlin, April 1934.

Borchmeyer, W.: *Hugenbergs Ringen in deutschen Schicksalsstunden*, 1949.

Borkenau, Franz: *Der europäische Kommunismus.* (Francke) Bern 1952.

Bracher, Karl Dietrich: 'Stufen totalitärer Gleichschaltung'. *Vierteljahreshefte für Zeitgeschichte*, Stuttgart 1/1956.

Brandes, Peter: 'Feuer über Deutschland'. *Der Stern*, Hamburg, 43/1957-52/1957.

Braun, Otto: *Von Weimar zu Hitler.* (Hammonia) Hamburg, 1949.

Brecht, Arnold: *Vorspiel zum Schweigen.* Vienna, 1948.

Bross, Werner: *Gespräche mit Göring.* (Wolff) Flensburg, 1950.

The Brown Book of the Hitler Terror and the Burning of the Reichstag. (Victor Gollancz) London, 1933.

The Second Brown Book of the Hitler Terror. (Bodley Head) London, 1934.

Buber-Neumann, Margarete: *Von Potsdam nach Moskau.* (Deva) Stuttgart, 1957.

Bullock, Alan: *Hitler.* (Odham's Press) London, 1952.

Crankshaw, Edward: *Gestapo.* (Putman) London, 1956.

Czech-Jochberg, Erich: *Vom 30. Januar zum 21. März.*

Dahlem, Franz: *Weg und Ziel.* Berlin, 1952.

Diels, Rudolf: *Lucifer ante portas.* (Deva) Stuttgart, 1950.

Dimitroff contra Göring. Die Vernehmung Görings als Zeuge im Reichstagsbrandprozess am 4. November 1933. (Tribune Druckerie) Leipzig n.d.

Dimitrov, Georgi: *Der Reichstagsbrandprozess.* (Neuer Weg) Berlin, 1946.

Dodd, William E.: *Ambassador Dodd's Diary*. (Victor Gollancz) London, 1945.

Duesterberg, Theodor: *Der Stahlhelm und Hitler*. Wolfenbüttel, 1949.

Effenberger, Gustav: *Welt in Flammen*. Hanover, 1913.

Ehrt, Adolf: *Entfesselung der Unterwelt*.

Ernst, Franz J.: *Der Reichstagsbrand*. Würzburg, 1948.

Eschenburg, Theodor: *Staat und Gesellschaft in Deutschland*. (Schwab) Stuttgart, 1956.

Fischer, Ernst: *Das Fanal*. (Stern) Vienna, 1946.

Fischer, Ruth: *Stalin and German Communism*. Harvard, 1948.

Flechtheim, Ossip: *Die KPD in der Weimar Republik*. Offenbach, 1948.

Forsthoff, Ernst: *Deutsche Geschichte seit 1918 in Dokumenten*. (Kröner) Stuttgart, 1938 (2nd edition).

François-Poncet, André: *Als Botschafter in Berlin*. (Kupferberg) Mainz, 1948.

Friedrich, G. and Lang, F.: *Vom Reichstagsbrand sur Entfachung des Weltbrandes*. (Promethée) Paris, 1938.

Frischauer, Willi: *Ein Marschallstab zerbrach*. (Münster) Ulm, 1951.

Gisevius, Hans Bernd: *Bis zum bitteren Ende*. a: (Claasen & Goverts) Hamburg, 1947. b: (Fretz & Wasmuth) Zürich, 1954.

Goebbels, Joseph: *Vom Kaiserhof zur Reichskanzlei*. (Eher) Munich, 1934.

Goebbels, Joseph: *Wetterleuchten*. (Eher) Munich, 1943. (5th edition).

Görlitz, Walter and Quint, Herbert A.: *Adolf Hitler*. (Steingrüben) Stuttgart, 1952.

Grimm, Friedrich: Politische Justiz. *Die Krankheit unserer Zeit*. (Bonn Univ. Press) Bonn, 1953.

Hager, Alfred: *Lehrbuch der Kriminalistik. Verhörtechnik und taktik*. (Hagedorn) Hanover, n. d.

Halle, Felix: *Wie verteidigt sich der Proletarier vor Gericht?* (Mopr) Berlin, 1929.

Hammerstein, Kunrat Freiherr von: 'Schleicher, Hammerstein und die Machtübernahme 1933'. *Frankfurter Hefte*, Frankfurt 1/1956–3/1956.

Hanfstaengl, Ernst: *Unheard Witness*. (Lippincott) Philadelphia, 1957.

Hays, Arthur Garfield: *City Lawyer*. (Simon & Schuster) New York, 1942.

Hegner, H. S. (Schulze-Wilde, Harry): *Die Reichskanzlei* (Frankfurter Bücher) Frankfurt, 1959.

Hegner, H. S. (Schulze-Wilde, Harry): 'Hinter den Kulissen der Reichskanzlei'. *Frankfurter Illustrierte*, Frankfurt 50/1948–8/1959.

Heiden, Konrad: *Die Geburt des Dritten Reiches*. (Europa) Zürich, 1934.

Hesslein, Pablo (Paul): 'Ich war im brennenden Reichstag'. *Stuttgarter Zeitung*, Stuttgart, 27th February, 1953.

Heydecker, Joe J. and Leeb, Johannes: *Der Nürnberger Prozess*. (Kiepenheuer) Cologne, 1958.

Hoegner, Wilhelm: *Die verratene Republik*. (Isar) Munich, 1958.

Hofer, Walther: *Der Nationalsozialismus. Dokumente 1933–1945*. (Fischer-Buch) Frankfurt, 1957.

Hohlfeldt, Johannes: *Dokumente der deutschen Politik*. (Juncker & Dünnhaupt) Berlin, 1933–1943.

Horkenbach, Cuno: *Das Deutsche Reich von 1918 bis heute*. (Presse-u. Wirtschaftsvlg.) Berlin, 1935.

Jäger, Hans: *Das wahre Gesicht der NSDAP*. Prague, 1933.

Jenke, Manfred: 'Die Wissenden schweigen'. *Frankfurter Rundschau*, Frankfurt, 25th February, 1956.

de Jong, G. T. J.: *De Brand*. (Blik) Amsterdam, 1934.

Kantorowicz, Alfred: *Deutsches Tagebuch*. (Kindler) Munich, 1959.

Kantorowicz, Alfred: 'Der Reichstagsbrand – Auftakt zur Weltbrandstiftung'. *Aufbau*, Berlin, 2/1947.

Katz, Otto: *Der Kampf um ein Buch*. (Carrefour) Paris, 1934.

Kaufhold, Friedrich: *Verbrennen und Löschen*. (Kohlhammer) Stuttgart, 1956.

Keesing's Contemporary Archives.

Knickerbocker, H. R.: *Deutschland so oder so?* (Rowohlt) Berlin, 1932.

Koestler, Arthur: *The Invisible Writing*. (Collins) London, 1954.

Koestler, Arthur: *The God that Failed*. (Hamish Hamilton) London, 1950.

Krivitsky, W. G.: *I was Stalin's Agent*. Amsterdam, 1940.

Kugler, Ferdinand: *Das Geheimnis des Reichstagsbrandes*. (Munster) Amsterdam, n. d.

Kuttner, Erich (Justinian); *Der Reichstagsbrand*. (Graphia) Karlsbad, 1934.

Last, Jef.: *Kruisgang der Jeugd*. (Brussel) Rotterdam, 1939.

Leber, Annedore: *Das Gewissen steht auf*. (Mosaik) Berlin, 1956.

Löbe, Paul: *Der Weg war lang*. (Arani) Berlin, 1949.

Lochner, Louis P.: *Stets das Unerwartete*. (Schneekluth) Darmstadt, 1955.

Lucian: *Die Abenteuer der Samosata*. (Allg. Verl. Anst.) Munich, 1924.

'Ludwig': *Der Reichstagsbrand. Ursachen, Wirkungen und Zusammenhänge*. (Défense) Paris, 1933.

Mantell, Ferdinand (Schneider, Wilhelm): 'Der Reichstagsbrand in anderer Sicht'. *Neue Politik*, Zürich, 20th January – 18th March, 1949.

Meissner, Otto: *Als Staatssekretär unter Ebert, Hindenburg und Hitler*. (Hoffmann & Campe) Hamburg, 1950.

Meissner, Hans Otto and (Schulze-) Wilde, Harry: 'Ein Toter spricht...' *Weltbild*, Munich, 23/1957-2/1958.

Meissner, Hans Otto and (Schulze-) Wilde, Harry: *Die Machtergreifung*. (Cotta) Stuttgart, 1958.

Mengering, Bob: '*Das Wahrheitsserum*'. (Kinau) Lüneburg, 1957.

Misch, Carl: *Deutsche Geschichte im Zeitalter der Massen*. (Kohlhammer) Stuttgart, 1952.

Niekisch, Ernst: *Das Reich der niederen Dämonen*. (Rowohlt) Hamburg, 1953.

Obbergen, Paulus van (Leers, Johannes von): 'Vom Reichstagsbrand zum Untergang des Reiches'. *Der Weg*, Buenos Aires, 12/1954.

The Oberfohren Memorandum. (German Information Bureau) London, 1933.

Papen, Franz von: *Der Wahrheit eine Gasse*. (List) Munich, 1952.

Picker, Henry: *Hitlers Tischgespräche im Führerhauptquartier 1941-1942*. (Athenäum) Bonn, 1951.

Rauschning, Hermann: *Conversations with Hitler*. (Butterworth) London, 1939.

Reber, Charles: 'Toxikologisches zum Fall van der Lubbe'. *Neues Tagebuch*, Paris, 1933.

Reed, Douglas: *The Burning of the Reichstag*. (Cape) London, 1934.

Reed, Douglas: *Fire and Bombs*. (Cape) London, 1940.

Regler, Gustav: *Das Ohr des Malchus*. (Kiepenheuer) Cologne, 1958.

Reitlinger, Gerald: *Die SS*. (Desch) Munich, 1956.

Roodboek (The Red Book). (Intern. Uitgeversbedrijf) Amsterdam, 1933.

Sack, Alfons: *Der Reichstagsbrandprozess*. With a foreword by Prof. Dr Friedrich Grimm. (Ullstein) Berlin, 1934.

Sauerbruch, Ferdinand: *Das war mein Leben*. (Kindler) Munich, 1956.

Schacht, Hjalmar: *Abrechnung mit Hitler*. (Rowohlt) Hamburg, 1949.

Scheringer, Richard: *Das grosse Los*. (Rowohlt) Hamburg, 1959.

Schlange-Schöningen, Hans: *Am Tage danach*. (Hammerich & Lesser) Hamburg, 1946.

Schulthess' Europäischer Geschichtskalender. (Beck) Munich, 1934.

Schulze-Wilde, Harry: 'Zur Geschichte der Technik der National-sozialistischen Machtergriefung'. *Frankfurter Hefte*, Frankfurt, 6/1957.

Schulze-Wilde, Harry: 'Van der Lubbes Rolle beim Reichstagsbrand'. *Süddeutsche Zeitung*, Munich, 25th-26th February 1956.

(Schulze-) Wilde, Harry: 'Der erste Schauprozess'. *Politische Studien*, Munich, 104/1958.

Schützinger, Hermann: 'Der Reichstag brennt'. *Neuer Vorwärts*, Bad Godesberg, 27th February, 1953.

Schwerin von Krosigk, Lutz Graf: *Es geschah in Deutschland*. (Wunderlich) Tübingen, 1951.

Sommerfeldt, Martin H.: *Ich war dabei*. Darmstadt, 1949.

Sommerfeldt, Martin H.: *Kommune*. (Mittler) Berlin, 1934.

Stampfer, Friedrich: *Die ersten vierzehn Jahre der Weimarer Republik*. (Auerdruck) Hamburg, 1953. (3rd edition).

Stampfer, Friedrich: 'Die Nacht des Reichstagsbrandes'. *Vorwärts*, Bad Godesberg, 20th December, 1957.

Stampfer, Friedrich: *Erfahrungen und Erkenntnisse*. (Politik und Wirtschaft), Cologne, 1957.

Stechert, Kurt: *Wie war das möglich?* (Bermann-Fischer) Stockholm, 1945.

Stein, Adolf (Rumpelstilzchen): *Gift, Feuer, Mord*. (Brunnen) Berlin, 1934.

Stephan, Werner: *Joseph Goebbels. Dämon einer Diktatur*. (Union) Stuttgart, 1949.

Sternberg, Fritz: *Kapitalismus und Sozialismus vor dem Weltgericht*. (Rowohlt) Hamburg, 1951.

Studnitz, Hans Georg von: 'Leben zwischen Macht und Gefahr'. *Christ und Welt*, Stuttgart, 5th December, 1957.

Taylor, A. J. P.: 'Who burnt the Reichstag?' *History Today*, London, August, 1960.

Thälmann, Ernst: *Der revolutionäre Ausweg und die KPD*. Quoted in *Wissen und Tat*, Düsseldorf, 5/1952.

Torgler, Ernst: 'Der Reichstagsbrand und was nachher kam'. *Die Zeit*, Hamburg, 21st October – 11th November, 1949.

Valtin, Jan (Krebs, Richard): *Out of the Night*. (Heinemann) London, 1941.

Wallot, Paul: *Das Reichstagsgebäude in Berlin*. (Cosmos) Leipzig, 1899.

White Book on the Executions of the 30th June, 1934. (Carrefour) Paris, 1934.

Wolff, Richard: 'Der Reichstagsbrand 1933. A Special Investigation'. Supplement to *Das Parlament*, Bonn, 18th January, 1956.

Wollenberg, Erich: 'Dimitroffs Aufstieg und Ende'. *Echo der Woche*, Munich, 12th August, 1949.

SOURCES CONSULTED

NEWSPAPERS AND JOURNALS:

Algemeen Handelsblad, Amster-
dam
Amtl. Preussischer Pressedienst
Berlin
Der Angriff, Berlin
Arbeitertum, Zeitung der DAF,
Berlin
Berliner Börsen-Courier
Berliner Börsenzeitung
Berliner Lokalanzeiger
Berliner Nachtausgabe
Braunschweiger Neueste Nachrichten
Braunschweigische Staatszeitung
Christ und Welt, Stuttgart
Daily Express, London
Deutsche Allgemeine Zeitung,
Berlin
Deutscher Reichsanzeiger, Berlin
Deutsche Rundschau, Stuttgart
Deutsche Woche, Munich
Echo der Woche, Munich
Feuerschutz
Frankfurter Hefte
Frankfurter Illustrierte
Frankfurter Rundschau
Das freie Wort, Bonn
Germania, Berlin
Hannoverscher Anzeiger
Hannoverscher Kurier
Hannoversche Presse
Het Volk, Amsterdam
History Today, London
Internationale
Kommunistische Internationale
Lichtpfad, Lorch
Lubecker Nachrichten
De Maasbode, Rotterdam
Manchester Guardian

*Ministerialblatt für die Preus-
sische innere Verwaltung*,
Berlin
*Monatsschrift für Psychiatrie und
Neurologie*, Berlin
Morning Post, London
Nationalsozialistische Partei-
Korrespondenz, Munich
Neue Arbeiter-Zeitung, Hanover
Neues Deutschland, Berlin
Neue Politik, Zürich
Neue Weltschau, Stuttgart
Neue Zürcher Zeitung, Zürich
Neues Tagebuch, Paris
New York Evening Post
Niedersächsische Tageszeitung,
Hanover
Niedersächsische Volksstimme,
Hanover
Das Parlament, Bonn
Politische Studien, Munich
Prager Montagsblatt
Pravda, Moscow
Reichsgesetzblatt, Berlin
La République, Strasbourg
Die Rote Fahne, Berlin
Saarbrückener Volksstimme
Safety at Work, London
Salzburger Nachrichten
Sender Freies Berlin
Der Spiegel, Hamburg
Der Stern, Hamburg
Stuttgarter Zeitung
Süddeutsche Zeitung, Munich
Der Tag, Berlin
De Telegraaf, Amsterdam
Telegraphen-Union, Berlin
The Times, London
Vierteljahreshefte für Zeitgeschichte,
Stuttgart

Völkischer Beobachter, Berlin-Munich
Vorwärts, Berlin
Neuer Vorwärts, Berlin
Neuer Vorwärts, Bad Godesberg
Vorwärts, Bad Godesberg
Vossische Zeitung, Berlin

Die Welt, Hamburg
Weltbild, Munich
Die Weltbühne, Berlin
Der Weg, Buenoes Aires
Wiener Arbeiterzeitung
Wissen und Tat, Düsseldorf
Wolffs Telegraphen-Büro, Berlin
Die Zeit, Hamburg

References

CHAPTER I
1. Martin H. Sommerfeldt: *Kommune*, p. 45.
2. *Vorwärts*, 20 December 1957.
3. Reported to the author by Buwert, now a police inspector.

CHAPTER 2
1. *Prelim. Exam.*, Vol. I, p. 57f.
2. De Jongh: *De Brand*, p. 54.
3. De Jongh: op. cit., p. 54.
4. *Prelim. Exam.*, Vol. I, p. 50.
5. *Niedersächsische Tageszeitung*, 29 September 1933.
6. *Brown Book I*, p. 112.
7. *Brown Book I*, p. 58f.
8. *Brown Book I*, German ed., pp. 55 and 57.
9. *Brown Book I*, German ed., p. 57.
10. *Red Book*, p. 52.

CHAPTER 3
1. *Prelim. Exam.*, Vol. I., p. 33.
2. Statement by Dr Zirpins on 26 December 1951.
3. *Prelim. Exam.*, Vol. II, p. 142.
4. *Brown Book II*, p. 47.
5. *Algemeen Handelsblad*, 11 March 1933.
6. *Völkischer Beobachter*, 15 March 1933.
7. *Red Book*, p. 36.
8. F. von Papen: *Der Wahrheit eine Gasse*, p. 303.
9. Franz J. Ernst: *Der Reichstagsbrand*, p. 12.
10. *Niedersächsische Tageszeitung*, 25 March 1933.
11. *Proc.*, 24 March 1933.
12. Picker, *Hitlers Tischgespräche*, p. 211.

CHAPTER 4
1. *Die Welt*, 24 August 1957.
2. Appendix to Dr Wolff's report, op. cit., p. 22.
3. IMT, Vol. XI, p. 489.

4. *Erinnerungen eines Reichstagspräsidenten*, p. 148f.
5. Gustav Regler, *Das Ohr des Malchus*, p. 21.
6. *Brown Book I*, p. 134.
7. *Prel. Exam.*, Vol. G, p. 46, Evidence of Engineer Krug.
8. *Prel. Exam.*, Vol. G, p. 48f.
9. Douglas Reed: *The Burning of the Reichstag*, p. 151.
10. Douglas Reed: *Fire and Bomb*, p. 20.
11. Douglas Reed: *The Burning of the Reichstag*, p. 150f.

CHAPTER 5
1. Cf. Ernst Hanfstaengl: *Hitler – the Missing Years*, p. 201f.
2. Goebbels: *Vom Kaiserhof zur Reichskanzlei*, p. 269.
3. *Völkischer Beobachter*, 28 February 1933.
4. Reported to the author by Ludwig Grauert on 3 October 1957.
5. *Völkischer Beobachter*, 5 November 1933.
6. Papen: op. cit., p. 302.
7. Martin H. Sommerfeldt: *Ich war dabei*, p. 25.
8. Rudolf Diels: *Lucifer ante portas*, p. 193.
9. Quoted in N. Hoegner: *Die verratene Republik*, p. 345.
10. J. Goebbels: op. cit., p. 254.
11. Rudolf Diels: op. cit., p. 194.
12. Rudolf Diels: op. cit., p. 195.
13. Dr Wilhelm Schneider: *Neue Politik*, Zürich, Nos. 2–5, 1949.
14. *Der. Spiegel*, 25 November 1959.
15. Reported by Grauert on 3 October 1957.
16. Martin H. Sommerfeldt: *Ich war dabei*, p. 26.
17. *Niedersächsische Tageszeitung*, 2 March 1933.
18. Sack: *Reichstagsbrandprozess*, p. 32.
19. Ernst Fischer: *Das Fanal*, p. 37.

CHAPTER 6
1. Keesing's Contemporary Archives, 11 December 1933.
2. Arthur Koestler: *The God that Failed*, p. 71.
3. M. Buber-Neumann: *Von Potsdam nach Moskau*, p. 199.
4. Arthur Koestler: *The Invisible Writing*, p. 198.
5. Arthur Koestler: *The God that Failed*, p. 71f.
6. Ruth Fischer: *Stalin and German Communism*, p. 613.

CHAPTER 7
1. *Manchester Guardian*, 26 April 1933.
2. *Völkischer Beobachter*, 28 April 1933.

REFERENCES

3. Sefton Delmer, *Trail Sinister*, p. 198.
4. Wolff: op. cit., p. 36.
5. *Brown Book I*, p. 82.
6. *Völkischer Beobachter*, 12 April 1933.
7. *Völkischer Beobachter*, 12 April 1933.
8. Dr Sack: op. cit., p. 40.
9. Dr Wolff: op. cit., p. 35.
10. *Neuer Vorwärts*, 29 October 1933.
11. Dr Sack: op. cit., p. 46.
12. Cf. Wolff, op. cit., note 63.
13. Dr Sack: op. cit., p. 49.
14. *Neue Arbeiter Zeitung*, Hanover, 25 February 1933.
15. Martin H. Sommerfeldt: *Kommune*, p. 85ff.
16. As reported in *Brown Book I*, p. 75.
17. *Völkischer Beobachter*, 3 March 1933.
18. Cf. Papen: op. cit., p. 291.

CHAPTER 8
1. *Aufbau*, No. 2, 1947.
2. A. Koestler: *The Invisible Writing*, p. 197f.
3. *Echo der Woche*, 12 August 1949.
4. *Die Zeit*, 4 November 1948.
5. Hays: *City Lawyer*, p. 341.
6. Dr Sack: op. cit., p. 240.
7. Dr Sack: op. cit., p. 116.
8. Hays: op. cit., p. 345.
9. Hays: op. cit., p. 377.
10. Hays: op. cit., p. 378.
11. Dr Sack: op. cit., p. 149.
12. Hays: op. cit., p. 388.
13. Dr Sack: op. cit., p. 154.
14. *Brown Book II*, p. 244.
15. Koestler: *The Invisible Writing*, p. 200.
16. Dr Sack: op. cit., preface.
17. *The Fight for a Book*, p. 16.
18. Hays: op. cit., p. 373.

CHAPTER 9
1. *Brown Book I*, p. 82.
2. *Brown Book I*, p. 52.
3. *Hannoverscher Kurier*, 8 November 1933.

4. Dr Sack: op. cit., p. 48.
5. Werner Stephan: *Joseph Goebbels*, p. 61.
6. R. Wolff: op. cit.
7. Martin H. Sommerfeldt: *Ich war dabei*, p. 30.
8. Martin H. Sommerfeldt: *Ich war dabei*, p. 57.
9. Martin H. Sommerfeldt: *Ich war dabei*, pp. 60–61.
10. Martin H. Sommerfeldt: *Ich war dabei*, p. 30.
11. Letter to *Der Spiegel*, 30 November 1959.
12. IMT, Vol. IX, p. 196.
13. *Echo der Woche*, 12 August 1949.
14. Meissner: *Staatssekretär*, p. 283.
15. Rudolf Diels, op. cit., p. 324.
16. *Völkischer Beobachter*, 5–6 November 1933.
17. Rudolf Diels: op. cit., p. 204.
18. *Die Zeit*, 21 October 1948.
19. *Niedersächsische Tageszeitung*, 20 October 1933.
20. J. Goebbels: op. cit., p. 271.
21. Keesing's Contemporary Archives: 19 April 1933.
22. *Völkischer Beobachter*, 28 February 1933.
23. *Brown Book II*, p. 303.
24. Douglas Reed: *The Burning of the Reichstag*, p. 121.
25. Letter dated 8 November 1957.
26. Douglas Reed: *The Burning of the Reichstag*, p. 122.
27. *Völkischer Beobachter*, 11 October 1933.
28. *Amtl. Preuss. Pressedienst*, 2 March 1933.
29. *Erinnerungen eines Reichstagspräsidenten*, p. 151.
30. *Ich war im brennenden Reichstag*, Stuttgarter Zeitung, 27 February 1933.
31. Annedore Leber: *Das Gewissen steht auf*, p. 106.
32. *Brown Book I*, p. 123.
33. *Berliner Lokalanzeiger*, 28 February 1933.
34. Letter by Puhle, 29 November 1957.
35. *Brown Book II*, p. 45.
36. *Niedersächsische Tageszeitung*, 12 October 1933.
37. *Brown Book II*, p. 298.
38. *Das freie Wort*, 21 February 1953.
39. *Lübecker Nachrichten*, 21 July 1954.
40. *Verdict*, p. 24.
41. *Neue Zürcher Zeitung*, 14 October 1933.

CHAPTER 10

1. *Neue Zürcher Zeitung*, 28 September 1933.
2. *Prelim. Exam.*, Vol. I, pp. 103–5.
3. *Prelim. Exam.*, Vol. I, p. 100.
4. *Indictment*, p. 33.
5. *Prelim. Exam.*, Vol. VI, p. 62.
6. *Prelim. Exam.*, Vol. VI, p. 63.
7. *Notes of Evidence*, 27 September 1933, p. 171.
8. *Neue Zürcher Zeitung*, 23 October 1933.
9. *Prelim., Exam.*, Vol: Reichstag III, pp. 156–7.
10. *Prelim. Exam.*, Vol: Reichstag IV, pp. 27–46.
11. *Notes of Evidence*, 27 September 1933, pp. 150–151.
12. *Notes of Evidence*, 27 September 1933, p. 155.
13. *Hannoverscher Kurier*, 23 November 1933.
14. cf. Buber-Neumann: op. cit., p. 238.
15. cf. S. Blagojewa: *Georgi Dimitroff*, p. 99.
16. *Brown Book II*, p. 57.
17. *Die Zeit*, 21 October 1948.
18. Dr Sack: op. cit., p. 218.
19. *Brown Book II*, p. 53f.
20. F. Kugler: *Geheimnis des Reichstagsbrandes*, p. 85.
21. *Notes of Evidence*, 27 September 1933.
22. *Brown Book II*, p. 59.
23. *Brown Book II*, p. 55.
24. Dr Sack: op. cit., p. 92.
25. C. Horkenbach: *Das Deutsche Reich;* entry of 21 March 1933.
26. *Neue Zürcher Zeitung*, 28 September 1933.
27. F. von Papen: op. cit., pp. 303–4.
28. *Die Zeit*, 28 October 1948.
29. Dr Sack: op. cit., pp. 96 and 288.
30. R. Diels: op. cit., p. 203.
31. Douglas Reed: *The Burning of the Reichstag*, p. 35.
32. *Die Zeit*, 4 November 1948.
33. *Niedersächsische Tageszeitung*, 24 September 1933.
34. *Die Zeit*, 4 November 1948.
35. *Neue Zürcher Zeitung*, 14 December 1933.
36. Otto Braun: *Von Weimar zu Hitler*, p. 100.

CHAPTER 11

1. op. cit., p. 41.
2. *Neue Zürcher Zeitung*, 5 November 1933.

3. Douglas Reed: *The Burning of the Reichstag*, p. 40f.
4. F. Kugler: op. cit., p. 29.
5. Dr Sack: op. cit., Preface, p. 9.
6. F. Kugler: op. cit., p. 23.
7. Dr Sack: op. cit., p. 155.
8. *Maasbode*, 31 October 1933.
9. Douglas Reed: *The Burning of the Reichstag*, p. 198.
10. *Neue Zürcher Zeitung*, 15 November 1933.
11. *De Telegraaf*, 7 October 1933.
12. *Het Volk*, 7 October 1933.
13. *Hannoverscher Anzeiger*, 7 October 1933.
14. *Hannoverscher Anzeiger*, 7 October 1933.
15. *Neue Zürcher Zeitung*, 8 October 1933.
16. F. Kugler: op. cit., p. 81.
17. *Neue Zürcher Zeitung*, 8 October 1933.
18. F. Kugler: op. cit., p. 100.
19. *Brown Book II*, p. 178.
20. *Neue Zürcher Zeitung*, 6 November 1933.
21. *Neue Zürcher Zeitung*, 6 November 1933.
22. Quoted in *Brown Book II*, p. 258.
23. *Brown Book II*, p. 193f.
24. Douglas Reed: *The Burning of the Reichstag*, p. 255f.
25. *Indictment*, p. 141.
26. Dr Sack: op. cit., p. 140.
27. Dr Sack: op. cit., p. 184ff.
28. *Neue Zürcher Zeitung*, 15 November 1933.
29. Dr Sack: op. cit., p. 198.
30. Army Medical Opinion quoted by Dr Sack: op. cit., p. 242.
31. *Indictment*, p. 160.
32. *Neue Zürcher Zeitung*, 1 November 1933.
33. *Neue Zürcher Zeitung*, 1 November 1933.
34. Kugler: op. cit., p. 136.
35. *Indictment*, p. 162.
36. Dr Sack: op. cit., p. 167.
37. Dr Sack: op. cit., p. 317.
38. Dr Sack: op. cit., p. 162.
39. *Prelim. Exam.* Vol. T III, p. 43.
40. *Indictment*, p. 136.
41. Dr Sack: op. cit., p. 310.
42. *Berliner Nachtausgabe* and *Neue Zürcher Zeitung*, 12 December 1933.

REFERENCES

CHAPTER 12

1. *Prelim. Exam. G.* p. 53ff.
2. *Völkischer Beobachter*, 23 October 1933.
3. *De Telegraaf*, 24 October 1933.
4. *Niedersächsische Tageszeitung*, 24 October 1933.
5. Douglas Reed: *The Burning of the Reichstag*, p. 187.
6. *Neue Zürcher Zeitung*, 24 October 1933.
7. Douglas Reed: *The Burning of the Reichstag*, p. 298f.
8. *Neue Zürcher Zeitung*, 13 November 1933.
9. *Neue Zürcher Zeitung*, 5 October 1933.
10. *Berliner Lokalanzeiger*, 28 February 1933.
11. *Hannoversche Presse*, 14 April 1956.
12. *Völkischer Beobachter*, 1 March 1933.
13. *Feuerschutz*, 1933, p. 50.
14. See M. J. Reaney: 'Give the Fire Air' in *Safety at Work*, London.
15. Effenberger: *Welt in Flammen*, p. 266.
16. ibid., p. 272.
17. *Völkischer Beobachter*, 1 March 1933.

CHAPTER 13

1. *Nationalsozialistische Partei Korrespondenz.*
2. *Berliner Börsen-Courier*, 23 December 1933.
3. Erich Kuttner: *Reichstagsbrand*, p. 34.
4. *Neue Züricher Zeitung*, 19 October 1933.
5. Adolf Stein: *Gift, Feuer, Mord*, p. 27f.
6. Kugler: op. cit., p. 25.
7. *Niedersächsische Tageszeitung*, 28 September 1933.
8. *Brown Book II*, p. 215.
9. *Brown Book II*, p. 173.
10. Douglas Reed: *The Burning of the Reichstag*, p. 264.
11. De Jongh: op. cit., p. 96.
12. Douglas Reed: *The Burning of the Reichstag*, p. 265f.

Index

AAU (General Workers' Union), 39
Adenauer, Dr, 160
Adermann, Paul, 26, 78
Agitprop (Communist Agitation and Propaganda Department), 75–6, 99, 101, 153
Ahrens, Councillor, 161, 163, 165
Albada, Piet van, 38, 39, 64–6
Albrecht, Dr Herbert, 92, 169
Albrecht, Police-sergeant, 47
Arnim, Professor von, 150
August Wilhelm, Prince, 84, 136

Bahn, Walter, 200
Bakker-Nort, Dr Betsy, 120, 126
Baling, Professor Fischer, 172
Bannert, Bruno, 243
Barbusse, Henri, 102, 103
Barge, Wilhelm, 55
Bell, Dr, 57–8, 126
Benario, Olga, 189
Bergery, Maître Gaston, 120, 127
Berliner Lokalanzeiger, quoted, 163
Berliner Nachtausgabe, 253
Berndt, Alfred Ingemar, 91
Bernhard, Professor Georg, 110, 125
Bernstein (witness), 236
Bienge, Paul, 182–4
Birkenhauer, Erich, 92, 244–5
Bismarck, Under-Secretary von, 88
Blagoi (Bulgarian Communist), 94
Blomberg, General von, 116
Bogun, Paul, 30, 194, 270–1
Böhmer, Judge, 165

Bonhoeffer, Professor Karl, 277, 279; quoted, 280
Borchardt, Otto, 260
Braffort (advocate), 121
Brandis, Judge, 198
Brandschutz, 265
Branting, Georg, 120–2, 126
Braschwitz, Detective-Inspector Dr, 180
Braun (Prussian Minister), 160
Braun, Otto, 203
Braune, Dr, 179
Breitscheid, Rudolf, 110, 125
Brown Book of the Hitler Terror (and the Second Brown Book), 130, 142, 200, 206, 230; publication of, 31; on the Sörnewitz legend, 54; on van der Lubbe's alleged homosexuality, 56–8; on Heisig, 69–70; on the underground passage, 75, 76; on Dr Oberfohren, 106; on Heines, 110; Münzenberg's masterpiece, 116; sponsors, staff and sources, 117–20; Leipzig Court's attempt to refute, 131–2; on Göring, 133, 222, 223; on Goebbels, 133, 222, 231; on the delay of the fire alarm, 154; on Gempp, 159, 162–5; on Dr Lepsius, 167–8; on Alexander Scranowitz, 169–71; on Judge Vogt, 193–5; on Dr Werner's indictment, 203; alleges that van der Lubbe was drugged, 281
Brüning, Professor Dr August, 64, 258, 259, 263, 274

339

341